10:50
1 EM

DATE DUE

APR 2 6 1972			
MAY 15			
DEC 17			
MAY 19			
DEC 16			
GAYLORD			PRINTED IN U.S A.

Psychological Factors

in Poverty

PSYCHOLOGICAL FACTORS IN POVERTY

Edited by

Vernon L. Allen
University of Wisconsin

Institute for Research on Poverty Monograph Series

MARKHAM PUBLISHING COMPANY
Chicago

The research reported here was supported by funds granted to the Institute for Research on Poverty at the University of Wisconsin by the Office of Economic Opportunity, pursuant to provisions of the Economic Opportunity Act of 1964.

Printed in the U.S.A.
Library of Congress Catalog Card Number: 70-111978
Standard Book Number: 8410-5003-1

PREFACE

A reader who thinks he may be interested in a book should know what it is *not*. Several things this book is not. It is not a broad and multidisciplinary coverage of the problems of poverty: the points of view of economics, law, social welfare, and political science are not included. The book is not a manual for the field worker struggling with the day-to-day problems of the poor; i.e., it is not a "how-to-do-it" book of applied psychology. Neither is the book an exhaustive nor comprehensive compendium of all psychological theory and research of relevance to poverty. The volume is not a collection of old or previously published papers collected from other sources; all were prepared for this book.

The book consists of a selective sample of some of the most important recent theoretical and empirical developments in behavioral science that have implications for poverty. Psychological factors in poverty is the theme of the book; nevertheless, the contributors come from several different disciplinary affiliations. The chapters vary in scope of the topic discussed, in intensiveness and detail of analysis, and in degree of immediate relevance and applicability to applied problems in the field.

With the exception of three papers, all the chapters published here were first presented at a conference held at Madison, Wisconsin, in June of 1967. The exceptions are the chapters written by Clinard and Allen. I should like to express my appreciation to the Institute for Research on Poverty, University of Wisconsin, for providing funds that made the conference possible. I am also grateful to Professor Harold Watts, Director of the Institute, for his help and advice throughout.

The extract in Chapter 1, from "Welfare as a Moral Category" by Bernard Beck, which was published in Volume 14 of *Social Problems*, is used with the permission of the Society for the Study of Social Problems. Chapter 7 in a longer version was published in the *Proceedings of the National Academy of Science*. The material by J.B.S. Haldane quoted in Chapter 8 is used here with the permission of Pergamon Publishing Company, the publishers of *Genetics Today: Proceedings of the XI International Congress of Genetics*, edited by S. J. Geertz. Chapter 11, by Urie Bronfenbrenner, was first published in *Child Development*, Volume 38; copyright,

Society for Research in Child Development, 1967. In Chapter 14 the quotations from Elliot Liebow's *Tally's Corner* are used with permission of Little, Brown and Company, publishers.

Mrs. Annette Stiefbold and Mrs. Jeanne DeRose deserve special acknowledgment for their role in making this book possible. For their invaluable contributions, my sincere thanks. The tireless and creative efforts of Annette Stiefbold contributed immeasurably toward making the conference a success. For her reliability, hard work, and constant good humor in time of crisis, I am extremely appreciative. I am also very grateful to Mrs. Jeanne DeRose who has so competently edited all the chapters of the book. To Jeanne fell the demanding task of serving as liaison among the publisher, the authors, and me, while also attending to the innumerable problems large and small that publishing a book entails. Moreover, she did all this in snowy Wisconsin without complaint while I had the pleasure of working on the book while living in merrie England!

VERNON L. ALLEN
University of Wisconsin
Madison, Wisconsin

CONTENTS

PART ONE

THEORETICAL
VANTAGE POINTS

INTRODUCTION

In 1846 Proudhon published a book on economic inequality titled The Philosophy of Poverty. *Answering the two-volume work the following year, Marx wrote a scathing attack in a small book derisively entitled* The Poverty of Philosophy. *In light of this historical precedent for alliterative license, it is with considerable trepidation that we present to the reader a volume arguing the importance of psychological variables in understanding poverty. Perhaps the dialectic of intellectual inquiry will inevitably provoke a reaction to this volume in the form of an article or book predictably called "The Poverty of Psychology."*[1]

And, admittedly, until recently, psychological contributions to understanding and improving the plight of the poor might justifiably have been interpreted as indicative of the poverty of psychology. If not yet excessively affluent in understanding and application, however, the psychological study of poverty at least shows healthy signs of growth and development. Within recent years, there has been a dramatic and vigorous research effort, launched by psychologists and other social scientists, directed toward investigating behavioral concomitants of poverty. The contents of this book are indicative of the range and diversity of current research activity.

The increased interest in research on poverty by social scientists parallels and in part reflects the heightened awareness and concern within society at large of the existence of festering social problems that have been neglected for too long. Poverty has a most peculiar way of being "rediscovered" about once every generation (Matza, 1966). That the poor are still with us, even in the affluent twentieth-century United States, is an unpleasant and stubborn fact that cannot be easily evaded. Michael Harrington's (1962) book The Other America *deserves considerable credit for most recently arousing the conscience of the nation about the plight of the underclass in America. Not surprisingly, Harrington's book bears a striking resemblance to a very influential book called* Poverty *published in 1904 by Robert Hunter. It is a distressing reflection on social progress to note how contemporary many sections of Hunter's 1904 book sound even today. Though the absolute level of deprivation and degradation was certainly much greater at the turn of the century, in relative terms the poor have experienced only slight improvement in their situation since then. In relation to the economic advances experienced by the rest of society, the condition of certain segments of the poor (e.g., the Negro) is in fact*

---

[1]Soon after the first draft of this introduction was written, Arthur Pearl sent to me the revised manuscript of his chapter for this book, a paper entitled "The Poverty of Psychology—an Indictment." Ever shorter becomes the time lag between prophecy and confirmation!

deteriorating (Kahn, 1964). Hence, in spite of the difference between the nature of poverty today and half a century ago, it is not surprising to find that many of Hunter's comments about the poor sound quite appropriate and sensible now, including his relativistic definition of poverty: ". . . those of our people who are underpaid, underfed, underclothed, badly housed and overworked."

Before proceeding, one point needs to be made perfectly clear: by concentrating on psychological factors we do not intend to imply that poverty can be understood and eradicated by employing techniques of the social sciences alone. It is almost too obvious to require mention that many aspects of our economic system and social structure contribute to the existence of poverty. Poverty would certainly qualify as an instance of multiple determination, or to use Lewin's (1951) term, "overdetermination," as opposed to a situation with a simplistic, unitary explanation. Proceeding from any one of several disciplinary vantage points, useful diagnoses and prescriptions for the treatment of poverty can be formulated. Thus, the economist may emphasize the need for more jobs and for retraining programs; the social worker may point to the role of physical and mental disability and old age, and thus to the need for rehabilitative services; the sociologist may analyze the social structure and social institutions and their attendant consequences to the individual; the psychologist may seek explanations in terms of characteristics of the individual. Without doubt, all analyses and corresponding change programs are correct, and just as surely, incomplete. Any program having the goal of eliminating poverty will have a significantly greater likelihood of success if relevant systems at all levels of analysis are brought to bear in a concerted fashion.

To repeat, if the psychologist emphasizes such variables as motivation, attitudes, and expectations, he is not attempting to minimize the role of economic, sociological, educational, and other relevant forces. As psychologists, however, we may most effectively contribute to the study of poverty by directing our efforts toward one portion of the problem on which we hold claim to some expertise—the behavioral—realizing all the while that the psychological analysis in itself will inevitably produce answers neither complete nor final. Nevertheless, if our understanding of poverty at the psychological level is inadequate, diagnoses and treatments undertaken at other levels may run aground upon the obstinate fact that human behavior is predictably complex and frequently unpredictable. Too many well-intentioned programs for ameliorating society have ended disastrously or with unintended and undesirable consequences because of our insufficient understanding of the psychological characteristics of individuals involved, or because of our inability to predict the psychological impact of programs conspicuously nonpsychological in nature.

The first part of this book delineates some of the theoretical issues involved in the psychology of poverty. Faced with the fact of the existence of poverty, the man in the street attempts to account for, and understand, the situation of the poor by using labeling processes that afford a folk diagnosis and remedy. Thus, poverty is due to being "lazy," "sinful," "sick," "stupid," "happy and irresponsible," or "the victim of environment." Scientific theory and research in poverty carries with it assumptions that are in many ways similar to folk analyses.

In the first chapter, Rainwater makes explicit some of the underlying —though frequently unstated—assumptions and theories about the poor accepted by both the scientist and the man in the street. From each of the five basic perspectives about the poor and about the nature of poverty, a particular set of policy implications or "therapies" seems most congruent and reasonable. It will be helpful, while reading other chapters, to keep in mind the five paradigms or perspectives on poverty that Rainwater has derived. Although they are usually not totally accepted in their pure forms by scientists working in the poverty area, most researchers probably would adhere to a somewhat greater extent to one perspective than to others. Many disagreements in theory and research in poverty probably stem from basic differences in the importance attributed to the five paradigms that Rainwater discusses.

In the second chapter, Sarbin applies the conceptual framework of role theory to the problems of poverty. Since role theory is a theoretical scheme that bridges the levels of culture (role), society (position), and individual (self), it may prove useful in analyzing poverty—a social problem that certainly penetrates these three levels. Role theory posits that behavior is a consequence of social organization, that is, of the positions in the social structure occupied by an individual. From an analysis of the situation of the poor, Sarbin concludes that the poor enact predominantly ascribed roles (nonchosen or granted) and very few achieved (chosen) roles. For describing the consequences of proper enactment of roles, Sarbin introduces the interesting distinction between esteem (positive valuation for enactment of achieved roles) and respect (positive valuation for enactment of ascribed roles). Improper enactment of ascribed roles—assigned disproportionately to the poor—results in very strong negative valuation or degradation. Thus, the poor experience degraded, negatively valued social identities, as indicated by the pejorative labels that are frequently applied.

The type of intervention program needed to transform degraded social identities emerges from role theory in a very straightforward way. The totality of role relationships defines one's social identity. Hence, to alter social identity it is necessary to change the social organization so that a greater proportion of achieved roles can be enacted by the poor. It is impor-

tant to note that the attack on problems of poverty taken by role theory emphasizes the impact on the individual of the antecedent social organiza- tion. Primary importance is not attributed to the individual's psycho- logical characteristics, which are viewed as outcomes of enactment of social roles.

The theoretical perspective discussed by Hunt in the third chapter represents the developmental-cognitive approach to the problems of poverty. Stress is placed on environmental conditions affecting development in early childhood, in contrast to the concern in role theory with the con- sequences of ongoing role enactments of adults. Recent empirical and theoretical advances in psychology make it quite apparent that many old assumptions are no longer tenable. For example, data reviewed by Hunt offer serious challenge to the belief that intelligence is fixed and that the sequence of development is predetermined. Impressive results from studies showing the effect on development of auditory, visual, and motor stim- ulation in early infancy have far-reaching implications for theory, as well as for the practical objective of facilitating cognitive development in lower- class children. Theory and data now available suggest that the damaging impact of poverty on the child could be vitiated by arranging conditions of optimal environment stimulation (both sensory and social) in early child- hood.

The revision of our assumptions about the fixed nature of intelligence and the predetermined sequence of development have direct relevance to early childhood educational programs. Hunt discusses the psychological bases of preschool enrichment and compensatory programs; it is, of course, not always easy to make specific program recommendations from theoreti- cal principles, but the broad outlines are clearly apparent. Lack of optimal environmental stimulation in the early childhood of lower-class children produces sequelae that are manifest later in life, as we shall see in Part 2, where learning processes in the poor are analyzed in some detail.

REFERENCES

Harrington, Michael, *The Other America—Poverty in the United States.* New York: Macmillan, 1962.

Hunter, Robert, *Poverty.* New York: Macmillan, 1904.

Kahn, Tom, *The Economics of Equality.* New York: League for Industrial Democracy, 1964.

Lewin, Kurt, *Field Theory in Social Science.* New York: Harper, 1951.

Matza, David, Poverty and Disrepute, in Robert K. Merton and Robert A. Nisbet, eds. *Contemporary Social Problems.* New York: Harcourt, Brace, World, 1966, pp.619-69.

Chapter 1

NEUTRALIZING THE DISINHERITED: SOME PSYCHOLOGICAL ASPECTS OF UNDERSTANDING THE POOR

Lee Rainwater*

INTRODUCTION

The central existential fact of life for the lower class, the poor, the deprived, and discriminated-against ethnic groups, is that their members are not included in the collectivity that makes up the "real" society of "real" people. They are not considered, and often do not consider themselves, quite part of the regular moral system taken in common as ordinary and regular society. They may not be allowed, or may not be able, to participate in those activities, or with those people, who are defined as integral to regular society. For this reason such groups can quite legitimately be considered "disinherited" in the sense that no valued and taken-for-granted place is made for them and their children in the society; they are on the

*Professor of Sociology, Harvard University, Cambridge, Mass. This chapter is based in part on research aided by a grant from the National Institute of Mental Health, Grant No. MH-09189, "Social and Community Problems in Public Housing Areas," to the Social Science Institute of Washington University. I am indebted to Herbert J. Gans for ideas contributed during a discussion of an earlier memo incorporating the view developed in this paper. In addition, in developing the ideas expressed in this paper I profited greatly from participating during the academic year 1966-67 in the "Poverty Seminar" supported by the American Academy of Arts and Sciences and chaired by Daniel P. Moynihan. Walter Miller's presentation to this seminar of his own typology of perspectives on lower-class culture stimulated me to work through some of these issues systematically.

outside looking in. Yet, at the same time, their activities are subject to surveillance and control by society in such a way that they are not truly
autonomous, not free to make a way of life of their own.

All of this is known, in a vague way, by everybody—the man in the
street knows it as well as the social scientist. To the extent that members
of regular society confront the reality of a disinherited group, they must
develop some understanding that "explains" the fact that there are people
among us who are not part of us. Social science views of these phenomena
are more elaborated, logically organized, and sophisticated versions of the
different common-sense understandings that develop about disinherited
groups. At the same time, to the extent that social science views derive
from reasonably adequate theory and empirical research, they are not
merely more elaborated, logically organized, and sophisticated versions,
but do indeed have a higher level of truth content than common-sense views,
even though they are not fully independent of these views.

When we seek to examine the various common-sense/social science
understandings of poverty, we are engaged in a study of what deviance experts call the *labeling process* (Lemert, 1967). In order to cope with the
presence of individuals who are not a regular part of a society, its members develop labels that signify the moral status of the deviant and carry
within them a folk etiology and diagnosis, and often a folk therapy. The
social scientist inevitably imports these folk understandings into his own
work. They yield both understanding and misunderstanding for him.

David Matza (1966) has neatly summarized the wide range of conceptions of the "disreputable poor" which social commentators have brought
to bear historically in their recurrent discovery of the poor. These labels
—be they *hard-to-reach, problem family, multiproblem family, lower-lower
class, lumpenproletariat, spurious leisure class,* or *paupers*—all can and
do exercise tremendous influence on the intellectual's grasp of the problems of poverty, and by extension also influence the kinds of policies that
are imagined whenever a "war on poverty" comes into being.

In Bertrand Beck's (1966, pp. 258-77)[1] analysis of "Welfare as a
Moral Category," what he has to say about the place of welfare and welfare recipients in the folk understandings of the social system (dare I say
"ethnosociology?") can be applied more generally to the situation of all
those who are in the position of the disinherited. Beck argues that in every
society individuals have a conception of how their system operates and
why it seems to operate that way that is parallel to, but not identical with,
an adequate sociological understanding of the social system. Thus he ob-
serves:

---

[1]See also the related articles by Simmel (1965) and Coser (1965).

Participants in the system, like scientific observers of it, postulate the structural coherence of most, if not all, the institutionalized roles. Like scientists, they have an interest in formulating a theory about the basic principles of this coherence. The folk theory of the participants will be called the Theory and is distinct from the sociologist's account of the structural coherence of the system of institutionalized roles. In fact, one of the most interesting sources of latent patterns should be in the gap between the publicly accepted Theory and the actual structure found by an observer. The Theory generates as its main result an object of public definition which we have called a "way of life," but which might be called in a more abstract vein the Theoretical structure, or even the ideal structure. In this paper, it will be called the Structure. Another important result generated by the Theory is a model of conduct with respect to the Structure. The belief that the Structure contributes to an orderly and predictable set of relationships among the persons who make up the population to a large degree explains its existence, according to the Theory. The implications of this notion are farreaching and constitute the basic building blocks out of which is constructed a folk model of conforming behavior and of the significance, explanation, and necessary treatment of deviations from conformity.

Beck goes on to observe that members of society inevitably run up against the fact that at least some individuals and groups do not conform to the folk Theory and Structure—that in fact the actual structure of the society does not always make a place that conforms to the folk Theory and Structure for each and every one of its members. This problem can be solved by fission (those who do not fit move out and form their own systems) or by the simple expedient of eliminating those who cannot be given a place in the system. But a situation short of this is more common and leads to a perplexing paradox for those who uphold the system:

> Those who are residual to the Structure will have to be provided with some defined place within it. They will have to be placed in some category created especially for them in order to bring them back within the system and allow the system to deal with them. What is paradoxical is that the role to which they are assigned is that of the roleless. In a sense being outside the Structure is a structural position.

Thus, new, jerry-built elements must be added to the Theory and Structure which give content to the role of the roleless and the structural position of being outside the structure. This is done through a variety of labels and common-sense understandings which these labels connote. But these additions to the Theory and Structure inevitably have a fugitive character because the very necessity to formulate them challenges the Theory. They tend to be shot through with contradictions and at the same time obsessively elaborated, in order somehow to rationalize the fact that the folk understandings break down when confronted with the hard reality that some of the individuals who live in the society's territory cannot be placed in the idealized system. Perhaps the most striking example we have of obsessive elaborations as efforts to rationalize such contradictions is the three-centuries-long effort on the part of southern slavery and Jim Crow advocates to formulate an adequate white supremacy ideology (Bailey, 1914; Bledsoe, 1856; Elliot, 1860; Fitzhugh, 1854; Shannon, 1907).

In the light of observations such as these it becomes apparent that the poor embarrass everyone. The Establishment is inevitably embarrassed, but the poor are no less embarrassing to those who seek concerted revolutionary action from the disinherited; thus the Marxist category of *Lumpenproletariat* is required to separate the honest revolutionary hero from the dregs who cannot be mobilized. In any elaborated radical ideology—that is, one that has existed long enough to have to seek to resolve some of its contradictions—the disinherited seem inevitably to become segregated in ideology, as they are in fact.

PERPLEXITY AND ANXIETY ENGENDERED BY DISINHERITANCE

We are accustomed to thinking of both the ordinary, common-sense understandings of the disinherited and the sophisticated, ideological, and social science understandings as having the psychological function of coping with the guilt feelings members of regular society develop because they know they derive various kinds of gains and gratifications from the existence of the disinherited. However, I think there is a more profound sentiment than guilt that motivates the search for an understanding of the disinherited. The individual who cannot avoid knowing about poverty and how the poor cope with their lives experiences a deep sense of *perplexity* and *anxiety* when he confronts his observations of how the poor live, or even when he ponders various unattractive stereotypes about them.[2]

---

[2]The salience of anxiety in common-sense perspectives on poverty and on Negroes was most clearly apparent to me in several anonymous telephone calls I received after being quoted in a St. Louis newspaper about the employment problems of lower-class Negro men in connection with the newspaper's background article on a proposal before the Missouri Legislature to provide for AFDC-U payments. In my remarks I had emphasized the desire of lower-class men to support their families, but had indicated the many ways in which economic and social arrangements interfere with the realization of this desire. Each of the white callers

The evidence available to regular people from experience with the disinherited and stereotypes about them leads to a deeply felt belief that "I would not live that way; I could not live that way." And this common-sense judgment that the disinherited way of life is "unlivable" in turn contributes to a perception of the situation of the disinherited as somehow unreal. Yet there they are; they do not lie down and die, they survive and they multiply. The original perception that their lives are unlivable is therefore called into question, which produces a great deal of anxiety. The disinherited *are,* yet they cannot be.

The calling into question of a perception which itself has important functions results in a highly unstable cognitive situation—an instability which the individual is strongly motivated to resolve. I think there are two very common kinds of resolutions (there may be others) which run somewhat along the following lines:

Initial Perception: "I could not live the way they live, but yet they seem to be able to do so—that is, as I understand my humanity I could not tolerate the experiences that they seem to have as I perceive those experiences to be. I cannot match my perceptions of normal humanity and of their conditions in any way that produces an understanding of their lives as livable." Therefore . . .

Solution 1: "Perhaps they do not actually live that way; perhaps my perception of their life circumstances is incorrect." Or . . .

Solution 2: "Perhaps they are not they. That is, perhaps they are not persons such as I. It is not possible to speak of us as we human beings. Since I am human and I have decided that humans (that is, persons like me) cannot live the way they live and survive, yet they do seem to live that way, then perhaps they are not human."

FIVE PERSPECTIVES ON THE DISINHERITED

If this analysis is correct, then we are justified in considering specific diagnoses of the condition of the disinherited as representing various amalgams of versions of "they don't really live that way," and "they are not human." From the popular literature dealing with problems of the disinherited and

---

said that I was wrong, that their own intimate knowledge of lower-class Negroes indicated that the men were simply lazy and uninterested in supporting their families. Although all of the callers seemed reasonably sane, I was struck by the fact that they expressed anxiety more than anger in their conversations, that my remarks seemed literally to disorient them in connection with their views about this group, and that they were almost pleading with me to admit that I was wrong so they might relax in the knowledge that their views were indeed valid.

from the social science literature, as well as from inevitable participant observation during discussions of these matters by lay people and by social scientists, I think it is possible to identify five different perspectives that are brought to bear on understanding the situation of the disinherited. In each perspective there can be discerned beliefs concerning the humanness or personality of disinherited persons and also beliefs having to do with their way of life somewhat apart from their individual personalities.

Before discussing in detail these five perspectives, I want to note that with one possible exception there are highly convincing portraits of each one of these points of view in both the popular and the social science literature. This suggests that each perspective may capture a certain amount of truth of the condition of the disinherited. But, by the same token, portraits hewing closely to any one of these views are often unsatisfactory both because it is easy to think of exceptions and because the characterizations tend to have the quality of making their subjects seem to be, in Harold Garfinkel's phrase, "conceptual boobs."

These five conceptions I will call the *moralizing,* the *naturalizing,* the *medicalizing,* the *apotheosizing,* and the *normalizing* perspectives. Four of them seem to me to represent combinations of two basic dichotomies about the situation of the disinherited, and one represents instead an effort to rise above these dichotomies. The relationship between these two dichotomous variables and the five perspectives is indicated in Figure 1. I suggest that the poor can be characterized as either weak or potent, and that they can be evaluated as either virtuous or lacking in virtue—as evil, if you will. The combination of a perception of the disinherited as evil and potent leads to what I will call the *moralizing* perspective; of virtuous and potent to the *apotheosizing* perspective; of evil and weak to the *medicalizing* perspective; of virtuous and weak to the *normalizing* perspective. The fifth—the *naturalizing* perspective—comes about as a result of an effort to rise above these

Figure 1: Five Perspectives on the Poor

The poor are evaluated as:	The poor are characterized as:	
	Weak	Potent
Virtuous	Normalizing	Apotheosizing
	Naturalizing	
Evil	Medicalizing	Moralizing

value judgments of virtuousness versus evil and weakness versus potency, and to develop a value-free conception that leans heavily on an impersonal, natural science perspective. (Of course, in this latter case, we are often able to see ample evidence that the explanation is neither value-free nor impersonal.)

Let us now examine each one of these perspectives in terms of what it stipulates about the personalities and way of life of the disinherited, and then in each case move on to a consideration of the policy implications, the "therapy," that seems to fit most easily with the diagnosis. However, a caveat is in order here. I think it is very likely that there is no necessary connection between the perspective as diagnosis and statements about the etiology and therapy that fit most easily with each perspective. Unique combinations can and do occur; probably a very careful analysis of the particular views of holders of a given perspective on all three issues would be necessary to specify the connection between etiology, diagnosis, and therapy. Thus, there may or may not be a predictable connection between a cataloging of causes of disinheritance—economic exploitation, political subjugation, ethnic discrimination, etc.—and any one particular perspective.

Similarly, I think that there are often "Left" and "Right" versions of most of these perspectives. This becomes clear in some of the controversies that revolve around questions of poverty war diagnosis and therapy. It seems to me that very often the perspective is more important to the holder than are his politics. One can sometimes detect alliances or at least parallel kinds of attack by Left and Right poverty warriors against a perspective that they find threatening for reasons that have little to do with basic political orientation.[3]

Finally, it should be noted that some of the most important functions, or at least effects, of these different perspectives relate to their role as social commentary quite apart from a specific therapy designed to deal with the poor. Each perspective allows secondary gains, so to speak, from the particular poverty diagnosis that is offered. Like other kinds of secondary gain, these may come to loom larger than the basic function of resolving perplexity and anxiety.

Poverty perspectives can become important to their users as a way of battling with one's enemies in regular society quite apart from their function for resolving the cognitive problems raised by becoming aware of poverty, or their rational functions of leading to the development of therapies for dealing with society's poverty problem. For example, social workers often use versions of poverty as a way of fighting a battle that pits them as welfare

---

[3]For a case study in which this kind of situation seems to obtain see Rainwater and Yancy (1967).

professionals against other kinds of professionals, particularly against the dominance of business institutions in American society. Similarly, white radicals often use poverty perspectives as a way of getting even with and irritating those they consider "square" and conventional. (And they, in turn, are often put down by Negro radicals who see through their inability to really do anything about the white squares.)

More recently, we have observed the possibility for black radicals to use their particular perspective on the disinheritance of the Negro poor as a way of retreating from antagonistic engagement with white society, or of retreating from cooptation into the white-dominated Negro middle class (Ladner, 1967).

Finally, everyone must by now be aware of the proclivity of some poverty perspectives for attenuating the commitment of liberals to the political goal of incorporating the disinherited into the society, and for rationalizing the metaphysical pathos of such liberals, which maintains that nothing can be done, or that whatever can be done can only be done very, very gradually. Furthermore, the disinherited are powerless to prevent themselves from being manipulated by members of the dominant society, be it the radical who wants to *épater le bourgeois,* the welfare professional who wants to assert his virtue over that of the entrepreneur, or the liberal establishmentarian who fights a two-front battle against radical and Republican alike.

The Moralizing Perspective

This is perhaps the oldest approach to understanding the disinherited. In this perspective a moral flaw is perceived in the disinherited or in their environment which explains the fact that they live unlivable lives—that is, they are able to live this way because they are morally different from regular people. The focus of the moralizing perspective can be on the individual disinherited person or on a quality of his environment (although, of course, the two are generally very much linked).

The Sinners.   In the moralizing view the disinherited are afflicted with the mark of Cain. They are meant to suffer, indeed must suffer, because of their moral failings. They live in a deserved hell on earth. As long as they do not renounce their immorality and allow themselves to be saved they must continue in the status of the disinherited. If they do renounce their immorality they may come into God's inheritance as members of the regular community.

An Environment of Sin. Regardless of the moral status of particular individuals, the disinherited live in a world in which immorality is the rule. Though innocent at birth, they do not stay this way long because of the seductions and temptations around them.

Therapy. Perhaps the most pressing claims for social action that stem from the moralizing perspective have to do with demands for punishment and control of the immorality lest it "infect" and "attack" the rest of the community.[4] Beyond punishment and control the therapies that go most naturally with this view emphasize efforts to redeem and "save" the disinherited sinners through evangelistic movements which may start either spontaneously within the community of the disinherited or be imposed from outside.

It would be difficult to overemphasize the extent to which the moralizing perspective undergirds seemingly more sophisticated views of poverty. It would also be difficult to exaggerate the extent to which the views of a great many of the disinherited themselves, about their own conditions and about the conditions of those around them, are informed by a moralizing perspective. Manifestations of this point of view are readily apparent at the popular level in the characterizations by lower-class people of themselves and their peers, more officially in the ideologies of fundamentalist churches, and particularly of movements such as the Black Muslims.

The Medicalizing Perspective

The medicalizing perspective is perhaps the most direct descendant of the moralizing one in the sense that it is relatively simple to replace the condition of "sin" with that of "sickness." In the medicalizing perspective the explanation of how the disinherited live unlivable lives lies in the understanding that normal people and normal social patterns have somehow been subjected to pathological processes. The disinherited and their way of life may be human, but sick. As before, various commentators will place primary emphasis either on the sickness of individuals or on the sickness of the environment.

Psychopathologizing. This perspective predicates that the disinherited live the way they do because their psyches are pathologically formed. This pathology can be taken to refer most directly to the personality: there will

---

[4]For example, the current widespread interest in federal crime control and juvenile-delinquency control activities can be seen as in part a political response to a moralistic critique of the "give-away" poverty and race programs.

be emphasis on mental illness, sociopathic behavior, apathetic or depressive orientations, disturbed child-rearing practices, etc. More recently, as psychology has become increasingly intrigued with mental processes rather than with personality processes in general, emphasis has shifted to the pathological character of cognitive development, to trained incapacities, to the absence of certain kinds of experiences that leave the child cognitively underdeveloped, and the like. In both cases the disinherited live as they do because of the way things are put together inside their heads. The human material from which they sprang has in the course of life been blunted and malformed; from this pathology results behavior that is destructive both to the individuals involved and to people around them. In this way, although it started out the same, the human material of the disinherited ends up different from that of the rest of us.

The Pathological Environment. Here the emphasis is on the sickness of the social environment. In contrast to the psychological emphasis on individual personality and mental processes, there is a sociological emphasis on social disorganization and pathology. Participation in this sick world, though in the extreme sociological view it may be considered not to rub off on the individual personality, nevertheless leads to unhappy and disorganized lives. The disinherited are seen as falling in, not with bad company, but with sick company. No matter how hard the individual tries he is constantly interfered with by a disorganized community which frustrates his constructive goals, and tends to replace them with deviant ones.

Therapy. In terms of therapy the implications of the first, more psychological, view are fairly straightforward. There is emphasis on psychotherapy and counseling for the disturbed personalities involved, or on the development of compensatory education and training programs that somehow repair cognitive damage. The choices this perspective leads to tend systematically to highlight the importance of clinical approaches and individual diagnosis.

With respect to the pathological environment, therapy will emphasize the building of a less pathological community of the disinherited. There will be emphasis on developing an organized, as opposed to a disorganized, community "infrastructure," and on generating community involvement in new institutions of various kinds which direct energies in a constructive, as opposed to a destructive, direction.

At the more extreme levels, however, where the perception is of a community that is hopelessly disorganized, the suggested solution may instead be to remove at least the children from the disorganizing environment   as in the underground suggestion one hears repeatedly from unself-conscious, usually nonprofessional, commentators on the War on Poverty that all poor children should be removed from their families and communities and put into government-run *kibbutzim* where they will learn proper ways.[5]

The Naturalizing Perspective

Here there is a great effort to gain evaluative distance from the situation of the disinherited. The emphasis is on discovering a "natural" explanation of how the disinherited live as they seem to. Science is to provide the answer in an impersonal, value-free way by the application of scientific knowledge about humans and their behavior.

Biological Determinism.   Thirty to forty years ago the emphasis on biological differences was probably the major alternative to the moralizing perspective. Great efforts were expended in demonstrating that the disinherited, particularly the darker racial groups but also the white disreputable poor, were biologically different and inferior to regular people. This inferiority was said to explain the fact that the disinherited are able to live in a way that regular folk cannot live. The disinherited were biologically below standard, were genetically inferior in one way or another. This was indeed unfortunate, and one should deal humanely with such people as one might with domestic animals, but it was believed unnatural to expect them to perform in regular ways and it was unwise (because of the stress on their inferior constitutions) to provide them with the regular rewards that society had to offer.

The major thrust of biological determinism as an explanatory perspective in this area had to do with intelligence—an effort was made to demonstrate inferior brains in those who are not part of regular society—but there were also congeries of other presumed traits that were believed to be genetically based: greater insensitivity to pain, greater ability to tolerate manual labor, lesser control of the emotions, etc. Biological determinism has not been very respectable intellectually for at least thirty years, but

---

[5]Indeed, at one point OEO was said to be considering the construction of large camps modeled somewhat along the lines of the Job Corps to which whole families would be assigned for resocialization. In the October 9, 1965, issue of the *Washington Star,* there appeared an article by Mary McGrory, "Job Corps Developing Plan for Whole Family," in which she said: "The Office of Economic Opportunity is working on a revolutionary scheme to resettle poor young couples in centers where the whole family would be trained to take its place in the Great Society . . . 'We would refurbish the whole family and set them on a higher plateau,' says Singletary (the Job Corps Director)."

that should not lead us to underestimate its influence as a lay perspective.[6]

The therapy that goes most naturally with biological determinism might be characterized as benign totalitarianism. Here a heavy emphasis is placed both on control of the activities of those who are biologically inferior since they obviously cannot judge best for themselves, and on a castelike social structure in which those who are marked as inferior are not allowed to weaken regular society by mating with it. From this perspective, eugenics is an important applied therapy in the progressive weeding out of the inferior.

The Cultural-Relativistic Perspective.   The other "natural" explanation of the situation of the disinherited is quite different. Not only is there a disinterest in biological determinism, but it is asserted that the way of life of the disinherited is perfectly valid, equally as functional as that of regular society. While the disinherited may have troubles from their way of life, just as every way has its characteristic difficulties, they are socialized into appropriate behavior for their world just as regular persons are socialized into appropriate behavior for theirs. The disinherited can be, and are, reasonably well-adjusted and happy within their world. They are neither inferior nor superior to regular society; they are just different. Their way of life has the same degree of organization and adaptiveness as has that of regular society. We are right in our initial perception that they are human, but we are wrong in our perception of the disinherited way of life, because we miss its inner coherence and validity.

The implications for action that flow from this view are less straightforward than in other cases because of the emphasis of cultural relativism on the inherent validity of each way of life. "Cultural pluralism" tends to be the main thrust, a request that regular society recognize the imperatives and the values of the culture of the disinherited, that it not be stigmatized, that regular society "get off their backs." In the conservative version of this view it may be argued that very little should be done in the way of special therapy, but that natural events should be allowed to run their course—if the disinherited want to buy into the regular society, they eventually will. A leftist view will hold that, despite the validity of the way of life of the disinherited, they do need resources of various kinds. This view will suggest a kind of "foreign aid" approach which turns over to the disinherited *as a group* certain kinds of resources that it will then use in whatever way seems appropriate given its cultural priorities rather than those of regular society.

---

[6]It is interesting that some genetic and some social scientists are very tentatively seeking to raise again as a scientific problem the question of genetically based differences in intelligence in relation to lower-status positions (but not with reference to racial groups for reasons that are too technical to note here). See, for example, Eckland (1967), and the references found there.

In its purest form, however, cultural relativism probably reinforces an emphasis on simply studying the disinherited, and tends to play down both the desirability and the possibility of regular society's doing anything about the situation in which the disinherited find themselves. The cultural relativist who also holds strong activist views will probably tend to be pushed in the direction of the next perspective, that of apotheosizing.

The Apotheosizing Perspective

This substitutes a perception of heroic adaptation for the initial perception of disinheritance—a kind of standing the initial perception on its head. The central myth that informs this perspective is that of the "natural man" in a "natural world." The villain is civilization which has deprived and alienated members of regular society while leaving the disinherited free to be natural. In a more moderate version apotheosizing asserts that "we're just as bad as they are, maybe worse."

The Natural Man. From this perspective the disinherited are perceived as stronger, as a kind of supermen who have developed special capacities (e.g., rhythm!), special philosophies, a special quality of existential humanity that eschews the artificiality of regular society. In a somewhat less complimentary, though still highly romantic version, the disinherited are seen as fortunately insensitive to pain and possessed of a natural self-assurance which allows them to endure the insult and derogation to which regular society subjects them. There are many representations of natural man among the disinherited (indeed, the myth of the "natural man" seems difficult to sustain except where the hero is among the disinherited). The ballad of John Henry, the hustler and the blues singer, the cowboy, the stoic sharecropper, the *macho* Latin, the newly conscious black man—all of these provide convenient symbolic representations of such a perspective.

Heroic Culture. When the emphasis shifts from the individuals involved to the social life of the group, the perspective tends to emphasize the heroic quality of the life of the disinherited. Heroic, not just in the sense of being able to cope with adversity and still maintain life, but in the sense that as a result of adversity the disinherited have been able to create a way of life that has beauty and virtue. The disinherited are seen as having a good thing going for them. Despite the fact that they are exploited, despite the punishment regular society dishes out, they have succeeded in constructing a way of life that actually has *more* validity, is *less* alienated, than regular middle-class society. Contrast to middle-class society becomes important for this perspective—"look at the pathology of the suburbs!" "Look at the disintegration of the sense of community in middle-class society!" In short, civilization dilutes the sense of both community and human individuality in regular society, but this sense is alive in the community of the despised.

Therapy. The most direct implication of these views involves the adoption by regular folk of natural man and heroic culture as symbols and the enjoyment of the superior inventions of the disinherited, whether these inventions be pizza, the hully gully, or the cool way of life. Beyond consumption, the apotheosizing perspective is tailor-made for use in attacking the rest of the society. The disinherited are held up to the rest of society not as an example of its destructiveness and barbarity, but rather of its self-destructiveness, its artificiality, and its unreal and alienated ways. Beyond these relatively passive uses of the apotheosizing perspective, it can become the core for an effort to create a new revolutionary man, to provide new hope for the old leftism and inspiration for a new radicalism. The apotheosized disinherited provide a source of human energy and creativity which can be organized to revitalize the total society, because only among them do human meaning and vitality persist. There is no more *lumpenproletariat,* for among the disinherited lie the real proletariat who have not been coopted and bought off by materialistic society. It is only necessary that the insightful members of regular society who perceive this throw in their lot with the disinherited and organize and manipulate them to provide a power base and an ideology for achieving the new society.

The Normalizing Perspective

Finally, there is the perspective that resolves the initial perplexity and anxiety by the simplest mechanism possible—denial. Following Fred Davis (1964), I mean by the normalizing perspective a process by which the individual who seeks to understand the situation of the disinherited "comes to view as normal and morally acceptable that which initially strikes him as odd, unnatural, 'crazy,' deviant, etc., irrespective of whether his perception was in the first instance reasonable, accurate, or justifiable." In the normalizing perspective the initial perception of disinherited individuals and their way of life as unlivable is simply denied, treated as the result of processes of middle-class projection and stereotyping. The disinherited are really just like you and me except perhaps that they are mistreated and poor, but these latter conditions do not result in other than superficial differences.

Ordinary People. In the normalizing perspective it is asserted that the disinherited have essentially the same hopes, wishes, goals, interests, joys, and sorrows that everybody else does and that they express these in the same way. Furthermore, they are just as law-abiding, self-controlled, sensitive, sensible, and intelligent as you and I. They are no more and no less than ordinary human beings, and their condition of disinheritance has only superficial impact on their personalities. They are deprived of the means to live in superficially conventional ways, that is, to have the same material goods, to participate socially in the same ways as the members of regular society. But these deprivations do not have any fundamental impact on their personalities and their world views, or on their values. From this perspective, then, the null hypothesis reigns—that is, except for behavior and attitudes that are simple, direct, and immediate responses to deprivation or prejudice, their views of life and their behavior are indistinguishable from those of others in the society.

An Adequately Coping Way of Life.   With respect to the social life of the disinherited, as opposed to their individual characters, the normalizing perspective suggests that while it is true that they have a great many troubles and the rest of society imposes many penalties and punishments on them, nevertheless they somehow manage their situation in such a way that their interpersonal relations and their ways of coping with the world are not deeply affected. Thus, in this perspective the disinherited love their children and their kin; help each other out (perhaps more than members of regular society because it is necessary to do so); and are reasonably well-adjusted and happy in their social relations, except that they have a realistic awareness of the problems that society makes for them. The anger that they may feel at their lot is simply healthy anger; it does not repercuss on their personalities or on the informal institutions of their day-to-day lives. In short, their lives are eminently livable, if somewhat restricted by lack of resources and barriers artificially imposed by the outside world.

Therapy.   In many ways the major effect of the normalizing perspective is to debunk other perspectives by denying the validity of their various conceptualizations of the disinherited life. This is often done to ward off or argue against the policy implications of the other perspectives, either out of a sense of identification with the essential humanity of the disinherited, or (probably equally common) out of a wish to do nothing and to underemphasize the deprivation and destruction that rejection from the conventional system involves.

In a more sophisticated way the normalizing perspective suggests therapies that emphasize "opportunity" rather than more radical alterations in the system. That is, it is argued that since the disinherited are really ordinary people who happen to be caught in an unfavorable situation for achieving their ordinary desires, it is necessary only to provide them with the ordinary means to the achievement of these desires. For example, such things as job-training programs, more thoughtfully and seriously under- taken education programs to replace the poorly equipped and poorly staffed schools that are available to them, and perhaps some counseling to make them aware of the opportunities that exist in the larger world should be pro- vided. In other words, the intervention that is required is basically the fairly superficial one of providing realistic access to means of achieving the level of income and other kinds of functioning that are necessary to be a part of regular society. To a great extent this involves not stereotyping the disin- herited or in any way emphasizing what little may be different about their way of life and their personal techniques for coping with their situation. In short, one wants to accentuate the positive both at the verbal level of the semantics of poverty and at the action level of making better-coordinated and -supported services and opportunities available.

CONCLUSION

Anyone who is well acquainted with the literature on poverty and race problems in this country probably would have little difficulty ticking off a number of authors to fit each of the perspectives presented above. However, for a number of reasons I have purposely avoided attaching specific authors to these views. Perhaps most important, almost none of the major writers on poverty and race could be neatly categorized as reflecting in pure type only one of these perspectives. By and large social scientists who seriously address the problems of race and poverty quickly become aware of the in- adequacy of any one of these views. Perhaps equally indicative of a writer's bias are the one or two perspectives that he most actively polemicizes *against*. Therefore, what is distinctive about any one poverty or race ex- pert is not so much the perspective to which he adheres as the particular combination of elements from different perspectives that his work repre- sents.

I have also tried to avoid any indication that one of these perspectives is correct, because it seems to me that each one has an irrational core which can serve to distort an adequate understanding of the condition of disin- herited people if pursued too single-mindedly. But it should also be noted that (with the probable exception of biological determinism) each one of these perspectives has something to offer in coming to a balanced appre- ciation of the life of the disinherited. I think it would not be at all difficult for the social scientist who has really intensive observational data from any one person or any one community of the disinherited to find data that support each of these perspectives.

One attractive solution to the problem of discovering that some poor people fit one perspective while others fit another is to develop a typology that apportions poor people to one or another type—in my schema we could have the immoral, the sick, the mentally retarded, the subcultural practitioner, the hero, and the normal. There may indeed be individuals who fit one of these perspectives not only at a given time but throughout their lives. However, I am much more impressed by the alterations in behavior and psychological state that poor people can experience as their situations change. The same individual can at one period of his life to all intents and purposes behave and feel like a conventional member of society, at another period seem the perfect example of the psychopathologically afflicted, and at another period seem content with a subculturally different existence. And, as Robert Coles has so sensitively shown, given particularly challenging circumstances, the disinherited child or adult can be truly heroic in ways that surprise and appall conventional people. For these reasons I suspect that the "typological solution" inevitably breaks down when we add a longitudinal dimension to our usual cross-sectional perspective.[7]

Finally, adherence to these perspectives either singly or in combination can very readily be found not only among social scientists and middle-class and stable working-class onlookers, but also among lower-class people themselves. Indeed, a very interesting study could examine the question of the ethnodiagnosis of the condition of poverty by people who themselves are afflicted with that condition.

More broadly, it should be noted that these five perspectives are probably fundamental explanatory categories for any problem in the way of life of a particular group. With some modifications this kind of schema could probably be applied to studying folk diagnoses of the situations of groups as different from the disinherited as business executives, the power elite, the artistically creative, and the government bureaucrat. We are probably always going to be confronted with the basic psychological issue of perplexity and anxiety which arises from trying to understand and account for the human condition. This issue comes to the fore when one concentrates on any particular group of human beings and discovers that his conception of what is human is so heavily personalized that he finds it difficult to empathize with the behavior of persons who are in notably different situations. It certainly would be true that the more conventional the group

---

[7]For my own efforts to resolve some of the contradictory impressions one gains from data about lower-class living patterns, see Rainwater (1970).

being studied, the more attractive will be the normalizing perspective unless one has a particular axe to grind. Nevertheless, I think it is also true that if one systematically surveyed the literature on exceptional groups in the society, whether they be exceptional by virtue of unusual achievement or (as in the case of the disinherited) lack of achievement, the issue of "they can't possibly be human in the way I am human" would come to the fore.

In the end we are confronted with a paradox: the effort to develop an understanding of the condition of the disinherited that will neutralize the perplexity and anxiety the observer experiences will, even when it is effective in accomplishing this goal, result in radical ambiguity in the rational task of developing an existentially grounded diagnosis of the condition of that group. We can satisfy ourselves, as well as those who are eagerly awaiting a diagnosis that will somehow get them off the hook, by developing a well-drawn portrait along the lines of one of these perspectives. However, we inevitably leave ambiguities, apparent to anyone who looks closely, because no one perspective can fully capture the complexity of life of the people in whom we are interested. I think these ambiguities can be tolerated as long as we are dealing with the scientific level of the problem. After all, we really are not at the point where we can expect social-scientific explanations that resolve all issues and neatly package reality.

On the other hand, once one moves over into the question of policy, these ambiguities become crucial because each perspective tends to encourage certain kinds of policy choices. Depending on how adequately the perspective copes with the reality of the disinherited, those policy choices may prove successful or unsuccessful. It would be my view that the perspectives that have dominated the formulation of the current War on Poverty have been the less powerful ones and that the policies that have been derived from social science research have been, by and large, the wrong ones (Rainwater, 1967a, b). Perhaps it is at this point that we need to be more flexible in the connection we make between diagnoses and policy prescriptions, or perhaps simply more profound. Perhaps we need to take our diagnoses a great deal more seriously than we do.

I do not think anyone studies the behavior of the disinherited out of solely scientific reasons, although there certainly is a wide range in the degree to which researchers are interested in an immediate policy follow-through. For the basic science goals, but even more for the policy goals, it seems to me that we somehow have to go beyond development of understandings that do an effective job of neutralizing the perceptions that make us (and everybody else) very nervous. We must strive first for a phenomenologically valid account both of the inner reality of personal life and of the social exchanges that constitute the pattern of social life of the disinherited. We must learn to become much more precise about how this inner reality and way of life came into being historically, and about how they are sustained by the larger social system in which they are embedded. The very gross paradigms that these five perspectives bring to bear can be useful in accomplishing this task if they are taken as starting points rather than as resolutions to the scientific and the policy problems.

But we will discover that a phenomenologically accurate account of the condition of the disinherited will make us and those who read us even more nervous because the more accurate the account, the more it will heighten, at least initially, the deeply human perception that "they cannot live like that because I could not live like that." Anyone who doubts that need only read the works of Erving Goffman, Harold Garfinkel, and their students.

Such accounts will inevitably present the social scientists and policy makers with what Alvin Gouldner (1966) has called "hostile information," that is, information that challenges their most deeply-held beliefs about what people are like, why they act as they do, and what this implies for political action. Yet if we are to provide a satisfactory intellectual grounding for systematic policy making in this area, we must somehow achieve such a complex, accurate diagnosis rather than merely a satisfying and anxiety-reducing one.

REFERENCES

Bailey, T. P. *Race Orthodoxy in the South and Other Aspects of the Negro Question.* New York: Neale, 1914.

Beck, Bernard. Welfare as a Moral Category. *Social Problems* 1966, 14: 258-277.

Bledsoe, A. T. *An Essay on Liberty and Slavery.* Philadelphia: Lippincott, 1956.

Coser, Lewis A. The Sociology of Poverty. *Social Problems* 1965, 8: 140-48.

Davis, F. Deviance Disavowal: The Management of Strained Interaction by the Visibly Handicapped, in H. S. Becker, ed. *The Other Side.* New York: Free Press, 1964, pp. 119-36.

Eckland, Bruce K. Genetics and Sociology: A Reconsideration. *American Sociological Review* 1967, 32: 173-94.

Elliott, E. N., ed. *Cotton is King, and Pro-Slavery Arguments.* Augusta, Ga.: Pritchard, Abbott and Loomis, 1860.

Fitzhugh, G. *Sociology for the South or the Failure of Free Society.* Richmond, Va.: A. Morris, 1854.

Gouldner, A. W. *Enter Plato.* New York: Basic Books, 1966.

Ladner, J. A Study of "Black Power" in Mississippi. Paper presented at the American Sociological Association meetings, August 1967.

Lemert, E. M. *Human Deviance, Social Problems and Social Control.* New York: Prentice-Hall, 1967.

Matza, David. The Disreputable Poor, in R. Bendix and S. M. Lipset, eds. *Class, Status and Power.* New York: Free Press, 1966, pp. 289-302.

Rainwater, Lee. *Behind Ghetto Walls: Black Family Life in a Federal Slum.* Chicago: Aldine, 1970.

————. The Lessons of Pruitt-Igoe. *The Public Interest* 1967, No. 8, 116-26.(a)

————. Policy Research, Applied Research, and Lower Class Culture. Paper presented at 26th annual meeting of the Society for Applied Anthropology, Washington, D.C., May 5-7, 1967.(b)

Rainwater, Lee, and Yancy, W. L. *The Moynihan Report and the Politics of Controversy.* Cambridge, Mass.: M.I.T. Press, 1967.

Shannon, A. H. *Racial Integrity and Other Features of the Negro Problem.* Nashville, Tenn.: Publishing House of the M. E. Church, South, 1907.

Simmel, Georg, The Poor. *Social Problems* 1965, 8: 118-40.

Chapter 2

THE CULTURE OF POVERTY, SOCIAL IDENTITY, AND COGNITIVE OUTCOMES

Theodore R. Sarbin*

INTRODUCTION

It is my aim in this chapter to establish four propositions concerning the so-called culture of poverty and to make clear their relations one to the other.

1. The first proposition is that criteria for identifying a culture may be specified in order to isolate for study and intervention a conceptual unit called the culture of poverty. As I shall argue, being a participant in the culture of poverty is not coterminous with being poor, or with being rated low on scales that index socioeconomic status.

2. The second proposition follows from the first: If there is a distinguishable culture or subculture, then certain regularities in conduct can be observed. These regularities may be of many kinds, some of interest to psychologists, such as beliefs about the locus of control

*Professor of Psychology, University of California, Santa Cruz. The initial development of the theoretical model employed in this chapter took place in 1965 as a collaborative enterprise with Professors K. E. Scheibe and Rolf O. Kroger (Sarbin, Sheibe, and Kroger, 1965). The model served as the basis for an analysis of the concept of danger (Sarbin, 1967) and of mental illness (Sarbin, 1968). In the spring of 1967, graduate students in a seminar on social identity and cognition were helpful in critically discussing many of the points raised here. The present version was completed during the writer's tenure as a Fellow of the Center for Advanced Studies, Wesleyan University, 1968-69.

of behavior, typical construing of time, linguistic codes, and un-
modulated forms of adaptive conduct.

3. The third proposition is that the conduct of participants in the culture of poverty follows from the type of social organization that
   characterizes the culture. I intend to suggest that a model derived
   from extensions of role theory and taking into account the form of
   social organization would predict the observed psychological outcomes.

4. The fourth proposition is in the nature of a prescription for action
   and follows from the other propositions: That interventions designed
   to modify the existing psychological outcomes should be directed to
   antecedent organizational components rather than to consequent
   psychological outcomes.

THE CULTURE OF POVERTY

There is a risk of belaboring the obvious in pointing to the need for regarding poverty as a culture. Oscar Lewis (1966) has popularized the term and
has argued that the culture of poverty may be observed in many parts of the
world where similar historical antecedents have resulted in a social organization that contains declassed or degraded persons. He is undoubtedly correct. My purposes are more limited, however. I shall maintain a more
restricted view and focus on the culture of poverty in the cities of America.
A continuity in the culture of poverty of the present and of past generations
in the United States is demonstrable through historical analysis, a continuity
that reaches across the centuries into the Elizabethan Poor Laws of the
seventeenth century. At least since that time there has existed a fine distinction between the reputable or respectable poor and the degraded or disreputable poor. The latter, when segregated and maintained, have formed subcultures lying adjacent to, or surrounded by, subcultures of nonpoverty. I
make the assumption that one may speak of the culture of poverty in the
same way that one may speak of the culture of the Alorese, the Hopi, or the
Kwakiutl. The imagery intended in such usage is that certain features
differentiate these collectivities one from the other. Some of the differentiating characteristics, such as geographical location, are relatively gross.
Examples are an island in the Pacific, a mesa in New Mexico, and an
area in New York City bounded by "Central Park and the East River
north of 99th Street and south of 125th Street." Other, less coarse, differentiating features include kinship systems, religious orientations, and
social organization. Still others are more fine-grained, such as language
structure, cognitive development, time perspective, and beliefs in locus of
control.

I agree with Lewis that the culture of poverty is not a phrase to refer to the absence of economic or social goods; it is not just a matter of economic deprivation, or low position on socioeconomic indicators. Rather, the definition that governs the employment of the word *culture* in contemporary anthropology is applicable here. A culture is a set of acquired patterns of conduct, a way of life that provides its participants with adaptive techniques to deal with a set of recurring problems. Viewed in this way, the focus is less exclusively on the individual victims of poverty but rather on the social organization that creates specific social types that reproduce and maintain themselves with predictable regularity.

With hardly an exception, psychological studies have not operated from the base suggested by the concept "the culture of poverty." Rather, interest has been focused on social class as the independent variable because it is readily quantifiable. Whatever system is used for assessing socioeconomic status as an independent variable, two facts emerge: (1) The classification of an individual or group as lower class or middle class carries a tacit or expressed criterion of earnings. That is, the underlying dimension is an economic one. (2) The classification of persons at the lower end of the dimension tends to homogenize the respectable poor and the degraded poor, the latter being participants in the culture of poverty.[1]

I might mention that the semantics of the social-class concept tends to conceal more than it reveals about social organization and about the probable psychological correlates of social organization. It was only at the end of the eighteenth century that the semantic structure of class in a social sense originated. Obviously, the introduction of class terms, such as *higher classes, middle classes,* and *working classes* (all between 1790 and 1815) did not indicate the beginnings of social distinctions. *Class* was employed to replace *rank* as a term to denote social divisions. The newer term was a more indefinite one than the older, and reflected some of the social effects of the industrial revolution (Williams, 1958). The concept of social classes and the concept of mobility developed interdependently and gave support to the notion of classes as way stations on the road to economic and social achievement. From this arose the notion of an underlying single dimension—socioeconomic status—that has tended to attenuate the recognition of the qualitative differences in ways of living—such differences being more noteworthy when the concept of culture or subculture is employed.

---

[1]The utility of the social-class concept has been repeatedly challenged. My own view is that social class has become a part of the conceptual structure of social scientists but not of the conceptual structure of the people studied by social scientists. Its utility as a reference group has not been established.

Space limitations do not allow a social historical analysis of the concept of the degraded poor—the recruits to the subculture of poverty in the United States. I can only refer briefly to the enlightening article by Matza (1966) entitled "The Disreputable Poor," in which he points to the stigmatization that occurs among certain classes of impoverished people. His social and historical analysis makes plain that pauperization follows certain predictable paths. The process of pauperization, i.e., assigning to a poor person a negatively valued identity, provides the basis for recruitment into the subculture of poverty. Focusing on one aspect of pauperization—the failure of some members of each cohort of immigrants to America to achieve a place in the upwardly mobile push out of the slum—Matza (1966, p. 645) refers to these as "the dregs." He says:

> Each experience of ethnic mobility leaves a sediment which appears to be trapped in slum life, whether as a result of insistence on maintaining traditional peasant values, or as a result of family disorganization, relatively lower intelligence, more emotional problems, or just plain misfortune. These are the dregs who settle into the milieu of disreputable poverty and perpetuate its distinctive characteristics.

PSYCHOLOGICAL OUTCOMES

Having presented a thesis that a sector of our pluralistic social system may be conceptualized as a subculture, in principle identifiable through the employment of determinate criteria, I turn now to some psychological characteristics which presumably are outcomes of immersion in the culture of poverty. A great number of characteristics could be listed that presumably differentiate between the poverty culture and other cultures, among them, attitudes toward child rearing, religious forms, beliefs about locus of control, level of moral development, time binding and time perspective, tolerance of ambiguity, ego-control, language development, and many others.

From my viewpoint, three of these variables are especially pertinent: (1) the conceptualization of time, (2) linguistic forms, and (3) beliefs about locus of control. At least initial support can be gleaned from the literature for the notion that such psychological outcomes are endemic to the culture of poverty.

Time Perspectives. Because psychologists have not been concerned with the culture of poverty as such, the published literature contains no explicit statement that conceptions of time are directly linked to cultural antecedents. However, the reported observations of experimental and social psychologists, when added to the observations of sociologists and anthropologists, all converge on the inference that persons reared in the culture of poverty construe time differently from persons reared in nonpoverty cultures. A series of studies conducted by Mischel (1958, 1961a, b) in which social class was used as the independent variable makes abundantly clear the notion that middle-class persons acquire the skill of deferring gratification under certain decision conditions, and that lower-class persons fail to acquire this characteristic.[2] The idea of deferring an immediate and less-valued reward for a more valuable outcome at a later time is alien to the culture of poverty. The hypothesis may be stated: The degraded poor are rooted in the present and are indifferent to the future.

Besides the deferral pattern, which reflects behavior in choice situations, observers have noted the absence of clear-cut future-time perspectives in the culture of poverty. This is to say, for the degraded poor, the future is vague, unstructured, ambiguous, and without consensual markers; in contrast, for persons not socialized to the culture of poverty, the future is conceptualized as formed, sequential, patterned, and with consensual markers.

A review of the literature on time perspective does not establish a direct link between the culture of poverty and unwillingness or incapacity to tolerate delay of reinforcement. However, such a review points to the characteristics that are logically associated with such unwillingness or incapacity. Among such associated characteristics are the following: perceiving time as unfilled (Simmel, 1963); having an undifferentiated structure of knowledge (Meade, 1959); having attitudes of indifference to achievement (Meade, 1966); reporting pessimistic attitudes (Teahan, 1958); having a low degree of confidence in reinforcing agents (Mahrer, 1956). Such intolerance of delay is more often seen in persons whose fathers are absent from the home (Mischel, 1961a), who are lower in terms of assessed intelligence (Mischel and Metzner, 1962), who are lacking in responsibility (Mischel, 1961b) and who are classified as juvenile delinquents (Davids, Kidder, and Reich, 1962; Stein, Sarbin, and Kulik, 1968). These are the same characteristics that have so often been associated with the degraded poor.

Until more direct evidence is reported, the conclusion appears warranted that participants in the subculture of poverty are unwilling or unable to defer to, or plan for, the future. Such temporal behavior is predictable from membership in social organizations that limit choice behavior, such as cultures of poverty.

---

[2]Hidden in my analysis is an orientation that places positive value on future-time perspective. We must recognize that a convincing argument can also be made favoring a present-time perspective. For the society of the future, "being" may be a more functional value than "becoming."

Linguistic Codes. The work of Basil Bernstein (1959, 1964) on linguistic codes is well known. When we consider his conclusions along with those of Deutsch (1963), Hess (1964), John (1963), and others, most of which have been based on social class as an independent variable, the inference is straightforward: being socialized into the culture of poverty leads to the development and use of linguistic systems different from those of the culture of nonpoverty. This is not the place to review the expanding literature on individual and group differences in the acquisition and use of language. A wealth of fact and theory is accumulating that supports the hypothesis that the linguistic code in the culture of poverty is restricted, relatively undifferentiated, simplex, lacking in modifiers, implicit, and aimed at reinforcing and implementing the social structure rather than conveying information.

It is clear that linguistic patterns reflect the monotony of sensory inputs characteristic of the culture of poverty. Where the world of occurrences is relatively invariant, the need to form and utter sentences that convey complexity and diversity does not arise. Bernstein's conclusions about working-class speech (as compared to middle-class speech) apply even more forcefully to the participants in the culture of poverty. Restrictions on conduct follow from "a form of spoken language in which complex verbal procedures are made irrelevant by the system of nonverbal procedures, and closely shared identifications which serve as a back cloth to the speech" (Bernstein, 1961, p. 176).

That these linguistic differences follow from the type of social organization in which a person is enculturated will be argued below. The undifferentiated pattern of language appears to be sufficient for communication purposes in social systems that are organized exclusively around roles-by-ascription; social systems that are organized around both ascriptive and achieved roles require the acquisition and use of elaborate linguistic systems.

Locus of Control.   A third psychological outcome of socialization to the culture of poverty is in the domain of beliefs and values. Rotter (1966) and his associates have, in a number of contexts, employed the concept "locus of control." Like most of the studies mentioned before, social class and ethnic background rather than poverty have been used as independent variables. The outcomes of the studies by Battle and Rotter (1963) together with the reports of day-to-day observers of the degraded poor suggest that participants in the culture of poverty would be more inclined to believe that external forces and agencies exclusively control the rewards they receive. The participant in nonpoverty cultures is more likely to believe that some of his reinforcements are contingent upon effort and skill, i.e., internal factors.

Rotter has recently reviewed the published studies on internal versus external control and has concluded that the individual who believes that he can
control his own destiny "is likely to (a) be more alert to those aspects of
the environment which provide useful information for his future behavior;
(b) take steps to improve his environmental condition; (c) place greater
value on skill or achievement reinforcements and be generally more concerned with his ability, particularly his failures; and (d) be resistive to
subtle attempts to influence him" (Rotter, 1966).

The translation of these conclusions to the culture of poverty would
help clarify the observations of the degraded poor made by Lewis (1966),
Irelan (1966), and others. They note that belief in fate and luck is evidenced
through lack of concern for upward mobility, frequency of gambling, and
apparently irrational risk taking.

Beliefs, like other outcomes of socialization and enculturation already
mentioned, arise as functional attributes of a social organization. In presenting a theory of social identity, it will be proposed that belief in external
control of events would follow from participating in a culture which degrades one's identity through restricting performances to those required
for ascribed statuses.

Recapitulation. First, I have argued that we may usefully employ
culture of poverty as a defining concept and that lower-social-class membership is related to, but not coterminous with, being a participant in the
culture of poverty. Second, I have asserted that certain psychological
outcomes are characteristic of the culture of poverty, among them, an exclusive time orientation to the present, a relatively undifferentiated language system, and a strong belief that events are controlled by external
forces.

Between these psychological outcomes and the antecedent condition
of the culture of poverty is the concept of degraded social identity, to which
we now turn.

INFLUENCE OF SOCIAL ORGANIZATION ON SOCIAL IDENTITY

To make sense of the relationship between the culture of poverty and psychological outcome variables, I turn to my third point, the presentation of a
three-dimensional model of social organization that has its origin in role
theory. In this model, it is argued that the culture of poverty tends to provide inputs to its participants that lead to self-definitions approaching the
nonperson. The culture is a mechanical rather than an organic one (Durk-

heim, 1893) and the roles enacted are for the most part intended only to validate the occupancy of statuses that are heavily ascribed. Restricted to the enactment of such roles, the participants run the risk of negative valuations for improper performance of ascribed roles without the potential esteem for proper performance of choice or achieved statuses.

These arguments are intended to show that a social organization characterized by negatively valued social identities provides the background for the acquisition of such cognitive outcomes as present-time perspective, restricted linguistic codes, and belief in the external locus of control of events.

A basic postulate in the model is that human beings constantly strive to locate themselves in their environments. In order to make efficient choices from among behavior alternatives, a person must locate himself with regard to the world of occurrences. This world may be differentiated into a number of ecologies, among them the social ecology, or role system. Constantly faced with the necessity of locating himself, a person's misplacement of self in the role system may lead to embarrassing, perilous, or even fatal consequences.

Locating oneself in the role system follows from an inferential process: on the basis of clues available and of his knowledge of the role system, the individual infers the role of other(s) and concurrently of self. The essence of the process is caught in the efforts of a person to find answers to the question, "Who am I?" The answer is achieved in constructing responses to the reflexive question, "Who are you?" Finding one's place in the social system is a reciprocal event—the answers to the question, "Who am I?" are determined by the answers to the question, "Who are you?" and vice versa. *It is the totality of such answers that defines a person's social identity.*

Answers to "Who am I?" questions are drawn from the categories of the role system, such as name, age, sex, occupation, memberships, religious affiliation, marital status, political party affiliation, and so on. It is important to note that all role categories imply relationships—there can be no role of teacher without the complementary role of student; no role of mother without the role of child, etc. Further, such relationships are imbedded in the social systems in which the person operates.

Role relationships being the definers of one's social identity, planned or unplanned changes in role relationships will alter the answers to the "Who are you?" questions and the simultaneous inference about social identity. Changes in social identity are the rule, occurring with changes in the roles of complementary others, e.g., one's location in social space is different when he interacts with an adult or with a child, with a policeman or with a physician. To understand the conduct of a participant in the culture of poverty requires a set of dimensions that makes it possible to determine the relative contribution of particular roles to a social identity; further, these dimensions should facilitate recognition of the effects of shifting placements in the role system. For this purpose, I have made use of a three-dimensional model that provides the means for assessing the total value of a person's social identity at any point in time (Sarbin, 1967; Sarbin, Scheibe, and Kroger, 1965). The three dimensions are: (a) the status dimension; (b) the value dimension; and (c) the involvement dimension. The appropriateness of this model to account for cognitive performances among the degraded poor will become apparent in the following paragraphs.

The Status Dimension. The term status is used in the sociological sense as being equivalent to position in a social structure. The relationship between role and status is governed by the conventional definitions: a status or position is an abstraction or set of beliefs defined by the expectations held by members of the relevant society; role is a set of public behaviors enacted by an individual in order to make good his occupancy of a particular status or position. Another way of differentiating these related concepts is to regard position or status as a cognitive notion, a set of expectations that is carried around in one's head, and to regard role as a unit of conduct, characterized by overt actions. The point of departure for this proposal is Linton's classification of statuses (and their corresponding roles) as *ascribed* or *achieved* (Linton, 1936). For conceptual analysis Linton separated statuses that are defined primarily by biological characteristics, such as age, sex, and kinship, which he called *ascribed,* from those statuses characterized by attainment or option, which he called *achieved.* Examples of ascribed statuses are mother, son, adult, child, uncle, male, and person; of achieved statuses, musician, teacher, ballet dancer, and voter. This two-valued classification is too limiting, however, primarily because of instances that show the contribution of both ascriptive and achievement factors. To be a candidate for the achieved status of President, for example, requires that one also occupy certain ascribed statuses in regard to age, sex, and nativity. Rather than being two-valued, the dimension is a continuum. *The underlying conception is the degree of choice prior to entry into any particular status.* At one endpoint of the dimension are statuses granted an individual, simply by virture of his membership in a society, i.e., cultural man, or person. Sex roles, age roles, and kinship roles are in the same region. The other endpoint is defined by statuses with high degrees of choice, such as member of a go-now-pay-later travel club or manager of a college baseball team. Several paths lead to filling a position at the choice end, among them election, nomination, training, revelation, and achievement.

At the granted end, statuses may be further defined as less differentiated. The skills required to validate the occupancy of statuses at the ascribed end are nonspecific. Such statuses are assigned to large numbers of members in a society. Thus, every adult member in principle is granted the minimal status of cultural participant or person; that is, he is expected to conform to certain propriety norms that have priority over specific expectations attached to any attained or choice status.

At the achieved end of the continuum, statuses may be additionally defined as optional and highly differentiated, their requirements applying to a very small number of potential candidates. Examples would be a Pulitzer Prize winner, a heavyweight champion, and the chairman of a conference for the study of poverty. The dimension is highly correlated with legitimate power. In addition to the bare minimum of rights granted by virtue of an individual's holding the ascribed status of person, he acquires grants of legitimate power according to the location of his statuses toward the achievement or choice end of the dimension. In general, then, the social identity assigned an individual may include several validated statuses located at different points on the status dimension, some carrying explicit grants of power, others little or none. It will soon be shown that in the culture of poverty, a person's social identity will not usually include validated statuses that carry any grants of power, hence the reported feelings of helplessness, powerlessness, and anomia.

The Value Dimension. The model becomes more fruitful when we add the second component, the value dimension. At the same time that public role enactments provide the cues for locating an individual's identity on the status dimension, they also provide the basis for declarations of value. The relevance of audiences that assign value to role enactments presents a special problem. For the culture of poverty, relevant audiences are those concerned with the effects of degraded identity—social workers, police, church personnel, politicians, the Establishment, etc.

The value continuum may be constructed at right angles to the status continuum. It has a neutral point and positive and negative endpoints. At different points of the status dimension, the range of potential value for proper role performance is different from the range of potential value for improper performance or nonperformance.

First, consider the range of potential value to be applied to the occupancy of statuses at the achievement end: The valuations declared on nonperformance or poor performance tend to be neutral. Negative valuations are not applied to persons whose enactments do not validate statuses heavily weighted with choice, such as occupational and recreational statuses. Being laid off from a job, dropped from a basketball team, or dismissed from school for poor grades does not enrage or perturb a community. The responses to such outcomes are formalized as failure, underachievement, poor judgment, or tough luck. On the other hand, the proper performance of role behaviors at the choice end earns high positive valuations, such as Nobel prizes, public recognitions, and monetary rewards. For role enactments that validate achieved statuses, then, the range of valuation is from neutral to positive. The word that best carries the meaning of valuation in this context is *esteem*. Thus, esteem is declared on performances, on actions that ratify a person's occupancy of a choice role.

Next consider role enactments aimed at validating statuses that are heavily ascribed or granted. Little or no positive value is declared for the enactment of granted roles. An individual is not praised for participation in a culture as a male, an adult, a father, a person. He is expected to enact such roles without incentive motivation. The status carries with it a form of valuation which may be canceled or withdrawn when the status occupant publicly fails to enact appropriate role behavior. The term that best connotes valuation at the ascribed end of the dimension is *respect*. The nonperformance of granted roles, however, calls out strong negative valuations, e.g., in place of respect for being a man, the male loses respect when he fails to perform according to the expectations for masculine sexuality. Other things being equal, a woman is respected for being a mother, for occupying the position of mother. If she fails publicly to show interest in the care and welfare of her children, she is devalued, disrespected. The same valuations apply to individuals who fail to act according to age standards or to kinship norms. The status of person—the very end point of the first dimension—carries with it silent expectations that the status occupant will engage in role behavior to meet minimal expectations. These minimal expectations may be listed as *propriety norms*. They deal with age-sex standards of behavior, kinship, reciprocal social interaction (communication), modesty, property, and ingroup aggression. When these norms are violated, the individual holding the minimal granted position becomes the target of negative valuation, he is disrespected, and marked with a pejorative label. There are many forms of pejorative labeling and they all connote the social identity of a nonperson. That is to say, if the label of disrespect is applied by an individual or group empowered to apply such labels, then the society goes to work to treat the individual as if he were a nonperson. A term widely used to represent nonperson is brute, sometimes rendered as beast, animal, or low-grade human (Platt and Diamond, 1965). Such labels are not a part of our scientific and professional lexicon because we have coined special euphemisms which only for a short time attenuate the strong negative valuational component—for example, the hard-to-reach, the disadvantaged, slum dwellers, clients, wards, charity cases, paupers, socially ill, welfare recipients, the masses, unemployed, problem families, damaged human material, immigrants, aliens, and so on. The euphemistic component fails to conceal the underlying reference of the label: that of nonperson. The labeled individual is likely to be perceived as if he were without grade on the first dimension and with negative value on the second.

Pejorative labels provide one means of codifying answers to the "Who are you?" question, of designating a degraded social identity. It is important to note that where ambiguity occurs in identifying a member of the degraded class, those in power legislate that appropriate emblems or identifying marks be worn. This is to say, stigmata of degradation must be visible to serve the purpose of identifying nonpersons. The brand has been used to designate such declared nonpersons as harlots, heretics, and slaves. Special clothing in prisons, tattooed serial numbers, and insignia are common examples. In England an act was passed in 1697 directing any man on relief to wear a pauper's badge (Holdsworth, 1956, Vol. X, p. 175). In this way the degraded poor could be publicly identified as different from the respectable poor.

Note that societies do not concern themselves with stigmatizing failures in achieved roles. Such failures, occurring as they do in a public context, are explained according to prevailing beliefs about entering and exiting from achieved roles. Loss of esteem is explicable. The difference between the two forms of evaluation, respect and esteem, should be underscored. Esteem is granted for the proper public performance of achieved roles; respect is granted, not necessarily on public performances, but on the assumption that the status occupant does not violate salient propriety norms.[3]

Psychological Involvement. The third component, involvement, may be recognized in two ways: (1) the amount of time a person spends in the

---

[3]At this point it is instructive to consider the theories of motivation brought forward to account for the nonperformance of granted roles, on the one hand, and for the nonperformance of chosen roles, on the other. The latter case is seldom taken as a starting point for elaborating a causal theory. When a champion loses his title, an industrial executive is demoted, or a politician defeated, explanations are drawn from rule-following models. Failure is attributed to lack of practice, aging, superior competition, economic considerations, etc. Just as the *acquisition* of an achieved status is explained through the application of rule-following models, so the *loss* of status is accounted for in the same way. The nonperformance of granted roles, however, calls out explanations of a causal kind, such as heredity, humoral displacements, depravity, constitutional psychopathic inferiority, unconscious conflicts, toxins, psychic forces, psychosexual complexes, etc. (Peters, 1958). The proper occupancy of ascribed statuses is fundamental to the maintenance of a collectivity. Ascribed statuses are the givens; rule-following models are not invoked to account for either enactment or nonenactment. Instead, the causal principles are sought in the nervous system, the germ plasm, the psyche, or even the stars.

occupancy of certain statuses, and (2) the degree of organismic energy expended in the role enactment. An individual whose identity includes a status of the achievement end of the continuum may sometimes be highly involved in the role enactment and not involved at other times. In short, the possibility exists for variation in time and effort expended in enacting attained roles. A teacher may be highly involved in his role when in the classroom, in the library, or when grading term papers. He may be relatively uninvolved in the teacher role when listening to music, when selecting a wardrobe, or when visiting friends. At the ascribed or granted end, involvement is typically high. To be cast in the role of adult male, for example, means occupying the status nearly all the time. To be cast in the role of "old maid," similarly demands high involvement. To be assigned to the extreme granted status of person, or its negatively valued counterpart, nonperson, similarly means being in role all the time. To use a current theatrical metaphor, the actor in the ascribed role is "on" all the time. Common examples of roles which are highly involving are prisoners in maximum security institutions, committed inmates of state mental hospitals, inmates of concentration camps, and the pauperized poor in urban ghettos. The social identity of a member of these classes of persons is made up of few, if any, achieved roles the enactment of which would be cyclical. Legitimate opportunities for obtaining multiple perspectives or role-distance (Goffman, 1961), are absent when one's identity is composed exclusively of a small number of granted roles.

From the preceding remarks, it follows that to degrade an individual's social identity, one need only remove from him the opportunity to enact roles that have elements of choice. Degradation can be implemented by placing the individual in a totalistic setting, such as a prison, or in a subculture that has little or no provision for achieved statuses. A similarity is to be noted here between Durkheim's categories of societies held together by mechanical solidarity and those held together by organic solidarity. The culture of poverty as described here is maintained by mechanical solidarity, by the ritual performance of ascribed roles. Organic solidarity occurs in more complex societies where choice enters the social organization and where demands are made on status occupants to create new solutions to problems engendered by complexity. The more a man's identity is made up of roles without choice components, the fewer opportunities he has of engaging in role behavior that may be positively valued, i.e., esteemed. The best he can hope for is to be respected (not disrespected) through engaging (usually before small audiences) in the minimal performance of granted roles, all of which are highly involving. Such valuation is attained, if at all, only at the cost of high degrees of strain, a neutrally valued social identity being the maximum possible reward.

At what point does the individual entertain the question of whether the payoffs are commensurate with the high degree of strain? Failure to meet normative requirements of the wider society is highest among subcultures that exhibit these characteristics. If a man has no access to jobs or to ceremonial positions that are vehicles for an achieved identity, then he has few opportunities to display conduct that may be positively valued by relevant others and, reflexively, by self. If a social organization is made up only of ascribed roles, then the members have little or no opportunity to be esteemed, nor do they have the opportunity of moving into and out of different achieved statuses. The difference is only one of degree between the degraded poor and the already cited common examples of degraded identities: inmates in a maximum security prison, patients in back wards of mental institutions, and prisoners of war in thought-control camps. A totalistic social organization that provides no place for achieved statuses sets the stage for the potential degradation to the identity of a nonperson.

The foregoing three-dimensional model of conduct is saturated with implications for the study of the psychological outcomes of the culture of poverty. The most important implication is that cultures maintained by a social organization characterized by few, if any, achieved statuses are likely to produce individuals with degraded characteristics. Such an implication follows from the fact that the participants act in relatively undifferentiated and ritualistic ways merely to validate their granted statuses. Among other things, such conduct provides limited models for the young to imitate, provides no opportunity for variations or novelty occasioned by social reinforcers of the esteem type, provides no need and no models for elaborate linguistic codes, provides no change in inputs that serve as the vehicles for time perspective. Since, in fact, degraded or declassed persons have no control over their destiny, they acquire the belief that outside forces, the Establishment, "they," magic, and luck control events. Thus the apparent hopelessness, lack of achievement motivation, and lack of future-time perspective.

MODIFYING THE EFFECTS OF POVERTY

The implications of this analysis should be transparent to those interested in modifying the effects of the culture of poverty. Rather than directing our efforts to the modification of outcomes, such as teaching more elaborate linguistic systems or skills or beliefs, we should set up conditions that favor the transformation of social identity. To do this means that the social organization must accommodate itself to the development of new statuses or redefinition of old statuses that have achieved as well as ascribed characteristics. Because achieved statuses are so closely tied to economic and occupational factors in the nonpoverty cultures, no less than a radical change in economic organization would be required to provide the means for increasing the enactment of roles that have achievement characteristics and therefore esteem-giving potential. That efforts are being made to bring the ghetto dweller into the mainstream of commerce and industry needs no documentation here. From my perspective, such efforts are successful in transforming the social identity of the participant in the poverty culture only because he is provided with the opportunity for choice. When the social conditions encourage, stimulate, and even demand a breakout from the narrow confinement of nonchoice statuses, then his performances can be judged as proper or improper, and expressions of esteem (social reinforcers) can be given or withheld. However, not all ghetto dwellers can be absorbed into commerce and industry, or establish their identities through the proper performance of economic roles. If, to call up the cliché of earlier times, "the poor will always be among us," it is not necessary that the poor be degraded and without opportunities for choice. The solution is to find other than economic statuses, the proper enactment of which would lead to positive valuations by others, and reflexively, by self. In the automated world of the future, it may be futile to insist on occupational statuses for everyone. New, noneconomic statuses must emerge, statuses that have choice components, that make possible the granting of esteem valuations for proper enactments. Such statuses may be ceremonial, they may be developed in the noneconomic contexts of athletics, art, and music, or they may be tied to existing ascribed statuses. As an example of the latter, one may point to the Latin-American cultures of poverty, where the exaggerated masculinity of the *machismo* custom exemplifies the accommodation of an ascribed status to an achieved one in which reported sexual prowess is the vehicle for acquiring esteem.

In this short chapter it would be presumptive to try to spell out a program for modifying social systems so that complexity, concern for the future, and competence are functional attributes. That the social policy implied in the present formulation can be implemented is illustrated in a report by Shaver and Scheibe (1967). They observed the interbehavior of student volunteers and mental hospital patients in a summer work camp. The patients were removed from the total institution where they were assigned the negatively valued status of the patient, a variety of nonperson. The student volunteers, in the context of assisting the patients in clearing the site, building the camp, and community living, did not treat the patients *qua* patients, but as individuals and coworkers. The conduct of the patients reflected their enactment of roles with choice components. Their "mental illness" behaviors diminished, their communications were understandable, their social identities had been transformed.[4]

If we have learned anything in the past decade, it is that direct efforts to modify the effects of immersion in the culture of poverty have negative utility. Providing free dictionaries, clocks, and calendars to the ghetto resident does not guarantee changes in linguistic competence or temporal orientation. Kindness, charity, welfare, or threat of punishment have no effect unless the degraded person is first removed from the status of non-person. To do this, the system must allow every participant some measure of choice through access to achieved roles.

---

[4]It is important to note that transformations are reversible. When the work assignment was completed and the men returned to the totalistic setting of the hospital (where patients are traditionally regarded as nonpersons) their social identities were retransformed. Their behavior and demeanor reflected the assignment to the ascribed role.

REFERENCES

Battle, E. S., and Rotter, J. B. Children's Feeling of Personal Control as Related to Social Class and Ethnic Group. *Journal of Personality* 1963, 31: 482-90.

Bernstein, B. A Public Language: Some Sociological Implications of a Linguistic Form. *British Journal of Sociology* 1959, 10: 310-23.

———. Social Structure, Language and Learning. *Educational Research* 1961, 3: 163-76.

———. Social Class, Speech Systems and Psychotherapy. *British Journal of Sociology* March 1964, 15: 54-64.

Davids, A., Kidder, C., and Reich, M. Time Orientation in Male and Female Juvenile Delinquents. *Journal of Abnormal and Social Psychology* 1962, 64: 239-40.

Deutsch, M. The Disadvantaged Child and the Learning Process, in N. Passow, ed. *Education in Depressed Areas*. New York: Teachers College Press, 1963, pp. 163-79.

Durkheim, E. *The Division of Labor in Society*. G. Simpson, trans., (original French edition 1893). New York: Macmillan, 1933.

Goffman, E. *Asylums*. Chicago: Aldine Press, 1961.

Hess, R. Educability and Rehabilitation: The Future of the Welfare Class. *Journal of Marriage and Family Life* 1964, 26: 422-29.

Holdsworth, W. S. *A History of English Law* (7th ed. rev.) A. L. Goodhart and H. G. Hansburg, eds. London: Methuen, 1956.

Irelan, L. M., ed. *Low-Income Life Styles*. Washington, D.C.: United States Department of Health, Education and Welfare, Publication No. 14, 1966.

John, V. P. The Intellectual Development of the Slum Child. *American Journal of Orthopsychiatry* 1963, 33: 823-31.

Lewis, O. The Culture of Poverty. *Scientific American* 1966, 215: 19-25.

Linton, R. *The Study of Man*. New York: Appleton-Century, 1936.

Mahrer, A. The Role of Expectancy in Delayed Reinforcement. *Journal of Experimental Psychology* 1959, 58: 275-79.

Matza, D. The Disreputable Poor, in N. J. Smelzer and S. M. Lipset, eds. *Social Structure and Social Mobility in Economic Growth*. Chicago: Aldine Press, 1966, pp. 310-39.

Meade, R. D. Time Estimates as Affected by Motivational Level, Goal Distance, and Rate of Progress. *Journal of Experimental Psychology* 1959, 58: 275-79.

———. Achievement Motivation, Achievement, and Psychological Time. *Journal of Personality and Social Psychology* 1966, 4: 577-80.

Mischel, W. Preference for Delayed Reinforcement: An Experimental

Study of a Cultural Observation. *Journal of Abnormal and Social Psychology* 1958, 56: 57-61.

———. Father Absence and Delay of Gratification. *Journal of Abnormal and Social Psychology* 1961, 63: 116-24.(a)

———. Preference for Delayed Reinforcement and Social Responsibility. *Journal of Abnormal and Social Psychology* 1961, 62: 1-7.(b)

Mischel, W., and Metzner, R. Preference for Delayed Reward as a Function of Age, Intelligence, and Length of Delay Interval. *Journal of Abnormal and Social Psychology* 1962, 64: 425-31.

Peters, R. S. *The Concept of Motivation.* London: Routledge & Kegan Paul, 1958.

Platt, A. M., and Diamond, B. L. The Origins and Development of the 'Wild Beast' Concept of Mental Illness and Its Relation to Theories of Criminal Responsibility. *Journal of History of the Behavioral Sciences* 1965, 1: 355-67.

Rotter, J. B. Generalized Expectancies for Internal Versus External Control of Reinforcement. *Psychological Monographs: General and Applied* 1966: 80 (Whole No. 609).

Sarbin, T. R. The Dangerous Individual: An Outcome of Social Identity Transformations. *British Journal of Criminology* 1967, 7: 285-93.

———. The Transformation of Social Identity, in Leigh M. Roberts, N. S. Greenfield, and M. L. Miller, eds. *Comprehensive Mental Health: The Challenge of Evaluation.* Madison: University of Wisconsin Press, 1968, pp. 97-115.

Sarbin, T. R., Scheibe, K. E., and Kroger, R. O. The Transformation of Social Identity. Unpublished paper, 1965.

Shaver, P. R., and Scheibe, K. G. The Transformation of Social Identity: A Study of Chronic Mental Patients and College Volunteers in a Summer Camp Setting. *Journal of Psychology* 1967, 66: 19-37.

Stein, K. B., Sarbin, T. R., and Kulik, J. A. Future Time Perspective: Its Relation to the Socialization Process and the Delinquent Role. *Journal of Consulting and Clinical Psychology* 1968, 32: 257-64.

Simmel, E. Time Estimation in Hospitalized Patients as a Function of Goal Distance and Magnitude of Reward. *Perceptual and Motor Skills* 1963, 17: 91-97.

Teahan, J. E. Future Time Perspective, Optimism, and Academic Achievement. *Journal of Abnormal and Social Psychology* 1958, 57: 379-80.

Williams, R. *Culture and Society, 1780-1950.* London: Chatto & Windus, 1958.

Chapter 3

POVERTY VERSUS EQUALITY
OF OPPORTUNITY

J. McV. Hunt*

INTRODUCTION

Poverty is coming to be viewed in a new perspective. Only two decades ago, those persistently poor were typically seen as just naturally inept or stupid, lazy, and irresponsible. Children of these persistently poor were observed to manifest a combination of such characteristics when they entered school at only five or six years of age. On tests of intelligence, they had low IQ's. Once in school, they gave poor attention to school tasks and to teachers' utterances. Moreover, they were hard to control. They were, in short, incompetent. Because these various indicators of incompetence were already present so early in the children of the poor, they were presumed to be inherited from their inept, stupid, lazy, and irresponsible parents. However, changes have occurred in the general conception of the role played by circumstances encountered during infancy and early childhood in the development of intelligence, of motivation, and of responsibility for desired patterns of conduct. The newly recognized role of circumstances has encouraged the current belief that the children of the poor first arrive at the public school with their various defects primarily because they have not had the opportunities required to master the linguistic and numeric skills basic to

*Professor of Psychology, University of Illinois, Urbana, Illinois. The work represented in and the writing of this chapter have been supported by USPHS Grants No. MH-K-6-18567 and MH-11321.

normal performance on intelligence tests, or the motivational systems required for attention to teacher talk, or the habits of conduct required for teacher control and approval. Let me give briefly the background of the problem.

HISTORICAL BACKGROUND

When our forefathers declared it to be self-evident that "all men are created equal," they uttered biological and psychological nonsense. But they were not thinking in terms either biological or psychological. Their concerns were ethical and political. In these terms, that equality of opportunity, which is the essence of their declaration, is the basic foundation for a democratic society.

So long as biological development and behavioral or psychological development were believed to be predetermined or preprogrammed, and intelligence was believed to be fixed by each individual's heredity, those persistently poor of the bottom social class could readily be accepted as just naturally inept, lazy, and irresponsible. In the light of these widely held beliefs, any improvements in this class of human beings had to look entirely to eugenics. So long as these beliefs in predetermined development and fixed intelligence prevailed, no reason existed to extend the ethical implications of equality of opportunity to those condemned by the accident of their birth to develop in the circumstances of poverty and under the child-rearing practices of parents of the lower class.

These beliefs in predetermined development and fixed intelligence never went unquestioned. They were questioned by those sociologists who took their lead from the thought and writings of Lester F. Ward (1883). They were also questioned, ironically, by Alfred Binet (1909), whose tests became standard in the intelligence-testing movement led by Americans who considered intelligence to be essentially fixed. Finally, they were called into question by Freud (1938), at least for the origin of emotional and motivational characteristics. Nevertheless, these beliefs in predetermined development and fixed intelligence dominated thought among a great majority of the leaders of psychology and education and among a major share of the intellectual leaders of America, from the days of the nineteenth century debates over Darwin's theory of evolution through World War II. Although evidence at odds with these beliefs began to appear before World War II, the leaders of psychological and educational thought—especially those in the intelligence-testing movement who had the greatest influence on education —held these beliefs so firmly that they made every effort to discredit any dissonant evidence. For instance, Skeels and Dye (1939) reported increases in the IQ of every one of a group of thirteen retarded infants from an orphanage who were transferred to a women's ward at an Iowa State School for the mentally retarded. These mentally retarded women doted on the infants, then aged from seven to thirty months. The infants thrived on the doting and exhibited increases in IQ ranging from 7 to 58 points, and all but four of these infants gained more than 20 points. These gains came with periods on the ward ranging from six to fifty-two months. Another group of twelve somewhat less retarded infants aged twelve to twenty-two months remained in the orphanage, and in periods varying from twenty to forty-three months all but one showed decreases in IQ varying from 8 to 45 points. When these findings were reported, they met with scathing derision and the most searching statistical criticism. To be sure, this pioneering study was not an ideal experiment, but the findings were highly suggestive and the derision largely obliterated any corrective value that they might have had.

But it was only for the time being. What follows is a synopsis of at least the nature of the various kinds of evidence that have been accumulating against the beliefs in preprogrammed development and fixed intelligence.

EVIDENCE DISSONANT WITH THE
BELIEFS IN FIXED INTELLIGENCE
AND PREDETERMINED DEVELOPMENT

The fatherhood of genetics has now come to be credited to Johannsen as well as to Mendel (Sinnott, Dunn, and Dobzhansky, 1958, Ch. 2,. Observable, measurable organisms, which Johannsen called *phenotypes,* have come to be seen as products of the interaction between the hereditary constitution, which Johannsen termed the *genotype,* and the circumstances encountered in the course of development. At Illinois, for instance, William Horsfall and his colleagues (Horsfall and Anderson, 1961) got what appeared to be phenotypic female snowpool mosquitoes from genotypic male larvae by exposing them continually to a temperature of 29° C. In consequence of such evidence, no longer is it seriously argued that the genotype guarantees either any given rate of development or any given outcome unless the organism encounters circumstances appropriate to bring out the genotypic potential at each phase of development. Obviously the genotype is both an essential and a tremendous factor in the product. One cannot get rats by breeding elephants. Rats may learn something in psychological laboratories, but they do not learn to talk or to do calculus problems. The genotype even determines much of the "how" of development and the nature of the developmental consequences of encountering any given kind of environmental circumstances. Horsfall's findings, for instance, apply only to snowpool mosquitoes. In human beings, however, the limits imposed by any genotype are unknown and basically unknowable. They depend in considerable part upon our educational ingenuity in arranging the circumstances to utilize varied "how" characteristics. The implication of Johannsen's interactionism, moreover, as Hirsch (1963, 1967) has pointed out, calls for an individualization of our educational efforts.

In coming to the view implicit in these last statements, studies of the role of early experience in the problem-solving ability of animal subjects have been important. Because both the genotype and the circumstances of the life history are easier to control in animal subjects, the results of such investigations have tended to be more convincing to many people than the evidence from such studies as that of orphanage infants by Skeels and Dye. It was the theorizing by Donald Hebb (1947) of McGill that instigated many of these animal studies. He also did the first of these experiments. Rats reared as pets, where they were provided first with a variety of auditory and visual experiences following the opening of their ears and eyes, and then with varied opportunities to act upon the environment, proved to be better problem solvers than rats reared in opaque laboratory cages (Forgays and Forgays, 1952; Forgus, 1955a; Hymovitch, 1952). When the problem-solving ability of pet-reared dogs was compared with that of their cage-reared littermates (Thompson and Heron, 1954), the differences were, if anything, more pronounced than the differences in problem-solving performances between pet-reared and cage-reared rats. This and other evidence suggests that the importance of early experience on later problem-solving ability probably increases up the evolutionary scale.[1]

A variety of investigations has also yielded evidence indicating that the longer a developing organism lives under any given kind of circumstances, the harder it is to alter the influence of these circumstances on its developing body or its developing behavior (Hunt, 1961, p. 321 ff).

I include *body* here on purpose. Since Austin Riesen (1958) first reared chimpanzee infants in the dark for sixteen months with resulting

---

[1]This suggestion may be untrue, for Margaret Harlow told me after my presentation that monkeys reared in solitude were no less able, presumably, to acquire learning sets than monkeys reared by their mothers, even though those reared in isolation did lack the normal repertory of social responses. Whether the learning sets utilized in the Wisconsin experiments demand the past acquisition of earlier learning sets and are thereby appropriate to bring out an intellectual deficit in the monkeys reared in isolation is unclear. I simply wish to warn the reader that the Wisconsin findings do call this suggestion into question, and that further analysis and investigation is needed.

failure of their retinas to develop properly, a number of investigators have found evidence that the circumstances encountered will influence even the anatomical maturation of the nervous system. These investigators include Hyden (1960); Hyden and Egyhazi (1962); the Swedish biochemist, Brattgord (1952) and his students; Bennett, Diamond, Krech, and Rosenzweig (1964), an interdisciplinary team of investigators at the University of California at Berkeley; and Hubel and Wiesel (1959, 1960, 1961), a team of neurophysiologists.

During these same years, evidence with a similar import from investigations with human subjects has also been accumulating. The rate of development during the first year following birth is especially plastic in human infants. At the Tewksbury State Hospital, for instance, Burton White (White and Held, 1966) has reduced the median ages of appearance of two landmarks in the development of eye-hand coordination (fisted swiping at object presented to view, and top-level reaching for them with the hand shaped in anticipation for grasping) from 72 and 145 days, respectively, to 55 and 87 days, respectively. In terms of the ratio of developmental age to chronological age used as the IQ, this latter change from 145 days to 87 days is an increase of sixty-seven points. It was achieved by turning the infants onto their stomachs for fifteen minutes after each of three feedings a day, twenty minutes of handling a day, and arranging a stabile on each crib for the infants to look at and feel with their hands. Probably the last of these three factors was most important. In my own laboratory, David Greenberg and Ina Uzgiris have found that the infant children of graduate students and staff in Champaign-Urbana who have had our objects hung within view over their cribs at 5 weeks of age begin blinking at an object approaching their eyes from a drop of 11.5 inches at an average of 7 weeks, while other infants, without such mobiles over their cribs, fail to show the blink response till an average age of 10.4 weeks. Such sensorimotor organizations as eye-hand coordination or the blink response may have no special significance in themselves for the ultimate level of competence, but these findings do illustrate the plasticity of that early development of human infants once considered predetermined in both rate and course. Moreover, these findings suggest that such increases in the rate of development may well be cumulative. This possibility must be investigated.

No one can now say how large such cumulative increases in the development of human ability might be, but Wayne Dennis has published (1966) some interesting findings based on the results from the Draw-a-Man test given to groups of typical children of from six to eight years in age from some fifty cultures over the world. The Draw-a-Man test, devised by Florence Goodenough (1926) to be culture free, was first called into question when typical Hopi Indian children aged eight to eleven years turned up with an average IQ of 123 on the test (Dennis, 1942). This mean IQ of 123 approximates the averages for samples of upper-middle-class suburban American children (125) and for samples of Japanese children (124) (Dennis, 1966). At the lower end of the distribution, Dennis (1966) has found Shilluk children of the Sudan with a mean IQ of 53, and Bedouin children of Syria with a mean IQ of 52. Here, then, we find a range of about 70 points in average IQ for typical groups of children from these various cultures. The most obvious correlate of mean IQ is amount of contact with the graphic arts. Among Moslem Arab children, where religion prohibits graven images, the range in average Draw-a-Man IQ's is from 52 to 98, and the most obvious correlate of this variation among the means for Arab children is amount of contact of the groups with Western culture. While the Draw-a-Man test is one that clearly requires but a limited set of abilities from a factor analytic standpoint, these variations in IQ are suggestive, nevertheless, of the remarkable degree to which circumstances may alter intelligence as now measured.

Clearly, the performance of a child on an intelligence test at one age cannot tell you what performance on such tests will be later without solid knowledge of the circumstances under which he is to live. In light of these various kinds of evidence, the beliefs in predetermined development and in fixed intelligence simply are no longer tenable.

ETHICAL IMPLICATIONS

Now, if circumstances can have effects of such magnitude on development during infancy and early childhood, the accident of being born to parents who have themselves grown up in a lower-class background of persistent poverty may well be depriving a child of the opportunity to develop the intellectual skills, the motivation, and the habits of conduct within his genotypic potential which are required for adaptive success in our schools and for later participation in the mainstream of our society. Thus, the ethical and political doctrine of equal opportunity takes on new implications. Such a child, by accident of birth, may well be deprived of the opportunity merely to participate in the mainstream of our society. If we take seriously the declaration of our forefathers that equality of opportunity is a birthright of all, we are ethically bound to try to equalize the opportunity of children born to parents in poverty with lower-class backgrounds. The new evidence makes of early childhood education an ethical matter and a political issue.

Two major challenges of our day emphasize the ethical importance of this issue. One of them is our advancing technology. The other is the recognition of the evils of racial segregation in the Supreme Court decision of 1954 which demands desegregation.

These two challenges are intertwined. The consequences of our advancing technology have probably been most evident during the past few years in agriculture. With the industrial revolution coming to the farms, it is said that more people have moved from the farms to the cities during the past twenty years than moved from the farms to the cities from the time the Pilgrims landed until 1947. Most of those moving have been marginal farmers: the rural poor, a large share of them Negro sharecroppers from the South. Here is a major source of the current dire plight of our cities. Here is also an instance in which our advancing technology is reducing—and reducing drastically—the economic opportunities for those with limited linguistic and numerical skills, with limited motivation to learn and to solve problems, and without the habit of accepting and carrying out tasks responsibly. At the very same time our advancing technology is markedly increasing the opportunities for those with such abilities and skills.

The intertwining of these challenges from our advancing technology and from the Supreme Court decision of 1954 derives from the fact that a major share of Negroes have been kept persistently poor ever since they were released from the legal bondage of slavery. Desegregation is an absolute necessity for that equality of opportunity for all men that our forefathers declared to be a birthright. But desegregation is not enough. Moreover, in the absence of compensatory opportunity for the children of the very poor, it may actually be harmful.

Let me explain. Children build a major share of their hopes for themselves by comparing their own performances with the performances of other children, as well as from what they are told about themselves (Diggory, 1966). When children aged five and six with markedly limited levels of ability to understand language, numbers, and rules of conduct are put together in our traditionally competitive schools with children having considerably higher levels of these abilities, no one has to tell the children of the poor that they are failing. Any light of hope they may have brought to the school is all too quickly dimmed or extinguished by their encounters with their own obvious failure. If frustration instigates aggressive behavior, as psychologists have long contended (Dollard et al., 1939), it is hardly surprising that aggressive behavior becomes common among these children. Neither is it surprising that as their own hopes are extinguished, they tend to drop out of school at the earliest opportunity. Unless something is done to change the traditional use of the lockstep and competition of our schools, merely putting those culturally deprived be they whites or blacks—together with those culturally privileged can only make matters worse. Where most of those culturally deprived are blacks, desegregation may actually exacerbate their problem.

WHAT IS LACKING IN CHILDREN OF THE POOR

It is fairly clear that something must be done to compensate the children of the poor for the lack of opportunities to learn language skills, number skills, motivation geared to initiative, achievement, and working for rewards that come only in the future, and the acceptance of those rules of conduct set largely in the middle class. Evidence from investigations of child-rearing practices in the various classes of British society by Bernstein (1960, 1961), of Israeli society by Smilansky (1961, 1964), and by Hess and Shipmann (1965) have made it quite clear that most children of the persistently poor of lower-class backgrounds do lack opportunities to learn these essential symbolic skills and motivational structures.

They lack, first of all, an opportunity to learn language. The parents of these children of lower-class background typically talk less often to their children than do parents of the middle class (Bernstein, 1960, 1961; Bronfenbrenner, 1958; Chilman, 1965). Since these parents themselves have never learned to utilize prepositional relationships with precision and their syntax is confused, they serve as poor models. Furthermore, these parents seldom ask questions designed to prompt their children to discern various kinds of relationships among things and people and to use language to describe these relationships and to communicate them. In fact, when their children do ask questions or talk out, parents of the lower class often tell them to "shut up," with no reason why. There is, incidentally, a world of difference between saying simply, "Shut up!" and saying, "Shut up, can't you see I am talking on the telephone?"

The basic psychological potential of the children of the poor may even be damaged before they are born. The dietary deficiencies and the emotional stress of mothers in poverty before conception and during pregnancy may hamper the development of their offspring during the embryonic and fetal stages (e.g., Pasamanick, 1962). The result is infants of high vulnerability, but the developmental fate of these children of high vulnerability is in considerable measure a function of the circumstances that they encounter during the first months and years after birth (Lois Murphy, 1961, 1968).

Children of the poor seldom have an opportunity to learn to take initiative, to be motivated toward future goals and toward status through achievement. The parents of the lower class themselves have never learned such kinds of motivation (Bronfenbrenner, 1958; Chilman, 1965; Davis, 1948; Davis and Havighurst, 1946; Lewis, 1961, 1966). Their responses to their children's actions and efforts at communication are dictated largely by their own immediate impulses and needs, not the child's. To them, a good child is a quiet child who does not bother them (Klaus and Gray, 1967). Such mothers send their young off to school with the command, "You be good and do like the teacher says." Since "good" is defined as being quiet and compliant, such treatment hardly encourages taking initiative, becoming orientated toward future goals, and acquiring the motivation to achieve.

So far as standards of conduct are concerned, the children of the poor typically learn their standards largely from their own peers or from other children somewhat older. Moreover, the conduct of their parents is hardly that prescribed by the middle class. What these children of the poor imitate of language, of motivation, and of conduct in the behavior of both their parents and their peers is often unsuitable for adaptation in the schools. This occurs despite the love that these poor parents have for their young. It is hardly surprising, then, that these children of the poor soon lose hope of succeeding in school, become fed up with it, and begin to drop out as soon as they can.

WHAT TO DO

Project Head Start was devised, of course, to provide compensatory education for the children of the poor to help to equalize their opportunities. The goal is perfectly correct, but having the proper goal and knowing immediately how to achieve that goal are different matters. While the behavioral sciences have uncovered evidence that makes the old beliefs in predetermined development and fixed intelligence untenable, this evidence is still insufficient to tell us with precision how to provide compensatory opportunities effectively. The first approach has understandably consisted all too often of providing traditional nursery school curricula which, unfortunately, have been devised largely for children of middle-class background and typically for other purposes.

Since psychologists and educators have considered it too softheaded during the past half-century to even try experimentally to increase the abilities of children from any background, we shall have to do our experimenting now. We shall have to try and fail, profit from our failures, and try again. We are being asked for readymade solutions which we do not have and which can only be provided through an extended program of research and development. The research should be directed toward better understanding of the factors influencing the development of intelligence, motivation, and conduct. Such understanding will lead toward innovations in educational practice. Those innovations which promise, from what we know of psychological development, to be effective, should be evaluated and the results widely disseminated to be implemented by the officials and teachers of Head Start, of the Centers for Children and Parents, and of our traditional schools.

However, even those of us who presume to have some expertise concerning early child development still disagree on major issues. Those approaching the problem from the standpoint of mental health have tended to emphasize emotional factors and the fate of instinctual needs and to place too little emphasis on the development of skills and competence. Those who have recently become concerned with fostering cognitive development may now be tending to underemphasize the emotional significance of conditions of learning. I sometimes wish Aristotle had never passed on to us the conception of triune man with affection, cognition, and conation separated. On the other hand, from the limited amount of information that I can glean from the evaluations of Head Start efforts and the evaluations of various curricular innovations for nursery education, I believe it is becoming clearer and clearer that these children of the poor gain most from curricula that do attempt deliberately to teach them skills required for coping with schools: cognitive structures, linguistic skills necessary to understand what teachers talk about, and rudimentary numerical skills. Those who do get these skills seem to be able to compete more evenly with their peers from more fortunate backgrounds in the kind of schools we now have. In the course of this competition, they seem to gain some of the self-respect and motivation required for continued participation, and to imbibe the standards of conduct which are required in school. These are the approximate and very tentative lessons to be learned from the evaluations of the various efforts in early childhood education about which I now know (O'Brien and Hunt, in prep.).

Various lines of evidence tend to support these lessons. In Champaign-Urbana, for instance, Carl Bereiter, Siegfried Engelmann, and their colleagues (1966) have had what appears to be substantial success with an academically-oriented nursery school geared to the teaching of both English and arithmetic as foreign languages and to the teaching of reading readiness.

The 15 four-year-old children with whom they started in the fall of 1964 all came from families below average in the socioeconomic scale, and all but two were selected because older siblings had been unable to succeed or were having severe problems in regular school classes. During the first six months of two hours of school each day, five days a week, these children gained some two years in psycholinguistic abilities as measured by the Illinois Test of these abilities (Kirk and McCarthy, 1961). Two of the original fifteen children left the group when one moved away and the other was judged unable to continue with the group and was put in a class for the retarded. Of the three new children who were added in the second year, one came from a family of middle-class background, and while the other two were considered able to learn readily, they also met the criteria for selection of the original group. During the second year, beginning in the fall of 1965, they continued to gain, and in the fall of 1966, these sixteen children were put into regular first-grade classes where the thirteen composing the two top tracks for Bereiter and Engelmann experienced varying degrees of success. Of the three children who were in the bottom group for Bereiter and Engelmann, all repeated first grade, one because she was young for her group and the other two because they seemed to learn very little.

Other innovators of educational practice with methods that differ from those of Bereiter and Engelmann but are aimed at the teaching of cognitive, linguistic, and numerical skills, have also been having considerable success. Which methods are most successful, either immediately or for the long pull, is not yet known. Proper evaluation must employ follow-up methods as well as measures of gain in symbolic skills.

Compensatory education after four years of age is very expensive. Moreover, even at best it may be too little and too late really to develop in the children of the persistently poor the potential to achieve full participation in the mainstream of our highly technological society. A way must be found, I believe, to intervene in the first three years of their lives. But how do we do it effectively? Parents are at least potentially the best teachers for these earliest years. Various federal agencies, however, have spent a great deal of money on projects wherein social workers, clinical psychologists, and psychiatrists have tried to change the child-rearing practices of lower-class parents by counseling them individually or in groups. Little or nothing, so far as I can ascertain, has come of it.

On the other hand, Klaus and Gray (1967) and their group at Peabody College for Teachers may be showing a promising way in their academically oriented nursery school. By getting the mothers of their young pupils to visit and observe at this school, the mothers can see the teachers' ways with their children and the children of their neighbors, and they can see the results of these ways in the behavior of their children. Moreover, they receive explanations of both the methods and the results. Coupled with such observation and imitative opportunity, these mothers have home visitors demonstrate methods similar to those of the nursery school teachers in their own homes.

Using the younger siblings of the children in the nursery school as controls, Klaus and Gray got larger improvements on test performance from the younger children of these mothers than they got with the children in the nursery school. Moreover, when they used other families in the neighborhood as controls for this within-family diffusion effect, these children, particularly the younger children in these neighborhood control families, also showed gains in test performance. This finding suggested that the mothers participating in the nursery school projects were communicating something of what they were learning about child-rearing practices to their neighbors, an interfamily diffusion. In order to test for their genuine existence, Klaus and Gray used families living in another town some forty miles away as controls and found no such gains in the children of these control families because they were living too far from those in the experiment to experience face-to-face communication. Thus, the improvement in the performance of the children of the neighborhood control mothers appeared to be genuine, providing a very hopeful suggestion that mothers involved in a teaching program for young children who have an opportunity to observe and imitate and to have new child-rearing practices demonstrated in their own homes, will not only improve their own child-rearing practices, but will also communicate these improved practices to those neighbors whom they see often in face-to-face contact. Other innovators, like Ira Gordon in Florida, are attempting to repeat the findings of the group at Peabody College.

Such suggestive results make it appear that a promising approach to the modification of child-rearing practices might be effected through Centers for Children and Parents. Each such center should provide an open door where the families to be served could obtain the full range of the services available within their communities. Moreover, each center should provide the leadership for forming day-care facilities for infants and toddlers, and also Head Start classes for older preschool children. Mothers and fathers and older children of the families served should be utilized as child-care and teachers' aides in these facilities so that they can, by observing and imitating relative experts, learn new methods for caring for children to utilize in their homes. These centers should also provide home visitors to demonstrate child-care practices in order to help bring the examples of these practices into the home setting.

But there is likely to be another kind of yield from an innovation such as the Centers for Children and Parents. As Bronfenbrenner (1967) has pointed out, such centers would utilize the love and concern which these parents of lower-class background—like all parents—have for their children in order to motivate the formation of interdependent cooperation in neighborhood groups like those which tend to develop naturally in rural communities and small towns. It is from such rural neighborhoods that most of those newcomers into the slums of our large cities have come. In the cities, they are all too often isolated. Their children grow up in households of fearful, frustrated, and isolated parents.

Families in both the unreconstructed ghettos and in the sterile new housing developments live largely apart from the work-a-day world where children come naturally and regularly in contact with adults other than their parents, with adults who know them and are concerned for them. As a consequence, the children of both the inner city and the poorer suburbs grow up with few adult models, and those models are largely unsatisfactory. Thus, they turn to peer groups for their socialization. The social and moral standards that develop in these peer groups of unattended children and adolescents are seldom those of established society. In fact, these standards are seldom of a kind that will permit an organized society to develop. We have witnessed some of the consequences in the mob violence of the Watts neighborhood in Los Angeles, and elsewhere, and we shall undoubtedly witness more examples of such mob violence. We can no more escape such explosions by repressive measures than middle-class parents who have failed to foster close ties of affection and identification can control their children by threats of punishment (Bandura and Walters, 1959). On the other hand, examples of aggressive ghetto adolescents who will fight to protect the facilities for the little children in their apartments or neighborhoods demonstrate the corrective motivational power of this interest in young children.

Centers for Children and Parents promise to help overcome the isolation of families in the slums and in the lower-middle-class housing developments by providing a motivational basis for cooperative organization for the care, education, and welfare of young children. By participating in such a center, by having relative experts as models, parents and older children should lose their isolation and hostility in constructive, cooperative effort. In the process, they should acquire some of that interdependence through which grow the values necessary for organized society, and some child-rearing practices that foster the development of those basic intellectual and motivational skills required to cope with and participate in the mainstream of our society.

We have now only the barest outline of what promises to be a fruitful approach. Twenty-five such centers have been established on an experimental basis to enable us to learn how to organize them on a more general level later. In neighborhoods of Negro people with de facto segregation, the centers will probably not be desegregated. What I believe is more important than immediate desegregation for children of the preschool period is that they develop those abilities and motives and skills which will better enable them to hold their own in desegregated schools with children of parents from middle-class backgrounds, be they white or black.

CONCLUSION

If the behavioral sciences have discovered anything that begins to approach in human significance the antibiotics and contraceptive pills of the biological and medical sciences and the atomic energy of the physical sciences, it may well be this new evidence of the great plasticity in infant and early childhood development. This new evidence is a basis for a justified hope that the cycle of poverty can be broken. No longer is it sensible to believe that those of lower-class background will inevitably be incompetent simply because of their biological inheritance and nature.

On the other hand, there is still a very long way to go in development of research in the behavioral sciences and in applying the research results to problems in education and mental health. We are probably only at the stage where Dr. Fleming was when he found that streptococcic bacteria adjacent to penicillin mold will die. But we do have justified hope, and if we follow the leads generated by data—even soft data—from our scientific experiments and from evaluations of promising innovations, and if we yield up the attitudes and beliefs we learned by hearsay from those who taught us, it should then be possible for us to learn how to compensate the children of the poor for their lack of opportunity. Furthermore, we should learn how to help parents reared in poverty to help their children, and in the process, how to help themselves overcome their own isolation and degradation.

If our impatient society does not lose hope and faith too soon, and if the violence of those of lower-class background does not destroy confidence in a positive approach, it is conceivable that we could bring a major share of the children of the persistently poor into the mainstream of our society within a generation.

REFERENCES

Bandura, A., and Walters, R. H. *Adolescent Aggression.* New York: Ronald, 1959.

Bennett, E. L., Diamond, M. C., Krech, D., and Rosenzweig, M. R. Chemical and Anatomical Plasticity of Brain. *Science* 1964, 146: 610-19.

Bereiter, C., Engelmann, S., Osborn, J., and Reidford, P. A. An Academically Oriented Pre-School for Culturally Deprived Children, in F. M. Hechinger, ed. *Pre-School Education Today.* Garden City, N. Y.: Doubleday, 1966. Chapter 6.

Bernstein, B. Language and Social Class. *British Journal of Sociology* 1960, 11: 271-76.

————. Social Class and Linguistic Development: A Theory of Social Learning, in A. H. Halsey, J. Floud, and C. A. Anderson, eds. *Education, Economy, and Society.* New York: Free Press, 1961, pp. 288-314.

Binet, A. *Les Idees Modernes sur les Enfants.* Paris: Ernest Flamarion, 1909 (cited from Stoddard, 1939).

Brattgard, S. O. The Importance of Adequate Stimulation for the Chemical Composition of Retinal Ganglion Cells, during Early Post-Natal Development. *Acta Radiologica.* Stockholm, 1952, suppl. 96, pp. 1-80.

Bronfenbrenner, U. Socialization and Social Class through Time and Space, in E. E. Maccoby, T. M. Newcomb, and E. L. Hartley, eds. *Readings in Social Psychology.* New York: Holt, 1958, pp. 400-425.

————. Early Deprivation in Mammals and Man, in N. Grant, ed. *Early Experience and Behavior.* Springfield, Ill.: C. C. Thomas, 1967.

Chilman, C. S. Child Rearing and Family Life Patterns of the Very Poor. *Welfare in Review* 1965, 3: 3-19.

Davis, W. A. *Social-Class Influences upon Learning.* Cambridge, Mass.: Harvard University Press, 1948.

Davis, W. A., and Havighurst, R. J. Social Class and Color Difference in Child-Rearing. *American Sociological Review* 1946, 11: 698-710.

Dennis, W. The Performance of Hopi Indian Children on the Goodenough Draw-a-Man Test. *Journal of Comparative Psychology* 1942, 34: 341-48.

————. Goodenough Scores, Art Experience, and Modernization. *Journal of Social Psychology* 1966, 68: 211-28.

Diggory, J. C. *Self-Evaluation: Concepts and Studies.* New York: Wiley, 1966.

Dollard, J., Doob, L. W., Miller, N. E., and Sears, R. R. *Frustration and Aggression.* New Haven: Yale University Press, 1939.

Forgays, D. G., and Forgays, J. W. The Nature of the Effect of Free Environmental Experience in the Rat. *Journal of Comparative and Physiological Psychology* 1952, 45: 322-28.

Forgus, R. H. Influence of Early Experience on Maze-Learning with and without Visual Cues. *Canadian Journal of Psychology* 1955, 9: 207-14.(a)

————. Early Visual and Motor Experience as Determiners of Complex Maze Learning Ability under Rich and Reduced Stimulation. *Journal of Comparative and Physiological Psychology* 1955, 48: 215-20.(b)

Freud, S. Three Contributions to the Theory of Sex, in A. A. Brill, ed. *The Basic Writings of Sigmund Freud.* New York: Modern Library, 1938, pp. 553-629.

Goodenough, F. L. *The Measurement of Intelligence by Drawings.* Yonkers-on-Hudson, N. Y.: World Book Company, 1926.

Hebb, D. O. The Effects of Early Experience on Problem-Solving at Maturity. *American Psychologist* 1947, 2: 306-7.

Hess, R. D., and Shipman, V. Early Experience and the Socialization of Cognitive Modes in Children. *Child Development* 1965, 36: 869-86.

Hirsch, J. Behavioral Genetics and Individuality Understood: Behaviorism's Counterfactual Dogma Blinded the Behavioral Science to the Significance of Meiosis. *Science* 1963, 142: 1436-42.

————. Behavioral Genetics, or "Experimental" Analysis: The Challenge of Science versus the Lure of Technology. *American Psychologist* 1967, 22: 118-30.

Horsfall, W. R., and Anderson, J. F. Suppression of Male Characteristics of Mosquitoes by Thermal Means. *Science* 1961, 133: no. 3467, 1830.

Hubel, D. N., and Wiesel, T. N. Receptive Fields of Single Neurons in the Cat's Striate Cortex. *Journal of Physiology* (London) 1959, 148: 574-91.

————. Receptive Fields of Optic Fibers in the Spider Monkey. *Journal of Physiology* (London) 1960, 154: 572-80.

————. Integrative Action in the Cat's Lateral Geniculate Body. *Journal of Physiology* (London) 1961, 155: 385-98.   .

Hunt, J. McV. *Intelligence and Experience.* New York: Ronald, 1961.

Hyden, H. The Neuron, in J. Brachet and A. E. Mirsky, eds. *The Cell: Biochemistry, Physiology, Morphology.* Vol. 4, *Specialized Cells.* New York: Academic Press, 1960.

Hyden, H., and Egyhazi, E. Nuclear RNA Changes of Nerve Cells during a Learning Experiment in Rats. *Proceedings of the National Academy of Science* 1962. Vol. 48: 1366-73.

Hymovitch, B. The Effects of Experimental Variations in Early Experience on Problem Solving in the Rat. *Journal of Comparative and Physiological Psychology* 1952, 45: 313-21.

Kirk, S. A., and McCarthy, J. J. The Illinois Test of Psycholinguistic Abilities. Urbana: University of Illinois Press, 1961.

Klaus, R. A., and Gray, S. W. *The Early Training Project for Disadvantaged Children: A Report after Five Years.* Nashville, Tenn.: George Peabody College, 1967.

Lewis, O. *The Children of Sanchez.* New York: Random House, 1961.

————. *La Vida; A Puerto Rican Family in the Culture of Poverty—San Juan and New York.* New York: Random House, 1966.

Murphy, L. B. Preventive Implications of Development in the Preschool Years, in G. Caplan, ed. *Prevention of Mental Disorders in Children.* New York: Basic Books, 1961.

————. Assessment of Young Children: The Concept of a Vulnerability Index, in C. A. Chandler, ed. *New Perspectives in Early Child Care.* New York: Atherton, 1968. Chapter 6.

O'Brian, R. A., and Hunt, J. McV. *Some of the Influential Factors in Compensatory Education* (in prep.).

Pasamanick, B. Determinants of Intelligence. Draft of paper presented at a symposium on "Man and Civilization: Control of the Mind—II," University of California San Francisco Medical Center, January 27, 1962.

Riesen, A. H. Plasticity of Behavior: Psychological Aspects, in H. F. Harlow and C. N. Woodsey, eds. *Biological and Biochemical Bases of Behavior.* Madison: University of Wisconsin Press, 1958, pp. 425-50.

Sinnott, E. W., Dunn, L. C., and Dobzhansky, T. *Principles of Genetics.* New York: McGraw-Hill, 1958.

Skeels, H. M., and Dye, H. B. A Study of the Effects of Differential Stimulation of Mentally Retarded Children. *Proceedings of the American Association on Mental Deficiency,* 1939. Vol. 44, pp. 114-36.

Smilansky, S. Evaluation of Early Education, in Unesco, *Educational Studies and Documents* 1961, no. 42, pp. 8-17.

————. A Program to Demonstrate Ways to Use a Year of Kindergarten to Promote Cognitive Abilities, Impart Basic Information and Modify Attitudes Essential for Scholastic Success of Culturally Deprived Children in Their First Two Years of School. Jerusalem, Israel: H. Szold Foundation, 1964.

Thompson, W. R., and Heron, W. The Effects of Restricting Early Experience on the Problem-Solving Capacity of Dogs. *Canadian Journal of Psychology* 1954, 8: 17-31.

Ward, L. F. *Dynamic Sociology* (2 vols.). New York: D. Appleton & Company, 1883.

White, B. L., and Held, R. Plasticity of Sensorimotor Development in the Human Infant, in J. F. Rosenblith and W. Allinsmith, eds. *The Causes of Behavior: Readings in Child Development and Educational Psychology* (2d ed.). Boston: Allyn & Bacon, 1966.

PART TWO

SOCIALIZATION AND LEARNING

INTRODUCTION

An individual comes to be the sort of person he is as a consequence of a long process of learning. Within the limits imposed by genetic and constitutional factors, the particular set of behavioral patterns acquired by an individual is extremely flexible, and determined to a large extent by the contingencies of reward and punishment that often occur naturally in the environment. In addition, direct attempts are made by other persons to inculcate specific skills and patterns of behavior in an individual.

The learning process, important to all areas of psychology, is relevant to poverty in two ways. First, processes of learning are of central importance to socialization. Socialization refers to those processes that lead to an individual's eventually sharing ways of acting, thinking, and feeling with other members of his culture or subculture. Processes of learning involved in socialization are varied and complex, ranging through simple conditioned responses, operant responses, and imitation to conceptual learning.

The goal of research in socialization—understanding the means by which an individual comes to share behaviors with other members of his group—is a most difficult and complex task. With respect to poverty, socialization research would pose the following broad question: How does a person born in poverty come to be noticeably different in a variety of ways from a person born in more advantaged circumstances?

There are probably at least three important agents of socialization. First, during early childhood paramount influence on the child comes from parents, and especially from the mother. Parents make conscious efforts to teach the child many specific responses, but more often learning occurs incidentally in the context of family interaction without parental intent to teach. As the child grows older, school becomes an important agent of socialization. The third socializing agent, an individual's peer group, continues to exert an influence throughout life. Though we usually think of socialization as the acquisition of cognitive and motivational patterns in childhood, it should be obvious that the socialization process continues throughout adulthood, as exemplified by occupational socialization (Brim and Wheeler, 1966).

A second area of poverty in which learning plays a central role is in understanding the mechanisms involved in the acquisition of new cognitive information in more formal environments, such as the school. The study of socialization attempts to discover how persons become the way they are; such research is not necessarily concerned with the consequences to the child and to society of his possessing certain characteristics at a given point in his life. Given the fact that disadvantaged children enter school with all the limitations imposed by socialization up to that point, research must then be directed toward ways of mitigating the learning problems they face. Research should attempt first to discover which particular aspects of the individual's present psychological state contribute to his school problems, and then to create the necessary conditions to increase motivation and to maximize the learning ability possessed by the students. Available evidence suggests that among the factors contributing to the disadvantaged child's learning difficulty in school are deficits in basic sensory discriminations, retardation in language development, insufficient motivation, and maladaptive attitudes and expectations about school.

In many cases it may be necessary to correct deficiencies in extremely basic and elementary skills before the learning of tasks involving more complex cognitive operations can be successfully undertaken. One interesting example of an approach to teaching students who have experienced extreme reading problems is the research of Staats et al. (1964), who used the operant conditioning paradigm. Monetary rewards were initially given for correctly making extremely simple visual discriminations, later for recognizing words, and finally only for correctly reading sentences and paragraphs. When the reward level was gradually reduced over time, performance tended to remain at a high level of efficiency. Hunt's chapter in the previous section describes other techniques for teaching disadvantaged children who have had grave difficulty learning in school.

One paper in this section deals with socialization, another with motivational aspects of learning, and one with social class differences in types of learning. The Hess paper focuses on the mother as an important socializing agent by analyzing the nature of the mother's interaction with her preschool child as a function of social-class level. Hess believes the nature of the mother-child interaction derives from structural properties of the environment in which the mother is immersed, a view congruent with the position taken by Sarbin.

Hess' research showed that social-class differences clearly emerged in the way the mother oriented the child toward authority figures. Likewise, expectations that the mother conveyed to her preschool child about school and her conception of the desired behavior of a child in school tended to vary by social-class level. Finally, differences among social-class levels were observed in techniques the mother used in teaching her child a specific and simple task. The ingenious experiments described by Hess show in miniature the nature of the learning environment (as represented by the mother) of the child from a poverty background. That the child is likely to encounter difficulties in school work is not surprising in view of his previous learning experiences. As Hess puts it, mother-child interaction among the lower class can be described as "socialization of apathy and underachievement."

Studying the association between child-rearing techniques and children's behavior has been a popular research problem in psychology for some time (Bandura and Walters, 1960; Sears et al., 1957). But Hess' studies differ in many significant ways from earlier research on the effect of parental behavior on the child. While previous research tended to obtain data by interviewing the mother concerning child-rearing practices—a procedure that suffers from the possibility of confabulation or forgetfulness —Hess directly observed the mother's behavior while she interacted with the child. Earlier research also tended to assess the mother's reported behavior in very global terms (e.g., "love-oriented"), whereas Hess used specific and simple tasks in observing the mother's behavior with the child in a standardized situation. Previous research emphasized general disciplinary techniques and their association with the child's motivational behavior (e.g., aggression or dependency); but Hess examined modes of communication and meaning conveyed by the mother and the relation of this behavior to the child's cognitive performance.

In the second article in this section, Katz starts with the fact that lower-class Negroes typically experience academic difficulty in school, then attempts to explain the problem of poor performance in terms of lack of motivation. Motivation is conceptualized as the internalization of standards of excellence and covert self-evaluation of performance. Katz describes research designed to study self-evaluation of high and low achievers subsequent to their performance on a simple task. Low-achieving boys were more self-critical than high-achieving boys, although the objective performance of the two groups did not differ. In a sense, these low-achieving boys were imposing failure on themselves by using more stringent critical standards for their own performance.

It is possible that students who achieve below acceptable standards in school have learned from past experience to be overly self-critical in evaluating their ability. Many years of discouraging failure in school must certainly be expected to cause a person to evaluate his own performance harshly. Continued failure and its accompanying frustration must surely have important consequences for the person's self-concept regarding ability in academic and intellectual matters in general. However, much additional research is needed to determine whether a negative self-concept, especially if not based on objective ability, contributes substantially to problems of classroom learning.

Evidence supports the assertion that lower-class persons do not attribute to themselves as much ability as they may in fact possess. In one relevant study (Wiley, 1963) junior high school students were asked to estimate their ability to perform school work and to go to college (assuming no financial barrier). The youngsters' own estimates of their ability were plotted against intelligence test scores as a measure of objective ability. Results showed that the majority of those from the lower class (excepting only persons with very high IQ scores) consistently underestimated themselves as compared to students from higher social-class backgrounds. In estimates of ability to do schoolwork, lower-class students in the lower

IQ range rated themselves as much as 20 percent lower than middle-class students who actually had the same score on intelligence tests. Self-estimates of ability for college work also showed discrepancies between students from middle and lower social classes who had the same IQ: at lower IQ levels a discrepancy of as much as 50 percent in estimates of ability existed between social classes for individuals with the same intelligence level.

Having unrealistically low estimates of his ability, the lower-class child is likely to acquire the general expectation that he cannot perform well and conclude that high aspirations are futile and doomed to failure. That these expectations often are not objectively based does not reduce their impact on performance.

In the last chapter in this section Jensen presents his research on the relations among educability, intelligence, and social class. Educability is a term used to refer to the benefit an individual can derive from formal instruction in school. There seem to be greater social-class differences in educability than in intelligence, which is less responsive to family and other environmental influences than is school performance. Jensen reports consistently finding the same intriguing result in several of his studies: intelligence test scores predict ability on simple learning tasks quite well for middle- and upper-class subjects, but not for lower-class subjects. Thus, lower-class children having IQ scores 20 points lower than middle-class children did equally well on direct serial learning tasks.

On the basis of extensive empirical data, Jensen proposes a simple conceptual model for explaining social-class differences in the relation between learning and intelligence test scores. Two levels or types of learning are simple stimulus-response association and more complex learning that involves verbal mediation between stimulus and response. It is assumed that social-class differences in ability exist in these two types of learning. The hypothesized relation among basic learning ability, intelligence, trainability, and educability contains many suggestions for leverage points that could be used to enhance the educability or scholastic performance of disadvantaged children. This model will no doubt stimulate additional research.

Finally, Jensen argues that we have tended to underestimate the role of hereditary and biological factors in determining intelligence and educability. He takes issue with the assumption that motivational factors are of primary importance in accounting for inferior classroom performance of the disadvantaged. Environmental factors have been considered by most psychologists to be the primary source of individual differences in educability and intelligence. Jensen would urge that we look closely at the facts of inheritance of mental ability in order to place the extreme environmental view in proper perspective. To this general question of heredity and environment we shall turn in the next section, where this complex issue will be confronted more directly.

REFERENCES

Bandura, A., and Walters, R. H. *Adolescent Aggression.* New York: Ronald, 1959.

Brim, O. G., Jr., and Wheeler, S. *Socialization after Childhood.* New York: Wiley, 1966.

Sears, R. R., Maccoby, E. E., and Levin, H. *Patterns of Child Rearing.* Evanston, Ill.: Row, Peterson, 1957.

Staats, A. W., Finley, J. R. Minke, K. A., and Wolf, M. M. Reinforcement Variables in the Control of Unit Reading Responses. *Journal of the Experimental Analysis of Behavior* 1964, 7: 139-49.

Wiley, R. C. Children's Estimates of their Schoolwork Ability as a Function of Sex, Race, and Socio-Economic Level. *Journal of Personality* 1963, 31: 203-24.

Chapter 4

THE TRANSMISSION OF COGNITIVE STRATEGIES IN POOR FAMILIES: THE SOCIALIZATION OF APATHY AND UNDERACHIEVEMENT

Robert D. Hess*

In the following observations about the impact of poverty upon children, the central themes of my arguments are: first, that children in poor families acquire patterns of learning and of relationships to authority which are maladaptive for later experience in the classroom; second, that these learning styles and authority orientations are acquired in the preschool years primarily through experience with the environment, of which the mother and other family members are the primary points of contact; and third, that the patterns of socialization in the home are rooted in the social and cultural matrix of which the family is a part, and are not amenable to significant remedy without some change in the social structure of the community. In their broadest sense, these remarks should be considered in the context of an inquiry into the relationship between social structure and

*Lee Jacks Professor of Child Education, School of Education, Stanford University, Palo Alto, California. The Research reported in this chapter was supported by Research Grant #R34 from the Children's Bureau, Social Security Administration, Department of Health, Education and Welfare, by the Ford Foundation Fund for the Advancement of Learning, and by grants-in-aid from the Social Science Research Committee of the Division of Social Sciences, University of Chicago, the office of Economic Opportunity, Division of Research, Project Head Start, and from the U. S. Office of Education. My colleagues on this project were Dr. Virginia Shipman, Dr. Roberta Bear, and Dr. Jere Brophy.

thought, with particular emphasis upon the functional connections between the social and cultural conditions in which the poor live, the socializing behavior of parents, and the consequent educability of young children. Perhaps these connections between social structure and individual behavior may usefully be considered in terms of (1) the nature of the physical and social environment, (2) the effects of this environment upon the adults who interact with small children, and (3) the behavioral outcomes that emerge in the child in his school achievement and his pattern of interaction with the school, its rules and representatives. In order to give some focus to the discussion, and to the project which will be described later, these comments will apply particularly to urban working-class populations.

THE SOCIAL ENVIRONMENT OF THE POOR

The economic poverty of families in the slums is, of course, the most visible and pervasive feature of life and is a dominating concern of many remedial programs. Its importance is assumed in this discussion, however, and the emphasis is upon social and psychological dimensions with which poverty and low status in the socioeconomic hierarchy are associated.

One significant dimension of social class and structure in the United States is the extent to which an individual can exercise power through status, prestige, or affiliation with an institution or organization. A sense of power has much in common with a sense of efficacy; the development of a sense of efficacy helps shape the types of social interaction that arise between the individual and his community. Powerlessness is one of the central problems of the poor. They are more likely to be arrested without justification and detained without adequate regard for individual rights. In mental health clinics, patients from working-class areas may be diagnosed as more maladjusted, with poorer prognoses, than the middle-class patients with similar records (Haase, 1965; Riessman, 1964). In hospital emergency wards, the poor get less adequate emergency treatment (Sudnow, 1967); and in many areas of their lives they have more difficulty defending themselves against invasions of privacy by welfare agents (Cloward and Piven, 1967).

Growing out of a condition of powerlessness and poverty is a vulnerability to disaster. The poor typically are without financial reserves of their own, and are most likely to be unemployed with little advance notice and to be victims of legislative and bureaucratic delay or interruption of welfare service. They possess little credit or borrowing power, and are less likely to have friends with resources (Cloward and Elman, 1966). In disaster situations they are less able to cope and recover (Koos, 1950). In a sense, they live on the edge of incipient tragedy which they are powerless to avert.

The circumstances of life also restrict the alternatives of action available to the poor. Lack of economic resources, of power, of education, and of prestige drastically reduce physical mobility and the opportunity for choosing among options concerning areas of residence, housing, and employment. As a group they are subject to economic control by federal, state, and local public health and welfare agencies who supply them with services. The medical and other services at their disposal are severely limited. Moreover, a low level of literacy and education and lack of knowledge about how to obtain information makes it difficult to discover and use those alternatives that technically may be available.

Another central dimension of social differentiation is the disparity in prestige enjoyed by members of different levels. The poor have little prestige in the society, and their awareness of this position is a mediating screen through which perceptions and information are filtered. This awareness is probably transmitted to children directly through their own observations, and indirectly through adults who define in verbal terms for their children their relative position in the community. This has its impact both on self-regard and on the type of responses that are generated in others. Its effect is part of the socialization process.

Another feature of the life of a lower-class adult is the relatively small overlap between his experiences and those of middle-class adults. Although there is sufficient contact to make the poor aware of middle-class values, the range of experiences is quite dissimilar. The details of daily routine at home are vastly different; the conditions of work are discrepant even (or perhaps especially) when they work in the same factory, school building, or university. The life of a university must look quite different to the maintenance personnel who sweep the floors, pick up the paper, and clean the toilets than it does to the students and faculty. The contact the poor have with the middle class is from a subordinate position. Similarly, middle-class persons typically have little exposure to the home life and extra-occupational activities of families from poverty areas.

ADAPTIVE CONSEQUENCES OF THE SOCIAL ENVIRONMENT

Among adults of poor neighborhoods, several adaptations and consequences emerge, partly as attempts to deal with the practical problems of survival, but also as inner consequences of the external conditions of life.

The relevance of the social, political, economic, and occupational situations in which members of any social status live is, for this discussion, the transformation of these external events and contacts into socializing behavior on the part of adults and their effects on children. Although the effects of experience are mediated only in part through adults, the current literature is dominated by a concern with the adult's role in the emergence of behavior patterns in children. This discussion, then, deals primarily with the consequences of social-class environments for adults, although there are effects that derive from more direct exchange between the child and the environment.

The adaptive consequences of socioeconomic conditions are more apparent at the lower extreme of society, and it may be most useful to focus upon the circumstances and style of life of the poor. However, in doing so, it should be recognized that comparisons of broad segments of society obscure the considerable variation within the lower status; the adaptations that one member makes may be fundamentally different from those of his neighbor.

The life style of the poor seems to show a preference for the familiar and a simplification of the experienced world. In a study by Cohen and Hodges (1963) of workers from different socioeconomic class levels, lower-blue-collar workers were found more likely to agree with statements such as "I'm not the sort of person who enjoys starting a conversation with strangers on the bus or train," and "It is easier not to speak to strangers until they speak to you." To the question "What things bother you most in everyday life?" they were most likely to answer that things and people are unpredictable and they prefer familiar, routine events. This is not so much an expression of indifference to popularity as an indication of lack of confidence and of fear of a social blunder. The lower-class adult apparently tends to level the contours of cognitive awareness and understanding and to interpret life in stereotypes, clichés, and familiar phrases (Bernstein, 1961).

Associated with this stance is a rejection of intellectuality (Cohen and Hodges, 1963), following in part from a mistrust of the unfamiliar—a sense of being unable to compete in modes of reasoning not familiar to them—and in part from a reluctance to accept standards of evaluation which would be to their disadvantage if applied to them. Also, the life circumstances of the poor orient them to practical action. Their participation at work has not typically been that of policy making; their gratification is not that of evaluating means and of developing ideas to guide action (Miller and Riessman, 1961).

A second consequence of lower-class life is the restriction of language and linguistic modes of communication. The interlacing of language with other forms of social behavior has been brilliantly stated by Bernstein (1962, 1964). Language serves behavior; to the extent that the life of the lower working-class is restricted and lacks opportunities for action and for selection among alternatives, its language has less need to be complex and differentiated. This does not imply that there is less communication in terms of frequency of speech or readiness to exchange messages, but that the patterning of speech differs in response to the nature of the interaction among participants (Schatzman and Strauss, 1955).

Relationships tend to be perceived and structured in terms of power. An orientation toward power among the poor has been described in a number of studies. Maas (1953) observed it in the interaction among members of adolescent clubs and their club leaders; Lipset (1960) regards it in part as a tendency for working-class individuals to select the least complex alternative. Whyte (1955) observed this tendency to use power to structure social interaction in his work with "street corner society"; it may underlie the greater incidence of physical punishment in working-class families (Bronfenbrenner, 1958). An orientation to power would seem to follow from the lower-class person's position in the society. In jobs he is likely to hold, instructions are given as specific commands. He has little opportunity to help make decisions which determine the conditions of his work. In other situations that involve interaction with bureaucratic structures (welfare, police, hospitals, credit agencies), the low-status person has relatively little voice in the decisions which affect his daily life; his most characteristic and most adaptive response is to comply and carry out instructions. Conversely, to have status and authority is to have power (Cohen and Hodges, 1963). In line with this orientation, the lower-class father tends to equate respect from children with their compliance and obedience to his wishes and commands (Cohen and Hodges, 1963; Kohn, 1959, 1963).

One of the consequences of lower-class life is a cluster of attitudes that express low esteem, a sense of inefficacy, and passivity. These are regarded not so much as stable personality traits as adaptive responses to frustration and unpredictability, to being acted upon, to being forced to wait for someone in authority to act. Contingencies linking action to outcome in the relation of middle-class behavior to community institutions are frequently missing or intermittent in the slums. The relatively dependent position of the lower working-class adult in the social structure, with its powerlessness, induces magical thought and a tendency to look to superhuman sources for support and assistance. There is a view of the environment as not responsive to individual effort (Hyman, 1953; Inkeles, 1960) and, perhaps consequently, the poor are more likely to accept events with resignation.

One adaptation to this is to elect short-term goals, seeking more immediately predictable gratification (Davis, 1948), and even to use illicit means (delinquent behavior) in achieving rewards usually not available (Cloward and Ohlin, 1960).

Another adaptive consequence of lower-class life is the reliance upon non-work-related friendships and kinship contacts for social support and resources. One expression of these sociometric choices is a lack of interaction with voluntary organizations and a consequent isolation from the institutions of the community (Wright and Hyman, 1958). Family life and social interaction outside the family are composed of a network of friends and kin to whom one can turn for assistance and support which, though limited, are significant. Nonparticipation in organizations may follow from the inability of the lower-class adult to see the relationship between the events and needs of his own life and the goals of the organization (with the possible exception of the union). Skills called for (verbal facility, administrative skill, knowledge of procedures, ability to organize groups in pursuit of goals) are not likely to be developed. As there is little he can do to contribute, and a limited perception of what the organization can do for him, there is little to be gained from membership (Cohen and Hodges, 1963). The world of social contacts is divided into friends and strangers. From strangers he has no reason to expect fair or benign treatment; friendships are salient.

The relative isolation of the lower-class person from the paths of experience of the dominant middle class is one antecedent of his relatively low level of skill and experience in obtaining and evaluating information about events and resources that affect or might affect his life. To put it more simply, he often does not know what to do, and does not know how to find out. This ignorance makes him susceptible to exploitation by members of his own social community and by con men, unscrupulous repair men, loan agencies, and other individuals, agencies, and groups. It may be, as Cohen and Hodges (1963) argue, that this lack of information makes him more inclined to be credulous, especially of the printed word, and more likely to believe TV commercials: ". . . [the lower-blue-collar worker] has *few independent criteria for evaluating the content of the message, little awareness of specific alternatives, and little disposition to weight evidence.*" (Italics in original.) They comment that the field of his experience is unstructured, increasing suggestibility and gullibility, as well as the possibility of eventual disappointment, frustration, and the feeling that life is unpredictable and that long-term probabilities of gratification are modest, at best.

These adaptations of the adults who are accustomed to poverty appear in their interactions with their children. In a study conducted at the University of Chicago, we examined the nature of this interaction and its effect upon the child through an analysis of certain aspects of maternal behavior through which the mother regulated or attempted to regulate the child's behavior and mediated his contact with his environment.

RESEARCH PLAN

For our project a research group of 160 Negro mothers and their four-year-old children was selected from four different social-status levels: Group A came from college-educated professional, executive, and managerial occupational levels; Group B came from skilled blue-collar occupational levels, with not more than high school education; Group C came from unskilled or semiskilled occupational levels, with predominantly elementary school education; Group D from unskilled or semiskilled occupational levels, with fathers absent and family supported by public assistance. These mothers were interviewed twice in their homes, and brought to the university for testing and for an interaction session between mother and child in which the mother was taught three simple tasks by the staff member and then asked to teach these tasks to the child.

One of these tasks was to sort or group a number of plastic toys by color and by function; a second task was to sort eight blocks by two characteristics simultaneously; the third task required the mother and child to work together to copy five designs on a toy called an Etch-a-Sketch. A description of various aspects of the project and some preliminary results have been presented in several papers and a final report (Brophy, Hess, and Shipman, 1966; Hess et al., 1968; Jackson, Hess, and Shipman, 1965; Olim, Hess, and Shipman, 1967; Shipman and Hess, 1965).

Only three aspects of maternal behavior are discussed in this paper: the mother's strategies of control, her role in orienting the child to the behavior that would be expected of him at school, and her teaching techniques in an experimental situation.

STRATEGIES OF MATERNAL CONTROL

One of the most significant aspects of the young child's experience with respect to its effect on cognitive functioning is the techniques he learns for controlling his own behavior. These are typically taught by the mother, or other adults who are responsible for him. In his interaction with them he learns to respond to discipline or control on the basis of three different types of appeal. These appeals are expressed in the techniques that mothers use —requesting, suggesting, arguing, commanding, pleading, scolding, punishing—to regulate their children's behavior. Some mothers use all of these techniques, with preference for one above the others. The significance of these control strategies by the mothers is in the type of response that the mother's strategy demands from the child. The techniques of control are:

1. Those based on appeal to norms, to status, and to generally accepted rules and regulations. The essential element of this strategy is that it accepts the status quo as appropriate and unquestionable, using such statements as "You'll do that because I said so," or "Don't do that—girls don't act that way," or "Mind the teacher and do what you are told." All of these statements (and many more) are based on the norms of the system and upon the position or status of members in it. For example, teachers are to be obeyed because they are teachers. This type of control is useful and necessary on certain occasions. It is essential to inform the child about authority structure and rules of the family, of the school, and, later, of the structure of more complex institutions—the army, the company, etc. However, it is a type of control that asks for no thought or reflection on the part of the child. He merely has to respond with compliance, not with understanding. He must obey, not think. If this type of control is used exclusively, or almost exclusively, with a child, his orientation is likely to be one of conforming (or rebelling), not of attempting to comprehend the rules and the system. This type of control defines his own role as passive, as waiting to be told, as accepting the instruction he is given, without curiosity and questioning. It may lead to a passive learning style when used by a family and subsequently used by the teacher at school.

2. Those based on subjective appeal to internal states of the child, the mother, or other persons with whom he interacts. In this type of control the mother calls attention to feelings and other internal reactions, using such phrases as "How do you think your sister will feel if you do that," or "You've hurt Bobby's feelings," or "The other girls won't like you if you . . . " or "When you do that, it makes me very sad," or "The teacher has a hard job taking care of so many kids. How would you feel if you were the teacher and the kids didn't mind?" These statements call the child's attention not to the rules so much as to the effects of his behavior on other persons and on himself. As a style of control, it orients the child toward the roles of other persons, asking him to put himself in another's place—to role play. This is a more complex cognitive process, and one which asks the child to be attentive to incoming clues from the environment, rather than to memorize a rule of behavior. It induces and encourages a different learning style—less passive, more alert to peers and authority figures, more able to see a situation from several vantage points.

   3. Those based on arguments relating to the task to be performed or on some future consequence of the behavior. This type of control calls the child's attention not to norms or feelings but to the eventual outcome of effects of the behavior. It is based on a rationale of cause and effect, and the notion that what the child does at present has a future result. It is thus much more complex than the first two strategies, for it asks the child to project himself into the future, and sometimes to another place, and to reflect on the long-range (relatively) effects of his behavior. The cognitive response this type of control requests from the child is to ask for reflection about the consequences of his action in relation to alternative actions and a decision based on a logical (no matter how simple) cause-effect consideration. For example, if a child asks to play with a classmate after school and the mother responds with "Will you have enough time to do your homework?" or a similar comment, the child is asked to weigh the consequences of alternative actions and to regulate his own behavior in accordance with a more complex plan than would be the case if the mother simply denied the request without linking her response to the other considerations she had in mind. This type of regulation thus gives the child a way to internalize control of a cognitive nature, providing him with general guidelines which he may himself apply to new situations.

   These regulatory techniques create complementary orientations in the children who live under them. In imperative, norm-centered approaches, the child learns to attend to authority figures as sources, rules, and enforcers; in subjective-personal systems, the child's attention is oriented toward expressive, internal reactions in others, and he is likely to become relatively more responsive to interpersonal features of behavior; in the cognitive-rational approach the child is more likely to be oriented toward tasks, toward goals, and toward logical principles. Although there is some overlapping in these orientations, they may be viewed as representing somewhat different arenas of emphasis and attention in the environment.

   There were differences among the four status groups in their tendency to use these different types of control strategies in reporting to us, in the research setting, how they would deal with their children in instances when some question of relationship to authority arose. The tendency to use imperative command appeared in responses to several different types of open-ended questions. Status differences are illustrated by Table 1, which indicates the percentage of imperative responses offered by the mothers when describing what they would say to their child to prepare him for his first day at school.

Table 1. Mean percentages of Imperative Responses in Maternal Control Technique Categories for the Four Social Status Groups

	Middle Class	Skilled	Working Class Unskilled	
			Father Present	Father Absent
Percent of imperative responses	14.9	48.2	44.5	46.9

There is a significant association between the pattern of regulatory or control strategies used by the mother and the cognitive performance of her child.

The effect is implicit in the description of the different control types: children of mothers who used imperative-normative regulatory techniques were associated with low performance in several areas (Table 2). First, there was a significant negative correlation between imperative responses on first day protocols and Stanford-Binet scores of the child ($r = -0.32$). Imperative responses were also correlated negatively with other variables such as the tendency to use relational categories ($r = -0.20$) and the tendency to offer scorable responses ($r = -0.24$) on the Sigel Sorting Task for children. Also mothers with high imperative scores had children who gave non-verbal responses to the Sigel Sorting Task ($r = 0.36$). This relationship holds for the three working-class groups as well as for the total research group. Conversely, mothers who are relatively high in their use of subjective responses have children who generally score somewhat higher than average on IQ and concept-formation tasks.

The picture presented by the data is congruent with the postulated relationship between maternal behavior and cognitive performance of children. Although the correlations are not high, they are, for the most part, significant and consistent. The measures of children's performance were taken from several quite different contexts using different tech-

Table 2. Correlations between Maternal Control Techniques and Children's Cognitive Performance

Cognitive Variables	Imperative A (first day)	Imperative B (school situation)
Block Verbal score	0.32*	0.25*
Binet IQ	0.32*	0.27*
Sigel nonverbal	0.36*	0.16†

*p < 0.01
†p < 0.05

niques, ranging from conventional intelligence testing to the more direct performance measures involving concept formation in a teaching situation.

MOTHERS' DEFINITION OF THE ROLE OF THE PUPIL

The conceptual categories with which the mother defines the school reveal which aspects of the new situation (i.e., new to the child) are most salient to her. Until he has entered and actually experienced this new realm, the preschool child's notions about school are likely to be hazy and inaccurate. He can, however, anticipate it by viewing it through his mother's eyes. Even if she does not tell her child in explicit terms what she thinks of school, nor describe the daily routine of a classroom, she will often express her attitudes and expectations indirectly, guiding him in developing attitudes and behavior she believes will be necessary for his success in school.

To obtain the mothers' definitions and perceptions of school, we asked them to imagine that it was the first day of school: "Your child is going to school for the first time, what will you do, what will you tell him?"

Responses to this question were scored in one of six categories. The "obedience" category includes responses in which the mother defined the classroom as a place where the child would have to behave in a socially-accepted and obedient manner toward the teacher and his peers; to conform to classroom routine; to follow a set of rules pertaining to health, safety, and property right; or simply to behave or be nice. For example, one mother said that she would tell her little girl,

> . . . to obey the teacher. Do what the teacher asks her to do and that's all to do or say. Just tell her to sit quiet and listen at the teacher and do whatever the teacher tells her to do and get her lessons.

Another, less concerned with school itself than with the problems of getting there and home safely, said,

> I would tell him to be aware of cars, you know, don't step out in front of a car is something that is dangerous. And don't pick up different things that don't concern him. Go straight to school and come straight home from school.

A less explicit statement of the importance of obedience was given by a Group C mother:

> Well, the first time I would tell him to be nice and learn to listen
> to the teachers and do what they tell him to do and mind.

A Group B mother listed a group of behaviors she expected her child to
remember when going to school for the first time:

> I'd tell him to go straight to school and stop at the patrol lady . . .
> don't cross, because she tells you to. Mind your teacher; be nice;
> raise your hand, and when you have to go to the bathroom ask her,
> you know, and don't talk in school, don't eat any candy or chew
> any gum. Be nice.

Mothers of middle-class background tended to elaborate more and to
suggest rather than to demand obedience.

> I will tell (her) that she is beginning her education. And here she
> will learn to listen to the teacher and how to act properly in a
> control situation such as not talking out any time she wants to
> . . . and I will tell her to be very cooperative and do whatever the
> teacher wants her to do. And try to be friendly and get along with
> the children.

The following middle-class mother drew an analogy between obedience
at home and at school:

> The only thing I will definitely stress to her is authority, that
> the teacher becomes the authority head. Mother and Daddy are the
> authorities at home, and that she has to respect and obey the
> teacher and likewise the teacher will respect and obey her wishes
> and I think this is mainly what I will tell her about it: that there is
> authority outside of the home and this is it, you are just going
> into it, your teacher will be your main center of authority at
> school and you must obey her as I want you to obey me.

A second response category defines school as an opportunity to attain
increasing levels of achievement in academic skills. A mother might say,
as did one in the public assistance group, "She's going there for to learn
things which will help her for whatever she might want to be when she
grows up." A Group C mother said, "I'd tell him that I want him to go to
school so that he can prepare himself how to work or help him get a good
job."

In addition to defining school as an authority system or as an educational system, some mothers were concerned with the beginning of school
as an emotional or affective experience. These mothers anticipated their
children's fears of the new and strange experience and stressed the adven-
turous aspects of meeting new people and the change in status from baby

to "big boy." One middle-class mother, concerned with affect, spoke only in positive tones:

> First of all, I would take (him) to see his new school, we would talk about the building, and after seeing the school I would tell him that he would meet new children who would be his friends, he would play and work with them. I would explain to him that the teacher would be his friend, would help him and guide him in school, and that he should do as she tells him to. That she will be his mother while he is away from home.

An eloquent statement of mixed emotions was given by a Group C mother:

> I know he gonna be frightened, you know, to stay there by himself, uh with the teacha. I just don't know what I would tell him. I try, I'd tell him that, uh, that he gonna have a lot of fun, you know, with the drawin' and everythin', and uh, playin' with the rest of the kids. Lots of kids there to play with—the rest of the kids. And I'll tell him that I'll be back for him, and uh, it's fun, it's a lot of fun to go to school, cause he looks forward to goin' to school, but I know that first day, I know how it is that first day, when your mother leave you, you just don't know what to do.

The coding system devised for responses to this question defines a unit as a completed thought, usually a subject-and-predicate clause. For each respondent the number of units devoted to each category of response can be expressed as the percentage of the total number of units contained in her response. It is for this reason that vague and irrelevant response units were included in the total score. Table 3 reports the average percent usage of each category obtained within each of the four status groups.

Although the total number of message units did not vary much among the four groups, the total response is partitioned differently in the four groups of mothers, with an especially marked difference in the use of obedience and affect categories by the middle-class mothers as contrasted with the other three groups. Middle-class mothers are apparently more concerned with the emotional aspects of the new situation, with its meaning to the child, than with his displaying good behavior, a finding congruent with previous research on Caucasian working-class mothers (Kohn, 1963).

MATERNAL TEACHING BEHAVIOR

The type of analysis of teaching styles used in the study may best be presented by examples rather than a description of the full range of variables used. In addition to the testing and interviewing of mothers and children, the

Table 3. Mother's Relative Use of Different Response Categories on the
First Day Technique (Mean Percentages)

Type of Response	Middle class (N-39)	Working class		
		Skilled (N-40)	Unskilled	
			Father Present (N-38)	Father Absent (N-40)
School relevant instruction:				
Obedience	21.3	49.1	44.2	46.7
Achievement	2.2	1.4	2.9	3.2
Noninstruction orientation:				
Affect	31.2	14.3	14.5	21.5
Preparation	8.6	3.9	1.1	1.3
Other:				
Vague	16.4	13.7	23.4	17.5
Irrelevant	19.6	15.2	13.2	12.8
Sum	99.3	97.6	99.3	103.0

last session of data gathering concluded with the mother attempting to teach her child three simple tasks which a staff member had previously taught the mother. The first of these was a sorting task, using plastic toys, which the children were asked to sort by color and by function. The second was a group of blocks which were to be sorted by two criteria—height of block and a symbol (O or X) on the top of the block. The third task used a commercially available toy, called Etch-A-Sketch. This is a little plastic toy consisting of a screen on which lines may be drawn by manipulating two knobs. When one of the knobs is turned clockwise a line appears on the screen moving to the right. Turning the knob counterclockwise traces a line to the left. The other knob may be used to move the line in a vertical dimension. If the two knobs are moved at the same time, the line moves in corresponding angles or arcs, depending on the degree to which one knob is moved relative to the other. The mothers were asked to copy five designs made up of connecting perpendicular lines. Mothers were assigned one knob; the children were assigned the other. The mothers were told that they could instruct the child but could not turn his knob for him. The success of the joint effort was dependent on the mother's ability to work with the child, using only verbal cues. When an error was made, the mother was given a fresh board and permitted to start the task again.

The data for selected measures for the four social status groups are summarized in Table 4. The group means are ordered by social-class level with significant differences between the middle-class group and the other groups. The differences in favor of the middle class are all in the direction associated with greater success at the task. Compared with the working-class subjects, middle-class mothers relied less on physical feedback, preferred motivating the child to controlling through implied threat, and gave more orientation to the task.

The effect of maternal teaching styles on the Etch-A-Sketch is perhaps best illustrated by two simple measures. The mothers were given cardboard cards on which were drawn the designs to be copied. One of the measures used was the mother's use of the design model. She could, at her own choice, show the child the card and design or not call his attention to it. Some mothers referred to the designs frequently, calling the child's attention to the shape and size of the model. Others placed the model where it could not be seen by the child and did not mention it in their instructions.

Table 4. Performance of the Four Groups on Measures of Maternal Teaching (Block Sorting Task)

	Middle class		Working class					
			Skilled		Unskilled			
					Father present		Father absent	
Variable	Mean (N = 40)	SD	Mean (N = 41)	SD	Mean (N = 40)	SD	Mean (N = 41)	SD
Providing needed information about the task	23.46	8.38	22.87	7.00	20.82	9.20	22.26	8.00
Motivating to perform well	5.30	4.49	3.46	3.67	2.73	2.57	3.08	3.16
Orienting	8.12	4.03	6.45	3.74	5.78	3.63	5.44	3.77
Requesting physical feedback	8.17	4.71	13.91	8.78	13.16	6.89	14.06	5.37

Note: Middle-class means significantly different from all working-class means on all variables.

Table 5. Means, SD's and Significant Differences among the Four Groups
on Etch-A-Sketch Measures

	Middle class		Working class					
			Skilled		Unskilled			
					Father present		Father absent	
Variable	Mean (N = 38)	SD	Mean (N = 37)	SD	Mean (N = 35)	SD	Mean (N = 35)	SD
Directions	17.21	5.95	10.89	7.40	8.86	7.00	9.74	8.16
Use of models	3.74	1.41	1.35	1.60	1.17	1.42	0.89	1.26

Note: Middle-class means significantly different from all working-class means on all variables.

The measure used in our analysis was the number of models, out of five, that the mother showed to her child at least once during the time they were working together to copy it.

The other measure was also a simple element in the task. It was the extent to which the mother gave the child directions for turning his knob when she was working with him to copy the designs. A sample of twenty-five directions from each mother was selected, and each was scored for presence or absence of specificity in indicating which way the child was to turn the knob. Such comments as "Okay," or "Now it's your turn" were non-specific; statements such as "Turn toward Mommy," "Turn the way you did last time," etc., were coded as specific. The measure was the total number of directions of twenty-five coded as specific. The summaries for the four groups for these two measures are shown in Table 5.

INTERRELATIONSHIPS AMONG THE MEASURES

The relationships between the maternal measures and the performance of the children are too extensive and detailed to present here, and are reported elsewhere (Hess et al., 1968), but the general features can be described. The mother's strategies of control and her teaching styles are related to the child's performance at a significant level, and are more highly related to it than is the mother's IQ. Such relationships hold, not only for the total group, but for the three working-class groups combined. Other maternal measures which are associated with the child's cognitive behavior are her sense of efficacy in relation to the school, her tendency to participate in activities in the community, her use of specific, complex, or abstract language models, and a number of other measures. These represent a life style of the working-class Negro mother which is restricted and shaped by the position she holds in the social structure. These measures correlate more highly with the child's cognitive performance (IQ, sorting behavior, verbal behavior) than do the mother's IQ, her social status, or the two measures combined. They also predict at a higher level the child's performance on cognitive measures in a follow-up study two years later when he is about to enter school. These data are to be reported in more detail in subsequent papers.

The problem of lack of meaning in the mother-child communication system is clearly exemplified in the behavior of many of the mothers on this task. Consider the plight of the child whose mother performs as follows: During the practice period, she demands that he turn his knob, but she fails to explain why or to relate it to events occurring on the screen; during the task she fails to show him the models, and typically fails to give specific turning directions. For such children, the learning situation is this:

1. The child is not given a goal to make his individual response meaningful (i.e., he is not shown the model).

2. The mother is not specific in her directions: each new response of the child is essentially a guess.

3. The sequence and pattern of response is not explained. The child has no way to tell ahead of time how to respond, and even after he does respond he cannot predict the mother's reaction. He is hindered in learning anything from one response which will generalize to the next.

4. Nevertheless, his responses are being rewarded or punished, typically with maternal praise or disapproval. This provides belated feedback for the individual response if the mother is not giving specific directions. In either case, it performs a motivating function.

As a result of the interaction of these factors, the child is in a position of being asked to produce responses which:

1. are not related to any discernible goal.

2. are not rewarding in themselves.

3. do not bring corrective feedback which will enable him to avoid punishment.

Nevertheless, reinforcement continues, and punishments are usually more frequent and intense than rewards. The parallel between this state of affairs and the experimental designs used by Maier (1949) to deliberately produce frustration in subhuman organisms is strikingly consistent. Given the conditions to which the child is exposed, the adaptive reaction for him is to cease producing responses and leave the field.

It appears, then, that in spite of a mother's good intentions, if she fails to inject sufficient meaning into her interactions with her child, she may structure the situation so that he not only fails to learn, but develops a negative response to the experience. It seems possible that for many children such experiences occur frequently enough to lead to generalization resulting in negative valence for many learning situations. By this route, then, a mother may induce negative attitudes, not by the child's imitating the mother or introjecting her views, but by his reacting adaptively to her well-meant but harmful teaching behavior. We believe that this kind of communication failure is a primary factor in the mother-child interaction patterns of socially disadvantaged groups, and that it has farreaching and cumulative effects which retard the child's educability in a formal classroom situation.

REFERENCES

Bernstein, B. Social Class and Linguistic Development: A Theory of Social Learning, in A. H. Halsey, et al., eds. *Education, Economy, and Society.* New York: Free Press, 1961, pp. 288-314.

————. Linguistic Codes, Hesitation Phenomena and Intelligence. *Language and Speech* 1962, 5:31-46.

————. Elaborated and Restricted Codes: Their Social Origins and Some Consequences, in J. Gumperz and D. Hymes, eds. *The Ethnography of Communication, American Anthropologist* 1964, 66: no. 6, part 2, pp. 55-69.

Bronfenbrenner, U. Socialization and Social Class through Time and Space, in E. E. Maccoby, et al., eds. *Readings in Social Psychology.* New York: Holt, 1958, pp. 400-425.

Brophy, J., Hess, R. D., and Shipman, V. C. Teaching Behavior of Mothers in a Structured Interaction with Their Four-Year-Old Children: A Study in Frustration. Paper presented at the 38th annual meeting of the Midwestern Psychological Association, Chicago, Illinois, May 1966.

Cloward, R. A., and Elman, R. M. Poverty, Injustice, and the Welfare States, Part 1. *The Nation,* February 28, 1966, 230-35.

Cloward, R. A., and Ohlin, L. E. *Delinquency and Opportunity.* Glencoe: Free Press, 1960.

Cloward, R. A., and Piven, F. F. Birth of a Movement. *The Nation,* May 8, 1967, 582-88.

Cohen, A. K., and Hodges, H. M. Characteristics of the Lower-Blue-Collar-Class. *Social Problems* 1963, 10: no. 4, 303-34.

Davis, A. *Social Class Influences Upon Learning* (The Inglis Lecture), Cambridge, Mass.: Harvard University Press, 1948.

Haase, W. Rorschach Diagnosis, Socio-Economic Class, and Examiner Bias. Doctoral dissertation, New York University, 1956.

Hess, R. D., Shipman, V. C., Brophy, J., and Bear, R. M. Cognitive Environments of Urban Preschool Negro Children. Report to the Children's Bureau, Social Security Administration, HEW, 1968.

Hyman, H. H. The Value Systems of Different Classes, in R. Bendix and S. M. Lipset, eds. *Class, Status and Power.* Glencoe: Free Press, 1953, pp. 426-42.

Inkeles, A. Industrial Man: The Relation of Status to Experience, Perception, and Value. *American Journal of Sociology* 1960, 66: 1-31.

Jackson, J. D., Hess, R. D., and Shipman, V. C. Communication Styles in Teachers: An Experiment. Paper presented at the American Educational Research Association, Chicago, 1965.

Kohn, M. L. Social Class and Parental Values. *American Journal of Sociology* 1959, 64: 337-51.

————. Social Class and Parent-Child Relationships: An Interpretation. *American Journal of Sociology* 1963, 67: 471-80.

Koos, E. L. Class Differences in Family Reactions to Crisis. *Marriage and Family Living* 1950, 12: 77-78.

Lipset, S. M. *Political Man.* Garden City, N.Y.: Doubleday, 1960.

Maas, H. S. The Role of Members in Clubs of Lower-Class and Middle-Class Adolescents, in J. M. Seidman, ed. *The Adolescent.* New York: Holt, Rinehart. Winston, 1953, pp. 294-304.

Maier, N. R. F. *Frustration, the Study of Behavior without a Goal.* New York: McGraw-Hill, 1949.

Miller, S. M., and Riessman, F. The Working Class Subculture: A New View. *Social Problems* 1961, 9: 86-97.

Olim, E. G., Hess, R. D., and Shipman, V. C. Role of Mothers' Language Styles in Mediating Their Preschool Children's Cognitive Development. *School Review* 1967, 75: 414-24.

Riessman, F., *New Approaches to Mental Health Treatment for Labor and Low Income Groups.* New York: National Institute of Labor Education, Mental Health Program, 1964.

Schatzman, L., and Strauss, A. Social Class and Modes of Communication. *American Journal of Sociology* 1955, 60: 329-38.

Shipman, V. C., and Hess, R. D. Social Class and Sex Differences in the Utilization of Language and the Consequences for Cognitive Development. Paper presented at Midwest Psychological Association, Chicago, April, 1965.

Sudnow, D. Dead on Arrival. *Trans-action* 1967, 5: 36-43.

Whyte, W. F. *Street Corner Society: The Social Structure of an Italian Slum.* Chicago: University of Chicago Press, 1955.

Wright, C., and Hyman, H. Voluntary Association Memberships of American Adults: Evidence from National Sample Surveys. *American Sociological Review* 1958, 23: 284-94.

Chapter 5

A NEW APPROACH TO THE STUDY OF SCHOOL MOTIVATION IN MINORITY GROUP CHILDREN

Irwin Katz*

What I should like to do in this chapter is bring to your attention an important social problem that up till now has, on the whole, been mysteriously ignored by social psychologists—mysteriously because it would seem to provide a unique opportunity to apply rigorous investigative techniques to a rich domain of social phenomena in their natural setting. I have in mind the problem of widespread academic failure among minority group children. Long a matter of common observation by teachers and school administrators, the racial gap in school achievement was recently documented by the Coleman survey (Coleman et al., 1966) of American public schools, which revealed that at every grade level studied, and in all regions of the country, average Negro scores on achievement tests were about one standard deviation below white averages. Until recently, the little research done on the causes of low Negro achievement tended to be narrowly concerned with the description of group differences in IQ. Fortunately, there is now discernible a more promising trend toward studies of cognitive development and the conditions that influence its course. However, very little is known, or is currently being learned, about the contribution of motivational factors to racial differences in school achievement.

Perhaps the first question to ask is whether Negro students are in

*Professor of Psychology, University of Michigan, Ann Arbor, Michigan. This chapter is based upon a longer and more detailed treatment of the subject that appeared in *The Nebraska Symposium on Motivation,* 1967.

fact less interested in formal learning than their white counterparts. The answer is not nearly as clear as one would wish, about the only available information being the qualitative impressions of educators. To my knowledge, there have been no systematic racial comparisons of academic motivation based on both psychological testing and classroom observations. However, at least with regard to the urban ghetto schools of the North, there is a high degree of consensus among teachers and principals that Negro children typically are not interested in schoolwork. Vivid, impressionistic descriptions of pupils from the inner-city slums are quite abundant. For example, a young teacher in a Harlem school (Levy, 1966) has written:

> What impressed me most was the fact that my children (9-10 years old) are already cynical and disillusioned about school, themselves, and life-in-general. They are hostile, rebellious, and bitter. . . . They are hyperactive and are constantly in motion. In many ways they can be compared with wild horses that are suddenly fenced in.

The picture conveyed in the above quotation does not apply to all predominantly Negro schools, even in slum areas, but it seems to be fairly typical of the lower socioeconomic levels. In less impoverished neighborhoods, teachers complain less about children's open hostility and rebelliousness, and more about their covert withdrawal into apathy, inattention, and laziness. If the prevailing view of teachers that Negro pupils lack adequate motivation for learning is accepted, the question then is whether greater interest in formal learning would really raise their level of attainment to a significant extent. So far as I know, there are no fully adequate data bearing upon this issue. However, in the absence of compelling evidence to the contrary, common sense suggests that a strengthening of the will to learn will lead to higher achievement. That is the assumption underlying my interest in studying nonintellectual determinants of academic success and failure. Concerning the nature of the Negro pupil's motivational deficit, a number of hypotheses have been advanced by various authors.

Some writers, particularly those who are psychoanalytically oriented, attribute the Negro pupil's learning difficulties to a basic failure of the socialization process in the home. Ausubel (1963) stresses two features of child rearing which he assumes to be typical of low-income Negro families. One is the harsh authoritarianism of parents, who emphasize punitive forms of control, and place considerable social and emotional distance between themselves and their children. The other feature is the early relaxation of close parental supervision, which makes the child precociously independent of adult influence but exposes him to the exaggerated socializing influence of the peer group. These conditions, in combination with the child's growing awareness of the stigma attached to being a Negro in a white-dominated society, are supposed to create a personality marked by feelings of unworthiness, lack of self-controlling mechanisms, and hostile rejection of adult values. Perhaps no one has stated this position as sharply as Bettelheim (1964), who believes "that human personality is shaped in infancy, and that the early characteristics are extremely resistant to change." In his view it is absurd to think that educational reform will change the outlook on life of the Negro child and improve his academic progress, "as if both were not determined before he entered kindergarten or first grade."

Another writer who postulates a failure of the socialization process in the Negro home is McClelland (1961). Negroes as a group, he maintains, are lacking in the achievement motive because of the matricentric structure of the Negro family, and the persistence of child-rearing practices that originated in slavery. McClelland takes for granted that strong mother-dependency weakens the development of need achievement (n Ach) in sons. Moreover, "Negro slaves . . . developed child-rearing practices calculated to produce obedience and responsibility not n Ach, and their descendants, while free, should still show the effects of such training in lower n Ach—which in fact is exactly the case. . . ."

A different type of cultural deprivation hypothesis stresses the importance for scholastic achievement of the motivation that is inherent in the information-processing or action components of the learning behavior itself. Hunt (1968) believes that the normal development of such intrinsic motivation, observable in children and animals as an interest in new experience, requires a variety of stimulation in early life that is lacking in lower-class environments.

Still another point of view has recently been advanced by Bereiter (1966), who denies the applicability of the sensory deprivation concept to lower-class children. He points out that sensory deprivation has nothing to do with the educational quality of the stimuli available, but only with their variety, intensity, and patterning. "On these purely quantitative bases," he comments, "automobiles passing in the street are as good as story books, old shoes are as good as dolls, and trash cans are as good as toy drums." Bereiter believes that the disadvantaged pupil lacks motivation because he does not possess the one essential tool of academic learning, hence is overwhelmed by the difficulty of the tasks that are put before him. What the child lacks is the ability to use language as a device for acquiring and processing the kind of information that is transmitted in the classroom.

In contradistinction to the various notions of cultural deprivation is the concept of cultural conflict. Inkeles (1966), Riessman (1962), Cloward and

Jones (1963), and others have pointed out that minority-group cultures have distinctive systems of values and goals that are not taken into account by the school. The lower-class Negro child may acquire the kind of competencies—the motives, attitudes, and skills—that are needed for optimal adjustment to the conditions of life that he is likely to encounter. The skills that are valued in his own culture may be intrinsically difficult, and require for their mastery a good deal of effort and persistence, yet be totally ignored by the educational establishment. Thus the low academic motivation of the Negro pupil may be a reflection of the fact that the competence goals of the school are not relevant to the competence goals toward which the child has been socialized by the transmitting agents of his own culture. In short, according to such writers as Inkeles, Riessman, and Cloward and Jones, the problem of motivating the Negro pupil is essentially one of accommodating the educational goals of the school to the values, goals, and learning styles that have been socially transmitted to the child in his home and neighborhood environments.

Clark (1965) presses the point further, by placing responsibility for the massive academic failure of ghetto school children squarely with the teachers and school administrators. To Clark, every one of the assumptions associated with the term "cultural deprivation" is "primarily an alibi for educational neglect, and in no way a reflection of the nature of the educational process." He believes that a key component of the deprivation which afflicts ghetto children is that generally their teachers do not expect them to learn, and have adopted custodial care and discipline as their concept of their function. Accordingly, the motivational problems of the children will be solved when teachers can be motivated to teach effectively—that is, to set high standards of scholastic performance, and to provide good instruction, combined with emotional acceptance and support.

Summarizing my brief survey of current assumptions regarding the low academic motivation of Negro children, the main emphases seem to be on (a) various types of personality and cognitive deficits associated with the notion of cultural deprivation, (b) the discontinuity of home and school competency training, and (c) the failure of predominantly Negro schools to provide the same quality of instruction that is provided in white middle-class schools. These assumptions have generated a heavy flow of speculative writing, but little in the way of research—a condition due mainly to a lack of suitable investigative techniques.

I think the crux of the motivational matter is the differential capability of children from different social backgrounds for vigorous and sustained effort on tasks that are not consistently interesting and attractive, and which offer no immediate extrinsic payoff, either positive or negative. In this view, effective scholastic motivation is largely reducible to self-control—an outcome of a socialization process involving the internalization of standards of excellence and of self-evaluations that have affective consequences. Presumably, these behavioral mechanisms both guide and energize performance whenever either immediate or delayed social evaluation is anticipated. Before discussing a new approach to the study of self-regulating behaviors I should like to mention three important types of related research. I refer to work on the achievement motive, material and symbolic rewards, and self-reinforcement.

An impressive body of research on determinants of academic effort has evolved from the notion of a general motive to achieve, as formulated principally by McClelland and Atkinson. As Atkinson (1964) puts it, ". . . the disposition called achievement motive might be conceived as a capacity for taking pride in accomplishment when success at one or another activity is achieved." It is supposed to be measured through scoring of fantasy productions elicited by pictures from the Thematic Apperception Test (TAT) and similar stimuli. From the standpoint of trying to ascertain the determinants of children's academic achieving behavior, I think the basic weakness of the McClelland-Atkinson approach is that it focuses exclusively on motive strength, and provides no useful information about the covert self-regulatory behaviors that are postulated in the definition of the achievement motive. What Atkinson (1964) alludes to as "a capacity for taking pride in accomplishment" can be regarded as a socially learned mechanism whereby the individual reinforces his own achievement efforts through affect-mediating self-evaluations, based upon comparison of his performance with internalized standards of excellence. Presumably it is these behaviors that enable a person to maintain certain activities (such as doing homework) in the absence of surveillance and immediate extrinsic reward. If standard setting, self-evaluation, and affect mediation constitute the core processes underlying the will to perform well in the classroom and elsewhere, then it is upon these processes and the social factors that influence their development that the investigator should concentrate his attention. What I am suggesting is the need for an explicit formulation of the organismic determinants of children's academic achievement-striving in terms of measurable self-regulatory behaviors, such as the dispensing of self-approval and self-disapproval in response to performance in various achievement situations. The usefulness of this type of formulation will of course depend upon the availability of techniques for assessing the covert behaviors inferentially. Let us consider two current approaches to the problem.

One well-known method for studying class and race differences in learning motivation is that which compares the effectiveness of different types of rewards, such as tangible versus symbolic, and person-centered versus response-centered. To account for various findings, Zigler and Kanzer (1962) have proposed that socially disadvantaged children lag behind their middle-class peers developmentally. They postulate a developmental hierarchy of reinforcers, according to which the dependency of early learning on primary need-gratification diminishes as social reinforcers (expressions of affection, attention, praise) become increasingly effective, until the social reinforcers, in turn, become less important motivationally than mere information that one's responses are correct. Thus in the final stage the child is more concerned about being right for right's sake than about receiving adult approval. According to Zigler and Kanzer, this process is central in the child's progress from infantile dependence to autonomy.

Let me briefly indicate what the reinforcement studies of Zigler and his associates, and of other investigators, tell us about social-class differences in the development of learning motivation. First, there is some evidence that tangible reinforcers are more effective than verbal ones with poor children, but not with middle-class children. Next, studies of age of subjects and reinforcer effectiveness tend to suggest that as children grow older they depend less on social stimuli and more on direct information about the correctness of their responses, the phenomenon being most evident when social and informational cues are most clearly separated. Thus these investigations can be said to point tentatively toward a kind of equivalence between social class and chronological age. That is, if one assumes that the socialization of intellectual motivation involves a progression from material to social to informational types of prepotent reinforcement, it could be argued that the lower-class child behaves as though he were at an earlier stage of development.

Unfortunately, the experiments that have compared groups of children on responsiveness to social reinforcers only—whether the reinforcers emphasized praise, correctness, or both—do not consistently support the developmental view. Indeed, these studies do not allow for any generalizations about class or race differences in motivation. It appears that the social reinforcement experiment is not a particularly appropriate technique for analyzing subcultural differences in the socialization of achieving behaviors. One reason is that the social-stimulus events (usually an experimenter's utterances) that are used as reinforcers can have widely discrepant meanings for children of different social backgrounds or of different chronological ages. The reinforcement properties of these social-stimulus events, as Stevenson (1965) has aptly observed, are incredibly complex. Stevenson has mentioned over a dozen broad types of variables that are known to influence children's responsiveness to social reinforcers. Yet research thus far has barely begun to unravel the mysteries of this behavior domain.

Recently a few investigators have tried to approach the problem of the self-regulation of performance more directly by operationalizing Skinner's (1953) concept of self-reinforcement. Their research has not been concerned with social background characteristics of individuals, but it constitutes an important methodological advance in the analysis of achievement socialization, and is therefore worthy of comment. The handful of experiments that have been carried out on self-reinforcement seem to fall roughly into two types: (a) studies on adults of factors that determine the way in which people self-administer signals for guiding their responses on bona fide learning tasks, and (b) studies (usually on children) of the influence of models on the standards employed for rewarding one's own performance on rigged tasks, where cues of excellence have no relation to actual effort or achievement. Both types of experiment have some obvious limitations for the empirical analysis of internalization. Two criteria for judging whether a particular type of socially learned behavior has become internalized would be, first, whether it occurs in the absence of surveillance, and second, whether it occurs in the absence of any external mediation of immediate affective consequences.

Neither the imitation experiments nor the experiments on self-administration of reinforcing signals meet the first criterion, inasmuch as subjects were apparently always aware that their responses would be known to the experimenter. Therefore, it could be argued that the subject's behavior was influenced by its anticipated effect upon a powerful authority figure. Moreover, none of the studies have met the second criterion by convincingly demonstrating intrinsic mediation of affect.

Recently I have been working with two colleagues, Reuben Baron and Gloria Cowan of Wayne State University, on the development of procedures for the direct observation of the covert responses of elementary school pupils to achievement situations. In the method we have used thus far, individual subjects are seated at a table alone in a cubicle. During a self-evaluation phase a series of tasks are presented with informal instructions that state: "We want to find out whether these things we will give you to do are interesting to kids your age." Near the child on the table is a metal box with three buttons. The buttons activate three small light bulbs of different colors, labeled *Good, Poor,* and *Don't Know.* Each time the subject completes a task he evaluates his performance by pressing one of the buttons. The self-evaluations are ostensibly private, unobserved, and for the child's own amusement. His instructions are: "We think you will enjoy doing these things more if you can tell yourself how nice a job you think you did. So after you finish each one you can press the button which shows how you feel about the kind of job you did. You can press *Good,* or *Poor,* or *Don't Know.* No one will know which button you are pressing." The instructions, of course, are deceptive, for the button pressings are mechanically recorded by counters concealed in the box.

In another phase of the procedure the extent to which the child's self-evaluations have affective consequences is investigated by testing whether the colored lights used in the self-evaluation box have acquired positive or negative incentive value by virtue of being associated with favorable and unfavorable self-evaluations. A rigorous test would require control of the frequency of the different types of self-evaluation, and before-after measures of the incentive value of the lights. However, in our exploratory work we have not fully met these conditions. Also, we did not bother to use a counterbalanced arrangement of light bulbs to neutralize preexperimental color preferences. In the self-evaluation series, blue, red, and amber, respectively, always designated "Good," "Poor," and "Don't Know." Two techniques of assessing acquired reinforcement value have been tried at different times. The first involved the introduction, after the self-evaluation phase, of a toylike gadget that the child was permitted to play with unobserved for a few minutes. It had three levers which activated bulbs when depressed. The bulbs corresponded in size, color, and position to those on the self-evaluation box, but were not labeled. The index of acquired reinforcement value was the number of times each lever was depressed, as recorded by concealed mechanical counters. The second technique required the child to fill in the outline of a clown with colored crayons both before and after the self-evaluation series, from which quantitative measures of the use of critical colors were obtained.

BEHAVIORAL FINDINGS

To date we have tested seventy-nine fourth-, fifth-, and sixth-grade Negro pupils in a virtually all-Negro public school in Detroit. Two types of subjects were used: those whom teachers regarded as high achievers, and those regarded as low achievers. Of the total sample, only ten were girls. Girls who were good and poor students showed little difference in their self-evaluations, hence were temporarily dropped from the research. However, among boys the poor students engaged in more self-criticism and were less favorable in their total self-evaluations than the good students. That the differences between groups were not created by a few extreme scores is evident from the data on thirty-six boys who evaluated their performance on a series of picture-assembly tasks: only three out of seventeen good students, but fully sixteen out of nineteen poor students used the "Poor" button at least once out of a total of six self-evaluations. Another male sample of roughly equal size that evaluated themselves on their constructions of simple words from Scrabble letters showed similar differences between high and low academic achievers.

Confronted with these results, my colleagues and I first looked into the possibility that the self-evaluations were reasonably accurate appraisals of actual performance on the picture-assembly and word-assembly tasks. We had judges who were unacquainted with the experimental procedures rate the pictures for quality. They detected no differences associated with academic achievement or self-ratings. Similarly, we could detect no differences in the accuracy of the constructed words. (I should mention, however, that we did not keep precise records of the amount of time subjects spent on the tasks, and it remains a possibility that the good-student groups did in fact work faster.)

We next looked into the question of observer effects. You will recall that we tried to make subjects believe that their self-evaluations were completely private—neither observed directly nor mechanically recorded. As a check on the success of this procedure we asked the children various questions in a terminal interview: whom they thought they were telling about their performance when they pressed the evaluation buttons, and so on. All but a few subjects indicated by their replies that they had accepted our cover story at face value. Of course one cannot be sure they were not telling us what we perhaps all too obviously wanted to hear. But one item of information leads me to believe that the pupils perceived the situation as more private than not. When several of them were requested to reveal their self-evaluations, the recollections they were willing or able to provide the interviewer bore virtually no relations to their actual behavior as recorded on the mechanical counters.

Let me turn to the findings on lever-pressing behavior in the postevaluative phase. Lever pressing, you will recall, was one of the techniques used to measure the acquired incentive value of the colored lights that had been associated with self-evaluative responses. Adequate lever-pressing data were available only for twenty-four subjects, evenly divided between high and low academic achievers. The most suggestive comparison was between the proportion of boys' responses to the lever that activated the red bulb (which previously was labeled "Poor"), and their academic status. When each child's responses to this lever were expressed as a proportion of his total responses to all three levers, and scores of high and low achievers were compared, greater avoidance of the red light by low achievers was just beyond the 0.15 level of significance for a two-tailed test. Given the smallness of the sample, the difference seems provocative. It suggests that the red light tended to become an aversive stimulus for the subjects who had actually used self-criticism and who were also low achievers.

The crayon-drawing technique also revealed an interesting, though again nonsignificant, tendency toward a stimulus-generalization effect. Among thirty-three boys who colored a clown before and after the self-evaluation experience, there were no pretest differences in the use of critical colors. However, when pre-post change scores were examined, low achievers showed a slight tendency, relative to high achievers, to avoid the use of red. The level of probability for the group differences was 0.10 for a two-tailed test. Thus the total evidence of self-reinforcement effects is weak indeed, but nonetheless encouraging at this stage of our investigations with regard to self-criticism.

Summarizing the findings thus far presented, low-achieving boys were more self-critical than high-achieving boys, and later showed a weak tendency to avoid a stimulus that had been associated with self-critical responses. There were no significant effects for girls. Let me consider some of the implications of the results for boys. First, it should be explained that the great majority of children, particularly of boys, in the school where we tested were in the low-achiever category. The teachers who selected our subjects were hard put to come up with thirty-five boys whom they could call high achievers—that is, whom they regarded as clearly competent in school work—and they were drawing on an aggregate pool of about 200 boys. Hence, it is fair to say tentatively that the typical male pupils in the school were both academically weak by teachers' standards, and critical of their own achievement efforts. Yet relative to pupils in other predominantly Negro schools in Detroit, these boys were no worse than average, according to the school principal. It is also noteworthy that the student body was not drawn from the lowest socioeconomic segment of the city's Negro population. The children seemed to be from homes of somewhat better-than-average socioeconomic status for Negroes.

What is intriguing about our results is the implication that among northern Negro children from homes of average quality, academic failure is not necessarily associated with low or unstable standards of evaluation. If standards are to be inferred from a predisposition to criticize oneself, then our low-achieving Negro boys had very high standards indeed. The data suggest that in the absence of clear external cues they had difficulty accepting their own performance as adequate. Conceivably, their standards were so stringent and rigid as to be utterly dysfunctional. What they perhaps had internalized was a most effective mechanism for self-discouragement. The child, in a sense, had been socialized to self-imposed failure. I use the term socialization in its technical meaning, for I believe what is involved is not merely a lack of prior rewards for achievement efforts, but also a history of punitive reactions by socializing agents to such efforts.

I have in mind Aronfreed's (1968) model for the socialization of self-criticism as a response to transgressions. Aronfreed is mainly concerned with accounting for the internalization of moral self-control, but his concepts are sufficiently general to apply to achievement situations as well. He defines self-criticism as the most common form of a class of reactions to transgression in which the child imitatively reproduces components of the punishment to which he has been previously exposed. Aronfreed's conception is basically quite simple. Once a child has had some contact with punishment for a particular type of behavior, he will experience anticipatory anxiety in the intervals which occur between subsequent enactments of such behavior and the occurrence of punishment. Certain of the stimulus components of punishment can then acquire value as signals for the attenuation of the child's anticipatory anxiety, since they mark the end of the interval of anticipation. Thus young children can sometimes be observed to verbalize self-criticism aloud, and to make the anxiety-reducing function of these responses quite transparent when they show signs of distress following a punishable behavior and then apparent relief after they have overtly censured themselves. Very likely, the extent to which self-criticism—rather than avoidance, withdrawal, or outwardly directed hostility—is acquired by a child as a technique for reducing anxiety will be governed to some extent by his dependency on adults for emotional security.

A theory of emotional blocks to learning that deals explicity with the conflict between emotional dependency and hostile impulses has been formulated by Sarason and his associates at Yale (Sarason et al., 1960) in connection with their investigations of test anxiety. Like Aronfreed, the Yale group offers an anxiety-reduction interpretation of self-blame. They regard the test-anxious child as one who typically reacts with strong unconscious hostility against teachers and others whom he thinks are passing judgment on his adequacy as a person. Because of his dependency on adults, the child does not express his feelings openly, but instead turns them inward upon himself in the form of self-derogatory attitudes. This is as far as the theory goes with regard to the adaptive function of self-blame. I would simply add that when inward-directed hostility expresses itself as self-criticism, the resultant discharge of the displaced impulses tends to be cathartic, hence anxiety-reducing.

Though the samples tested by the Yale group were vastly different from ours, being drawn from predominantly white middle-class schools in suburban communities, their theoretical linkage of anxiety and self-deprecation made it desirable to administer the Test Anxiety Scale which they had devised to our Negro subjects. We found in our Negro boys that test anxiety was greater among low achievers than among high achievers, and that it was directly related to propensity for self-criticism in the experimental situation. These results suggest that anxiety was a factor of importance in the behavior of the low-achieving Negro boys.

We also investigated the notion that the parents of self-critical children are inclined to withhold positive reinforcements, while dispensing negative reinforcements all too abundantly. Subjects were administered a Reinforcement History Questionnaire which my coinvestigator Reuben Baron had designed. It contains twenty-one items dealing with characteristic reactions of the father or mother to the child in a variety of situations. The results clearly show that low achievement, anxiety, and self-devaluation, which are all interrelated, are each in turn related to perceptions of low parental acceptance and high parental punitiveness. It would of course be worthwhile to obtain comparable scores on the child's perceptions of the reactions of teachers and peers. Future research should also include direct observations of parent-child and teacher-child interactions.

Space does not permit me to discuss in detail the directions that are indicated for future research. Clearly, a first order of business will be an effort to devise an adequate technique for demonstrating the self-reinforcement properties of self-evaluations. Then it will be appropriate to explore certain parameters of the behavioral situation, including the kind and amount of information given subjects about their task performance, the degree of perceived surveillance of both task performance and self-evaluations, the nature of the task, and characteristics of the experimenter. Beyond that, there seem to be manifold possibilities for examining developmental phenomena, sex and cultural differences, the effectiveness of interventions involving different types of behavior by adult and peer models, and so on.

To conclude, my basic proposition has been that the child's capacity for sustained academic effort depends heavily upon an internalized mechanism of affect-mediating self-evaluations. Pilot research encourages me to believe that this is a core motivational process, the study of which can provide a fruitful scientific entry into the problem of widespread academic failure among socially underprivileged children in the United States. By assessing the self-regulatory process, and relating its characteristics to classroom performance on the one hand, and to school and home background variables on the other, it may be possible to test adequately for the first time a broad range of hypotheses regarding the in-school and out-of-school sources of the disadvantaged pupil's motivational difficulties.

REFERENCES

Atkinson, J. W. *An Introduction to Motivation.* New York: Van Nostrand, 1964.

Aronfreed, J. M. *Conduct and Conscience: The Socialization of Internalized Control over Behavior.* New York: Academic Press, 1968.

Ausubel, D. P., and Ausubel, P. Ego Development among Segregated Negro Children, in A. H. Passow, ed. *Education in Depressed Areas.* New York: Bureau of Publications, Teachers College, Columbia University, 1963, pp. 104-41.

Bereiter, C. E., and Engelmann, S. *Teaching Disadvantaged Children in the Preschool.* Englewood Cliffs, N. J.: Prentice-Hall, 1966.

Bettelheim, B. Review of B. S. Bloom's *Stability and Change in Human Characteristics,* in *New York Review of Books* Sept. 10, 1964, pp. 1-4.

Clark, K. B. *Dark Ghetto.* New York: Harper & Row, 1965.

Cloward, R. A., and Jones, J. A. Social Class: Educational Attitudes and Participation, in A. H. Passow, ed. *Education in Depressed Areas.* New York: Bureau of Publications, Teachers College, Columbia University, 1963, pp. 190-216.

Coleman, J. S. et al. *Equality of Educational Opportunity.* Washington, D.C.: U.S. Department of Health, Education and Welfare, U. S. Government Printing Office, 1966.

Hunt, J. McV. The Psychological Basis for Preschool Cultural Enrichment Programs, in M. Deutsch, A. Jensen, and I. Katz, eds. *Social Class, Race, and Psychological Development.* New York: Holt, Rinehart & Winston, 1968, pp. 296-336.

Inkeles, A. A Note on Social Structure and the Socialization of Competence. *Harvard Educational Review* 1966, 36: 265-83.

Levy, B. An Urban Teacher Speaks Out, in S. W. Webster, ed. *The Disadvantaged Learner.* San Francisco: Chandler, 1966, pp. 430-36.

McClelland, D. C. *The Achieving Society.* New York: Van Nostrand, 1961.

Riessman, F. *The Culturally Deprived Child.* New York: Harper, 1962.

Sarason, S. B., Davidson, K. S., Lighthall, F. F., Waite, R. R., and Ruebush, B. K. *Anxiety in Elementary School Children.* New York: Wiley, 1960.

Skinner, B. F. *Science and Human Behavior.* New York: Macmillan, 1953.

Stevenson, H. W. Social Reinforcement of Children's Behavior, in L. P. Lipsit and C. C. Spiker, eds. *Advances in Child Development and Behavior.* Vol. 2. New York: Academic Press, 1965, pp. 97-126.

Zigler, E., and Kanzer, P. The Effectiveness of Two Classes of Verbal Reinforcers on the Performance of Middle-Class and Lower-Class Children. *Journal of Personality* 1962, 30: 157-63.

Chapter 6

LEARNING ABILITY, INTELLIGENCE, AND EDUCABILITY

Arthur R. Jensen*

When viewed in conjunction with other research on the nature of intelligence, data gathered in my learning laboratory over the past few years suggest an interesting hypothesis relevant to the educational problems of children currently called culturally disadvantaged. The model presented here has grown directly from results of a variety of experiments and is best regarded merely as an attempt to make sense out of the data. The experiments originally were not specifically designed to test this hypothesis, but the simple model may make possible useful predictions related to the educability of culturally disadvantaged children. The purposes of this discussion are: (a) to present relevant empirical data; (b) to describe a theoretical model that integrates these data; (c) to consider the biological and environmental determinants of individual differences in ability; (d) to explore the concept of educability.

EMPIRICAL DATA REQUIRING EXPLANATION

Learning Abilities in Mexican- and Anglo-American Children

My active interest in this problem began during a casual conversation with a school psychologist and an elementary classroom teacher working in

---

*Professor of Educational Psychology University of California, Berkeley

a school district with a substantial proportion of Mexican-American pupils, the majority of whom performed below the average in learning school subjects. Both agreed that Mexican-American children seemed brighter than Anglo-American children of the same IQ, and that this was especially true when comparing low IQ Mexican-Americans with low IQ Anglo-Americans. Though these groups performed equally poorly in school tasks, much as might be expected on the basis of their low IQ's, the Mexican-Americans seemed distinctly brighter on the playground than their Anglo-American counterparts. The school psychologist had been unable to find any test—verbal or nonverbal, culture-free or culture-fair, administered either in English or in Spanish—that reflected this interesting difference.

Standard intelligence tests, of course, measure mostly knowledge and skills which the child must already have acquired before taking the test. If children's opportunities for relevant experiences are unequal, the tests will measure opportunity for learning rather than intelligence. Therefore, it seemed to me that the best way to assess the educational potential of children of differing backgrounds might be to measure their learning ability directly. The proper test would give the child a new learning task that minimizes the importance of individual differences in acquired skills.

A number of simple learning tasks were devised which more or less met this criterion. The tasks consisted essentially of free recall and serial learning. Two kinds of stimulus materials were used, but were never mixed together in the same learning task: familiar objects (e.g., water glass, bar of soap, paint brush, ball, candle, toy airplane, toy gun, comb, spoon, etc.); and abstract materials consisting of three-dimensional colored geometric forms (triangles, circles, squares, and diamonds colored red, blue, yellow, and green).

In the recall test for familiar objects the examiner showed the child a dozen objects one at a time and asked him to name each object. The name that the child gave to an object was unimportant so long as it was consistent and distinct. After naming the twelve objects laid on the table before him, the child was told to view them for 10 seconds and to name as many as possible after they were removed from sight. The objects were then covered, and as the child named each one the examiner placed it again in view. When the child made no further responses for approximately one minute, the remaining unrecalled objects were exposed one at a time and the child was asked to name them again. The whole process was repeated until the child could recall all twelve objects. The child's score was the total number of unrecalled objects on all trials up to the first perfect trial. The recall test for abstract objects was the same, except that only seven objects were used in any single test, and some of the children had to be told their names.

In the serial learning test, the objects that were used in the recall test were placed under a row of small identical boxes. The child had to anticipate which object would appear under each box, going in serial order from left to right. Each box was lifted immediately after the child guessed which object was under it. The procedure was repeated until the child attained one perfect trial. The score was the total number of errors up to the first perfect trial. The serial test with abstract forms was the same except that the series consisted of only seven items.

Mexican-American and Anglo-American children in the fourth grade were matched at two levels of IQ on a standard test (California Test of Mental Maturity). Both groups were of relatively low socioeconomic status (SES), although the Mexican-American group was probably slightly lower than the Anglo-American in ways not likely to show up in crude indices of SES such as father's occupation. Results are shown in Figures 1 to 4 (Jensen, 1961).

The significant feature of these results is that the IQ test predicts learning ability quite well in the Anglo-American group, but not in the Mexican-American group. Low-IQ Anglo-Americans were much poorer learners than their Mexican-American counterparts, while the above-average-IQ Mexican-American group showed no consistent superiority in learning scores.

That this result could have been due to the fact that the Mexican-American children came from bilingual homes, and therefore were seriously underestimated by the usual verbal IQ tests, was a real possibility. But children in this group generally perform as poorly on intelligence tests given in Spanish as in English, so the results may represent something more fundamental than a problem of bilingualism.

Learning Ability as a Function of Social Class and Intelligence

Would results be similar for upper-middle and lower SES Anglo-Americans in whom there is no question of bilingualism or ethnic discrimination? One of my students, Dr. Jacqueline Rapier, investigated this matter using serial and paired-associate learning tasks (Rapier, 1968). Her tests (serial and paired-associate learning, using pictures of familiar objects) all showed essentially the same results. Though the high (i.e., upper-middle) and low SES groups were closely matched on both individual and group IQ tests, these tests failed to predict learning ability (both serial and paired-associate) in the low SES group; but IQ did predict learning ability in the high SES group. Correlations between IQ and learning ability ranged between 0.01 and 0.22 for the various tasks and experimental conditions in the low SES group, and from 0.41 to 0.60 in the high SES group. These are very substantial correlations, considering that the reliability of these short

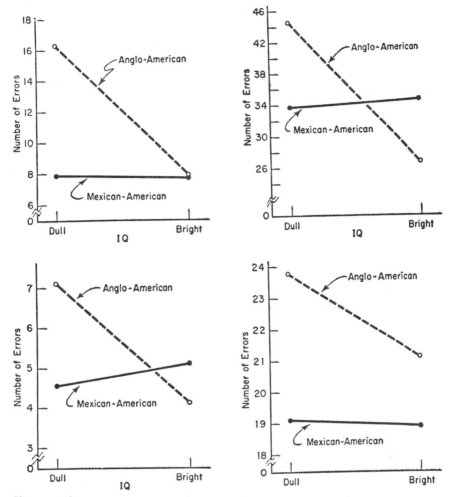

Figure 1 (left): Mean error scores of dull (IQ's 73-89) and bright (IQ's 111-126) Mexican-American and Anglo-American fourth-grade children on the recall test for familiar objects. Figure 2 (right): Mean error scores of dull and bright Mexican-American and Anglo-American children on the serial learning of familiar objects. Figure 3 (left): Mean error scores of dull and bright Mexican-American and Anglo-American children on the recall test for abstract objects. Figure 4 (right): Mean error scores of dull and bright Mexican-American and Anglo-American children on the serial learning of abstract objects.

learning tests is in the range of 0.60 to 0.70. In the low IQ range, results showed a higher average level of learning ability in low SES children, while in the IQ range above 100, low SES children performed no better on the learning tests than middle-class children of the same IQ. This is essentially the same picture that emerged from the Mexican-American data.

Learning Abilities in Retarded, Average, and Gifted Children

In a study conducted in a junior high school having a great diversity of socioeconomic levels and racial groups, all children in special classes for the mentally retarded (Stanford-Binet IQ from 50 to 75) were compared with groups of average (IQ 90 to 110) and gifted (IQ above 135) children in a trial-and-error selective learning task (Jensen, 1963). The apparatus consisted essentially of a stimulus-display screen and a response panel of pushbuttons (Jensen, Collins, and Freeland, 1962). Colored geometric forms appeared in random sequence on the screen, and the subjects had to learn by trial and error which pushbutton corresponded to each colored form. Reinforcement for correct responses consisted of a one-second flash of a green light located below the display screen. Each subject worked at his own pace. Subjects were given preliminary practice trials on simpler forms of the task, involving fewer stimulus-response (S-R) connections. No subject was tested on the final form of the task (with six S-R connections) until the examiner had clear evidence that the subject was able to learn in the situation and was at ease with the apparatus.

As should be expected, the learning rates of the three groups, shown in Figure 5, correspond to their IQ levels. But these ordinary-looking learning curves fail to reveal the great range of individual differences in learning ability among children in the retarded group. Four of the thirty-six subjects in the retarded group performed above the mean of the gifted group. In fact, the two fastest learners from all three groups had IQ's of 147 and 65! On the other hand, the average and gifted groups showed much less variability. None of the children in the average group (IQ 90 to 110) approached the mean of the gifted group in learning ability, and none of the gifted were as poor in learning as the mean of the average group.

Inquiry into the family backgrounds of the slowest and fastest learners in the retarded group revealed that the low IQ children who were fast learners were, without exception, from a low SES. Low IQ children from more advantaged backgrounds were the slowest learners.

To obtain further confirmation of this observation a number of retarded young adults in a sheltered workshop (none of whom would be called culturally disadvantaged) were given the same learning test. They learned at an extremely slow rate; none exceeded the mean of the retarded junior high school pupils, although their IQ's were in the same range.

Another experiment, based on a picture form of serial and paired-associate learning, showed that these forms of learning are clearly correlated with IQ among middle-class subjects (Jensen, 1965a). IQ rather than mental age seemed to be the main correlate of learning rate. We should expect this, of course, since traditional tests like the Stanford-Binet primarily test the amount of knowledge the child possesses, which is based on

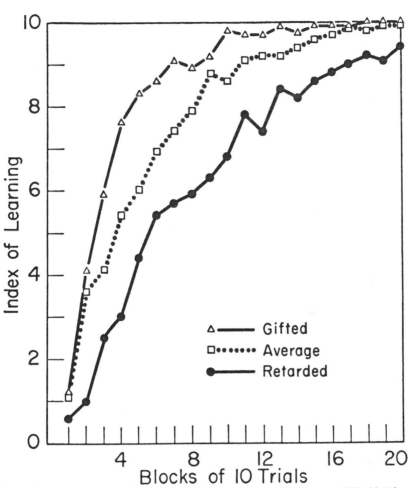

Figure 5: Learning curves of gifted (IQ's 135+, mean = 143), average (IQ's 90-110, mean = 103), and retarded (IQ's 50-75, mean = 66) junior high school students on a trial-and-error selective learning task involving six S = R connections (Jensen, 1963).

his experience and therefore related to mental age. Dividing amount of knowledge (mental age) by time taken to acquire it (chronological age) yields a measure of rate of acquisition, the IQ. According to this line of reasoning, it was not surprising to find that normal nine-year-old children with a mental age of nine learned serial and paired-associate lists much faster than young adults whose mental age was nine years but whose IQ's placed them in the mentally retarded category.

All these results are wholly consistent with the previous studies. *Laboratory learning tests are highly correlated with IQ except when the subjects are of low socioeconomic status.* Furthermore, lower-class children, although generally averaging some 15 to 20 points lower in IQ than middle-class children, perform about as well as middle-class children on the direct learning tests.

Learning Ability of Negroes and Whites

In the course of an experimental investigation of the determinants of verbal mediation or mnemonic elaboration in paired-associate learning, Dr. William D. Rohwer, my coworker in much of this research, compared the performance of low and middle SES children in classes from Head Start and kindergarten to sixth grade. More than 90 percent of the low SES children in Rohwer's study were Negro; all the middle SES children were white.

The learning task used by Rohwer consisted of twenty-four paired-associate pictures of familiar objects presented by means of a motion picture projector. The series of twenty-four picture pairs was presented twice, each pair being shown for three seconds; after each presentation of the entire list only one item of each pair was shown, and the subject asked to name the object that was paired with it. The score is the total number of correct responses in two trials. Rohwer's results are shown in Figure 6. There is a significant age trend in learning performance, but the slight SES differences are negligible and nonsignificant despite the fact that the low and middle SES groups differ by almost 20 points in IQ.

Rohwer explored the question of whether this particular learning task is in any way related to intelligence by giving the test to mentally retarded young adults with an average mental age of close to ten years, which is more than twice the mental age of the Head Start children. As can be seen in Figure 6, the adult retardates were the poorest learners of all.

The same paired-assocate test was administered to one hundred middle SES children in private nursery schools and to one hundred low SES children (mostly Negro) of comparable age in day-care centers. The two SES groups were both four to five years in age, but differed 19 points in mean IQ.

The correlation between mental age and learning scores (with chronological age partialled out) was 0.10 for the low SES group and 0.51 for the middle SES group (corrected for attenuation, these correlations are 0.13 and 0.67, respectively). Again it is clear that learning scores are related to measured intelligence, but much more so in the middle than in the low SES group.

Learning Ability and Digit Span

Items making up most standard intelligence tests bear little resemblance to our direct-learning tasks, most of them requiring either past

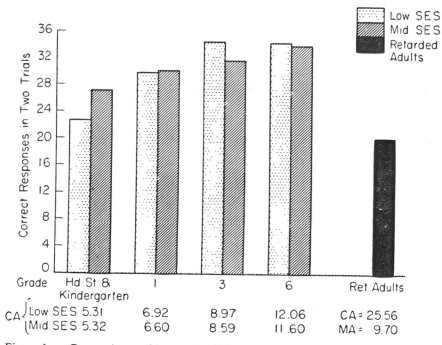

Grade	Hd St & Kindergarten	1	3	6	Ret Adults
CA { Low SES	5.31	6.92	8.97	12.06	CA = 25.56
{ Mid SES	5.32	6.60	8.59	11.60	MA = 9.70

Figure 6: Comparisons of low- and middle-socioeconomic groups at various ages with retarded adults on a paired-associate task (24 picture pairs presented two times at a rate of 3 sec. per pair). (Permission of Dr. Wm. Rohwer.)

learning and ability to recall knowledge or the ability to apply past knowledge to the solution of relatively complex problems. The individual's learning rate can only be indirectly inferred from performance on items of this type. In making this inference the individual's chronological age and experiential background must be taken into account.

Of all the items in standardized individual tests like the Stanford-Binet and Wechsler tests, digit span has more in common with our direct-learning tests than any of the other subtests. But clinical psychologists have a widespread misconception that digit span (i.e., the ability to repeat a series of n digits after hearing or reading it only once) is one of the poorest measures of intelligence in standard IQ batteries. One reason for this is probably the relatively low reliability of digit span due to the extreme brevity of the test as commonly used in clinical practice. When the correlation of digit span with total IQ on the Wechsler Intelligence Scale for Adults is corrected for attenuation (i.e., the unreliability of the test is statistically removed from the correlation), it is 0.75. A factor analysis of the Wechsler subscales shows that in the 18- to 19-year age group (the peak age for this ability), digit span has a factor loading (corrected for attenuation) of 0.75 on g, the general factor common to all subtests (Wechsler, 1958, p. 122). The Stanford-Binet digit-span test has loadings on g about as high as its reliability permits. At age two-and-a-half the digit-span test consists of repeating only two digits, scored simply pass or fail; this brief test has a biserial correlation of 0.63 (not corrected for attenuation) with total IQ (Terman and Merrill, 1960, p. 342).

A factor analysis of individual differences in digit span and serial learning has shown that these two types of tasks comprise very much the same abilities; that is, practically all the individual-differences variance in serial learning (of meaningful words, nonsense syllables, or color forms) is predictable from scores on digit-span tests (Jensen, 1965b). Furthermore, twelve factor scores derived from a battery of digit-span and serial learning tasks yielded a multiple correlation with college grade-point average of 0.76 (0.68 after correction for shrinkage) in a group of fifty undergraduates in the University of California, Berkeley. Thus, most of what we have been measuring by means of our direct-learning tests might be measured more easily and efficiently by means of digit-span or similar short-term memory tests.

There is already some evidence that digit span behaves much like our learning tests in relation to social class and ethnic variables. For example, we can compare the vocabulary and digit-span subtest of the Stanford-Binet in the white normative population and in the Negro norms collected by Kennedy, Van de Riet, and White (1963). Vocabulary is a good test with which to compare digit span in this context, since vocabulary has the highest correlation with total IQ and the highest loading on g of any of the Stanford-Binet subtests. Negro and white children differed markedly in vocabulary at every age level, but they differed much less in digit span.

The fact that digit span is undoubtedly a much more culture-free test than vocabulary could account for a relatively greater discrepancy between vocabulary and digit span in the Negro than in the white population. But the same argument does not suffice to explain the relative lack of correlation between IQ and learning ability as measured by our learning test (and presumably also measured by digit span). Even if scores on vocabulary and other culturally loaded tests were depressed in a given segment of a population because of environmental disadvantages, one should still expect that whatever true variance does exist in, say, vocabulary, would be as highly correlated with learning ability in a disadvantaged as in a more advantaged population.

One other fact about the digit span should be noted, since it is probably the main reason for its being so often discredited as a measure of intelligence by clinical psychologists. Clinicians report that occasionally a person with a very low IQ and a history of school failure nevertheless shows quite normal or even superior performance on the digit-span test.

But the reverse almost never seems to occur, except in aged or senile persons and in cases of brain damage incurred after maturity. Wechsler (1958, p. 72) also comments that clinicians believe digit span is best for detecting mental defectives since, barring emotional disturbance, brain damage, and senility, poor digit span almost invariably means low intelligence by all other criteria, while good digit span is not invariably associated with superior or even average general intelligence.

This combination of facts strongly suggests that short-term memory (the chief process measured by digit span) is a necessary but not sufficient condition for the development of functional intelligence of the type measured by tests highly loaded on g and tapped in its purest form by tests like Raven's Progressive Matrices.

THEORETICAL INTERPRETATION OF EMPIRICAL FINDINGS

Level I and Level II Abilities: Associative and Cognitive Learning

A conceptually simple model is now proposed as a means of systematically comprehending the array of phenomena discussed in the first section. Two levels of ability are posited for the psychological processes involved in learning and problem solving (hereafter referred to as Level I and Level II). Level I ability is characterized by attention, short-term memory, and associative learning. Level II ability is characterized by symbolic or abstract thinking, conceptual learning, semantic generalization, and the use of language as a tool of thought in learning and problem solving. A digit-span test, the speed of serial rote learning, or the rate of operant conditioning would all presumably measure Level I abilities. The question "How are an apple and a banana alike?" or "Which number goes in the blank in the following series: 2, 3, 5, 8, 12, 17,   ?" or problems requiring the proper combination of previously acquired bits of knowledge or skill are all examples of items that measure Level II ability. In brief, Level II can be characterized in much the same way as Spearman characterized g—"the education of relations and correlates"—in short, the ability to see relationships.

There is now considerable experimental evidence for these two levels of ability and for the fact that during the period from infancy to childhood the Level II abilities become increasingly prominent in relation to Level I. Level II is closely related to the development of language and particularly to the transition from the use of language merely as a form of social communication to its internalized use as a means of representing and interpreting one's own experiences to oneself, ordering events, anticipating, planning, and solving problems. This transition from associative learning to what has been called *cognitive learning* is manifest most conspicuously between the ages of five and six. It is interesting that throughout history all societies that have had a system of formal education have chosen the ages of five or six to begin the child's formal instruction. Pavlov (1927) referred to Level II functions as the "second signal system," meaning that instead of the direct control of behavior by external stimuli, verbal responses mediate behavior at this level of development.

Sheldon White (1965) has reviewed most of the experimental evidence for the transition from Level I to Level II process and has found about twenty various psychological phenomena that show a marked qualitative change between the ages five to seven, the younger pattern of behavior being more similar to the learning of subhuman species and the older pattern being characteristic of adult humans with fully developed language functions.

In normal adults both levels of functioning and the relative prominence of each process at any given time depend upon the nature of the task. Most intelligence tests tap a mixture of Level I and Level II functions, but predominantly Level II. Our direct-learning tests, although also a mixture, involve predominantly Level I.

In terms of our theory, we postulate that Levels I and II are essentially independent functions that are interrelated only in actual performance. In the language of physiology, they are structurally independent, but functionally interdependent. In the language of genetics, they are genotypically independent but phenotypically correlated. Level I processes, furthermore, are seen as a necessary but not sufficient condition for the development of Level II processes. Individual differences in Level II abilities are dependent upon individual differences in Level I abilities in much the same way that the amount of liquid in a container depends upon the amount poured into it—up to the capacity of the container.

Social Class and Level I and Level II Abilities

Since IQ tests measure functional intelligence, which depends upon both Levels I and II, we are not able to assess Level II functions either directly or independently of Level I. To proceed with the development of our hypothesis, imagine that we can completely separate Levels I and II; they are indeed conceptually separable in the same way that genotype and phenotype are conceptually separable to geneticists.

The performances of low SES and middle and upper-middle SES children on the IQ and direct-learning tests suggest the hypothesis that Level I and Level II abilities are distributed unequally in the population partly as a function of social class. The hypothesized distributions of genotypes for Levels I and II as a function of social class are illustrated in Figure 7. The precise form of these hypothetical distributions is not a crucial issue at this point. If this assumption concerning distributions is essentially correct, along with the assumptions concerning the two genotypically independent levels of ability, the model should predict the empirical findings described previously.

To simplify exposition of the model, let us deal with only two classifications of abilities at Levels I and II: above-average and below-average. We can assume proportions of each SES group that fall above and below the average of Levels I and II to illustrate the hypothesis, as shown in Table 1.

If Levels I and II are independent, then the joint probability of any combination of the two in a given population is a product of their independent probabilities. Thus we arrive at the following fourfold contingency tables for lower and upper SES groups (Table 2). The lower right-hand cell theoretically contains no subjects, since in Level II performance they look like subjects in the lower left-hand cell; thus the arrow indicating they are added to the other group, since tests which involve Level II do not distinguish these subjects from the group which is below average in both Levels I and II.

These tables show some of the interesting features we have noted in our data. The main points are: (a) the low SES contingency table yields a larger proportion of below-average subjects in functional intelligence (85 percent versus 52 percent in the middle SES table); (b) a larger proportion of the low than of the middle SES falls into the category, *above*, on Level I, and *below*, on Level II, and if persons were selected at random from the below-average IQ group, there would be about twice as great a chance of getting an above-average child on Level I abilities from a low SES group as from a high SES group; (c) the correlation between performance measures of Levels I and II is much less in the low than in the middle SES group (0.42 versus 0.78 in the example above); (d) the form of the correlation scatter diagram is not symmetrical—a relatively greater proportion of the off-diagonal cases fall into the upper left quadrant, and this effect is more exaggerated in the low SES group.

This, in fact, is what we find in examining our actual correlation scatter plots: for both SES groups the lowest frequency is in the lower right quadrant. Table 3 shows the proportions obtained in an experiment reported previously in which four- to five-year-old children of low and middle SES groups were given a picture paired-associate test (the Peabody Picture Vocabulary Test was used to measure mental age). These tests are, of course, not pure measures of Level I or Level II processes, but the paired-associate test reflects predominantly Level I and the PPVT reflects predominantly Level II. Why should there be any subjects at all in the

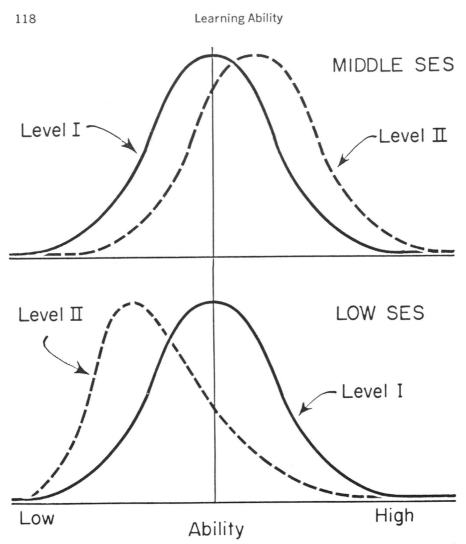

Figure 7:   Hypothetical curves of the distributions of Level I (solid line) and
             Level II (dashed line) abilities in middle-class (upper curves) and
             culturally disadvantaged (lower curves) populations.

lower right quadrant when the theory predicts none in this quadrant for
either SES group? Probably because there is a great amount of noise in
these rough data. As pointed out before, the tests themselves are far
from being pure measures of Levels I and II abilities. Furthermore, the
learning task is somewhat more demanding and stressful than the intelligence test. We also know that laboratory tests are often quite sensitive in
reflecting anxiety and emotional disturbance, so that even a child who
scores high in the intelligence test but who is anxious or emotionally dis-

Table 1. Proportions of SES Groups Falling Above and Below the Mean of
Level I and Level II Abilities

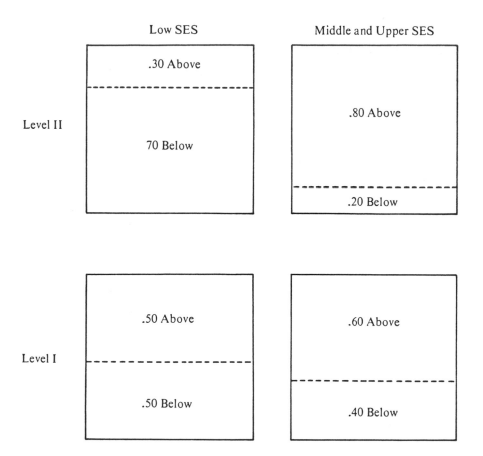

turbed may perform poorly on the learning task (Eysenck, 1967; Jensen, 1962). More carefully controlled and refined experiments are needed to decrease the noise and provide rigorous tests for the hypothesis proposed here; this work is now in progress.

Rates of Development of Level I and Level II

In terms of the hypothesis of Levels I and II and their different distributions as a function of SES, the following conjecture is made concerning the growth curves of these two classes of mental processes (shown in Figure 8). Level I abilities are depicted as developing early and rapidly approaching their asymptote during childhood. We have some evidence that

Table 2. Contingency Tables Showing Proportion of Population Falling Above
and Below Mean of Level I and Level II for Different Social Classes

	Low SES				Middle and Upper SES		
	Level II				Level II		
	Below	Above			Below	Above	
Level I Above	.35	.15	.50	Level I Above	.12	.48	.60
Below	.35	0	.50	Below	.08	0	.40
	.15 ←—(.15)				.32 ←—(.32)		
	.85	.15	1.00		.52	.48	1.00

this is actually the case. Serial learning ability, for example, although re-
vealing great individual differences at any age level, shows little improvement with age beyond eight or nine years (Jensen and Rohwer, 1965). Level
II abilities, on the other hand, are shown getting off to a slow start, then
developing rapidly between ages four and seven, and later assuming a negatively accelerated growth rate. Intelligence testing below the ages of two or
three taps mostly perceptual-motor and Level I abilities; beyond age three
the tests become increasingly loaded with content that taps Level II functions. Furthermore, individual differences in Level II become increasingly
manifest after three or four years of age. Consequently, tests of intelligence
given prior to age two or three show negligible correlations with test
scores obtained in adolescence or adulthood, and it is not until the Level II
functions are clearly manifest in the child's behavior that IQ correlates
substantially (i.e., over 0.60) with later assessments of intelligence. It is
during this period from ages four to seven years, in which for most children
the Level II functions show their most rapid development, that children
called culturally disadvantaged begin to evince progressive retardation, that
is, a progressively slower rate of intellectual development than that of
typical middle-class children. This increasing divergence of Level II growth
for lower- and middle-class children is also depicted in Figure 8. These
hypothetical curves suggest that the optimal age of children on whom to test
the hypothesis described in the preceding section is about eight or nine

Table 3. Contingency Tables Showing Relationship between Paired Associate Learning and Mental Age in Low and Middle SES Children of Four to Five Years of Age (N = 100 in each SES Group)

Low SES

Paired Associate Learning	Mental Age: Below	Mental Age: Above	
Above	20	24	44
Below	46	10	56
	66	34	100

Middle SES

Paired Associate Learning	Mental Age: Below	Mental Age: Above	
Above	15	41	56
Below	32	12	44
	47	53	100

years, for by this time there is clear separation of the means of low and middle SES groups on Level II abilities.

Implications of the Theoretical Model for Motivation

The question often arises whether, in general, children from low SES backgrounds obtain relatively low scores on tests and do poorly in school mainly because they are not as highly motivated as middle-class children, or because they have a lower average level of the necessary abilities. The fact that low SES children perform about as well as middle SES children on our direct-learning tasks strongly suggests that their difficulty with the usual intelligence tests and with school subjects such as reading and arithmetic is due primarily to intellectual rather than motivational factors. It was found, for example, that certain children who performed very poorly on a selective learning task dramatically improved their performance after being briefly coached in some cognitive skills relevant to learning the task, such as labeling the stimuli by overt verbal responses (Jensen, 1963). This was not a motivational but a cognitive change that led to better learning. The evidence suggests that the learning difficulty that low SES children show in school subjects is more or less proportional to the importance of what we have called Level II processes for the performance of the particular

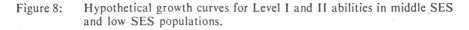

Figure 8:   Hypothetical growth curves for Level I and II abilities in middle SES and low SES populations.

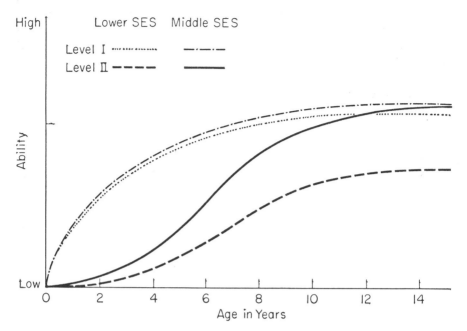

task. The acquisition of connotative reading skill (i.e., reading comprehension), as contrasted with denotative reading (i.e., word recognition), apparently makes especially great demands on Level II abilities.

Failure in learning due to ability factors leads to a diminution of rewards for successful accomplishment, so important in reinforcing and maintaining the attentional behavior that promotes learning. After repeated experiences of failure in the classroom, learning deteriorates into inattentiveness, apathy, or aimless hyperactivity, with consequent frustration of the teacher's instructional efforts.

BIOLOGICAL AND ENVIRONMENTAL DETERMINANTS OF ABILITY

The evidence for the major role of heredity factors in determining individual differences in mental ability is now so consistent and conclusive that it should require little further explication. However, literature on the culturally disadvantaged has largely ignored or discounted this body of research, despite its direct relevance and the fact that the findings and conclusions are among the least ambiguous topics in psychology (Burt, 1958;

Erlenmeyer-Kimling and Jarvik, 1963; Fuller and Thompson, 1960; Huntley, 1966; Jensen, 1967, 1968a, 1968b; Vernon, 1960, 1966). The main
conclusion to be drawn from research on the inheritance of mental ability is
that in European and American societies most of the individual-differences
variance in measured intelligence is attributable to genetic variation, while
only a minor portion can be ascribed to differences in environments. For
intelligence, heritability estimates generally range from 0.70 to 0.80. That
is to say, 70 to 80 percent of the individual-differences variance in intelligence in the population is attributable to genetic factors, while the remaining variance is due to environmental influences (both prenatal and
postnatal).

The eschewal of hereditary factors in ability has generalized to other
biological factors as well, particularly the importance of prenatal factors
in determining individual differences in intelligence and educability. The
recent emphasis in the literature on the disadvantaged has been almost exclusively on postnatal social environmental factors, despite the fact that
years ago intensive large-scale researches (e.g., Burks, 1928) found that
this class of environmental factors accounts for relatively little (less than
20 percent) of the variance in intelligence and no subsequent research has
contradicted this conclusion. Recent work by Stott (1966) makes a strong
case for the importance of prenatal stress during the last months of pregnancy as a causal factor in learning and behavior disorders which may
appear at various times in the child's later development.

The remarkable research of Heyns (1963) on abdominal decompression suggests that the prenatal environment can be improved in ways that
give infants whose mothers are subjected to this treatment a marked developmental advantage. This research is of tremendous potential importance
and should be pursued by qualified investigators in the United States. By
means of a special mechanical device, Heyns reduces intrauterine pressure
for an hour or two each day during the last months of pregnancy and during labor. Infants born to women so treated show more rapid early development than a control group of infants whose mothers were not subjected
to such treatment. The developmental quotient (DQ) of the treated infants
is, on the average, 20 to 30 points higher than that of the controls. Heyns
believes that the greater blood supply to the brain during the later stages of
fetal development and the lessening of the risk of brain damage during labor
are largely responsible for this boosting of the DQ in the experimental
group. It is not yet known whether the early advantage of these children
will manifest itself later in higher levels of intelligence and this, of course, is
the more important issue.

In recent years there has grown up an inordinate emphasis on the belief
that environmental factors are the main cause of individual and group differences in traits relevant to educational potential. This exaggerated emphasis

on the critical importance of even subtle environmental effects in the child's early environment as determinants of quite gross differences in mental ability and scholastic performance is belied by the preponderance of evidence. Children whose early years were spent in extreme deprivation have later shown normal mental development, scholastic achievement, and success in adult life (e.g., Skeels, 1966). Helen Keller experienced extreme sensory deprivation between nineteen months and seven years of age. Furthermore, there are children born into families in which either one or both parents are mentally retarded (i.e., IQ under 70) and whose environment has been described as "extremely deprived," who have been found to have IQ's in the "bright" and "superior" range—above 120 or 130 (Reed and Reed, 1965). The prevailing doctrine found in much of the current literature on the culturally disadvantaged, based on an overriding environmental determinism, does not accord with facts such as these or with the evidence on the inheritance of mental ability.

One important consideration which has not been adequately investigated is the consequences of the hypothesis that the importance of environment as a factor in individual differences in intelligence becomes much less important beyond a certain threshold of environmental stimulation. That is to say, the environment may influence intelligence in much the same fashion that nutrition affects stature. Beyond the minimum daily requirement of the essential vitamins, minerals, and proteins, further amounts of these elements or wide variations in diet have negligible effects on stature; hereditary factors then become all-important in determining people's heights. The psychological dimensions of environmental impoverishment-enrichment we do not yet well understand nor, except for the most extreme cases, do we know the region on this vague continuum below which environmental variations become increasingly important as determinants of individual differences in intellectual development.

The Heritability of Level I and Level II Abilities

The abilities measured by standard intelligence tests, which reflect largely Level II, have been shown to have high heritability in the general population. But there is also the possibility that Level II abilities are entirely learned through appropriate environmental input and that it is the associative learning abilities (Level I) that are primarily inherited. If this were the case, the essential difference between disadvantaged and advantaged children would be not in their biological potential for the development of Level II abilities, but in the opportunities afforded by the environment for the acquisition of such abilities. The interesting question, however, is why there are children who are apparently equal in simple associative learning ability but quite unequal in their acquisition of mediational habits and abstract conceptual ability. We have been able to instruct individuals in techniques of verbal mediation and thereby temporarily boost their learning performance. It has been possible, for example, to get mentally retarded subjects to perform at a nearly normal level by such techniques, and to boost performance of second-graders to equal that of twelfth-graders (Jensen and Rohwer, 1963a, 1963b, 1965). But children still differ markedly in their capacity to acquire these techniques, either from their natural environment or from specific training, and in their ability to retain them. One gets the impression that although Level II functions may have to be learned, there are great individual differences in the speed and ease with which they can be learned, and that these differences are relatively independent of Level I learning abilities. The direct training of Level II abilities is territory which we are just beginning to investigate. So far, the most direct application of closely related techniques to the early education of culturally disadvantaged children has been described by Bereiter and Engelmann (1966) in their important book *Teaching Disadvantaged Children in the Preschool.*

Although there have been no studies on the heritability of Level I abilities, there is no reason to believe they would not be at least as heritable as the abilities measured by intelligence tests, and very probably even more so, since the techniques for assessing Level I appear considerably more culture-free and less affected by prior experience than the usual intelligence tests.

The critical evidence for deciding whether Level II abilities are mainly learned from the environment by means of Level I ability is to be found in the study of middle-class children from culturally enriched environments who are average or above in Level I but retarded in Level II abilities. (It would be even better if such cases could be found with siblings of at least average ability on both Levels I and II; this would tend to confirm the adequacy of the environment for satisfactory Level II development.) The fact that such subjects do occur in some of the previously cited studies suggests the hypothesis that Level I abilities are necessary but not sufficient for the development of Level II—that the neurological structures for Level II must be innate if these abilities are to develop out of associative learning and appropriate environmental inputs. This hypothesis has not yet been subjected to rigorous tests.

Social Class Differences in Heritability of Levels I and II Abilities

If individual differences in both Levels I and II are largely due to heredity, why do social classes differ relatively little on Level I but considerably on Level II abilities? A strictly environmental theory does not account for SES differences in intelligence nearly as well as a theory which attributes part of the differences to genetic and part to environmental factors.

Since SES is closely linked to occupational and educational levels, the criteria of successful performance in this realm act as a crude screening device for abilities. This fact, along with the possibilities for social mobility and assortative mating (i.e., marrying within one's social class, educational level, etc.) results in some degree of genetic segregation among social classes. Since the correlation between parents and children is only 0.5 to 0.6, there is considerable dispersion about the mean intelligence level of each social class, and the means of the children from various SES groups will be closer together than the means of their parents. This is the well-known phenomenon of regression towards the mean of the general population.

The same phenomenon is found for stature and other polygenically inherited traits. The regression from parents to children is almost perfectly one-half the difference between the parental and the population means. A rather simple genetic model, involving polygenic inheritance with dominance, precisely predicts these results. But no theory of the environmental determination of social-class differences yields this prediction. The genetic explanation of this phenomenon is further substantiated by the findings that the IQ's of orphanage children who have never known their parents correlate almost as highly with their father's occupation as do the IQ's of children reared by their own parents (Lawrence, 1931).

Since occupations (and the types of educational preparation that they require) are ranked in prestige and economic reward roughly in accord with the amount of Level II abilities that they involve, it should not be surprising that the lower and middle SES groups differ more on Level II than on Level I abilities. Level I abilities should be related to effectiveness in any occupation, while Level II would be of little importance in many types of work not involving the interpretation or manipulation of symbols or other abstract abilities nor depending upon much formal education.

EDUCABILITY

The term educability as used here means the ability to learn traditional school subjects through ordinary classroom instruction. Individual differences in educability are at least as great as individual differences in intelligence. Also, some groups in the population are clearly less educable than others, and one of the characteristics of the segment of the population called "culturally disadvantaged" is their relatively low average level of educability.

Although the IQ is the single best predictor of educability, it still accounts for only about half the variance in measures of school achievement. Therefore, the abilities measured by intelligence tests are not the only determinants of school performance. Other nonintellectual factors generally described under such labels as achievement motivation, attitudes, interests, and the like, play an important part in educability. These are not to be thought of as "drives" or psychic entities which individuals possess in different amounts, but are broad descriptive categories of kinds of behavior that seem to be correlated with achievement in any learning situation. The most basic common denominator of these forms of behavior and the environmental factors that seem to govern them is that they control the amount of time that the individual actually spends in a particular form of learning activity. (It is important that this be understood as meaning only the time actually spent in behavior that promotes learning.)

Another important fact about educability is that it has lower heritability than general intelligence. Studies of the heritability of scholastic achievement show that it is determined only about half as much by hereditary factors as is intelligence; that is, on the average, about 60 percent of the variance in scholastic achievement is attributable to nongenetic factors (Jensen, 1967). These nongenetic factors seem to originate largely from influences from within the family unit. We know, for example, that siblings reared in the same family are much less alike in intelligence than in scholastic achievement; the contrast between differences in intelligence and in scholastic performance is even more obvious among unrelated adopted children reared in the same family. In one study, for example, the correlation between unrelated children reared together was 0.56 for scholastic achievement as compared with 0.26 for intelligence (see Jensen, 1968a, 1968b). Also important is that social-class differences are somewhat greater for scholastic performance than for intelligence (Wiseman, 1964).

Taken all together, the facts reviewed above would seem to have at least one important implication for the education of the culturally disadvantaged: focus on improving those factors in educability that constitute the large proportion of the variance not predicted by IQ and not determined by genetic factors. This could prove more difficult than it may seem at first glance, however. The environmental sources of variance may be no more accessible or amenable to change than the genetic variance. Variance in educability which is unpredicted by IQ may be due to so many diverse and minute influences that the sum total of these effects could be highly immune to any appreciable degree of systematic control. Family size and birth order, for example, have some nongenetic effects on intelligence and educational attainment, but it seems highly unlikely that anything can be done about these sources of variance, at least not within the province of education.

Figure 9:   Schema to illustrate relationships among four educationally important
            constructs.

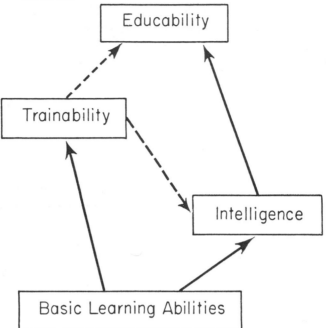

Our tests of associative learning are correlated with school performance in the same way that they are correlated with intelligence: average or
superior Level I learning ability does not produce average or superior
school performance unless general intelligence is also average or superior.
Basic learning processes surely are involved in school learning, but serve
educability only through the agency of developed intelligence. The probable
relationships among these variables are shown in Figure 9. The solid arrows indicate known relationships; the dashed arrows indicate probable,
but as yet not fully substantiated, relationships. Note that the basic learning abilities (Level I) do not serve educability directly, but must work
through intelligence. But there is a possible alternate route from raw
learning ability to educability via trainability, which is the ability to acquire
knowledge or skill in an instructional situation in which the learner's behavior is under direct, immediate control of the instructor or instructional me-
dium (such as a teaching machine). Trainability differs from educability in
that the former requires far fewer of the self-initiated information-processing skills necessary to classroom instruction: the voluntary control of
attention, the perception of order, self-initiated rehearsal of newly acquired
responses, recognition of and self-reinforcement for correct performance,

autonomous symbolic mediation, and other related processes (Jensen, 1968b). In short, educability implies that the learner is already able to act upon the instructional input in order to master it. Trainability, on the other hand, assumes basic learning ability as a prerequisite, but the focusing of the learner's attention, his active engagement in the task, and the immediacy of recognition and reinforcement of correct responses are not entirely left up to him, but are essential features of the instructional procedure. Such instruction is possible on a private tutorial basis, or by means of computerized, automated teaching devices.

What needs to be explored more fully is the possibility of actually training some of the components we recognize as constituting intelligence (Level II processes). It now seems unlikely that this can be accomplished by merely exposing disadvantaged children to an enriched environment for a year or so before they begin school. Quite precise training conditions may have to be established to inculcate some of the fundamental skills of self-initiated attention, perception, and verbalization that constitute educability (Jensen, 1966a, 1966b).

Individuals have different patterns of abilities that can determine the effectiveness of various instructional procedures. At present, however, we have practically no systematic knowledge of how our teaching methods can capitalize on individual differences. Finding answers to this problem is now generally seen as the major task of educational research, especially as it applies to the education of the disadvantaged.

REFERENCES

Bereiter, C., and Engelmann, S. *Teaching Disadvantaged Children in the Preschool.* Englewood Cliffs, N. J.: Prentice-Hall, 1966.

Burks, B. S. The Relative Influence of Nature and Nurture upon Mental Development. *National Society for the Study of Education Yearbook* 1928, 27: 219-316.

Burt, C. The Inheritance of Mental Ability. *American Psychologist* 1958, 13: 1-15.

Erlenmeyer-Kimling, L., and Jarvik, L. F. Genetics and Intelligence: A Review. *Science* 1963, 142: 1477-79.

Eysenck, H. J. Intelligence Assessment: A Theoretical and Experimental Approach. *British Journal of Educational Psychology* 1967, 37: 81-98.

Fuller, J. L., and Thompson, W. R. *Behavior Genetics.* New York: Wiley, 1960.

Heyns, O. S. *Abdominal Decompression.* Johannesburg: Witwatersrand University Press, 1963.

Huntley, R. M. C. Heritability of Intelligence, in J. E. Meade and A. S. Parkes, eds. *Genetic and Environmental Factors in Human Ability.* New York: Plenum Press, 1966, pp. 201-18.

Jensen, A. R. Learning Abilities in Mexican-American and Anglo-American Children. *California Journal of Educational Research* 1961, 12: 147-59.

————. Extraversion, Neuroticism, and Serial Learning. *Acta Psychologica* 1962, 20: 69-77.

————. Learning Abilities in Retarded, Average, and Gifted Children. *Merrill-Palmer Quarterly* 1963, 9: 123-40.

————. Rote Learning in Retarded Adults and Normal Children. *American Journal of Mental Deficiency* 1965, 69: 828-34. (a)

————. *Individual Differences in Learning: Interference Factor.* Cooperative Research Project No. 1867. Washington, D.C.: U.S. Office of Education, 1965. (b)

————. Verbal Mediation and Educational Potential. *Psychology in the Schools* 1966, 3: 99-109. (a)

————. Social Class and Perceptual Learning. *Mental Hygiene* 1966, 50: 226-39. (b)

————. Estimation of the Limits of Heritability of Traits by Comparison of Monozygotic and Dizygotic Twins. *Proceedings of the National Academy of Sciences* 1967, Vol. 58, pp. 149-56.

————. Social Class, Race, and Genetics: Implications for Education. *American Educational Research Journal* 1968, 5: 1-42. (a)

————. The Culturally Disadvantaged and the Heredity-Environment Uncertainty, in J. Helmuth, ed. *The Disadvantaged Child.* Vol. 2. Seattle, Wash.: Special Child Publications, 1968, pp. 27-76. (b)

Jensen, A. R., Collins, C. C., and Vreeland, R. W. A. Multiple S-R Apparatus for Human Learning. *American Journal of Psychology* 1962, 75: 470-76.

Jensen, A. R., and Rohwer, W. D., Jr. Verbal Mediation in Paired-Associate and Serial Learning. *Journal of Verbal Learning and Behavior* 1963, 1: 346-52: (a)

————. The Effect of Verbal Mediation on the Learning and Retention of Paired-Associates by Retarded Adults. *American Journal of Mental Deficiency* 1963, 68: 80-84. (b)

————. Syntactical Mediation of Serial and Paired-Associate Learning as a Function of Age. *Child Development* 1965, 36: 601-608.

Kennedy, W. A., Van De Riet, V., and White, J. C. A Normative Sample of Intelligence and Achievement of Negro Elementary School Children in the Southeastern United States. *Monographs of Social Research in Child Development* 1963, 28, No. 6.

Lawrence, E. M. An Investigation into the Relation between Intelligence and Inheritance. *British Journal of Psychology.* Monograph Supplement, 1931, 16: No. 5.

Pavlov, I. P. *Conditioned Reflexes.* Trans. by G. V. Anrep. London: Oxford University Press, 1927. Paperback: New York: Dover, 1960.

Rapier, J. L. The Learning Abilities of Normal and Retarded Children as a Function of Social Class. *Journal of Educational Psychology* 1968, 58: 102-10.

Reed, E. W., and Reed, S. C. *Mental Retardation: A Family Study.* Philadelphia: W. B. Saunders Co., 1965.

Skeels, H. M. Adult Status of Children with Contrasting Early Life Experiences: A Follow-Up Study. *Child Development Monographs* 1966, 31: No. 3. Serial no. 105.

Stott, D. H. *Studies of Troublesome Children.* New York: Humanities Press, 1966.

Terman, L. M., and Merrill, M. A. *Stanford-Binet Intelligence Scale: Manual for the Third Revision, Form L-M.* Boston: Houghton Mifflin, 1960.

Vernon, P. E. *Intelligence and Attainment Tests.* London: University of London Press, 1960.

————. Development of Current Ideas about Intelligence Tests, in J. E. Meade and A. S. Parkes, eds. *Genetic and Environmental Factors in Human Ability.* New York: Plenum Press, 1966, pp. 3-14.

Wechsler, D. *The Measurement and Appraisal of Adult Intelligence,* 4th ed. Baltimore: Williams & Wilkins, 1958.

White, S. H. Evidence for a Hierarchical Arrangement of Learning Processes, in L. P. Lipsitt and C. C. Spiker, eds. *Advances in Child Development and Behavior,* Vol. 2. New York: Academic Press, 1965, pp. 187-220.

Wiseman, S., *Education and Environment.* Manchester, England: Manchester University Press, 1964.

PART THREE

HEREDITY AND ENVIRONMENT

INTRODUCTION

The possibility of hereditary factors contributing to basic learning ability and educability was raised in the last chapter by Jensen, who admonished psychologists not to ignore the well-established facts concerning the hereditary basis of intelligence. In the present section the heredity-environment issue in relation to poverty is faced squarely by three authors representing diverse scientific backgrounds and points of view. The question of the potential contribution of a hereditary component to poverty (particularly chronic or cross-generational poverty) is sooner or later raised when serious inquiry into the etiology of poverty is undertaken. It behooves us to make explicit the possible role of genetic factors in poverty and to explore the implications of our present theoretical and factual knowledge.

Earlier generations quite readily attributed poverty to hereditary inferiority. Today we are not as willing to acknowledge a genetic basis for poverty. It is fair to say that throughout the twentieth century social scientists have adopted an extreme environmentalist position that minimizes the role of heredity in behavior. Within psychology the environmentalist view was popularized largely by John B. Watson (1924) and the behaviorists who followed him. The nature-nurture argument, as it was called, became one of the more active arenas of psychological research and controversy during the first half of this century, and has continued to evoke interest up to the present. It has become abundantly clear after years of research and controversy that questions of the sort, "Does heredity or environment—nature or nurture—determine behavior X?" not only are unanswerable, but are not in fact scientifically meaningful issues (Anastasi, 1958).

Rather, both heredity and environment contribute and interact in determining a behavioral characteristic. The absurdity of the "either-or" question can be seen when one of the components is reduced to zero. The more reasonable question is to ask how genetic and environmental factors operate in interaction. As McClearn (1964) puts it, the "nature-nurture controversy" must be replaced by the "nature-nurture collaboration."

The complexity of problems in this area is staggering. An adult characteristic does not simply appear full-blown; at innumerable steps during the projected course of development both genetic and environmental influences have been exerted. And environment consists, it must be remembered, of much more than postnatal physical and social conditions. The prenatal embryological, chemical, and cellular environments are crucial to later behavior, though often overlooked. The importance of these aspects of environment can be appreciated by remembering Jensen's report of the apparent striking effect of prenatal oxygenation on postnatal behavioral (and possibly intellectual) development.

When the nature-nurture argument is applied to poverty, it is particularly these prenatal facets of the problems that are slighted, though they are of direct relevance and utmost importance. Since they lack economic resources for adequate nutrition and prenatal medical care, it is especially among the poor that prenatal environmental complications might occur with greatest frequency, and hence be more likely to influence subsequent behavioral development. (See Chapter 11 by Bronfenbrenner for a review of relevant data and for some evidence that adherents of the hereditary explanation of poverty would find hard to accommodate.) Add to prenatal environmental factors the crucial effects of birth injury and early infant care (e.g., inadequacy of early sensory stimulation as discussed by Hunt) and one can immediately see the difficulties of trying to sort out components of the nature-nurture dilemma.

In spite of the obvious difficulty of behavioral investigation, there is no reason research should be avoided. As mentioned earlier, social scientists have typically taken a polar position on the environmental side, and thus have not been eager to seek genetic bases for complex behavior. The environmentalist preference is a reflection of values: it is congruent with democratic ideals to assume that manifest differences among people are due to environmental circumstances rather than to inborn traits. And, of course, adherence to the environmentalist position is congenial also because it offers the possibility of improvement by changing the environment. Acceptance of genetic determinism of behavior tends to generate less optimism regarding social change or social betterment.

Recently a sociologist took his colleagues to task for neglecting the genetic bases of behavior, and pointed out several implications of the heredity-environment interactions for sociological problems (Eckland, 1967). Having reviewed the data, Eckland concluded that difference in intelligence across social classes probably is to some extent due to heredity and assortative mating. Marriage tends to occur between occupational and educational, and therefore intellectual, equals. He concluded that differences among races is probably not due to hereditary factors, since assortative mating based on color is likely to result only in the random distribution of other traits. So there is a possibility that in our meritocracy, social-class membership may be somewhat determined by intellectual ability. But poverty is probably less correlated with intellectual ability among Negroes than among whites, due to objective barriers that limit opportunity.

Attempted analysis of the heredity-environment problem is enormously complex when dealing with possible social-class differences, and is yet more complex in the case of racial comparisons. In discussing potential genetic differences among races, the obvious drastic environmental differences that exist would seem to provide a parsimonious and sufficient ex-

*planation. Considerable data exist demonstrating that observed racial dif-
ferences in intelligence are easily accounted for by environmental factors.
The well-known studies by Klineberg (1935) and Lee (1951) found that
children of Negro migrants from the South increased in IQ score as a
function of years of school attended in the North. Moreover, studies have
shown that infant and preschool Negro and white children differ little in
IQ (Gilliland, 1951; Knobloch and Pasamanick, 1953; Pasamanick, 1946).*

*In the first chapter in this section Shockley calls for more research
on the heredity-environment problem. This physical scientist believes that
the environmentalist orientation of social scientists has prevented them
from objectively and impartially pursuing research on this problem,
particularly research on racial differences. He asserts that such research is
both needed and possible with presently available techniques. In arguing
thus Shockley proposes four research techniques that might yield useful results. He is also worried about the possible detrimental effect on national
intelligence that may result from large birthrates among the poor. This
problem receives some explication from data presented by Vandenberg in
Chapter 9.*

*Shockley constructs a social capacity index to explore racial differ-
ences on a continuum ranging from prosocial behavior and achievement to
antisocial behavior. The value of such an index is, of course, wholly dependent upon the quality of the original data from which it is derived.
And who is bold enough to claim that, for example, criminal statistics are
entirely objective concerning racial differences among offenders? The behavior of police and the disposition of arrest cases are known to depend
to some extent on the race of the offender. Similarly, at the positive end
of the index the usefulness of Who's Who information for racial comparison is limited severely, perhaps fatally, by difference in the quality of
schools according to racial composition of the neighborhood, and by
racial differences in access to higher education, upon which nomination
to Who's Who to no small extent depends.*

*Even if it were to be assumed that available statistics on racial differ-
ences in behavior are really reliable, the problem of attributing environmental or hereditary causal priority to a specific behavior would remain
as ambiguous as ever. The difficulty of nature-nurture research on human
social behavior is shown by the long controversy about the adequacy and
meaning of data collected by the twin-study technique, a fairly rigorous
method compared to research designs in racial differences that confound
an enormous number of uncontrolled variables.*

*In recent years there has been a reexamination of the role of genetics
in social science. Several sociologists have argued that a closer relationship should exist with genetics (Eckland, 1967; Bresslaer, as reported in*

*Glass, 1967), and others have noted that ideological barriers have contrib-
uted to the rejection by social scientists of hereditary explanations of
human behavior. Within psychology, too, extreme environmentalism is
being challenged or tempered by the vigorous growth of behavior genetics.
Genetic factors in social behavior is now a very active area of research
(Fuller and Thompson, 1960; McClearn, 1962). The contemporary view
of the nature-nurture issue does not claim that a person's behavior is fixed
by genetic endowment, but on the other hand it is realized that genetic differences among persons are not insignificant and cannot be ignored. A
more balanced view of the interaction of environment and heredity is now
being achieved. Shockley's chapter reminds us again to be alert to our
possible theoretical biases, and urges social scientists to engage more actively in research in this area.*

*In Chapter 8 a geneticist gives his views on the heredity-environment
problem in relation to poverty. In contrast to Shockley's position, Crow
does not believe that the question of the role of genetics in poverty and
racial differences is an urgent one. He suggests that the techniques used
by society in attacking its social problems would probably be identical
whether scientific evidence were to point to heredity or to environment as
being the more important in determining a particular behavior.*

*The difficulty of obtaining simple answers in this area is stressed by
Crow. He points out that the determination of the precise hereditary contribution to behavior is difficult even in well-controlled studies. Many assumptions of the theoretical model underlying the heredity-environment
analysis are probably not met in animal studies, much less in human research. The fact that social behavior and intelligence probably involve
numerous rather than single genes is a further complication. Crow is very
pessimistic about the possibility of precisely measuring the contribution of
heredity to human behavior. And the possibility of making adequate racial
comparisons would seem to be even more remote.*

*Serious discussions of the possibility of man's influencing his future
development by genetic intervention goes back to Francis Galton. The
chief obstacle to improving a population by selective reproduction (eugenics)
is not at present imposed by a limitation of genetic knowledge. For despite
the complexities mentioned above, geneticists can easily predict qualitative
effects, even if knowledge of the amount and rate of change is unsatisfactory. Crow concludes that there is available sufficient genetic knowledge
to predict and control successfully in a general way the future course of
human development—if society should desire to do so. Significant changes
derived from a eugenics program would be slow, however, and not detect-
able for several generations. But society is apparently loath to make the
necessary social changes to accommodate a eugenics program. Even if*

practical, improving behavioral characteristics through genetic means cannot be expected to produce desirable social behavior naturally among people living in a degrading and deprived environment. Improving intelligence within a population continuing to live in a social milieu conducive to crime and other antisocial acts will not necessarily lead to behavior beneficial to society, but perhaps to more ingenious antisocial behavior.

A psychologist discusses the possible role of hereditary factors in poverty in the last chapter in this section. Vandenberg examines relevant empirical data on several questions raised in Shockley's chapter. Is the national intelligence level decreasing as a result of higher birthrates among lower social classes or certain racial groups? Data reviewed by Vandenberg indicate a negative answer to this question. Birthrates across social-class levels seem to be narrowing, and Negro birthrates apparently respond to the same factors (education, rural-urban background, etc.) that affect birthrates in the white population.

Vandenberg explores two bodies of research for relevance to the heredity-environment question, and particularly to racial differences. Some interesting research has been conducted in Africa, but whether these data have relevance to performance of different racial groups within a single society is questionable. Twin-studies are also examined, including data collected by Vandenberg. One interesting result from Vandenberg's research is that certain intellectual abilities seem to be more strongly controlled by heredity than others. Yet even twin-studies may have little direct implications for possible racial differences. After discussing the evidence Vandenberg concludes that of the many traits controlled by genes perhaps minor differences in frequencies exist among major racial groups, but the differences are not clear-cut. It seems reasonable to suggest that observed differences in IQ scores between races may to a great extent be due to a larger proportion of Negroes than of whites being in the lower socioeconomic levels. Improvements for Negroes in such factors as education and income (i.e., in socioeconomic level) might well eliminate any racial differences presently found in IQ scores.

Available psychological research, then, offers no firm and simple answer concerning genetic factors either in poverty or in race (which overlap considerably in the United States). This section underscores the inadequacy and oversimplification of the simple nature-nurture dichotomy. The usual call for further research is applicable here. The degree of urgency felt about research on the nature-nurture question relative to other problems in poverty will, however, differ considerably among researchers.

REFERENCES

Anastasi, A. *Differential Psychology*, 3d ed. New York: Macmillan, 1958.

Eckland, B. K. Genetics and Sociology: A Reconsideration. *American Sociological Review* 1967, 32: 173-94.

Fuller, J. L., and Thompson, W. R. *Behavior Genetics*. New York: Wiley, 1960.

Glass, D. C. Genetics and Social Behavior. *Social Science Research Council Items* 1967, 21: No. 1, 1-12.

Gilliland, A. R. Socio-economic Status and Race as Factors in Infant Test Scores. *Child Development* 1951, 22: 271-73.

Klineberg, O. *Negro Intelligence and Selective Migration*. New York: Columbia University Press, 1935.

Knobloch, H., and Pasamanick, B. Further Observations on the Behavioral Development of Negro Children. *Journal of Genetic Psychology* 1953, 83: 137-57.

Lee, E. S. Negro Intelligence and Selective Migration: A Philadelphia Test of Klineberg's Hypothesis. *American Sociological Review* 1951, 61: 227-33.

McClearn, G. E. The Inheritance of Behavior, in L. J. Postman, ed. *Psychology in the Making*. New York: Knopf, 1962, pp. 144-252.

———. Genetics and Behavior Development, in M. L. Hoffman and L. W. Hoffman, eds. *Review of Child Development Research*. Vol. 1. New York: Russell Sage Foundation, 1964, pp. 433-80.

Pasamanick, B. A Comparative Study of the Educational Development of Negro Infants. *Journal of Genetic Psychology* 1946, 69: 3-44.

Watson, J. B. *Behaviorism*. New York: Norton, 1924.

Chapter 7

A "TRY SIMPLEST CASES" APPROACH TO THE HEREDITY-POVERTY-CRIME PROBLEM

William Shockley*

Two aspects of humanity are quantity and quality. Mankind is now beginning to face the quantity problem of the world population explosion realistically, whereas ten years ago in this country it was rejected as not a fit
subject for governmental concern. My conjecture is that there are also
grounds for worry about the quality problem. Let me mention one modern
development in human evolution, and let me say I approve of this development; I applaud its humanitarian benefits. In 1840, a male child born in
America had four chances in ten of dying before age twenty; now this
chance is ten times less. This tenfold reduction of an elimination mechanism
must inevitably have had some evolutionary effect.

Human quality problems, with their environment-heredity uncertainties and their racial aspects, are on the front pages almost daily. When
someone says, "Research results in this area cannot conceivably be of
value to mankind," it expresses to me an undemocratic contempt for public
wisdom that is quite in keeping with totalitarian regimes and wholly out of
harmony with the free-speech and free-press principles of our constitution.
The lesson to be learned from Nazi history is the value of free speech, not

*Alexander M. Poniatoff Professor of Engineering Science, Stanford Uni-
versity, Palo Alto, California. The original and longer version of this chapter was
read before the National Academy of Sciences in June 1967, and was, including
reference, printed in the *Proceedings* of that academy, Vol. 57, No. 6, pp. 1767-74.

that eugenics is intolerable. A form of eugenics has been in effect in Denmark for thirty years but I have found no one in this country who has studied it really seriously. Thinking about human quality problems is blocked in this country by the wishful-thinking microbe that produces the disease I call inverted liberalism. True liberalism means an open-minded search for truth and free speech in expressing ideas, whereas inverted liberalism opposes these courses on the basis of purportedly noble principles.

One thought-blocking viewpoint that I analyze as a symptom of inverted liberalism is this often-expressed view: "Suppose we did find out there are important adverse genetic effects occurring now; what would be the value of this knowledge to mankind? Any social action would be intolerable."

Within the last couple of years, the Idaho Legislature passed a sterilization law for mental defectives who, after being sterilized, would then be permitted to leave institutions and return to public life. Thus it is obvious that the representatives of the American public are prepared to take action. I doubt if the public feels that any individual has a right to produce a child if the probability is high that the child will never be self-supporting. Although passed by 40 votes to 2 in the Idaho House, this law passed by only 18 to 16 in the Senate and was vetoed by the Governor. I conjecture that lack of knowledge of well-established facts on inheritance of mental retardation led to this unwise outcome. This situation constitutes an example of why I recommend further research on the research which already exists.

"TRY SIMPLEST CASES" APPROACH

The "try simplest cases" approach that I discuss here was provoked in part by my finding that in 1966 only 7 percent of the Negro scores on the Armed Forces mental tests exceeded or overlapped the white median score. Fifty years ago, the overlap was 13 percent. This decrease in overlap from 13 to 7 percent would be expected if the difference between median IQ's for Negroes and whites had increased by five IQ points during the intervening two-and-one-half generations. In 1964, Secretary of Labor Wirtz stated: "There is a strong indication that a disproportionate number of unemployed come from large families, but we do not pursue evidence that would permit establishing this as a fact or evaluating its significance." My inquiries directed to the Secretaries of Labor and Health, Education and Welfare, to the Surgeon General of the Army, and to the Commissioner of Education have produced no evidence that anyone has learned or has been concerned with learning about the decrease in overlap, and no evidence that anyone has been looking at its possible genetic aspects.

The facts of behavioral genetics, and what information I could obtain relevant to Secretary Wirtz's large-families statement, led me to conclude that a drop of five IQ points in average Negro intelligence could easily have occurred in the course of the two generations since World War I as a result of higher birthrates of disadvantaged, improvident people. My inquiries to eminent anthropologists convinced me further that objective studies were not in progress and were even being discouraged. I adhere to the principle that man's destiny should be shaped by the application of intelligence to determine realistic goals for human progress, rather than by forces man has let get beyond his control. My call is for vigorous attempts to establish fact, not for any form of social action.

These thoughts provoked me to a "try simplest cases" approach to see how far an all-genetic model would go toward explaining existing facts. I find a surprisingly consistent picture, which does not, of course, necessarily prove the correctness of an all-genetic model.

The results I obtained in a few days of research convinced me that it must be a thinking-block, rather than the difficulty of doing research, that has kept such research from being done. Speaking as a scientist and as a World War II operations researcher, I was amazed at the orderly relationship that came from data obtainable from a reference library.

SOCIAL CAPACITY INDEX

One very significant feature of the analysis is that my proposed social capacity distribution appears to correlate, on the basis of a single universal pattern, the statistics of a very diverse assemblage of behaviors. For whites social capacity ranges from an index of plus 4.9 near the top of the scale for the eminence of listing in *The International Who's Who* down through study for a law degree, illegitimacy rates, arrests for crime, narcotic addiction, and finally, down to a social-capacity index of minus 5.7 for commission of murder. Furthermore, the universal distribution pattern employed is not simply a normal distribution pattern, but one that has been experimentally established for scores on IQ tests. This distribution was published in 1963 by Sir Cyril Burt (1963). This observation suggests that IQ test results may actually be a deeper measure, at least on a statistical basis, of a distribution of some more fundamental social capacity.

When social-capacity index values are obtained from my extrapolation of Burt's distribution, and applied separately to the populations involved, I find a substantially consistent offset for the Negro distribution compared to the white distribution of about 1.2 social capacity units. For example, with respect to whites, Negroes perform at about ten times lower frequency in eminent accomplishment, and at nearly ten times higher frequency in antisocial behavior, such as narcotics addiction and murder. In contrast, Chinese- and Japanese-Americans are almost equally offset above whites, at least with regard to scientific achievement on the one end and arrests on the other. Two exceptions are eminence in science, in which the offset for Negroes is about two units, and in unemployment, in which it is about one-third of a unit. The lower offset for unemployment might be taken to mean that sociological forces are overcoming statistical disadvantages in placing Negroes in jobs.

I do not conclude that my studies prove a genetic offset actually exists. The conclusions are consistent with a model that assumes a genetic off-set of 1.2 units equivalent to about 18 IQ points is the principal cause. However, the agreement of this model with the facts does not prove that the effects are not principally environmental.

The environment-heredity uncertainty for American Negroes reminds me of the absolute motion problem of pre-Einstein physics. No matter how the earth was moving on its orbit, and no matter how one attempted to measure speed through the hypothetical ether that filled all space, the results came out as if the earth were standing still. Can it be that no studies can ever resolve the environment-heredity uncertainty about the American Negro offset? If so, what underlying principle is the cause? I see this as a question worthy of imaginative, constructive scientific attention.

RECOMMENDATIONS

Having terminated discussion of the statistical analysis I shall now present some of my personal values. I have placed emphasis on Negro aspects for two reasons: (1) data are available, and (2) the racial problem is nationally prominent.

Until acceptable facts are established, the truth or falsity of the predominantly genetic simplest-case model is obscured by the environment-heredity uncertainty. I deplore this uncertainty. If environment is the main cause, the present uncertainty will inhibit our overcoming unreasonable prejudice. If genetics is the main cause, the uncertainty will cloud public discussions and the search for solutions. Furthermore, vast expenditures in our well-intentioned War on Poverty may not accomplish a solution but instead create a larger problem—a situation comparable to providing economic aid to underdeveloped countries and at the same time disregarding the population explosion.

Let me make it clear that I favor all environmental improvements possible for all humanity. I approve of antipoverty programs in general, and Head Start in particular. I intend my actions in raising these questions to have the effect of a visitor to a sick friend, who strongly urges a diagnosis, painful though it may be, which seeks to expose all significant ailments. If study shows that ghetto birthrates are actually lowering average Negro intelligence, objectively facing this fact might lead to finding ways to prevent a form of genetic enslavement that could provoke extremes of racism.

What can be done to make a diagnosis? I have two recommendations. First, I believe a national study group should be set up to do research on the research that has already been done. The facts on which definitive conclusions may be based may already be available, if not in this country, perhaps in Denmark's genetic records. Second, a study of drastic changes in environment on the most disadvantaged children of improvident backgrounds should be undertaken. This study would be based on data from adoption programs and should be planned to answer a key question that lies at the very core of the war against poverty: *Can improved environment remedy the obviously enormous disadvantages afflicting the illegitimate 25 percent of Negro babies, or will genetic inheritance produce such a low social-capacity index that most will perform at frustratingly low social levels?*

At a cost of probably less than ten million dollars and in a time span of less than a decade, I believe a highly reliable answer to this question could be obtained. If existing adoption programs are so administered that relevant data cannot be obtained, I feel confident that eminently humanitarian, appropriately subsidized, voluntary experimental programs could be designed to produce the needed facts. These facts could so reduce the present environment-heredity uncertainty about the causes of poverty that they could easily pay off a thousand times their cost in increased effectiveness of programs costing tens to hundreds of billion dollars contemplated over the next twenty years.

I have confidence that the intellectual power of our nation that set up a ten-year program to place a piece of the moon in the hands of our scientists can also set up programs to establish facts on the environment-heredity uncertainty that will contribute to our national competence to deal with the problems of the city slums. But this intellectual power can do so only if it can be freed of fears of emotional slogans and brought to bear with courage to ask the questions, do the necessary research, find the facts, and discuss them objectively and publicly.

REFERENCE

Burt, C. Is Intelligence Distributed Normally? *British Journal of Statistical Psychology* 1963, 16: 175-90.

For more recent research and an extensive list of references, see:
Shockley, W. *Human Quality Problems and Research Taboos: New Concepts and Directions.* Greenwich, Conn.: Educational Records Bureau, 1969.

Chapter 8

DO GENETIC FACTORS CONTRIBUTE TO POVERTY?

James F. Crow*

My main thesis is almost an internal contradiction: we know a great deal about the basic principles of genetics and a great deal qualitatively about human heredity; yet our quantitative knowledge about the traits of greatest importance is very poor. Furthermore, it is not likely that further research along existing lines will make quantitative predictions much more precise.

Current understanding of the gene and its manner of action is as deep as anything biology has to offer. We have the most fundamental chemical knowledge of why "like begets like." Furthermore, in specific diseases special cytological and chemical knowledge make possible very precise assessment of genetic risks. For more complex traits, we "understand" that they are the result of genotype and environment and the interaction between these; our statistical methods are quite sophisticated. We know enough in general to predict in a qualitative way the effects of selection for complicated traits. We can be quite confident that if those individuals who are parents have considerably lower IQ's than the population mean, there will be a decrease in average IQ next generation—unless there were a compensatory environmental improvement. If the parents have higher IQ's, an increase of the next generation's average over this generation's could be confidently predicted.

But when it comes to predicting how much change would occur there is considerably more doubt. When many genes are involved, as is likely for traits such as intelligence and overall health, it is almost impossible to iso-

---

*Chairman, Department of Medical Genetics, University of Wisconsin, Madison, Wisconsin.

late individual gene effects. Furthermore there is the environmental influence, which would be hard to assess even if we could do the kind of controlled-environment experiments that are possible with experimental organisms. Finally, there is almost certain to be an interaction between genetic and environmental causes so that knowledge of either one by itself is insufficient. So I conclude that we already know enough to make confident predictions as to the direction in which the population would change under genetic selection, but there would be considerable uncertainty as to the rate or amount of change.

When it comes to assessing the role of heredity in determining racial differences in intelligence and attainments of various kinds (including wealth), the difficulties seem almost prohibitive. I differ from Professor Shockley both in the assessment of how easy it would be to arrive at precise heritability measures, and also about the social urgency of removing the heredity-environment uncertainty about racial differences.

Even at the phenotypic level, without trying to determine the extent to which heredity is involved, there are difficulties of definition. I quote from J. B. S. Haldane (1965, p. xcii-xciii).

> The primitive genetical idea that noble blood, or whatever similar phrase is used, is a qualification for ruling, is now rapidly being abandoned, but it has had an immense historical influence, and curious vestiges of it, such as hereditary monarchy, remain in otherwise advanced countries.

> The notion that one race is genetically superior to another has been of equal historical importance, and perhaps caused even greater injustices than the aristocratic idea. As I have pointed out elsewhere the statement that race A is superior in some respect (say in music) to race B may mean any of at least five different things, if we are simply judging on performance, without trying to decide whether the superiority is genetic or not. We may mean that the worst of A exceeds the best of B, that there is no overlap. This never occurs in fact. The most musical nations include some deaf mutes. We might mean that the median performance of A was superior to that of B. Such differences are commonly found, but the medians rarely differ by a quartile. Thirdly we might mean that exceptional performance is commoner in race A than B. When we say the ancient Greek were great mathematicians we are in fact thinking of about 20 men. We know nothing about the average Greeks in this respect. For cultural achievements high variability may be more important than a high average. Fourthly we might mean that bad performance was rarer in race A than race B. This is generally what we mean when we ascribe to a race or nation bad characters such as drunkenness or thieving. No sane person believes that all members of some race are drunkards. Or finally we might mean that heredity or environment placed some upper limit on the achievement of the inferior race.

But when we ask whether observed differences in cultural achievements are due to genetical or other causes, we are faced with enormous difficulties. We say that we could judge of genetical differences if samples of two races were compared in the same environment. Because children of Chinese and Japanese stock do about as well as those of European origin, but no better, in American schools, we say that their genetical equipment for school work is much the same. This may be true, but if we compare different breeds of an animal species we generally find that each is pre-adapted for some special environment, for example, cattle adapted for mountain or for valley pastures, dogs for hunting or for tending sheep. Perhaps we could find an environment X where race A would prove superior to B, and an environment Y where B would prove superior to A. This is almost certainly the case for disease resistance. Many tropical races seem to be more resistant to malaria than the peoples of northern Europe, and some members of them certainly carry genes at at least three different loci which confer such resistance. In presence of malaria they are therefore superior to Europeans. However, Europeans seem to be more resistant than tropical peoples to tuberculosis, doubtless partly through selective mortality in the last two centuries.

WHY HAS EUGENICS NOT BEEN POPULAR?

There is wide agreement that most human traits that we value highly, such as intelligence, health, special talents, and learning ability, have both genetic and environmental causes. I believe there is also agreement that these traits could be changed by selection in a chosen direction, although there would be the uncertainties as to the amount of change that I mentioned before. Why, then, is it that society has enthusiastically adopted all sorts of environmental means of influencing these traits, but has attempted genetic means hardly at all?

The reasons sometimes given are that we do not know enough about human heredity to predict the results of selection, that we are not sure what traits are desirable, that we do not know enough about future environments, that genetic changes are irreversible so that mistakes cannot be righted, that there may be unexpected and unwanted byproducts, that if we only wait much more precise methods of genetic improvement will become available through cellular and molecular discoveries, and finally that genetic changes are too slow to be practical.

Genetic change is slow relative to many changes affecting our lives. The threat of genetic deterioration by an increased mutation rate, through the relaxation of natural selection, or through possible differential birthrates, is much less urgent than the threat of decimation by nuclear war or mass starvation because of overpopulation. Likewise, any genetic improvement that might occur must be measured with thirty-year human generations as time units whereas an environmental improvement could start immediately.

Yet, I find myself in agreement with Kingsley Davis (1966) when he says that such reasons as I have listed are mainly rationalizations, and that the basic reason is society's resistance to change in social customs. Eugenics is a social movement, and any wide-scale application would upset social conventions that are deeply ingrained. We fear not the genetic unknown as much as the intrusions caused by the means of eugenics.

Since the issues are those of desirability of ends and acceptability of means, they are not for the geneticist to decide. His role is that of technical advisor. The decisions are for society at large, with its collective wisdoms and decision-making processes.

HOW VALID ARE BIOLOGICAL ARGUMENTS AGAINST EUGENICS?

How much uncertainty is there about the probable effects of selection in the human population? How valid are the genetic, as opposed to social, arguments against man's attempting to influence his genetic future?

One argument is that we do not know enough to make any meaningful predictions about the results of selection. For those conditions that are determined by single, identifiable genes one can make accurate predictions. But what about complicated, multifactorial traits? Here, we certainly do not know as much as we would like to. Yet, we see from the experience of animal breeding that almost any trait can be changed by selection, and moreover, by selection based on a principle no more complicated than resemblance of parent and progeny. Selection programs in animals have often been slower than the breeder had hoped, but almost always the direction of change has been as expected. When it has not been, the cause is usually chance fluctuation due to small numbers or an unexpected environmental factor (e.g., an epidemic) that is more than balancing the genetic improvement. The same would surely be true for selection in man. The predictions would be as good as they were in pre-Mendelian days for animal selection experiments, and would be better to whatever extent newer knowledge is applicable.

Another argument is that we should not try to influence human evolution because we do not know what is desirable, because we disagree about the aims. To some extent this is undoubtedly true; we certainly differ in our concepts of the ideal human being, or the ideal population. This is especially true if we are to be less parochial in our outlook and consider the views of people in India, South America, China, and Africa. Yet I believe that there is a considerable area of agreement. For one thing, we must surely agree on a number of negative aims. No one will argue that we should maintain greater than the present incidence of muscular dystrophy or severe mental retardation. There probably is also agreement that man should continue to be genetically diverse—that it is better to have many tastes and talents rather than only a few. I suspect also that there is general agreement that at least a moderate increase in average intelligence is good. We spend enormous amounts of our resources on education, and even force children to attend school (in some cases against their deep social and religious convictions, thereby violating what they regard as basic human rights). How can we seriously argue that education is good while educability is not? I am sure that there would be agreement that physical and mental health and delayed onset of senility are desirable. So I do not think disagreement on ends is the major deterrent to public acceptance of modest eugenic suggestions.

What about the argument that we cannot predict the future environment and that a selection program might be producing people unfitted for that environment? This is also a possibility, but the human genotype is already poorly adapted to many aspects of our environment, such as the common cold virus, smog, and perhaps the stresses of noise, high-speed transport, and overcrowding. Primarily, we need to adapt the environment to man. But whether we can or cannot, there is no reason why selection for, say, fewer mentally-retarded would materially change our ability to adapt to a new kind of environment.

The question of unexpected byproducts of selection is often mentioned. It is argued that the bulldog has trouble breathing, that a dairy cow would have trouble surviving in the wild, and that highly selected domestic animals in general are particularly susceptible to disease. But I assume that any discussion of eugenics more serious than science fiction foresees much less drastic changes. The experience of animal breeders is that unexpected side effects happen only after rather extreme changes. Often, such things as disease susceptibility in selected strains are a consequence of a high level of inbreeding, something that any intelligent human selection program would avoid. Because many traits that society conventionally regards as desirable tend to be positively correlated, the byproducts might be beneficial. For example, by selecting for greater educability we might also get improved health.

The assertion that the effects of selection are permanent and irreversible is, I think, simply wrong. The whole history of selection in animals has shown that it is almost always easier to reverse a selection program than to continue it. For example, strains of mice selected for large size respond very rapidly to reverse selection for small size. In fact, this often happens when selection is stopped, even in the absence of reverse selection. It is so typical that it has been given a name, *genetic homeostasis*.

Most of the objections thus far mentioned assume that a selection program would produce results. Many laymen, I believe, have an exaggerated idea of how fast selection works. We must remember that Galton's principle of filial regression is just as true now as when he discovered it. The offspring of selected parents tend to deviate from the population average in the same direction as their parents, but in lesser amounts.

But despite all this, as I said earlier, I think the real reason that eugenics has not found acceptance is that society does not like the means. We do not want to interfere with the reproductive customs of this generation in order to change the genetic composition of the next generation. Furthermore, we fear, I believe, not so much unexpected genetic consequences of the future as we do unwise human choices of aims. We also fear further intrusions of a highly undesirable sort once the door is opened to any control over human reproduction.

For all these reasons I think that a discussion of eugenics is very much in order. Man's capacity to influence his own evolution will undoubtedly increase greatly in the future. We must examine the desirability of the means as well as the ends, and the probable success in attaining them. How can we respond intelligently to big opportunities for both good and bad later if we do not discuss the smaller ones that are available now? I do not think that increased genetic knowledge will make the social decisions much easier.

HOW CAN GENETIC PREDICTIONS BE MADE?

To understand the role of genetic factors in determining traits like intelligence and in causing social problems like poverty, or to predict the effects of a eugenic program, we can proceed at three levels.

The first stage is purely empirical. We observe what kinds of children come from particular kinds of parents. With adequate data we could measure the average IQ of children whose parents' IQ's average 110. These kinds of data would have considerable predictive value provided that other factors remain the same. If the sole object were to select parents in such a way as to give a specified distribution of phenotypes next generation this would probably do reasonably well. For example, there are data on the average IQ of children whose parents had IQ's below 80. We could therefore make a reasonably accurate prediction of what would happen if the reproductive rate of parents below 80 were to change.

The disadvantage of this is that we are making no distinction between genetic and environmental causation. We might be changing the IQ, not by changing the gene frequency, but by changing the number of children brought up in environments conducive to low IQ. This is not necessarily bad, but it does destroy our confidence in long-range predictability in a changing environment.

The second stage is to attempt to separate the genetic and environmental factors and measure them statistically. The animal breeder does this by measuring a quantity called the *heritability*. I will discuss this in more detail in the next section.

The third stage is to learn more about the individual genes. The chemical defects in phenylketonuria or galactosemia are well known. We can hope to identify some of the component genes associated with intelligence or other desired traits. Such understanding will gradually come, but it is hard to know how soon it will produce any real improvement in predicting the effect of selection on traits with complex inheritance.

But, as I emphasized earlier, to understand the mechanism is not sufficient for making accurate predictions in individual instances. There is a random element associated with the Mendelian mechanism that makes each meiotic event a lottery. Until Mendelian inheritance is replaced—as it one day probably will be—individual predictions will have a large random error. However, this does not by itself preclude important social benefits, for we are often more interested in major trends than in statistical fluctuations around these trends.

HOW WELL CAN HERITABILITY BE MEASURED IN MAN?

The term *heritability* is used in two different ways. In both cases the basic methodology is correlation and variance analysis, but the psychologist usually uses heritability in a broader sense than the animal breeder. The psychologist-geneticist is usually interested in the extent to which the trait under consideration is determined by hereditary versus environmental differences. The animal-breeder-geneticist is usually interested in predicting the effects of a selection program, and hence uses the narrower definition.

Heritability in the broad sense can be understood as follows. We measure the population variance (i.e., average of the squared deviations from the mean) for some trait of interest and call this the total variance, V_T. Now, if we could somehow have held the genotype constant (if somehow all the population could be made into identical n-tuplets), the remaining variance would be entirely due to environmental differences, which we designate as the environmental variance, V_E. Alternatively, we could in principle hold the environment constant, in which case the remaining variance would be entirely due to genetic differences. We call this the hereditary or genotypic variance, V_H. If genetic and environmental influences act additively on the trait being measured, and if they are independent in occurrence, then there is no genotype-environment interaction, and $V_T \doteq V_H + V_E$. Heritability in the broad sense is defined as V_H / V_T.

Heritability in the broad sense is not a good predictor in selection experiments. To whatever extent dominance and gene interaction enter, V_H overestimates the effect of selection. The animal breeder is interested only in that part of V_H that directly reflects the gene makeup, for it is a random half of the genes, not the intact genotype, that is transmitted to the next generation in Mendelian inheritance. To estimate this part, he measures the genic or additive genetic variance, V_G. This cannot be measured directly, but is inferred from the least-squares estimates of regressions and correlations between relatives placed in randomized environments.

With simplifying assumptions (mainly the independence of genotype and environment mentioned before) we can write

$$V_T = V_H + V_E$$
$$= V_G + V_D + V_I + V_E \tag{1}$$

where V_H is subdivided into the genic variances (V_G),. variance due to dominance deviations (V_D), and that due to gene interaction (V_I). For a description of the methods, see Falconer (1960).

Figure 1 shows three situations. In A, genetic progress under selection is slow, since V_G is small. In B, selection will produce rapid results, since V_G is large. Situation C is frustrating. Selection will be relatively ineffective because of the low value of V_G; but environmental change is not promising either because V_E is too small. Heritability in the broad sense, V_H/V_T, is high, but in the narrow sense, V_G/V_T, it is low. The trait is largely determined by heredity, but the genes interact in such a way that there is not much prediction of offspring from parent. The simplest example is a trait caused by a rare recessive gene; even though the cause may be entirely genetic, selection is not effective in changing the incidence of the trait, because most of the individuals showing it come from normal parents and could not therefore have been identified in advance.

Comparison of monozygous and dizygous twins can, under certain simplifying assumptions, give an estimate of heritability in the broad sense. Unfortunately twin studies do not distinguish B from C in Figure 1.

The correlation between monozygous twins is

$$r_{MZ} = \frac{V_H + V_e}{V_T}$$

where V_e is the part of V_E that measures environmental differences between families, but not those within families. The correlation between twins is, of course, enhanced by the environmental similarities within sibships.

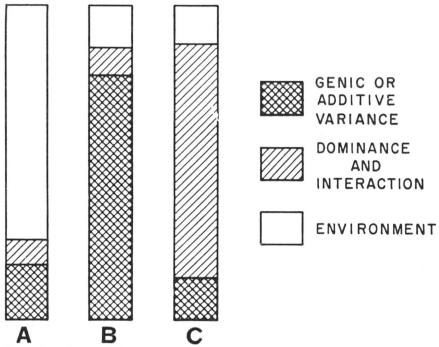

Figure 1.   Three different heritability situations. In A the cause of variability is mainly environmental and progress under selection would be slow. In B selection would produce rapid results. In C there is a large degree of genetic determination but since the gene action is complicated selection is ineffective.

The correlation between dizygous twins is

$$r_{DZ} = \frac{1/2\, V_G + 1/4\, V_D + \kappa V_I + V_e}{V_T} \qquad (3)$$

provided that marriage is random with respect to this trait. The quantity κ is less than 1/4. So we can write

$$r_{DZ} = \frac{\rho V_H + V_e}{V_T} \qquad (4)$$

where ρ is an unknown quantity that is, however, less than 1/2.

Combining equations (2) and (4) we obtain

$$r_{MZ} - r_{DZ} = \frac{(1 - \rho)\, V_H}{V_T}$$

from which heritability in the broad sense can be written as

$$\frac{V_H}{V_T} = \frac{r_{MZ} - r_{DZ}}{1 - \rho}$$

This is the same equation used in Jensen's article.

The value of ρ is usually taken to be $1/2$. Its actual value is unknown, but this may often be a reasonably good estimate. But if V_D and V_I are appreciable, then ρ is less than $1/2$ and taking it as $1/2$ will overestimate the heritability. On the other hand, in man there is often assortative marriage, and this will increase ρ. So the two principal errors are in opposite directions and there is some cancellation.

However, in addition to uncertainty regarding the value of ρ, there is uncertainty about the assumptions. One of these is that the environmental similarities within the sibship are the same for monozygous and dizygous twins. This is likely to be a poor assumption for many behavioral traits where genetic identity can produce environmental similarity (as happens if identical twins tend to stay together more than fraternals) or difference (as might happen if one twin became the leader). Furthermore, there may be prenatal differences in monozygotic and dyzygotic twins, e.g., circulatory anastomoses may produce an unequal blood suppy.

Another unwarranted assumption is that environmental effects, measured collectively by V_E, are additive to each other and to the genetic effects, and are independent in occurrence. The animal breeder can get around the latter difficulty by allotting his experimental subjects to environments in some properly randomized way. But he may not be able to circumvent the possibility of nonadditivity. The human geneticist can do very little about it either.

I conclude that, even with refinements, the twin method does not give an unambiguous estimate of V_H/V_T. Even if it did, it would not offer much guidance for predicting the results of selection, since V_G/V_T is what we want.

If twins could be reared in random environments, one could do considerably better. Then, as can be easily verified from equations (2) and (3),

$$\frac{V_H}{V_T} = r_{MZ} \tag{6}$$

$$\frac{V_G}{V_T} = 4r_{DZ} - r_{MZ} \tag{7}$$

since V_e becomes zero with proper randomization. Again there is the assumption of no assortative marriage, and no gene-environment interaction.

Twins reared in different environments are very rare, and the environments can hardly be regarded as properly randomized. So, again, there is not much hope for good quantitative information.

Better information would be from sibs reared in different environments, as might be obtained from adopted children. There is a question of the representativeness of adopted children and adopting parents; it is likely that they are both far from a random sample of the population.

The best data would be from half-sibs reared in independent environments. There is no dominance component in the correlation between half-sibs, so we can estimate the (narrow) heritability from

$$\frac{V_G}{V_T} = 4r_{HS} \tag{8}$$

where r_{HS} is the correlation between half-sibs.

The usual prediction formula used by livestock breeders is

$$0 = M + H(P - M) \tag{9}$$

where 0 is the predicted average of the progeny, M is the population mean, H is the heritability in the narrow sense, and P is the mean of the parents. It is likely that H, when measured from correlations between randomized half-sibs, includes just about the same fraction of epistatic error as the prediction formula should include, so the neglect of epistatic variance is probably not too important.

Clearly a large number of sets of half-sibs reared in randomized environments is not attainable in the human population. We must conclude, I think, that precise heritability studies are out of the question at present. We shall have to be content with crude measures which are only approximate, and which depend on unverified simplifying assumptions.

With All These Uncertainties, How Predictable are the Effects of Selection in Man?

After this dreary recitation of the difficulties in measuring heritability in man, is the situation hopelessly bad? I do not think that it will be possible, certainly not in any obvious way, to remove these uncertainties in the interpretation of human heritability measurements. At best, the estimates will have to serve as rough guides.

On the other hand, I do not want to conclude that because of this the results of selection would be chaotic. We do not have to know the heritability to predict the direction of selection. Many social decisions would be the same whether the heritability value is 20 or 80 percent. Furthermore, we have or can obtain empirical data that have value in predicting the phenotypes of children of selected parents, although the cause will be an unknown mixture of genetic and environmental factors.

I conclude that, despite all the difficulties mentioned above, a eugenic program designed to change almost any measurable trait would be, in some measure, successful. In particular, greater reproduction by persons with high IQ's would increase the mean IQ next generation, unless there were some counteracting environmental change for the worse. I am also sure that continued selection could, depending on its intensity, make large changes if carried on a long time. Man cannot be this different from the rest of nature. Furthermore, aside from greater difficulties of reproducible measurements, there is no reason why selection for behavioral traits should be appreciably different from selection for physical traits.

I come back to my earlier point. We know enough about selection, despite all the uncertainties, that if we were sure of the ends and found the means acceptable, we could confidently embark on a selection program. The predictions would be qualitatively correct, but uncertain in magnitude. Thus, I think the discussion should be on these points: (1) What do we want for the next few generations? (2) Is society willing to try to influence the reproduction of this generation in order to achieve this? (3) Should it do so?

WHAT EUGENIC STEPS SHOULD WE TAKE?

I now come to the question of what we should do. These are matters on which opinions differ widely, and I am giving my own, which are not necessarily representative. They are applicable, I think, to the poverty problem, but are also applicable in a wider context.

First, I would advocate the extension of genetic counseling. Until recently the genetic counselor could really do very little. Now, thanks to new cytological techniques and new chemical knowledge, he can do much more. Furthermore, knowledge is increasing rapidly. Most aspects of genetic counseling have wide social acceptance. The counselor ordinarily does not tell people that they should or should not have children, but rather points out what the risk is of having an abnormal or diseased child. The family can then make its own decision depending on the severity of the disease, the likelihood of a cure, the magnitude of the risk, and their own desire for children.

This is creating one situation that will call for a difficult social decision. It is becoming increasingly possible to detect genetic abnormalities before birth. This may be done by either cytological or chemical tests on cells obtained from the amniotic fluid. Therapeutic abortion could save a number of genetic tragedies. At the same time it would permit parents who know they are carriers of hidden genetic diseases, and therefore fearful of having any children at all, to have normal children, for all abnormal embryos could be aborted. I hope that abortion can be made easily available in such circumstances.

Genetic counseling usually involves rare diseases. As great as the importance is in individual cases, it still is not making any significant impact on the overall statistics of human health and intelligence. For this, a much larger influence on the birth pattern would be needed.

I am not ready to advocate any overall eugenic program at present. For one thing, I do not think society would accept any program that is extensive enough to make any substantial change. For another, the genetic risks to the population from possible existing differential birthrates or mutation accumulation are likely to be changing gene frequencies only very slowly. If we do nothing, it is much more like a missed opportunity than failure to avoid a genetic catastrophe.

I *would* like to urge, though, that we remove the present legal and social barriers to the *means* of eugenics. At present the wide distribution of contraceptives if often prohibited, especially to the unmarried. Abortion is severely restricted legally, though rather widely practiced. The net effect is that abortions under good medical conditions are available only to the privileged. Finally, artificial insemination is of such questionable legal and social standing that we do not even have any idea of the number of children conceived this way.

I urge that contraceptive information and, when this fails, abortion, be easily available to any who desire them. My reason is not primarily eugenic. It is rather the belief that freedom not to have an unwanted child is as basic as the right to have one that is wanted.

As regards artificial insemination, the present system of relying on anonymous donors chosen by the doctor seems to me to leave much to be desired. I should think the mother might well wish to know something about the donor. H. J. Muller (1967) has advocated using sperm from persons dead at the time of use. This would permit selection of donors on the basis of lifetime performance (for example, potential donors who developed physical or mental disease or premature senility later in life could be rejected). It might also mitigate some social problems that could possibly arise if the identity of living donors were known.

Finally, let me emphasize that genetic and environmental means of improvement are not mutually exclusive. More likely they are mutually reinforcing. There is an immediate social acceptability of environmental improvement in almost all areas of concern. So I hope that any discussion of genetic possibilities will not be used as an excuse to reduce efforts at environmental improvement.

REFERENCES

Davis, K. Sociological Aspects of Genetic Control, in J. D. Roslansky, ed. *Genetics and the Future of Man.* New York: Appleton-Century-Crofts, 1966, pp. 173-204.

Falconer, D. S. *Introduction to Quantitative Genetics.* New York: Ronald Press, 1960.

Haldane, J. B. S. The Implications of Genetics for Human Society, in S. J. Geertz, ed. *Genetics Today: Proceedings of the XI International Congress of Genetics.* The Hague, Netherlands, Sept. 1963. New York: Pergamon Press, 1965, pp. xcii-xciii.

Muller, H. J. What Genetic Course Will Man Steer? *Proceedings of the Third International Congress of Human Genetics.* Baltimore: The Johns Hopkins Press, 1967, pp. 521-43.

Chapter 9

GENETIC FACTORS IN POVERTY: A PSYCHOLOGIST'S POINT OF VIEW

Steven G. Vandenberg*

Before we can discuss genetic factors in poverty, we have to clarify what we mean by poverty. Poverty is, of course, a relative concept. It is often said that compared to conditions in other parts of the world, there is little real poverty in the United States. What is meant is that there is little starvation in the United States, and that is probably true.

Poverty is as much an evaluation as a statement of fact. To proceed with a discussion of genetic factors, we will have to agree that there is a segment of the United States population that is poor, even though each of us might draw the lines somewhat differently. For example, one might debate whether graduate students should be included, or struggling artists, or persons who retired on what at the time seemed adequate pensions. We can probably also agree on some of the causative factors in poverty. Poverty can be the result of a variety of circumstances, including persistent bad luck, physical or psychological handicaps, or minority ethnic status. Other causes include ignorance of rights, opportunities, or sources of assistance that leads to apathy and makes the person an easy victim of exploitation. Ignorance also contributes to poor economic judgment and bad management of otherwise adequate finances. Poverty can be a chronic condition, or it can be temporary. Chronic poverty tends to seek out the weak, including

*Professor of Psychology, Department of Psychology, University of Colorado, Boulder. The research reported here was supported by grants K3-MH-18, 382, and HD 00843 of the National Institute of Health.

the poorly educated, the unskilled, the ugly, the clumsy, the borderline ill—whether physically or mentally—and the ethnically or culturally different. These factors are cumulative, and the presence of two or more greatly increases the likelihood of poverty. For the purposes of our present discussion, it is this category of poverty with which we shall be concerned.

Although some of the above attributes can to some degree be related to low intelligence or defective character structure, it is erroneous to equate poverty with low ability and character defects. There are many poor people, particularly in economically-depressed areas, who would not fit such a description. Yet it is probably these two characteristics that are in the minds of those who raise the question of genetic factors in poverty. While I do not subscribe to this more limited view of poverty, it is the one we can best deal with in considering whether hereditary factors play any role in being poor.

IS THE NATIONAL AVERAGE IQ DECLINING?

William Shockley has argued in the past that there may be a considerable genetic factor in poverty, due to hereditary differences in ability. He has also expressed concern that the national intelligence level may be lowered by the higher-than-average reproductive rate of the poor. Higher birthrates in the lower classes were reported as early as the seventeenth century, but intelligence test scores have been available only since about World War I. Anastasi (1956) reviewed this question in considerable detail and concluded that there was no indication that the higher birthrates and lower intelligence scores of the lower social classes will, in fact, gradually depress the intelligence of the population.

The empirical evidence that there is no lowering of intelligence is rather sparse. The main factual support for the idea comes from *The Trend of Scottish Intelligence,* a report published in 1949 by the Scottish Council for Research in Education. The report is primarily a comparison of the 1932 and 1947 surveys of the intelligence of eleven-year-old pupils. Almost ninety thousand children were tested in 1932, and almost seventy-one thousand in 1947. Of course, all of these children could not be tested individually. Instead they were given the identical group-administered paper-and-pencil test. Compared with an average score of 34.5 in 1932, the 1947 average score was 36.7. To convert these scores into measures of increase in IQ additional tests were administered to the children.

In each survey a subset of children (1,000 in 1932 and 1,200 in 1947) was also tested individually with a Binet test, making it possible to calculate regression equations allowing conversion of the group-test scores into IQ estimates. After converting the scores on the group test into IQ scores, the results for the two years showed a small increase for boys (0.62 IQ points) and an almost equal decrease for girls (0.67) over the period. Anastasi questioned whether this procedure gave any better understanding than did the original results, but her criticism would not affect the Scottish investigators' conclusion that there had been no decline in intelligence in recent times. This inference certainly seems warranted, even though the time interval from 1932 to 1947 was a rather short one.

The early report of the Scottish investigators also provided a good illustration of the negative correlation between intelligence test score and the size of the family in which the child is reared. Anastasi (1956) pointed out that the negative correlation between a child's IQ and the number of brothers and sisters he has may be partly due to the fact that many of the families included in such studies are incomplete. Some of the high-scoring children from small families may actually belong in one or another category of larger families where they would raise the average IQ. Anastasi also called attention to the fact that, although a negative relation between the size of sibship and IQ is well established, in all studies in which parental IQ correlated with number of offspring the relation was positive. (These studies were usually of small, selected samples.)

Further evidence of the fact that the relation between the size of a person's sibship and his IQ differs from the relation between the number of his offspring and his IQ comes from reports of large studies by Bajema (1963), Gibson and Young (1965), and Higgins, Reed, and Reed (1962), all of whom studied intact families. Higgins, Reed, and Reed (1962) found a bimodal distribution for the number of children born to persons of different IQ levels, with greater number of offspring for the higher and the lower IQ levels. Gibson and Young (1965) in Great Britain also found a bimodal distribution of the number of offspring for different IQ groups. Bajema (1963) studied the reproductive pattern of 969 whites born in 1916 or 1917 who were given an intelligence test as sixth-graders in the Kalamazoo (Michigan) public schools. He found no simple negative correlation between the number of offspring and IQ, but rather a curvilinear relation. The correlation between the IQ of an individual and the number of his offspring was 0.05, even though the relation between his IQ and the size of the family he came from was -0.26. To take the age of death of deceased individuals into account, Bajema (1963) also calculated the intrinsic rate of natural increase and the relative fitness of the five IQ groups. These are two technical indices from population biology in which a correction is made for the fact that an individual who dies young may not leave as many children as someone who lives longer. These results, presented in Table 1, show even more clearly that in this population there is a positive relation between IQ and fertility.

Genetic Factors in Poverty

Table 1. The Relation of IQ to the Intrinsic Rate of Natural Increase and Relative Fitness, Using the Average Number of Offspring as the Measure of Population Growth (from Bajema, 1963).

IQ range	Intrinsic rate of natural increase	Relative fitness
≥ 120	0.008885	1.0000
105-119	0.003890	0.8614
95-104	0.000332	0.7771
80- 94	0.007454	0.9484
69- 79	-0.010001	0.5774

That there is no real reason to worry about a decline of ability in the population, even if the so-called upper classes were to fail completely to reproduce, is shown convincingly by the results of a Belgian study by Nuttin (1965). The author analyzed the performance on four ability factors of 1,514 children whose parents were in the following five socioeconomic strata: (1) upper-class occupations, most of which require graduate, professional, or higher technical training; (2) middle-class occupations generally requiring a completed secondary school education; (3) lower-middle-class occupations requiring only three years of secondary school; (4) skilled manual occupations; (5) unskilled occupations.

Four abilities—vocabulary, number, perceptual speed, and spatial visualization—were measured by a Belgian adaptation of Thurstone's Primary Mental Abilities Scale for the five- to seven-year age range. The number of children in each of the five strata was 91, 226, 343, 457, and 397. The average scores on the four abilities for each group are shown in Table 2. In order to allow a direct comparison, I have converted the means to percentages of the possible maximum score, which varied among the four abilities.

Table 2. Mean Scores for Five Socioeconomic Groups on Four Abilities, Expressed as Percentage of Maximum Score

Socioeconomic Group	Vocabulary	Number ability	Perceptual speed	Spatial visualization
1 (Highest)	62.9	52.8	43.7	49.6
2	56.9	44.0	49.7	50.8
3	52.9	38.8	35.3	45.8
4	46.9	33.6	23.7	40.0
5 (Lowest)	44.3	30.0	26.0	35.8

Nuttin (1965) also calculated the proportion of children from each of the socioeconomic backgrounds who scored in the top 10 and top 20 percent of the total distribution. It is clear that loss of Group 1 would not lead to serious consequences for the distribution of intelligence, because nearly 85 percent of the top-scoring children come from middle- or lower-class homes. The elimination of the majority of the upper class during the French and Russian revolutions are actual examples of this situation, and do not seem to have affected the ability distribution of these countries.

Further evidence on social mobility and on the presence of overlapping ability distributions in offspring of fathers from different socioeconomic groups comes from a study by Cliquet (1963) in which Flemish recruits (N = 3,621) were measured on seven abilities, thirty anthropometric variables, and a large number of body-build indices based on ratios between two or more original measures. In general the recruits from higher socioeconomic origins were taller, heavier, etc., than those of lower classes.

Of more interest to our present concern is the finding that, while there is a clear-cut relation between socioeconomic status and the scores on the

Figure 1. Mean scores (and range of one standard deviation above and below the mean) for seven ability measures of Flemish recruits from nine socio-economic levels (after Cliquet).

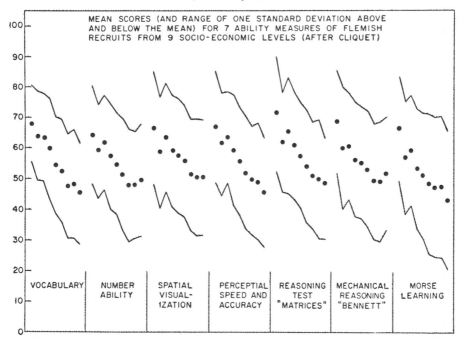

seven ability measures, there is at the same time much overlap between the abilities of recruits from different socioeconomic origins, as shown in Figure 1. In fact, on most of the seven abilities those scores for the lowest group that are one standard deviation above their group-mean fall above the mean score obtained by all groups of higher socioeconomic origin. In other words, assuming normal distributions, one-sixth of the members of the lowest group scored above the mean for the highest group. Cliquet's data also permit us to ask whether the differences in ability among various classes are similar for all seven abilities, or whether some abilities are more affected than others. My recalculation of Cliquet's data shows that socioeconomic status affects vocabulary most, and mechanical reasoning least. It seems probable that these findings hold true, if perhaps with less clarity, for other countries besides Belgium, where the class distributions may be greater than in the United States of America.

The apparent paradox of a negative correlation between a child's IQ and the number of siblings of that child, but a positive correlation between parental IQ and number of offspring can best be understood as being due to a psychological effect. Growing up in a larger family apparently has a tendency to depress intelligence. Several other facts support this hypothesis. First, we frequently read that the oldest child in a family tends to have a higher average ability score when compared with children in the second, third, and later positions. Second, twins have been found to have slightly lower average IQ's just as do closely spaced sibs (Gille et al., 1954; Tabah and Sutter, 1954). This effect is more pronounced on measures of verbal ability than of nonverbal ability, as shown for twins by Helen Koch (1966) and for sibs by Scott and Nisbet (1955); these findings suggest that it is again the lessened opportunity for verbal contact with adults that is responsible.

But geneticists would argue that it may not even be necessary to invoke such a psychological effect to deny that we need worry about a decline in intelligence. Penrose (1948, 1950a, b) has shown that a negative correlation between IQ scores and number of children need not lead to a decline over time in the intellectual level of the population, because some parents of average or even borderline IQ have children of above average ability. Intelligence is presumably controlled by so many genes that the average and below-average person will carry a number of genes for high ability which at times will transmit to his offspring. In addition, high ability may be due to a particular constellation of genes which can be produced just as often by the combination of genes of two low ability parents as of high ability parents.

In recent years the difference in birthrate between various socioeconomic groups has narrowed in both Great Britain and the United States (Benjamin, 1966). For example, the ratio between the family size of college graduates and the family size of those who failed to complete elementary school has decreased from 2.4 to 1.4. A similar trend was reported for Japan, where the standard deviation of the average family size classified by father's occupation dropped from 0.90 in 1955 to 0.16 in 1960, while the average dropped from 3.0 to 2.3 (Kimura, 1966). Perhaps we may expect increasing industrialization to produce similar trends over the entire world.

RACIAL FACTORS

So far we have considered (and intentionally minimized) the effect on intelligence of differential fertility within the white population alone. But of all Negro families, 40 percent are "poor" according to Social Security Administration criteria, whereas the figure for white families is only 11 percent (Comer, 1967). As far as I know, no studies have been made of the relation between IQ and family size specifically within the Negro population. However, I would expect it to be roughly the same as for whites. For instance Lee and Lee (1952) did find that fertility rates of Negroes were affected in ways very similar to those of whites of comparable socioeconomic status, education, and urban-rural residence. Whelpton et al. (1966) found that nonwhites desire no more offspring than whites, but do delay using contraceptives, or use them inefficiently. Nonwhites who have little education or who ever lived on farms bear atypically large numbers of children. On the other hand, they found that the fertility of nonwhite women having either a high-school education or no southern farm background resembles that of comparable white women. This suggests that when migration of Negroes to the North has passed its present peak, the Negro differential birthrate will tend to disappear. Moreover, the conditions in the South that favor migration to the North are beginning to change, so that urban ghetto formation in the North may not surpass the existing situation. When considering the effect of the differential fertility of Negroes compared to whites on the distribution of intelligence in the United States it would be useful to have some hard facts about the nature and origin of differences in IQ distribution in the two groups, but such information is unfortunately still incomplete. The problem is badly complicated by the simultaneous existence of large economic, educational, and cultural differences between Negroes and whites—the very factors known to affect present ability measures. A good deal of the research on this topic of "race differences in ability" has been of poor quality because these complications have not been adequately dealt with, which is not to say that they can be easily controlled. Eliminating the effect of environmental factors, for instance, by matching selected Negro and white subjects on income and education of the parents and grandparents, would probably also eliminate a substantial part of the differences in

Figure 2. Mean algebraic error in size constancy for five groups

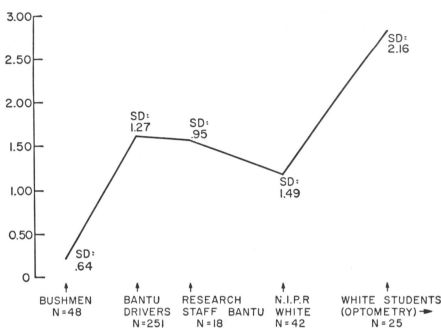

ability distributions observed in studies in which no matching is used. Yet, such matching can usually be criticized as inadequate or begging the question.

Nor has evidence from cross-cultural studies in other parts of the world been informative about racial differences. The major findings from such studies have been that nonacculturated African adults do very poorly on Western ability measures, mainly because of basic difficulties of motivation and understanding of the testing situation, but that African children who have gone to Western-style schools do about as well as white children. I would like to describe briefly a few studies that demonstrate why the available studies from Africa cannot help us at present.

Mundy-Castle (1966) showed Ghanaian children four drawings in which different cues were used to suggest distance or perspective, and asked them to describe what they saw. Many children failed to see distance, because the Western convention of abstract representation of distance by converging lines, or by depicting distant objects as smaller, is not familiar to them. It would be extremely interesting to repeat a similar study with photographs or film strips rather than schematic drawings.

This work was a partial replication of a study by Hudson (1960), who found that Bantu school children and teachers in South Africa did equally as well as white children on a test of depth perception, but that adult

Bantus of various low levels of education did not see depth in drawings. A sample of white laborers also did very poorly.

There have been several studies of the accuracy of size estimation in different cultures. Wendy Winter (1967) summarized unpublished studies of size constancy by Renning in which the amount of texture in the setting of the study was varied. African subjects did very well on this task, performing even better when the terrain varied in texture than when it was bare and open. Several white and African groups living in similar settings were also studied. Figure 2 shows a comparison of the average error of each group, and Figure 3 shows the average setting. The Bushmen did far better than any other group. There was no meaningful difference between noneducated and educated Bantus, nor between the latter group and white members of the research staff. Yet white optometry students did considerably poorer—perhaps because, due to their training, they were too aware of possible sources of errors.

In many cross-cultural studies the validity for that culture of the psychological tests used was not ascertained. My earlier discussion has shown that validity in the American culture is no guarantee of validity in another culture. In recent years investigators have become more aware of this restriction, and have at times started their research program by demonstrating the validity of their test for the culture under study.

The largest cross-cultural study of psychological variables attempted so far is reported in a monograph by Segall, Campbell, and Herskovits (1966). Prompted by an environmentalist hypothesis, they focused within

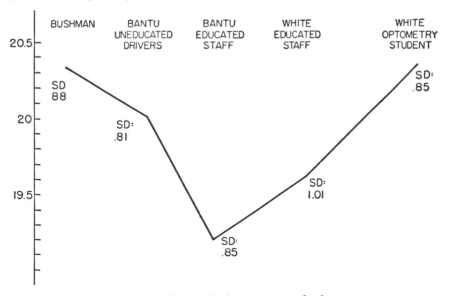

Figure 3. Average threshold (size constancy) for five groups

this framework on ecological factors such as the prevalence of open vistas compared to dense vegetation in the subject's habitat, and the frequency of "carpentered" (i.e., rectangular) structures. Ethnic samples studied came from fourteen locations in Africa (including one group of European extraction), one from the Philippines, two from the Australian aborigines, and three from the United States. For several of the tasks, Europeans were most subject to the illusion; some "primitive" cultures performed much more accurately. There were strong differences among various ethnic groups in their response to diagrams that evoke visual illusions in western subjects. In view of these findings, can we expect that materials even more structured by Western cultural traditions, such as conventional intelligence tests, can be culture-fair? Yet it is possible to obtain interesting results by relating differences in performance to ecological and cultural differences among groups.

Perhaps the most thorough study to date of the ecology and culture of a group of people, conducted in such a way that appropriate psychological experiments could be performed, is the study in central Liberia by Gay and Cole (1967). A few of the findings relevant to our topic are reviewed here.

Kpelle culture was studied intensively to provide a basis for recommendations concerning necessary adaptations of Western educational curricula. An analysis of the language revealed the absence of some concepts, without which the customary teaching of arithmetic degrades to rote learning. For instance, while the Kpelle language does have the concept of sets, the distinction between countable and uncountable nouns is less clear than in English. We say "a house" or "horse," but "water," and not "a water." In Kpelle such a distinction has to be supplied through the context.

One experiment demonstrated the Kpelles' lack of proficiency in classifying objects into different sets. After adults and children had used one principle to sort cards with designs differing in color, number, and form, into two categories, they found it difficult to sort according to another category, and very difficult to do so according to the third principle. Yet no special preference was shown for any of the three categories; it was the change of category that produced the difficulty.

Similar findings suggest other problems in teaching arithmetic by conventional methods. Thus, the Kpelle language includes words for one through ten, for one hundred, and a borrowed term for one thousand, but only a few ordinal terms; fractions are described by elaborate construction, indicating the infrequent nature of their use. Familiarity with arithmetic is uncommon, and somewhat of a trade secret of merchants. Yet the smaller numbers are quite familiar, as was shown by some experiments on number recognition. Ten piles of stones with from ten to one hundred stones were shown in the same random order to adult Kpelles and to several groups of

Americans. Subjects were asked to estimate the number in each pile. The Kpelles were more accurate than the Americans. However, after one group of Yale students was told the number of stones in a pile containing sixty, their performance improved up to the Kpelle standards.

On a tachistoscopic display of random dots, Kpelle and American children gave very similar results when asked to estimate the number of dots. However, unlike Americans, Kpelle subjects do not seem to use patterns of grouping such as 2 × 4, and therefore do less well. Apparently they are not as familiar with the multiplication tables.

Until recently the Kpelles did not have a cost or money economy, but used a system of barter. This means that they are more accustomed to considering the relative value of various amounts of commodities than to quantifying everything in the way Westerners do. Another experiment demonstrated this: when Kpelle and American subjects were asked to estimate the number of cups of rice in several containers, the Kpelles were better. Kpelle adults also did better at estimating the length of a stick. Lest one think that these findings are peculiar to Africa, similar conditions exist in other parts of the world, and existed in Europe before general education became universal. We must conclude for the moment that neither studies from the United States nor those from other parts of the world provide useful information about the comparative intelligence of Negroes and whites.

CAN TWIN-STUDIES HELP?

In the absence of valid comparisons of Negroes and whites one is tempted to fall back on the evidence from twin-studies that indicates clearly that hereditary components are responsible for a major share of the observed individual differences in the normal range. Arthur Jensen (1967) has presented results of a study by Burt (1958) that shows the regular increase in concordance between pairs of persons of increasingly close blood relationship. Similar results were found in a summary of a large number of studies compiled by Erlenmeyer-Kimling and Jarvik (1963).

In my own work I have generally not calculated an index of heritability, which gives an estimate of the proportion of the within-pair variance attributable to heredity. Instead I have calculated a variance ratio (F), which can be tested for significance in the usual way. The ratio is between the fraternal (DZ) and the identical (MZ) within-pair variances, with degrees of freedom N_{DZ} and N_{MZ} where N is the number of pairs. Tables 3 and 4 present some results from studies of twins with two well-known batteries of ability tests. In both tables there is replication. These results provide evidence, first of all, for the significance of the increased within-pair

Table 3. F Ratios of DZ and MZ Within-Pair Variances for the Six
Scores of the Chicago Primary Mental Abilities Test

Name of score	Blewett, 1954	Thurstone, 1955	Vandenberg, 1962a	Vandenberg, 1968
Verbal	3.13*	2.81*	2.65*	1.74†
Space	2.04†	4.19*	1.77†	3.51*
Number	1.07	1.52	2.58*	2.26*
Reasoning	2.78*	1.35	1.40	1.10
Word fluency	Not used	2.47*	2.57*	2.24*
Memory		1.62†	1.26	Not used
N_{DZ}	26	53	37	36
N_{MZ}	26	45	45	76

* $p < 0.01$
† $p < 0.05$

variance in fraternal twins, and second, for the contention that certain abilities are controlled to a higher degree by hereditary components than are other abilities.

However, evidence for hereditary components in ability does not, in itself, prove that there are hereditary differences in ability between Negroes and whites. We know that many traits today are entirely controlled by genes, and for most of these there are no clear-cut differences between major racial groups, but only relatively minor differences in frequencies.

We are thus left at an impasse. However, we know, or are reasonably sure, that factors operating among Negroes are the same as those we reviewed for studies of the white population: there are hereditary factors in ability, and there is a difference in average ability between social classes, as well as perhaps a difference in birthrates. (Statements by recent investigators indicate that this differential birthrate is disappearing.) Yet the few directly-relevant studies found no decline in average ability in whites. This paradox is resolved if we remember that extremely low-ability persons are more likely not to marry and thus have no offspring at all. Since the same factors are at work, we can probably expect that the same answer is correct when we consider Negroes or the total population. Many laymen apparently believe that there is a difference in ability between Negroes and whites. Most scientists who have studied this area believe that any existing difference is due to environmental factors. Because the difference in the distribution of socioeconomic status for Negroes and whites is so very obvious, and because the differences in ability, largely due to those same differences in socioeconomic status, are also easily observed, fears about the effect of differences in birthrates are accentuated.

Perhaps looking at a different trait about which we have less strong

Table 4. *F* Ratios between *DZ* and *MZ* Within-Pair Variances on the Subtests of the Differential Abilities Test Obtained at Michigan and in Louisville

Name of score	1961	1965
Verbal reasoning	2.29*	2.38*
Number ability	1.39	1.37
Abstract reasoning	1.47	1.23
Space relations	1.67	2.19*
Mechanical reasoning	1.36	1.46
Clerical speed and accuracy	2.54*	3.25*
Language use I: spelling	3.64*	2.58*
Language use II: sentences	3.06*	2.00†
N_{DZ}	25	86
N_{MZ}	47	109

*p < 0.01
†p < 0.05

emotional feelings will help us understand the situation. Although the genetics of stature or height is not as completely understood as the genetics of color blindness, for instance, the former makes a better analogy for our purpose. Let us review briefly a few generalizations known about height. From twin-studies we learn that over 90 percent of the variation is due to heredity (Vandenberg, 1962b), although environmental factors such as improved diet, especially in childhood, also tend to lead to some increase in height (Kaplan, 1954). There is a significant difference in the average height of persons from different socioeconomic classes. Of course, there is a great deal of variation within each socioeconomic class. To give one example, let us look at the study of Cliquet (1963) cited earlier. The study showed a correlation between height and socioeconomic status: height and breadth of the chest drop steadily as one goes down the social-class ladder. The same relationship holds true for many other anthropometric measures. Cliquet summarized many earlier studies that showed similar correlations between social status and height.

Because of the differential birthrates among socioeconomic classes, one might fear a gradual lowering of the average height in the total population. Yet suits of armor and uniforms from earlier times are too small for the average male of today. There are no clear-cut relations between skin color and height or between height and any other racially distinctive features that would give reason to expect changes in the distribution of height in the population due to racial differences in birthrate. Is it not reasonable to expect that the relationship between intelligence and race may be analogous to the relationship between height and race?

REFERENCES

Anastasi, A. Intelligence and Family Size. *Psychological Bulletin* 1956, 53: 187-210.

Bajema, C. J. Estimation of the Direction and Intensity of Natural Selection in Relation to Human Intelligence by Means of the Intrinsic Rate of Natural Increase. *Eugenics Quarterly* 1963, 10: 175-87.

Benjamin, B. Social and Economic Differentials in Fertility, in J. E. Meade and A. S. Parkes, eds. *Genetic and Environmental Factors in Human Ability*. New York: Plenum Press, 1966.

Blewett, D. R. An Experimental Study of the Inheritance of Intelligence. *Journal of Mental Science* 1954, 100: 922-33.

Burt, C. The Inheritance of Mental Ability. *American Psychologist* 1958, 13: 1-15.

Cliquet, R. L. Bijdrage tot de kennis van het verband tussen de sociale status en een aantal antrobiologische kenmerken (Contribution to the knowledge of the relation between social status and a number of anthrobiological characteristics). Verh. Kon. Vlaamse Acad. Wetensch., Kl. Wetensch. No. 72, Brussels, 1963.

Comer, J. P. The Social Power of the Negro. *Scientific American* 1967, 216: 21-27.

Dreger, R. M., and Miller, K. S. Comparative Psychological Studies of Negroes and Whites in the United States. *Psychological Bulletin* 1960, 57: 361-402.

Erlenmeyer-Kimling, L., and Jarvik, L. F. Genetics and Intelligence: A Review. *Science* 1963, 142: 1477-79.

Gay, J. H., and Cole, M. *The New Mathematics and an Old Culture; A Study of Learning among the Kpelle of Liberia*. New York: Holt, Rinehart & Winston, 1967.

Gibson, J., and Young, M. Social Mobility and Fertility, in J. E. Meade and A. S. Parkes, eds. *Biological Aspects of Social Problems: A Symposium Held by the Eugenics Society in October, 1964*. Edinburgh: Oliver & Boyd, 1965, pp. 69-80.

Gille, R., Henry, L., Tabah, L., Sutter, J., Bergues, H., Girard, A., & Bastide, H. *Le niveau intellectuel des enfants d'age scolaire: la determination des aptitudes; l'influence des facteurs constitutionnels familiaux, et sociaux*. Paris: Presses Universitaires de France, 1954.

Higgins, J., Reed, E., and Reed, S. Intelligence and Family Size: A Paradox Resolved. *Eugenics Quarterly* 1962, 9: 84-90.

Hudson, W. Pictorial Perception in Subcultural Groups in Africa. *Journal of Social Psychology* 1960, 52: 182-208.

Jensen, A. R. Family Background and Educability. Paper presented at a conference on psychological factors in poverty, Madison, Wisconsin, June 22-24, 1967.

Kaplan, B. Environment and Human Plasticity. *American Anthropologist* 1954, 56: 780-800.

Kímura, M. Current Fertility Patterns in Japan, in *World Population Con-ference, 1965*. New York: United Nations, 1966.

Koch, H. L. *Twins and Twin Relations*. Chicago: University of Chicago Press, 1966.

Lee, E. S., and Lee, A. S. The Differential Fertility of the American Negro. *American Sociological Review* 1952, 17: 437-47.

Mundy-Castle, A. C. Pictorial Depth Perception in Ghanaian Children. *International Journal of Psychology* 1966, 1: 289-300.

Nuttin, J. De verstandelijke begaaftheid van de jeugd in de verschillende sociale klassen en woonplaastsen (The intellectual ability of youth in different socioeconomic classes and urban and rural backgrounds). Mededel. Kon. Vlaamse Akad. Kl. Lett. 27: No. 7, Brussels, 1965.

Penrose, L. S. The Supposed Threat of Declining Intelligence. *American Journal of Mental Deficiency* 1948, 53: 114-18.

———. Genetical Influences on the Intelligence Level of the Population. *British Journal of Psychology* 1950, 40: 128-36. (a)

———. Propagation of the Unfit. *Lancet* 1950, 259: 425-27. (b)

Scott, E. M., and Nisbet, J. D. Intelligence and Family Size in Adult Sample. *Eugenics Review* 1955, 46: 233-35.

Scottish Council for Research in Education. *The Trend of Scottish Intelligence*. London: University of London Press, 1949.

Segall, M. H., Campbell, D. T., and Herskovitz, M. J. *The Influence of Culture on Visual Perception*. Indianapolis: Bobbs-Merrill, 1966.

Tabah, L., and Sutter, J. Le niveau intellectuel des enfants d'une meme famille. *Annals of Human Genetics* 1954, 19: 120-50.

Thurstone, T. G., Thurstone, L. L., and Strandskov, H. H. A Psychological Study of Twins. Report No. 4 from the Psychometric Laboratory, University of North Carolina, Chapel Hill, N.C., 1955.

Vandenberg, S. G. The Hereditary Abilities Study: Hereditary Components in a Psychological Test Battery. *American Journal of Human Genetics* 1962, 14: 220-37. (a)

———. How Stable are Heritability Estimates? A Comparison of Six Anthropometric Studies. *American Journal of Physical Anthropology* 1962, 20: 331-38. (b)

———. The Nature and Nurture of Intelligence, in D. C. Glass, ed. *Genetics; Proceedings of a Conference*. New York: Rockefeller University Press and Russell Sage Foundation, 1968, pp. 3-58.

Whelpton, P. K., Campbell, A. A., and Patterson, J. E. *Fertility and Family Planning in the United States*. Princeton, N. J.: Princeton University Press, 1966.

Winter, W. L. Size Constancy, Relative Size Estimation and Background: A Cross-Cultural Study. *Psvchologia Africana* 1967, 12: 42-58.

PART FOUR

BEHAVIORAL
CONCOMITANTS

INTRODUCTION

The four chapters included in this section represent a sampling of some of the most important behavioral consequences of poverty. Research has documented the great range and diversity of behaviors associated with poverty, including mental illness, attitudes and beliefs, patterns of social interaction, techniques of childrearing, and sexual habits.

Psychological concomitants of poverty often impose severe handicaps on the individual, making it extremely difficult to overcome poverty by personal effort alone. For example, low achievement motivation typically found among the poor decreases the possibility of escaping from poverty through educational or occupational success. This vicious circle indicates the central importance of psychological correlates of poverty. The vicious circle is further complicated in the case of Negroes because of their castelike position within American society. It is likely that all blacks, whether poor or not, share many of the psychological consequences of discrimination and segregation; and the Negro poor are recipients of the doubly debilitating impact of poverty and race.

There is one correlate of poverty that has usually been ignored as superficial and as being peripheral to the central concerns of psychological theory. The fact is, however, that a pervasive and not unimportant concomitant of poverty is unhappiness and worry (Bradburn and Caplovitz, 1965). The poor are clearly more unhappy and worry more than persons in the middle class. And things the poor worry about are directly connected with their precarious economic situation. Illness and old age are important sources of worry because of the financial crisis that would be likely to ensue. Consistent data were reported from Rainwater's (1966) study of sexual happiness. Contrary to popular belief, lower-class married couples experienced less satisfaction and happiness from sexual behavior than did middle-class couples.

To state that a particular behavior is associated with poverty does not imply direction of causation, i.e., it does n.. clarify whether the behavior was responsible for the person's being poor, or whether poverty caused the behavior. It seems more reasonable and plausible, however, to assume that poverty causes the observed behavior, rather than the opposite. Some psychological correlates of poverty can certainly be linked quite directly to the mere absence of money. One of the early studies of the psychological effects of unemployment showed that apathy and feelings of helplessness resulted from loss of a job and the resulting financial insecurity (Zawadzki and Lazarsfeld, 1935). The origin of behaviors associated with poverty cannot always be precisely ascertained. The nature of the external physical environment is probably of great importance in determining many aspects of behavior. Other behavior patterns are acquired by the child from par-

ents, other family members, and peer groups, as mentioned in an earlier section.

Living in poverty for a long period of time produces habits and behavioral dispositions that may be fairly permanent and quite resistant to change unless special intervention programs are initiated. The problem of individual and social change will be discussed in the last section of this book.

Chapter 10 explores the impact of poverty on the degree and type of impairment in personality functioning during childhood and adolescence. Langner and his associates report preliminary results from a large-scale psychiatric study based on a random sample of children and adolescents varying in ethnic background, income, and education. The advantage of obtaining a sample from a normal population is that prevalence rates for psychological impairment can be much more accurately estimated than by studying only patients receiving treatment. We know from previous research that social-class level is related to the probability of receiving treatment for psychological problems (Hollingshead and Redlich, 1958). The rich and complex data reported in Chapter 10 were collected by two-hour home interviews, supplemented by direct psychiatric examinations of the children. It should be kept in mind that degree of psychiatric impairment was determined by psychiatrists' ratings, and is therefore dependent on currently-accepted psychiatric concepts regarding the nature of the healthy and of the impaired personality.

Results of the psychiatric survey revealed prevalence of impairment in the total population and across different ethnic, income, and educational levels. The rather large proportion (38 percent) of the sample judged "moderately" impaired, i.e., experiencing difficulties severe enough to cause concern, should perhaps be considered a comment on the nature of our times. Few who were in need of treatment were actually receiving it, and the probability of receiving treatment (and the type of treatment given) depended on race, income, and ethnic background. Corroborating a review of relevant research summarized by Bronfenbrenner in Chapter 11, results of Langner's study found that boys showed a greater proportion of "marked" or "severe" incapacitation than did girls. Moreover, trends indicated that girls may improve as they get older, while boys are likely to get worse. Ethnic differences in psychiatric impairment were found, and remained even when appropriate controls were introduced for difference in income across ethnic groups. Interestingly, a strong relation was also observed between mental health and mother's character, though the effect of specific patterns of childrearing was negligible.

Many studies with adults have found that severity of impairment of *psychological functioning is strongly related to income. Langner's results with white children are no exception: the impact of poverty is manifested again, with low-income groups of whites displaying much greater psychological impairment. An exception to the foregoing statement constitutes one of the most interesting findings discussed in Langner's chapter. No difference in adequacy of psychological health was found between high- and low-income Negro and Spanish children; possible explanations for the finding are suggested by Langner.*

Bronfenbrenner summarizes in Chapter 11 many of the motivational, emotional, and educational problems that the disadvantaged child—and in particular the Negro child—brings with him to the school. These difficulties spring from multiple sources and include parental absence from the home, impoverished home environment, and possibly pre- and postnatal organic complications due to inadequate medical care.

Recurring throughout this volume have been indications of the overlapping of racial membership and poverty. All who are poor are not black by any means—look at Appalachia—but a greater proportion of the Negro population is economically deprived than of the white. Therefore, discussions of problems of discrimination and segregation are relevant to a large segment of the poverty population. By desegregating schools, and thereby helping to insure equality of opportunity, one important step can be taken towards the goal of eliminating poverty. Bronfenbrenner cautions that merely desegregating schools may not constitute a sufficient condition to improve school performance quickly, since the disadvantaged Negro child (and especially the Negro male) possesses enormous psychological handicaps. It must be realized, too, that there are psychological costs to the middle class that will accompany racial integration. For example, on the basis of previous research on peer influence, school performance of middle-class children could be expected to be influenced detrimentally by behavior of the disadvantaged students. Hope for breaking the cycle of poverty among the Negro poor will be greater if middle-class parents will accept the inevitable psychological costs of integration.

Bronfenbrenner suggests several very interesting ideas for programs to help reduce the impact of poverty and discrimination on the Negro child. A plea is sounded for greater involvement of both poor and middle-class parents in out-of-school activities with children. With parental absence being more common among disadvantaged families, the role of a positive adult male model assumes unusual significance for the child. Bronfenbrenner describes, from first hand observations, the Soviet Union's system of parental involvement in numerous school-related activities. In the United States, the role of the peer group and of respected adult models in influencing children's behavior has been insufficiently acknowledged, and when acknowledged has failed to be translated into practical programs to complement the classroom.

In Chapter 12 Caplovitz describes some of the intricate financial arrangements in which the poor frequently find themselves enmeshed. Problems associated with getting and spending money cost the poor a great deal in time, effort, and worry. Caplovitz summarizes the numerous ways that patterns of consumer behavior of the poor differ from those of the middle class, and discusses several features of the economy of poverty. For instance, one of the interesting aspects of economic behavior in poverty areas is the existence of various entrepreneural activities of questionable degrees of legality. This type of behavior, known as "hustling," seems to play an important part in the economy of the slum.

It is apparent that a central role in the economic behavior of the poor is played by installment buying, a pattern of behavior that often leads to problems resulting in legal action. In many respects the law seems to be biased against the poor consumer when he is confronted by the legal process as a consequence of a financial entanglement. In enforcing contracts drawn under dubious circumstances and in allowing garnishment of wages by an employer, the legal system confers singular hardships upon the poor.

The poor have accepted the American dream of having the good (material) things in life, but unfortunately do not possess the means for obtaining them. Thanks to the system of easy credit, however, material manifestations of the good life are made available even to the poor. For the benefits of easy credit the poor pay dearly in exorbitant interest charges and in excessive prices for inferior quality merchandise. Caplovitz (1963) hypothesizes in an earlier book that the poor engage in "compensatory consumption," in which the purchase of major durables such as appliances and automobiles may serve as a compensation, a substitute, for blocked social mobility. Merchants in slum areas use a variety of appalling schemes (including deception) to insure that such compensatory consumption remains at a high level. The title of Caplovitz's (1963) book, The Poor Pay More, *aptly describes the plight of the poor as consumers.*

In the last chapter in this section Allen reviews the state of empirical knowledge concerning the relationship between poverty and certain personality characteristics. Most psychologists would accept Gordon Allport's (1964) definition of personality as ". . . the dynamic organization within the individual of those psychophysical systems that determine his characteristic behavior and thought." Personality theorists have not assigned an important place in their systems for the role of socioeconomic status in personality. Sigmund Freud (1920) made a passing remark in an early book, suggesting that socioeconomic status might influence personality, but did not develop the thought further. One of the earliest empirical studies was, possibly, the 1927 research by Gesell and Lord, who investigated the effects of economic status on personality traits of nursery-school children. Since the 1930's, however, an enormous number of studies have attempted to assess the relationship between social class and personality.

A large number of personality traits are widely believed to be associated with poverty; a critical examination of research shows that some of these beliefs are not strongly supported by empirical data. Unfortunately, much of the research on personality correlates has not progressed beyond attempting to demonstrate the existence of a difference between the poor and the nonpoor on some isolated trait. It is quite clear that a great deal more empirical research and improved theoretical conceptualization are needed in this area before satisfactory general conclusions can be reached.

REFERENCES

Allport, G. *Pattern and Growth in Personality*. New York: Holt, Rinehart & Winston, 1964.

Bradburn, N. M., and Caplovitz, D. *Reports on Happiness*. Chicago: Aldine, 1965.

Caplovitz, D. *The Poor Pay More*. Glencoe, Ill.: The Free Press, 1963.

Freud, S. *A General Introduction to Psycho-Analysis*. New York: Liveright, 1920, pp. 308-309.

Gesell, A., and Lord, E. E., Psychological Comparison of Nursery School Children from Homes of Low and High Economic Status. *Journal of Genetic Psychology* 1927, 34: 339-56.

Hollingshead, A. B., and Redlich, F. C. *Social Class and Mental Illness*. New York: Wiley, 1958.

Rainwater, L. Some Aspects of Lower Class Sexual Behavior. *Journal of Social Issues* April 1966, 22: 96-108.

Zawadski, B., and Lazarsfeld, P. The Psychological Consequences of Unemployment. *Journal of Social Psychology* 1935, 6: 224-51.

Chapter 10

CHILDREN OF THE CITY: AFFLUENCE, POVERTY, AND MENTAL HEALTH*

Thomas S. Langner[1], Joseph H. Herson[2], Edward L. Greene[2], Jean D. Jameson[2] Jeanne A. Goff[3]

Little is known about the prevalence of mental disorders in children, and even less is known about the extent of mental disorders in children from differing socioeconomic statuses. Whether a child grows up in an environment of affluence or poverty is likely to have a significant effect on his mental health. The few studies of mental health in the general child population have not been oriented toward investigating types of behavior that psychiatrists and child psychologists believe are truly indicative of mental disorders.

10241024
*From the Columbia University School of Public Health and Administrative Medicine, (CUSPHAM) Division of Epidemiology. This investigation is supported by Public Health Service Project Grants #MH11545 and #MH18260 of the National Institute of Mental Health, Center for Epidemiologic Studies and Project Grants #348 and #10-P-56006 from the U.S. Department of Health, Education, and Welfare, Social and Rehabilitation Service, Division of Research and Demonstration Grants. Support for the Principal Investigator has been given by Career Scientists Grants #I-338 and #I-640 of the Health Research Council of the City of New York.

Statistical analysis had been done under the guidance of Prof. Jacob Cohen, New York University, and Dr. Patricia Cohen. Data processing has been handled by Fred Palm of Abacus Associates.

[1]Professor of Epidemiology, CUSPHAM, and Principal Investigator

[2]Research Associate, Department of Psychiatry, Columbia University College of Physicians and Surgeons

[3]Staff Associate in Epidemiology, CUSPHAM.

Often such studies deal only with symptoms, and do not make a total assessment of degree and type of impairment. In the following discussion a study is reported in which an attempt was made to determine the degree of psychiatric impairment within a population of urban (Manhattan) children. Among the goals of the research were to: (1) make prevalence estimates of the degree and type of psychiatric impairment and health in children and adolescents in a metropolis; (2) relate impairment to environmental and biological factors, especially familial and broader social variables, such as socioeconomic status; (3) compare estimates of impairment based on mother's reports with those based upon direct examination; (4) raise questions concerning our current definitions of mental health and disorder, and test their validity in several ways; (5) develop a relatively short, inexpensive screening instrument for use by schools, welfare departments, and other agencies that deal with large numbers of children.

RESEARCH METHODS AND PROCEDURE

Sample

Children used in the study were selected by a clustered random sample of 1,034 households on the East and West sides of Manhattan, New York City. One child was selected randomly from each household containing one or more children between the ages of six and eighteen. The 400 cases that form the basis of this report are in most respects representative of the final sample of 1,034, although the background characteristics may change somewhat in the final analysis. For instance, the initial ethnic distribution was 65 percent white, 16 percent Negro and 14 percent Puerto Rican. In the total sample, however, the proportions will be closer to 58 percent white, 12 percent Negro and 30 percent Puerto Rican and Spanish-speaking. The 1 to 1 sex ratio is expected to remain, and the age distribution is fairly even, with the exception of eighteen-year-olds (males are harder to come by, for obvious reasons). The average age of 11.7 years is about what might be expected.

Among mothers of children in the sample, 68 percent were born in the United States, 14 percent in Puerto Rico and 18 percent in other areas. Most (95 percent) of the respondents were the natural mothers of the children, and 83 percent were married at the time of the interviews. The widowed, divorced, and separated accounted for 5 percent each, the abandoned and never married for only 1 percent each. Nine children in ten had been in the natural mothers' care without interruption since birth. However, since 52 percent of the children were aged eleven years or less, there is reason to expect that a much larger proportion of them will have had some interruption in maternal care by the time they are eighteen. Stepmothers, female relatives, and grandmothers accounted for about 1 percent each of the respondents, and adoptive mothers for 2 percent. It is of interest to note that 36 percent of the midtown Manhattan adults studied in an earlier investigation had not lived with both parents through age eighteen (Langner and Michael, 1963). While not including any Negro adults, and only about 1 percent of Puerto Rican background, the sample did include a large proportion (about one-third) who were immigrants. Since family structure frequently suffers with migration from country to country, this might account for the high rate of "broken homes" in the present sample. It is doubtful that the final rate would reach as high as 20 percent, despite the low income of many families, if these children were all followed through age 18.

Mothers' education appeared similar in distribution to that of fathers', with the exception of graduate school (13 percent of the mothers, 23 percent of the fathers). Nineteen percent of mothers and 21 percent of fathers had grade-school education only. The model group for both was high school and trade school (43 and 35 percent, respectively), although a high proportion went as far as college (25 percent of mothers, 21 percent of fathers).

Average income is deceptive, for the large group of families with incomes of $15,000 and over (32 percent) is out of line with usual income distributions. However, the long tail found in most studies of income becomes bimodal here with a hump around $4,000 and another around $15,000. What this substantiates is that urban areas are rapidly becoming the homes of the rich and the poor and what has long been recognized as the flight of the middle class has become virtually an exodus. By a conservative estimate, two-fifths of the families visited in the initial sample fell below the "adequate health and decency budget" based on a standard of $7,200 as the minimum for a four-person family (Keyserling, 1967).

A large proportion (46 percent) of the mothers were employed. However, this might be considered somewhat low in terms of the total sample in view of the large number of families needing a second source of income. In 1952, one study showed that nationally 40 percent of mothers with school-age children were working (Applebaum, 1952). In the total sample it is expected that there will be a larger proportion of the Negro mothers working than of the white or Puerto Rican mothers. Of the fathers (or husbands), 91 percent were working, 4 percent were accounted for by unemployment and retirement, and another 2 percent by illness.

Psychiatric Interview

A two-hour home interview was conducted by a psychiatric social worker or the equivalent with the mother of each child in the sample. The interview covered the following areas: the child's current behavior with mother, father, peers, siblings, and in school; symptomatology that might be considered neurotic, psychotic, psychophysiological, and sociopathic; the mother's pregnancy and the child's development, including his medical history, his self-confidence and organization; parental practices and attitudes and parents' relationship to each other; and details of the family background. Special attention was given to the psychotherapeutic treatment history of the child, his parents, and siblings, and to the presence of any untreated psychological problems in the siblings.

Once the data were edited and punched, a special computer program produced three printed reports covering the questionnaire data. The first report covered symptomatology and role functioning, the second covered sociocultural background, and the third parental behavior. Using the first report, the psychiatrist rated impairment "blind" on a five-point scale (well-to-minimal, mild, moderate, marked, and severe-to-incapacitated) in each area of behavior. The psychiatrist initially used only the symptom printout, identifying the child only by age and sex. (It would have been impossible to judge whether any behavior was appropriate without knowing the sex or age of a child.) The psychiatrist (not the same person who had actually seen the child) next inspected the second printout of social background (race, socioeconomic status, religion, etc.), and made a second set of ratings that might or might not coincide with the first set. A third set of ratings was made upon seeing the parental behavior and attitude printout. After seeing each printout, ten areas of impairment, one global rating of impairment, a "caseness" rating (see below), and a diagnostic impression were assigned to the child. At the third rating, general etiological factors in the child's life—somatic, biological, physical, and psychological—were coded along with ten special stress factors, recommendations for intervention with child or family members, and prognosis with and without intervention.

The first rating permits correlating social data with impairment. The second allows the clinician to take into account mitigating circumstances which are exogenous, such as an immigrant child with language difficulty. Ratings may also be corrected in the direction of greater illness. The third rating gives an idea of what a total psychiatric evaluation might be if all information were present—it is closest to a rating based upon direct examination using all clues. This rating is useful for estimating the actual proportion of mental disorder assuming that a satisfactory cutoff point on the rating scale can be found—an unwarranted assumption, in our experience. Inter-rater agreement has been satisfactory on the five-point impairment scales. One psychiatrist examined the child directly, and two others rated the child from the protocol of the direct examiner. Average correlations between paired raters ranged from 0.69 to 0.77, based on data from one hundred cases.

Another approach to the distinction between health and illness is made through a "caseness rating." With each set of impairment ratings a five-point caseness rating is made, similar to the four-point scale used in the Stirling County Study (Leighton et al., 1963). This is an estimate of the confidence of the psychiatrist, in percent (using five categories: 10, 25, 50, 75 and 90 percent), that there should be some form of therapeutic intervention in this child's situation. The confidence rating gives the rate of potential "cases." Impairment and caseness are not identical, of course. For example, a child may show little overall impairment, but have early first-grade reading difficulties caused by sensory problems, as in specific dyslexia. Current impairment would be only moderate, yet caseness would be high, perhaps 90 percent sure, since special visual and other sensory training is strongly indicated.

In addition to interviews with 1,034 mothers, about three hundred of the children were given a direct one-and-one-half-hour psychiatric interview by Dr. Greene or Dr. Herson, and in some cases by Dr. Jameson. These examinations followed a detailed guide, responses were recorded on this guide, and some interviews were tape-recorded and rated independently for reliability purposes. In addition, all the principal symptoms were coded on an extensive precoded list to facilitate the comparison of symptoms elicited by direct examination of the child with those given by the mother during the interview.

Certain methodological emphases and methodological improvements over previous surveys should be mentioned.

1. Direct examination was conducted on about 30 percent of the children in addition to the evaluation through use of a mother's questionnaire.

2. Emphasis was placed on role functioning, as opposed to heavy emphasis in previous adult surveys on psychophysiological symptoms. We noted the strengths of the child—hobbies, awards, and special interests. The child was rated in ten functional areas, most of them involving role expectations: relationship to mother, father, siblings, and peers. Symptom impairment (general impairment not confined to one behavior setting), and impairment of self-confidence were also rated. The weight of the ratings, however, was on the side of role performance.

3. There was a built-in attempt to compare or calibrate the mother's report of the child's behavior with direct psychiatric examination, school records, and with standard tests such as Draw-a-Person and Bender-Gestalt. The direct examination cannot be viewed as a validation method, but as a different method of evaluating the child.

4. Stress scores were based not only on the mother's questionnaire data, but also on five-point psychiatric ratings of severity of each stress made after an hour and a half with the child and a half-hour with the mother.

5. An elaborate rating system was used that initially withholds background data from the psychiatrists to assure that relationships between social variables (such as class or race) and impairment or diagnosis are not built in to the ratings, except in the direct examination.

6. Diagnostic impressions were made of each child and also of the mother. The revised diagnostic list makes it possible to effectively diagnose well children into personality types; thus, a child may be well but shy. Most of the labels usually employed in diagnosing personality disorders were attached to the label *well;* for example, "well with compulsive personality." Thus, diagnostic impressions could cover the full range of disorder and health in the general child population.

7. In addition to using, with minor revisions, the diagnostic definitions of children's disorders given by the American Psychiatric Association (Group for the Advancement of Psychiatry, 1966), our psychiatric team produced a series of cue points for the rating scales. Since these scales specify the types of role and other behavior in all areas of the child's life, we approach an explicit and public, hence replicable, measure of mental disorder in children.

RESULTS OF DATA ANALYSIS

Prevalence of Emotionally Disturbed Children in the Midtown Area of Manhattan

One hesitates to present, perhaps prematurely, the distribution of total impairment ratings. There is a natural desire to cut distributions of this sort into "sick" and "well," but these labels cannot be assigned to portions of a continuum of impairment without doing injustice to the data. Intervention and the confidence (expressed in percentages) that it should be undertaken is expressed in caseness ratings which are separate from total impairment. In actual fact, the two ratings are highly correlated, yet the distinction must be made, for there are some cases where a specific treatment may be strongly recommended for a child with mild total impairment.

With these caveats in mind, the distribution of impairment for the four hundred children in the part of the sample reported here may be examined. Immediately striking is the fact that well children (or those with minimal impairment) constitute only 9 percent of the sample. Next is the modal group, mild impairment (40 percent), and it seems logical that the usual child would have mild impairment, would not be symptom-free, and would have some problems. Also striking is the low proportion of children with severe impairment or incapacitation (1 percent). Those of us who rate the children and who have examined several hundred directly in the community feel that a rating of three, or moderate impairment (38 percent), is some cause for concern. Children with marked (12 percent) or severe impairment may be in serious condition and should have some type of clinical consultation. Together these constitute 13 percent of the sample, and are surely more than our child psychiatric facilities could presently service. It is clear that not all of these children would be effectively treated by clinical intervention alone.

The reader should be alerted at this point to an important methodological adjustment made in the distribution of impairment ratings. In order to maximize the number of cases that could be analyzed at this time, we pooled the ratings based upon direct examination with the indirect ratings made from the computer printout of the mother's report. This immediately gives rise to the possibility that the two methods, though highly correlated, produce two distributions that are a certain distance apart. The suspicion that the methods yielded two distinct distributions was tested, employing the ridit. This is a cumulative percentile ranking, based on the total distribution of ratings, that can be averaged (Bross 1958). The computation of the ridits for the direct psychiatric examinations and the printout ratings showed that the impairment risk of children rated by the printout method was significantly greater (at the 1 percent level of confidence). This meant that our methods might to some extent be responsible for the distribution of ratings. We find that 14 percent of the direct and only 4 percent of the indirect cases were rated well. This is doubtless a function of several factors: (1) the tremendous impact of seven hundred symptoms printed out in booklet form for the psychiatrist; (2) the mitigating effect of the child's speech, looks, manner, and tone of voice, as opposed to a disembodied case record; and (3) the inability of the psychiatrist to elicit the large number of symptoms from a child in about half the time that the interviewer spent with the mother. For example, several suicide attempts were mentioned in the mothers' interviews that did not come out in the direct examinations, simply because this particular question was not asked routinely by the psychiatrists.

The more data one sees, the more pathological the individual looks. This is an old saw of psychological testing. A recent study also showed that direct methods usually uncover less pathology than indirect methods (Buehler, 1966).

Analysis of direct and indirect ratings does not yield a great discrepancy at the other end of the scale, however. The tendency to rate children as "worse off" is concentrated mostly in the middle of the distribution. Eleven percent and 12 percent of the direct and indirect ratings were in the marked category (a rating of four), and 0 percent and 3 percent fell in the severe group (a rating of five). Thus the most impaired end of the scale shows only 11 percent, using the direct examination, and 15 percent for the indirect. This is not a significant difference, unlike the well proportions. The resolution of the problem lies in the comparison of the same cases, rated by both methods. Preliminary impressions indicate that the indirect method "screens" more impaired children. Since one purpose of the study is to develop instruments to screen children prior to their being seen by a psychiatrist, the error of including more children for possible examination is preferable to missing some who are severely impaired.

The various types of disorders can be measured by areas of impairment and by diagnostic impressions. The seriousness of some disorders in the largely untreated sample of community children can be seen in the primary diagnostic distribution. Organic developmental conditions were not considered as primary diagnoses. Thus the proportions of children with brain syndrome (1 percent) and mental retardation (25 percent) are much lower than the actual proportions of such children in the community. Added to these two serious categories is the 5 percent estimated to have psychotic disorders. A total of 6 percent can be considered to have serious disorders, even if their current impairment is not severe. There are, in addition, many children with markedly impaired personality disorders and some impaired psychoneurotics.

Only 8 percent of the children were considered neurotics, but an unexpectedly large group (45 percent) exhibited personality trait disorders. Developmental deviations involved only 5 percent. The large percentage of reactive disorders (15 percent) as compared to less than 1 percent found in the adults in the Midtown study (Langner and Michael, 1963, pp. 403-404 and Table 15-1) is consistent with the diagnostic approach which states that individuals react to situations in their environment at an early age. Such situations then are either resolved or become internalized or crystalized into personality disorders or neurosis.

A factor to be taken into consideration in examining the low percentage of neurotic diagnoses in the children is the feeling among many child psychiatrists that the presence of well-crystalized neurotic-like symptomatology in children is indicative of a profound defect in personality. Many feel that to be so fixed in mode of adaptation at an early age is indicative of an underlying psychotic process. In view of this, it might be that we use neurotic diagnoses which mean one thing in adulthood and another in childhood. This problem can only be resolved by a longitudinal examination of these cases.

Before proceeding to more detailed analyses of these data, a word should be said about the parents of children in our sample. It was not unexpected that measures of the mother's mental health are closely related to the child's impairment. On a pilot sample of fifty-four cases which were selected for home visits by the psychiatrist, the mother's total impairment rating (assigned by the psychiatrist after seeing the child) was shown to be highly related to the child's total impairment. Mothers rated one, two, three, and four had children with impairment risks (ridits) of 0.33, 0.50, 0.66, and 0.85. This result might have been circular, since an interview with a disturbed child might have biased the psychiatrist against the mother if he thought, perhaps rightly, that such a child could not belong to a healthy mother. This halo effect has been avoided by utilizing symptoms elicited independently by the interviewer—mother's symptoms which the psychiatric rater does not see when assigning Rating I.

Father's absence shows a strong and definite relationship to the child's impairment. Children of absent fathers (without a stepfather) were worse off than those with fathers, in almost every impairment area, whether they were boys or girls (fourteen of eighteen comparisons showed increased impairment). However, it is of great theoretical and practical significance that the presence of a surrogate father seems associated with impairment which is greater than that found with the father merely absent but not replaced. This is true of total impairment, where 29 percent with surrogates and 26 percent with no father are impaired among boys, while 27 percent with surrogates and only 11 percent with no fathers are impaired (4+) among girls. This trend in total impairment is reflected in most of the functional areas, for impairment among children with surrogate fathers is greater than among those with father absent in eleven of eighteen comparisons.

What about sex differences? Boys without fathers are slightly better off than those with surrogates (26 percent versus 29 percent are 4+), while girls without fathers are much better off than those with surrogates (11 percent versus 27 percent). The simplest explanation seems to be in terms of identification patterns, for the mother remains as a model for girls who have lost their fathers, but boys have lost a role model.

Background Characteristics of Children with Impairment

Boys showed a greater proportion of 4+ impaired (marked or severe) than girls (16 percent versus 10 percent). This is in accord with most studies of "treated" populations, which indicate that boys in treatment outnumber girls by two or three to one. Interestingly, no age differences were found when data were grouped in six-to-nine-year-olds (13 percent); ten-to-thirteen-year-olds (12 percent); and fourteen-to-eighteen-year-olds (13 percent). Although studies of adults have shown increasing impairment with increasing age, we have found no sharp differences, at least within the age range studied.

Sharp differences by ethnic background appeared: in the marked + group were 11 percent of the white children, 19 percent of the Negro children, and 16 percent of the Spanish-speaking children. At a later point it will be seen that income and other social-class factors do not vitiate these findings.

Differences among children of various income groups were distinct, showing a rapid rise in impairment in lower-income groups. This finding has been repeated in some eighteen out of twenty-two studies of mental disorder in adults (Dohrenwend and Dohrenwend, 1965). The impairment of children (8 percent of the higher-, 12 percent of the middle-, and 21 percent of the low-income group) mirrors the impairment of adults who are their parents. This finding is important, for it has been argued that adults who are mentally ill drift downward, and that this drift, or social selection, accounts primarily for the association between mental disorder and socioeconomic status. Our data suggest that the social selection process may take place in adolescence through school dropouts, but essentially the die is cast long before the older teenager succeeds or fails to take his place in the occupational world. If our figures stand up, a child whose parents are in a low-income bracket has more than twice the chance of being psychiatrically impaired than a child whose parents are in a high-income bracket.

Is this impairment a function of income, or of ethnic background, or both? Data showed that there is a distinct income difference within the white group, for 20 percent of the low-income (under $6,500) whites and only 8 percent of the high-income (over $6,500) whites exhibit marked impairment or worse. However, contrary to our expectations, there are no real differences between Negro children of low income (18 percent) and those of high income (19 percent). What this suggests is that as Negroes attain higher incomes, various environmental forces such as prejudice and job discrimination, which in turn may have effects on family organization and relationships, prevent their children from obtaining a commensurate reduction in impairment. The source of income probably varies among groups, and must have a profound effect on family life. Among high-income Negroes income is clearly the result of the husband's and wife's combined low wages, with almost all mothers working full time. Spanish-speaking children of high income (15 percent) also do not show a sharp reduction in impairment over low-income peers (17 percent). Later analyses will attempt to indicate what aspects of parental character, child-rearing practices, and other factors might account for the surprising impairment of high-income Negro and Spanish-speaking children.

Mother's birthplace can be used as a rough indicator of nationality background at this point. The data suggest that mother's immigration alone is not the important factor in the elevated impairment rate of Puerto Rican children (20 percent were 4+). When compared with the impairment rate of children of immigrant German mothers which is half that high (10 percent), the Puerto Rican rate suggests that poverty and discrimination are the determining factors, rather than immigration itself. The midtown adults who were wealthy immigrants showed little impairment, while poor immigrants had a high risk of impairment. Of course, the circumstances under which one migrates constitute the stress of migration, not the fact of migration alone. The reception the migrant receives is also crucial.

Interruption of maternal care shows a moderately strong relation to impairment. Twenty percent of the children who had not been in their mother's care since birth were impaired, against only 12 percent of those who had been constantly in her care. This relationship is stronger than that found for adults who were or were not in their mother's care through age 18 (Langner and Michael, 1963). Perhaps the immediate effects are seen in these children, but the long-range effects of separation are not as great as we had imagined.

Marital status of the mother is related to impairment, but not in a simple fashion, such as married versus unmarried. Children of divorced mothers show high impairment (18 percent). However, children of separated or widowed mothers show no elevation of impairment (9 and 11 percent, respectively). These data do not support the hypothesis that paternal death is interpreted by the child as abandonment. One would expect resentment of the fathers in such cases, and consequent impairment. We know that adults who lost their fathers before they were eighteen were not significantly worse off than adults who did not. In contrast, many studies indicate that the disunity of the parents which leads to divorce is a primary factor in impairment. The impairment associated with quarrelsome homes is much greater than that associated with homes broken by death.

Parents' education is dramatically related to the child's impairment. While 21 percent with grammar-schooled mothers were impaired, only 14 percent of those whose mother completed high school, 10 percent of those with semiprofessional and college-level education, and 4 percent of those whose mothers had graduate-school education were impaired. If education were broken down into complete and incomplete, its discriminating power for impairment of the child would be even higher. This is because the educational attainment of the mother is closely related to her physical and mental health, and this is particularly true if she is a dropout. Many low-income children discontinue their schooling for financial or motivational reasons, or because schools they attend are poor. However, as one ascends the income ladder, the dropout is more likely to be a psychiatric casualty, rather than a social one. Father's education shows a similar trend.

There was no relationship between the mother's paid employment and the child's impairment. Adults in the midtown sample whose mothers worked part time (rather than full time or not at all) were healthiest. In this preliminary sample, 46 percent of the mothers had paid employment.

The number of different addresses at which the child had lived in the city bears a slight relationship to impairment. There is a definite increase from those who have lived at one address since birth (9 percent) to those who have lived at two addresses (16 percent). After this point, there is no clear-cut evidence of a trend.

Impairment in Relation to Age, Sex, Income, and Ethnic Background

The various types of impairment were first examined in relation to age, sex, and income simultaneously. Sex and income (three levels: low = under $6,500, middle = $6,500-$15,499, high = $15,500 and over) were examined first. If any relationship to age was apparent, special note was taken. It is clear that low-income males had a higher rate of developmental impairment (9 percent are 4+, as opposed to a range of 3 to 7 percent in the other cells). Among low-income males we found that impairment of development was concentrated mostly in the young (19 percent of the six-to-nine-year-olds). Other sex and income groups did not show this clear pattern of impairment of development in the younger age groups.

Boys alone showed marked or severe school impairment. Two-thirds of the nine boys with marked + school impairment were in the low-income group, one-third in the middle-, and none in the high-income group. These boys are mostly in the fourteen to eighteen age group, the age of the school dropout. Serious school problems clearly center in teenage low-income boys, not girls.

There was only a slight tendency for low-income children to show increased impairment in peer relationships. Impairment of sibling relationships was more common among high-income boys and girls, and income differences were more pronounced among high-income girls. The proportion of moderate + ratings (three or over) was used, since few children received 4+ ratings in the sibling area. Among high-income females there was a slight increasing trend with age, and the opposite trend for high-income boys. The increasing intensity of sibling rivalry as income increases fits with our observations, and has been contrasted with peer group formation among low-income siblings, who may band together against their parents. Low-income females showed twice the average impairment of the relationship to their natural mothers (6 percent), but high-income males show no marked + impairment in this sphere. Other groups showed 2 percent or 3 percent marked *plus*.

The older low-income females show more impairment in their relationship to mothers than the younger females. However, 13 percent of middle-income, fourteen- to eighteen-year-old males were in the 4+group, the highest single rate. The obvious inference of an Oedipal attachment in the middle-income group ("the middle-class male child and neurosis") is misleading, for this is a rare diagnostic category in the first place (8 percent). The trend is toward an increase in impairment of the relationship to mothers with increasing age of the child. This much is in accord with our expectations.

Impairment in relation to natural fathers was marked among low-income children of both sexes. However, low-income females (19 percent) showed almost twice the impairment of the males (11 to 12 percent). Most striking is the absence of such ratings in middle- and high-income girls, which further accentuates the high rate for low-income girls. The relationship to natural fathers was strikingly poor in a study of Negro and Puerto Rican teenagers (Langner, Gould, and Miller, 1963). Fathers were seen as authoritarian, as interfering with girls' dating, as often cold, and as absent a great deal. Teenage females had no higher proportion of impaired relations with father (21 percent) than the six- to eight-year-olds. Again, the older children of each sex and income level showed an increase in impairment with father. While this sounds like adolescent rebellion, it is all too easy to write off long-term impairment as temporary *Sturm und Drang,* or growing pains. Masterson (1967, p. v) has expressed this well:

> The symptomatic adolescent, as suggested by Thoreau's theme, is believed to step to a different drummer only temporarily under the surge of adolescent growth process. However, the music to which the adolescents we studied stepped was not a transient melody orchestrated by growth and development, but a persistent and pervasive symphony arranged by psychiatric illness. Its somber cadence pursued these patients through their adolescent years into adulthood.

Impairment associated with symptoms (ranked on the number of areas of functioning affected and amount of distortion or crippling of the child's life by these symptoms) is clearly predominant among low-income males (24 percent). High-income males (contrary to most types of impairment) also showed an elevated rate (15 percent). The proportion in this group, however, increases with increasing age. Thus both younger low-income males and older high-income males were affected. Low- and middle-income females had about twice the rate of the highs (10 and 11 percent versus 6 percent). However, no consistent age pattern appeared among girls.

Self-confidence is at its worst among the low-income boys (15 percent).

This impairment decreases with higher income among males. Females show no differences across income and, in general, the low-income males alone have elevated rates. No consistent pattern with age is apparent. This is our most difficult rating, and agreement is usually lowest here; nevertheless, it shows the same general pattern, in that low-income males have the greatest risk.

Total impairment shows the expected trend in relation to income among girls (6 percent of the highs, 10 percent of the middles, and 12 percent of the lows). However, among boys, the lows and highs are elevated, the middles not as impaired (low = 24 percent, middle = 9 percent, high = 13 percent). The absence of relationship between age and total impairment noted previously obscures the fact that there are some sex and income cells with definite age trends. Lumping these trends together, we get the impression that girls are more likely to improve with age, while boys are more likely to get worse with age. Part of this is due to cultural patterns, for the very definition of manhood and the life goals of the male are often awry. The pseudotoughness required for male emancipation and the unique quality of our "sissy complex" attest to this. This break with the mother may, however, be reflected in our ratings of impairment with natural mother, which should increase with age but did not show a trend. Perhaps our definition of illness still depends too much upon what gets the individual into trouble with society. Girls, being more prone to aches and complaints than to acting out their problems (as many studies of psychophysiological complaints have shown), are less likely to get into trouble. Their overall impairment is less than that of boys, their treatment rate lower, and impairment in their roles in the later teens and especially after marriage less easy to detect.

The caseness rating follows the total impairment pattern very closely (except among middle-income males). Looking at age as well, the difference in the proportion of children of different groups rated five for caseness ranged from 0 percent (high-teen females) to 35 percent (low-six- to-nine-year-old males). If, for one reason or another, these problems must be approached by mass methods focused on a single group, it would be advisable to choose a group such as the six-to-nine low-income males, since a larger proportion of children would be getting help at one time. In essence this is the philosophy behind programs such as Head Start. Yet, looking at the various categories, this leaves a great number of other children of all types in need.

A usually very fruitful combination of two control variables is ethnic background and income, which we will now discuss. Although there was a large difference in the proportion of 4+ impaired between high- and low-income whites (20 versus 8 percent), there was no difference among Negroes

(18 and 19 percent) and little among Spanish-speaking children (17 and 15 percent). Since most studies show a difference in symptomatology, impairment, or related measures that favor the higher-income or higher-status groups, our data need explanation. One of the first tasks was to check our methods. Perhaps this was an artifact of the direct examination, which includes the bias of recognizing the child's racial background or ethnic background. Ratings based on the direct examination of the child showed essentially the same relationships. There was apparently no psychiatric bias, which would probably have acted to lower the impairment rating of a Negro child in a more luxurious apartment. The proportion of Spanish-speaking children rated marked + was also not diminished greatly by better clothing, neater surroundings, and other characteristics of the wealthier environment.

The indirect ratings were made without any information concerning the ethnic background or income of the child. Analysis by ethnic background and income showed essentially the same relationship emerging from this blind procedure. There was a sharp income difference among whites (25 percent of the lows versus 11 percent of the highs). The Negro children rated blind showed the beginnings of a reversal, for 20 percent of the lows and 25 percent of the highs were rated 4+ using a blind method. (An inadequate number of Spanish cases was rated from the printout to assess whether the same relationship holds true for them in the blind-rating system.) The lack of bias in the direct ratings and the similarity of pattern (despite general elevation of the ratings) found in the blind (printout) ratings reaffirms our feeling that the elevation of the high-income Negroes and to some extent the high-income Spanish is not an artifact.

Another source of error might be found in the statistics. A different impression might be obtained if the ridit, which gives an average figure for each subgroup, were substituted for the percentage of marked +. The measures describe different things—one proportion deals only with the extreme cases, while the ridit covers the entire range, assessing subtler shifts within the distribution. We can examine the ridits for the six ethnic and income groups. The larger the ridit, the worse off the group in question. White children again showed improvement in the high-income group (lows, 0.56; highs, 0.45). Negro children showed no improvement (lows, 0.59; highs, 0.61). If anything, the high-income Negro children run a slightly greater (though not statistically significant) risk. Spanish children, however, showed a decrease in risk that they did not show in the percentages of marked + (lows, 0.53; highs, 0.38). The shift in the Spanish group was in the middle ratings, at which the ridit is sensitive.

The ridits for the direct examination alone showed the same pattern for whites and Negroes as shown by the indirect ratings. The whites showed a decrease (lows, 0.48; highs, 0.40) and the Negroes showed a sharp increase (lows, 0.46; highs, 0.55). The Spanish, however, showed the same decrease in the higher-income group (lows, 0.55; highs, 0.38). The indirect ratings alone showed the same pattern as the direct ratings, but there were no Spanish high-income cases. Since this rating was blind, and the use of a different statistic did not affect the relationships involved for whites and Negroes, we have again confirmed the results.

If we have uncovered an unexpected increase in impairment among higher-income Negro children ($6,500+), does this same trend hold in all areas of impairment? Is it exaggerated in particular roles, reduced in others? Data showed that developmental problems were reduced among high-income whites and Spanish, but not among Negroes. And the only high-income child with marked + school impairment was Negro, which is in keeping with our impressions. Peer relationships, however, were consistently worse in the low-income Negro group.

We found previously that high-income whites showed an increase in sibling impairment. This area and the area of self-confidence are the only two in which high-income whites showed no great improvement over the lows. Both white and Negro highs showed a slight elevation of sibling impairment. Only the Spanish group showed a decrease. The latter group's patterns are perhaps unstable, due to the small number of cases (13) of high-income Spanish.

Impairment in relation to natural mother was elevated only among high-income Negroes. Implications are that the matriarchal family is stressful for the male child, and this result could certainly have been expected. While relations to natural father were worse among low-income Negroes (and no marked + ratings were made in the low white group), the high Negroes again were alone in having 5 percent in this category. Relations to both parents were poor among Negroes, but more so in the high group in contrast to whites and Spanish.

Symptom impairment showed the typical sharp reduction in the high-income group among whites, 23 versus 9 percent, but not among Negroes, 21 versus 19 percent, and Spanish, 11 versus 8 percent. Self-confidence, as mentioned before, did not show the reduction of 4 + ratings among high whites. However, whites in general and high Spanish children exhibited low rates. High Negroes showed little improvement in self-confidence. One cannot help but feel that all these data point to the consequences of discrimination against Negroes, which robs the family of cohesion, and has its repercussions in interparental and parent-child conflicts.

If we consider only those children rated with 90 percent confidence, about half as many high as low whites were judged "cases" (8 versus 15 percent). However, 33 percent of high Negroes and only 21 percent of low

Negroes were considered as "cases." The Spanish, like the whites, showed a decrease among the highs. In most impairment areas, then, the high-income Negro child is particularly unfortunate, and one-third of this group could be considered likely candidates for some type of help. Whether this intervention is social or psychiatric or financial (in relieving the working mothers so prevalent in this subgroup) is largely irrelevant, since a multi-factorial attack to the problem is the only successful approach. We will attempt later to sort out some of the familial and social factors associated with this unexpectedly high incidence of pathology. Parents' awareness of their child's impairment is indicated, but only very roughly, by the question, "Does anything about your child's behavior worry you?" It is evident that both high-income whites and high-income Negroes are much more likely than lows to worry about their children's behavior, while the Spanish show no income differences. About one-third of the whites, two-fifths of the Negroes, and one-fifth of the Spanish tried to get help for the problem. Among high-income whites and all Negroes, a much greater proportion worried about their child's problem than did anything about getting help. This may be fortunate, since the proportion worrying mounts as high as 81 percent of the high-income Negroes. In general, there was a slight trend for the low-income parents to seek more help. This might be expected, in view of the greater need of their children, Negroes excepted.

Parental and Child Characteristics According to Ethnic Background and Income

The problematic increase of impairment in high-income as opposed to low-income Negro children was discussed briefly above. The background characteristics of parents, particularly income and ethnic origin, are closely related to the child's impairment, but in rather complex ways. Understanding the dynamic aspects of the unexpected increase of impairment in a higher-income group is a challenge that is hard to meet in a preliminary report based upon less than half the sample. By selecting not only parental characteristics, but also characteristics of the children (behavior) and examining the differential distribution of these characteristics within each ethnic and income group, a better understanding of the unexpected distribution of impairment may be obtained.

The cutting point of $6,500 annual family income was used because it not only approximates the $6,000 level below which Medicaid can be obtained for families with two children, but is high enough to allow us a sizeable group of low-income whites (thirty-nine cases). The high-income Spanish group, however, becomes very small due to this cutoff (thirteen cases). It was deemed better to use a cutting point across the board, rather than adjust it within ethnic groups. This still does not mean that differences in income are on the same scale, since family size and number of people working will have to be considered in developing a final index.

The highest educational level attained by the mothers showed a five-fold increase in the proportion of college-educated (or higher) in the high-income whites over the low-income whites (13 percent versus 63 percent). The ratio for Negro mothers was only 1.4, however (11 versus 15 percent). The expected increase in higher education among high-income Negro mothers was not confirmed. We know, of course, that Negroes in general do not have the educational opportunities of whites, nor do their parents have the ability to make higher education seem meaningful when another wage earner is needed, when many available colleges are second-rate, or when funds are short. None of the Spanish-speaking mothers had any college, so no income comparisons are possible.

Father's education again showed the highs with more than five times as many college-educated as the lows among the whites (13 versus 73 percent). High-income Negro fathers, however, have about half the proportion of the college-educated that we find in the lows (5 versus 11 percent). Thus the high-income Negro fathers may be earning more money, but they have even less education than some of their low-income counterparts. Higher education, then, may not be the best way for Negroes to achieve financial stability, while for the white high-income male a college education is virtually the norm (73 percent). Again there is a possible factor in the greater impairment of high-income Negroes: the status disequilibration of their fathers, usually a higher income accompanied by a lower education. Having one foot high and the other foot low is believed by many to be more stressful than having both feet low. Whether this is true or not may be tested only by measures of mental disorder. We have little such information for fathers, but a fair amount for mothers. This includes a direct psychiatric estimate of total impairment on a large series of mothers seen in the home for a half hour or more.

The higher income of the high Negroes and Spanish is bought at a price. While equal proportions (49 and 48 percent) of high and low white mothers were working (and many of these on a volunteer or career basis), 81 percent of high Negroes and 69 percent of high Spanish were working. It was mentioned that children of working mothers who were "bread-winners" showed a very high impairment rate. Obviously, many of the Negro mothers in particular fill this role. High-income Spanish mothers, working in the needle trades, have often had an easier time getting skilled jobs than their husbands, a fact often cited as a possible cause of the breakdown of the fathers' authority among Puerto Ricans. The proportion of children not constantly in their natural mother's care since birth decreased slightly in the higher-income bracket of each ethnic group. However, between two and three times as many Negro and Spanish children as white children have not been with their mothers constantly.

High-income mothers, regardless of ethnic background, are more likely to be married than low-income mothers. For example, only 50 percent of low-income Negro mothers are married now, compared with 95 percent of high-income Negro mothers. Marital status, per se, does not explain the increased impairment of high-income Negro children.

Low birth weight (three to five pounds) was reduced in the higher-income groups (white, 12 percent; Negro, 10 percent; Spanish, 16 percent); low-income Negroes had the highest proportion (29 percent) compared with 16 percent and 18 percent of white and Spanish. Thus, income differences in low birth weight were greatest among Negroes. Premature births (seventh month or before) were scarce, but were reported for 5 percent of high and low Negroes, 8 percent of low Spanish, and 1 percent of high whites, but not by low whites or high Spanish. High-income Negroes, again, showed no "improvement" in rates in this relatively objective report of biological functioning.

More high Negro mothers have been in mental hospitals. Their husbands are less able to show affection, but this is a complaint of higher-income Spanish mothers, too. More high Negro fathers have seen a psychiatrist than lows, but this is expected. Disagreement over bringing up the children was proportionally five times greater among high than among low Negroes, but equal among whites. That 43 percent of the parents should disagree in this area is surprising, and no other subgroup approaches it. Negro marriages were more likely to be reported as less happy than those of the respondent's parents. The mother was most likely to be the "boss of the family" among Negroes, and least likely among Spanish. There were equal proportions of fathers and mothers acting as "boss" among Negro families, while twice as many fathers were the boss among low whites, four times as many among high whites, and seven to eight times as many among the Spanish. This corroborates the hypothesis of the matriarchal Negro family in very tangible terms. The range was from the Negro ratio of 1:1 to between 2:1 and 8:1 for other groups, signifying increasing paternal dominance.

High-income rather than low-income mothers all tend to say they "expect too much of their children." The increase is most striking among the Spanish (4 versus 39 percent). The highest proportion was among high-income whites, and this was previously shown to be related to lowered impairment, as well as "strictness." These expectations and demands, when not excessive, show the child that the parent is involved and cares for him. High-income Negroes do show some increase in demands, but not as great as the other two groups.

Fewer low-income Negroes get their children to do things by threatening, while more high Negroes employ this method than other highs. No Negro mothers spontaneously mentioned rewarding the child, while some whites and Spanish did at both income levels. About three-fifths of the white mothers used no physical punishment, compared to about one-third of Negroes and Spanish. Income differences here were of less importance than ethnic background. While spanking with a strap was fairly common among the lows (8, 16, and 19 percent of white, Negro, and Spanish, respectively), it was almost absent among the high except for 10 percent of the Negroes. Again this category seems to share the pathology and practices usually associated with lower-income levels, as if the parental socialization via Dr. Spock and television had not yet fully penetrated the practices of older generations.

Negro mothers were about five times more likely to punish by depriving the child of things or privileges than white or Spanish mothers. From 8 to 15 percent of the other mothers used deprivation, but 45 percent of the low and 52 percent of the high Negro mothers used some form of depriving the child. Note that a somewhat larger proportion of high mothers employed this method, when a reduction of such practices with greater income might well be expected. This reduction was present among the white and Spanish. Mothers punished more than fathers in all groups, particularly the high Negro and Spanish. The low Spanish group contained the greatest proportion of fathers who punish more than mothers (21 percent), while proportions of mothers ranged from 51 percent to 81 percent. Due to absent fathers the proportions would not always add to 100 percent, even if those who did not know or did not answer were listed. A fair proportion of white parents alone punished equally (10 and 17 percent of the low- and high-income group).

White mothers were most likely to use hugs and kisses when their child was unhappy (26 and 29 percent versus 9 percent or less of the other groups). Between 26 and 50 percent said they would "cheer them up." Fewer high- than low-income Negro mothers used this approach. Distraction was also used, but more by both whites and Negroes than by Spanish. More   the lows punished when their child was rebellious, but scolding was commonest among high whites (39 percent). "Talking about it" was reported most by high whites and Negroes. The McFarlane et al. (1954) study found that children of mothers who used verbal communication were healthier. Yet "tries to talk about it" was commonest among high whites, whose children are indeed the healthiest, and also among high Negroes, whose children were greatly impaired. Talking at a nonverbal child is known to be a poor method for a middle-class teacher to employ when dealing with children who have not been reared in this fashion. Yet it seems that the high-income Negro mothers do talk, at least by their own reports, and this poses a logical dilemma.

A few of the children's symptoms can be reviewed, though they are part of total impairment. More children lacked pride in their fathers than lacked pride in their mothers. We would expect that a greater proportion of low-income children were "not proud," due to the rejection of their parents by society in general. However, this was true for more high-income children among whites and Negroes in relation to mother, and again among Negroes in relation to father. The largest proportion of children hostile to their mothers was reported among high-income Negroes (14 percent). Hostile white children were reported by only 8 and 9 percent of their mothers. No Spanish mothers reported any feelings of hostility emanating from their children. The expression of those feelings, of course, is very limited in the Puerto Rican family.

As if to reinforce our argument that real environmental stresses exist in high Negro families leading to the greater impairment rates, 29 percent of these mothers reported that their child was hostile toward the father. Whites came next (10 percent), the lowest proportion being found among low Spanish (4 percent), the most traditionally patriarchal. Only 8 percent of low Negro children were reported as hostile to father (though they have more missing fathers and more divorces than the highs). Assuming that expression of such feelings is more permissible in Negro homes, how can we account for the income difference which is threefold (8 versus 29 percent)? Our guess is that although the Negro home has been matriarchal, the high-income Negro home is attempting to break this pattern through greater prestige and earning power of the father. This attempt to shift the pattern may cause more conflict in the family during the generation which is upwardly mobile.

Poor or fair health of the child was reported more by the high Negro and Spanish and less by the high whites. The difference is primarily only among Spanish: more high Negro mothers thought they might hurt their child. This and other negative aspects of mother's character structure can be measured by combining several questions concerning the mother's handling of the child or her own psychophysiological complaints. For brevity's sake these items have been considered as aspects of her character, and the highest proportion found in any subgroup has been given the rank of 1. These ranks were cumulated, and averaged. For low white, Negro, and Spanish they were 3.61, 3.14, and 2.89; for high white, Negro, and Spanish they were 4.32, 2.93, and 4.11. Ranking these in turn, it is clear that the Spanish lows had the highest proportion of mother's character and coping problems (rank 1), while Spanish highs had much less (rank 5). White highs and lows also showed an income difference in the expected direction (lows rank 4, highs rank 6). However, the Negro ranks were reversed, so that high-income Negro mothers had more problems on the average (rank 2) than low-income Negro mothers (rank 3). This finding alone makes us feel that a real elevation in impairment exists in high-income Negro children, and that it may be partially accounted for by the emotional impairment and coping difficulties of their mothers. Body complaints, lack of understanding of the child, changeableness, dissatisfaction in general and lack of enjoyment of her child, and a poor self-image all contribute to a picture of poor mothering in this higher-income Negro group. Behind this, we hypothesize, is the second-class citizenship, the ghetto, and its more devastating effects on the people who try to rise above it. Perhaps we are seeing in some small measure the price paid for upward mobility across what has been called caste, rather than class, lines.

In summary, there can be no doubt that our preliminary data show that low socioeconomic status and minority ethnic background are associated with greater impairment in urban children. The information also suggests that an increase in family income at the expense of having both parents work full time, without improvement of parental education, or without social acceptance of the family in the wider community, is not enough to diminish the rates of impairment among Negro and possibly Puerto Rican children.

Social Class and Psychotherapy

An attempt was made to determine the degree and type of therapy being received by children from different social classes. Mothers were asked if their child had had any therapeutic contact with a school counselor, psychologist, social worker, or psychiatrist. If they answered yes to any of these, they were asked how long ago the child was seen, and the duration of the treatment contact. A more meaningful assessment of the contact is obtained by including duration as well, for only 11 percent of the sample can be considered as having had a meaningful treatment contact (two months or more).

Level of income was controlled and treatment analyzed by degree of impairment, using three categories of impairment (one and two, three, four and five). Let us assume that the first group is not in need of intervention, that the third is, and that the middle group is on the fence and can be ignored temporarily. Results showed that only 36 percent of the low-income marked + (four and five) had therapeutic contacts, against 46 percent of the high-income marked +. While this is not a sharp difference, the highs may be getting a better share of treatment when need is held constant. This has been a fairly consistent finding. On the other hand, considering the fact that less than half of the high-income children in need have had any contact, our energies should obviously be directed toward providing facilities and an atmosphere conducive to their use for all social levels.

If a more meaningful measure (a two months' contact or longer) is used, only 25 percent of the low marked + against 34 percent of the high are included. If a year or more of contact is used as the criterion, the difference between low- and high-income groups disappears. Among the impaired, those children with long-term therapy must be the most severely damaged, or at least those causing the greatest difficulty in management at home and in school.

What of those children having therapy with little need (ratings one and two)? Thirteen percent of the highs with mild or minimal impairment versus 5 percent of the lows had some contact. In other words, almost three times as many children from high-income families had a contact which might be unnecessary. If the two month or longer contact is considered, 6 percent of the highs and none of the lows in the well-mild-impairment group were included. This is reminiscent of the large proportion of higher-income adults in therapy in psychiatrists' private offices in Manhattan (Srole et al., 1962) who fell into the well or mild rating categories when rated blind (without knowledge of their treatment status).

The type of therapeutic contact varied widely with income and ethnic background. Negro children were three to five times as likely to see a school counselor as white children, while few Spanish children saw one. Negroes also were more apt to see a social worker than Spanish. Whites, regardless of income, were most likely to see a psychiatrist. In fact, low- and high-income whites were the only groups receiving psychiatric therapy while still exhibiting low impairment (well or mild).

In all cases children with greater impairment were more likely to be getting therapy. While low, impaired whites were seeing psychologists (15 percent) and psychiatrists (11 percent) in fairly large numbers, low, impaired Negroes saw only a social worker (17 percent), and low, impaired Spanish saw only a school counselor (4 percent) or a social worker (4 percent). Therapeutic contacts are not likely to be wasted on Negro or Spanish-speaking children who are not in need.

When mothers of children who had a therapeutic contact were asked if it had been helpful, 47 percent of the low-income group (under $6,500) said yes compared with 65 percent of the high-income group. In interpreting this, one must take into account several factors: the original level of impairment, the quality of private versus public treatment, the greater average length of therapy for the high-income child, and the greater proportion of families self-referred among the high-income families. Our data show that it is typically the lower-income families who are forced to bring their children into therapy through the schools or the courts. Their reaction therefore is not likely to be positive.

The person or agency sending the child for help initially is most likely to be the mother alone (12 percent of both high- and low-income groups). The father alone is involved less than 1 percent of the time. However, both parents initiated the search for help in 2 percent of the lows, and 8 percent of the highs. This is a reflection of the differences in family structure, and the lack of communication between husband and wife in the blue-collar families. Here the sex division of labor is sharper, and mothers bear the primary responsibility of caring for the children and make decisions concerning them. Moreover, in some of these families the father is missing or merely a visitor, especially if the family is on welfare.

The school and the court sent 4 and 5 percent, respectively, of the low-income children, but none of the highs. Children referred by the court or the school exhibited greater impairment than those referred by the family. Less than 1 percent of the children were self-referred. The web of attitudes leading to therapy is even more complex in the case of children than it is among adults, for the parents' views of themselves and their children and their attitudes toward help, in addition to the degree of the child's impairment, are of primary importance.

REFERENCES

Applebaum, S. B. Working Wives and Mothers. *Public Affairs Pamphlet* November 1952, no. 188.

Bross, I. D. J. How to Use Ridit Analysis. *Biometrics* 1958, 14: 18-38.

Buehler, J. A. Two Experiments in Psychiatric Inter-Rater Reliability. *Journal of Health and Human Behavior* 1966, 7: 192-202.

Dohrenwend, B. P., and Dohrenwend, B. S. The Problem of Validity in Field Studies of Psychological Disorder. *International Journal of Psychiatry* 1965, 1: 585-610.

Group for the Advancement of Psychiatry, Committee on Child Psychiatry. *Psychopathological Disorders in Childhood: Theoretical Considerations and a Proposed Classification,* Vol. 6, Report no. 62. New York: Mental Health Materials Center, 1966.

Keyserling, L. United Federation of Teachers Research Report, quoted in an article by Gene Currivan, *New York Times,* June 9, 1967.

Langner, T. S., Gould, R. E., & Miller, B. S. *The Teenage Leadership Program: A Study in Personality and Social Change.* 1967. Mimeographed.

Langner, T. S., and Michael, S. T. *Life Stress and Mental Health.* New York: Free Press, 1963.

Leighton, D. C., Harding, J. S., Macklin, D. B., Macmillan, A. M., & Leighton, A. H. *The Character of Danger: Psychiatric Symptoms in Selected Communities.* New York: Basic Books, 1963.

McFarlane, J. W., Allen, L., and Honzik, M. P. *A Developmental Study of the Behavior Problems of Normal Children between Twenty-One Months and Fourteen Years.* University of California Publications in Child Development, Vol. 2. Berkeley and Los Angeles: University of California Press, 1954.

Masterson, J. F. *The Psychiatric Dilemma of Adolescence.* New York: Little, Brown, 1967.

Srole, L., Langner, T. S., Michael, S. T., Opler, S. T., and Rennie, T. A. C. *Mental Health in the Metropolis.* New York: McGraw-Hill, 1962.

Chapter 11

THE PSYCHOLOGICAL COSTS OF QUALITY AND EQUALITY IN EDUCATION

Urie Bronfenbrenner*

The costs of quality and equality in education—calculated, as they usually are, in dollars and cents—invariably turn out to be higher than expected. Not infrequently the public is unwilling to pay the price, and even when it does so, it is often with reluctance, pain, and resentment, both toward those who impose the payment and toward those who receive the benefits. The reasons for resistance are well known. Personal financial resources are slow to acquire, the demand invariably exceeds the supply, and what little we have is urgently needed to provide for ourselves and our families.

The sobering burden of this discussion is to show that all these considerations apply with even greater force when the costs of quality and equality are reckoned in psychological rather than in economic terms. Here, too, the price turns out to be far higher than anticipated, but the available resources are even more limited, the needs of self and family more pressing, and the pain and resentment at having to pay the price far more acute. Yet these costs will have to be met, for unless they are, no increase in school budget, however generous, no regrouping of pupils, however democratic, no new curriculum, however adapted to the child's environment, can bring either quality or equality in education to those who do not have them—nor, as I hope to demonstrate, even to those who do.

*Professor of Child Development and Family Relationships, Cornell University, Ithaca, New York. This paper was first published in *Child Development* Vol. 38 (1967).

To understand why this is so, we must come to terms with an unwelcome but nonetheless inexorable reality: whatever their origin, the most immediate, overwhelming, and stubborn obstacles to achieving quality and equality in education now lie as much in the character and way of life of the American Negro as in the indifference and hostility of the white community. The basis for this assertion follows.

THE PSYCHOLOGICAL CHARACTERISTICS OF THE NEGRO CHILD

Recognition in actual practice of the critical role played by psychological factors in the education of the Negro child begins with implementation of the 1954 Supreme Court decision that separate facilities are inherently unequal. Unfortunately, it all too often ends there. In many American communities enlightened leaders, both Negro and white, and their supporters operate on the tacit assumption that once the Negro child finds himself in an integrated classroom with a qualified teacher and adequate materials, learning will take place, and the deficiencies of the American Negro, and the judgments of inferiority which they in part encourage, will be erased.

Regrettably, this is not the case. Neither the scars of slavery which the Negro child still bears nor the skills and self-confidence of his white companion rub off merely through contact in the same classroom. This is not to imply that integration is impotent as an instrument of change. On the contrary, it is a desperately necessary condition, but not a sufficient one. Objective equality of opportunity is not enough. The Negro child must also be able to profit from the educational situation in which he finds himself. This he cannot do if he lacks the background and motivation necessary for learning. And the evidence indicates that these essentials are often conspicuously absent.

Lett us examine the data. Fortunately, most of the relevant facts a e already brought together for us in Pettigrew's (1964) *A Profile of the Negro American,* a masterful compendium and interpretation of the available research findings. We shall not concern ourselves here with the full array of facts that Pettigrew presents; they are eloquent testimony to the crippling psychological costs to the Negro of the inequality imposed upon him by slavery and its contemporary economic and social heritage. For our purposes those findings that bear directly and indirectly on the educability of the Negro child of poverty have been selected.

The first of these is the sobering statistic that the longer such a child remains in school, even in integrated classrooms, the farther behind he falls in relation to the norms for his age and grade. Such progressive retardation is reported not only for measures of academic achievement (Coleman, 1966; Deutsch, 1960; Kennedy, Van de Riet, and White, 1963) but also for scores on tests of general intelligence (Coleman, 1966; Deutsch and Brown, 1964; Kennedy et al., 1963; Pettigrew, 1964, Chapter 5). Moreover, the discrepancies between Negro and white children are not limited to poverty-stricken families. They are not only present across the socioeconomic spectrum but "the Negro-White differences increase at each higher SES level" (Deutsch and Brown, 1964, p. 27).

In analyzing the factors producing these results, investigators call attention to the inappropriateness of many test items to lower-class Negro culture. But at the same time they make clear that improvements in test construction will not change the fact of the Negro child's inferiority; he suffers from handicaps that are real and debilitating. For example, Deutsch (1960) cites evidence that, in comparison with white children from deprived socioeconomic backgrounds, lower-class Negro youngsters are especially retarded in reading and language skills. They also show a shorter attention span in any task that requires concentration and persistence. Deutsch's observations indicate that the lack of persistence reflects not only an inability to concentrate but also a lack of motivation and an attitude of futility in the face of difficulty. Thus he reports (Deutsch, 1960, p. 9):

> Time after time, the experimental child would drop a problem posed by the teacher as soon as he met any difficulty in attempting to solve it. In questioning after, the child would typically respond "so what?" or "who cares?" or "what does it matter?" In the control group (white children of "similar socio-economic level"), there was an obvious competitive spirit, with a verbalized anticipation of "reward" for a correct response. In general, this anticipation was only infrequently present in the experimental group and was not consistently or meaningfully reinforced by the teachers.

Deutsch's observations are confirmed by a series of studies, cited by Pettigrew, showing that "lower-class Negro children of school age typically 'give up the fight' and reveal unusually low need for achievement" (1964, pp. 30-31).

Not only does the Negro child feel powerless; he feels worthless as well. At the core of this sense of inferiority is the awareness of being black. From the age of three onward, Negro children begin to prefer white skin to black and to think of Negroes in general and of themselves in particular as ugly, unwanted, and "bad." Results of the numerous studies of this phenomenon, summarized by Pettigrew (1964, Chapter 1) are epitomized in an example he cites of a small Negro boy who served as a subject in one of these investigations. Asked if he were white or colored, he hung his head and hesitated. Then he murmured softly, "I guess I'se kind o' colored" (Pettigrew, 1964, p. 8).

It is this "mark of oppression" (Kardiner and Ovesey, 1951) that distinguishes the personality development of the Negro child from that of his white counterpart, especially in lower-class families. The psychological process and its consequences are summarized by the following excerpt from a more extended analysis by Ausubel (1958, p. 35):

> The Negro child . . . gradually becomes aware of the social significance of racial membership . . . He perceives himself as an object of derision and disparagement, as socially rejected by the prestigeful elements of society, and as unworthy of succorance and affection. Having no compelling reasons for not accepting this officially sanctioned, negative evaluation of himself, he develops ingrained feelings of inferiority.

The Negro child brings all of these intellectual, motivational, and emotional problems with him when he goes to school. The obstacles they pose to the learning process are reflected in the marked contrast in classroom atmosphere reported by Deutsch (1960) in his study of schools in Negro and white lower-class neighborhoods. In the former setting, 50 to 80 percent of all classroom time was devoted to disciplinary and other essentially nonacademic tasks, whereas the corresponding percentage for the white control group was about 30 percent.

What factors account for the special debilities and behavior difficulties of Negro children? The thesis, still militantly upheld by some investigators (Garrett, 1960, 1961, 1962a, 1962b; McGurk, 1956, 1959; Shuey, 1958; Van den Haag, 1964), that such deficiencies have an innate basis in race differences, has been so thoroughly discredited (Anastasi, 1956; Chein, 1961; Pettigrew, 1964) that it needs no extended consideration here. We would call attention, however, to one additional fact which, if acknowledged, presents an interesting problem to those who seek to account for Negro inferiority in genetic terms. The intellectual, emotional, and social deficiencies observed in Negro children are considerably more pronounced in boys than in girls. Systematic data on this point are cited by Deutsch (1960). For instance, in his sample of Negro school children in grades four through six, 38 percent of the girls and 68 percent of the boys scored below fourth-grade norms on the Stanford Achievement Test, the discrepancies being greatest on the reading subtest. No differences approaching this magnitude were found for the white controls. Similarly, in repeating digits forward or backward, Negro girls performed at about the same level as white controls, whereas Negro boys were markedly inferior to their white counterparts. Deutsch stresses the psychological significance of this difference in view of "the importance of attention for any academic learning and therefore the potential contribution of lowered attentivity to the achievement differences found" (Deutsch, 1960, p. 12). It is noteworthy that these sex differences in achievement are observed among southern as well as northern Negroes, are present at every socioeconomic level, and tend to increase with age (Kennedy et al., 1963, see especially Tables 68 and 60).

THE SOURCES OF INADEQUACY

Clearly any satisfactory explanation for the debilities of the Negro child must also account for the special ineptitude of the Negro male. Several lines of evidence are pertinent in this regard: the first is biological, the remainder social.

Organic Bases of Inadequacy

Though the Negro infant is not biologically inferior at the moment of conception, he often becomes so shortly thereafter. The inadequate nutrition and prenatal care received by millions of Negro mothers result in complications of pregnancy which take their toll in extraordinarily high rates of prematurity and congenital defect (Knobloch, Rider, Harper, and Pasamanick, 1956; Pasamanick, Knobloch, and Lilienfeld, 1956; Pasamanick and Knobloch, 1958). Many of these abnormalities entail neurological damage resulting in impaired intellectual functioning and behavioral disturbances, including hyperactivity, distractibility, and low attention span. Of particular relevance is the significant role played by paranatal and prenatal factors in the genesis of childhood reading disorders. In a retrospective comparison of hospital records, Kawi and Pasamanick (1959) found that instances of two or more complications of pregnancy were over nine times as frequent in the records of mothers whose children later exhibited severe reading difficulties as in a control population matched in social class and other relevant variables. Finally, it is a well established, though not thoroughly understood, fact that neurological disorders resulting from complications of pregnancy and birth are considerably more frequent for males than for females. This differential rate has been identified as a major factor in contributing to the consistent sex differences observed in incidence of neuropsychiatric disorders and psychological disturbances in children (Kawi and Pasamanick, 1959, p. 19). Of special relevance in this connection is the statistic that "behavior disorders are two to three times more common in boys, reading disorders as much as eight or nine times" (Pasamanick and Knobloch, 1958, p. 7). These authors see in "reproductive casualty" and its sequelae a major factor contributing to school retardation in Negro children generally and Negro males in particular. Organic debilities of course result not only in intellectual dysfunction but also in discouragement. In this manner they play a part in evoking the expectations of failure, the readiness to give up in the face of difficulty, and the low level of aspiration observed in Negro children, especially among boys.

The Impact of Paternal Absence

Even where organic factors do not set in motion the vicious circle of defeat and uninterest in achievement, social circumstances can be counted on to instigate and accelerate a similar downward spiral. A growing body of research evidence points to the debilitating effect on personality development in Negro children, particularly males, resulting from the high frequency of father-absence in Negro families. The extent of such absence is eloquently reflected in census figures summarized by Pettigrew (1964, pp. 16 and 17):

> Census data for 1960 illustrate the depth of this family disorganization among Negroes: over a third (34.3 per cent) of all non-white mothers with children under six years of age hold jobs compared with less than a fifth (19.5 per cent) of white mothers with children under six; only three-fourths (79.9 per cent) of all non-white families have both the husband and the wife present in the household, as compared with nine-tenths (89.2 per cent) of white families; and only two-thirds (66.3 per cent) of non-whites under eighteen years of age live with both of their parents as compared with nine-tenths (90.2 per cent) of such whites. . . .

The vast majority of incomplete Negro households lack the husband. Frazier estimated in 1950 that the male parent was missing in roughly 20 percent of Negro households. In addition to divorce and separation, part of this phenomenon is due to a higher Negro male death rate. The percentage of widows among Negro women fifty-four years old or less is roughly twice that among white women (Pettigrew, 1964).

The consequence of this state of affairs for the personality development of the Negro child is indicated by several lines of investigations. First, a series of studies conducted in the United States (Bach, 1946; Barclay and Cosumano, 1967; Kuckenberg, 1963; Sears, Pintler, and Sears, 1946; Sears, 1951; Stolz, 1954) and in Norway (Gronseth, 1957; Lynn and Sawrey, 1959; Tiller, 1957, 1961) showed that father absence has far greater impact on sons than on daughters. The results and their implications are summarized by Pettigrew (1964, p. 18):

> . . . father-deprived boys are markedly more immature, submissive, dependent, and effeminate than other boys. . . . As they grow older, this passive behavior may continue, but more typically, it is vigorously overcompensated for by exaggerated masculinity. Juvenile gangs, white and Negro, classically act out this pseudo-masculinity with leather jackets, harsh language, and physical "toughness."

Consistent with this line of evidence are the results of a substantial number of studies pointing to the importance of paternal absence and inadequacy in the genesis of delinquent behavior (Bacon, Child, and Barry, 1963; Bandura and Walters, 1959; Burton and Whiting, 1961; Glueck and Glueck, 1950, 1956; Miller, 1958; Rohrer and Edmonson, 1960; Scarpitti, Murray, Dinitz, and Reckless, 1960). In seeking an explanation for this relationship, several of the major investigators have concluded that the exaggerated toughness, aggressiveness, and cruelty of delinquent gangs reflect the desperate effort of males in lower-class culture to rebel against their early overprotective, feminizing environment and to find a masculine identity. For example, Miller (1958, p. 9) analyzes the dynamics of the process in the following terms:

> The genesis of the intense concern over "toughness" in lower class culture is probably related to the fact that a significant proportion of lower class males are reared in a predominantly female household, and lack a consistently present male figure with whom to identify and from whom to learn essential components of a "male" role. Since women serve as a primary object of identification during preadolescent years, the almost obsessive lower class concern with "masculinity" probably resembles a type of compulsive reaction-formation . . . A positive overt evaluation of behavior defined as "effeminate" would be out of the question for a lower class male.

The special relevance of this dynamic for public education is indicated in a similar conclusion drawn by Rohrer and Edmonson in their follow-up study of Negro youth in New Orleans. "The gang member rejects this femininity in every form, and he sees it in women and in effeminate men, in laws and morals and religion, in schools, and occupational striving" (Rohrer and Edmonson, 1960, p. 163).

Despite their desperate effort to prove the contrary, a latent femininity is nevertheless present in "fatherless" youngsters and results in a confused sex identity. Substantial support for this argument is found in the impressive number of studies, summarized by Pettigrew, that show that Negro men, especially those from lower-class homes, obtain high scores on indirect measures of femininity. Additional evidence points to father-absence as a critical factor. In comparison with a control group from intact homes, Negroes whose fathers were absent during early childhood were far more likely to be either single or divorced; in addition, "they also felt more victimized, less in control of the environment, and more distrustful of others" (Pettigrew, 1964, p. 20).

Nor are the consequences of paternal absence limited to the emotional and social sphere. A series of investigations by Mischel (1958, 1961a, 1961b, 1961c) points to the crucial role of this factor in the development of a capacity essential to achievement generally and to academic achievement in particular—the ability to delay immediate gratification in order to obtain a later reward. The systematic investigation of this phenomenon was suggested to the investigator by anthropological reports alleging "a major personality difference" between Negro and East Indian groups on the island of Trinidad. Numerous informants reported that the Negroes are impulsive, indulge themselves, settle for next to nothing if they can get it right away, and do not work or wait for bigger things in the future, but instead prefer smaller gains immediately (Mischel, 1958, p. 57).

In a series of ingenious experiments (e.g., a child is offered a choice between a tiny candy bar now, versus a larger bar in a week's time), Mischel (1958, 1961c) demonstrated that preference for immediate gratification was a distinguishing characteristic observable in Negro children of ten years of age and that the cultural difference could be attributed primarily, but not entirely, to the greater absence of the father among Negro families. In addition, the same investigator has shown that the desire for immediate gratification is associated with poorer accuracy in judging time, less achievement drive, lower levels of social responsibility, and a greater propensity toward delinquent behavior (Mischel, 1961a, 1961b).

The impact of paternal absence on actual school performance is reflected in Deutsch's (1960) finding that lower-class Negro children from broken homes were far more likely to score below grade level on tests of academic achievement than their classmates from intact families, and that the higher frequency of broken homes among Negro families accounted for most of the difference in achievement between the Negro and the white samples. Moreover, children from intact families did better in school than those from broken homes despite the fact that intact homes were more crowded, a circumstance that leads Deutsch to conclude that "who lives in the room is more important than how many" (Deutsch, 1960, p. 10). In a subsequent study, Deutsch and Brown (1964) showed that a significant difference of about eight points in IQ is specifically attributable to absence of the father from the home.

Finally, it is not only the absence of the Negro father that prevents the son from seeing the future realistically. Also relevant is the inferior position held by the adult Negro male in the economic world. In the matter of occupational choice the Negro boy has few models to emulate that are actually within the realm of possible achievement. This circumstance is reflected in a study of occupational aspirations among lower-class children (Deutsch, 1960, pp. 11-14). When asked what they wanted to be when they grew up, 25 percent of the Negro boys named high prestige professions such as doctor or lawyer, etc.—goals completely beyond practical realization and hence reflecting idle wish-fulfillment rather than an active achievement drive. In contrast, Negro girls were more realistic in scaling down their aspirations to occupations within their reach. Deutsch accounts for this difference in terms of the greater availability for the girls of an accepted role model both within the family and in the outside world.

The Impoverished Environment

We see, then, that the high incidence of both pathology and paternal absence among lower-class Negroes has produced psychological deficits and disturbances in Negro children, particularly boys. But there are other early influences, equally baneful, that do not discriminate between the sexes. Among these is another product of poverty, the absence of an educationally stimulating environment during the preschool years. Studies of this phenomenon, summarized in Bloom, Davis, and Hess (1965), indicate that the lower-class Negro home is barren of objects (books, newspapers, pencils, paper, toys, games) and of coherent social interaction. For example, in a study of the "Social World of the Urban Slums," Keller (1963) reports that the children had little sustained contact with adults, few organized conversations, and little shared family activity. In the same vein, a comparison of Negro and white lower-class children (Deutsch, 1960) revealed that the former had fewer books in the home, got less help with their homework, took fewer trips beyond a twenty-five-block radius from their home, ate less frequently with their parents, and spent less time with them on Sundays. Also, such verbal interaction with parents as did occur tended to be limited in complexity and completeness. For example, commands were likely to be one or several words rather than complete sentences, and were typically given without explanation or elaboration.

Patterns of Child-Rearing

An additional factor contributing to the inadequacies and problems of the Negro child is the alternately repressive and indulgent pattern of upbringing found in lower-class families in general (Bronfenbrenner, 1958) and in Negro lower-class families in particular (Davis, 1941; Davis and Dollard, 1940; Davis and Havighurst, 1946; Frazier, 1957; Rohrer and Edmonson, 1960). Discipline is exercised principally by the mother, is focused on overt acts rather than on motives or goals, and is mainly inhibitory in character; that is, the child is told not to do this or that, to keep quiet, not ask questions, stay out of trouble. The effect of such negative reinforcement is to discourage early initiative, curiosity, and exploration, as well as cooperative interaction with a guiding adult.

The Legacy of Slavery

It is noteworthy how many of the characteristics of the Negro family of today that are dysfunctional for modern society were functional for or at least adaptive to the conditions of bondage (Frazier, 1957). With the father constantly in jeopardy of being sold to another owner, a matriarchal family structure became almost inevitable. But since the mother, too, had to work, it was necessary to keep the child from interfering by his activity, questions, or misbehavior. Moreover, as McClelland (1961) has pointed out, slavery is incompatible with and destructive of a high drive for achievement, since the rewards of the slave come not from initiative and independence but from compliance. "Negro slaves should, therefore, have developed child-rearing practices calculated to produce obedience and responsibility not n-Achievement, and their descendants, while free, should still show the effects of such training in lower n-Achievement" (McCelland, 1961, pp. 376-77). In keeping with this prediction, Negro adolescents have the lowest scores in achievement motive among youth from six different ethnic groups in the United States (Rosen, 1959).

But the most important legacies of slavery were the conditions in which the American Negro found himself upon release from bondage—economic poverty and racial discrimination. The three together—slavery, poverty, and discrimination—lie at the root of the biological and social forces that produce widespread psychological debility and disturbance in the Negro child. From this perspective it is the white man who is in the first instance primarily responsible for the inadequacies of the Negro and his way of life.

THE INTEGRATED CLASSROOM AND THE DISINTEGRATED CHILD

But attribution, or even acceptance, of responsibility for damage does not eliminate the Negro child's deficiencies. Nor does placing him in an integrated classroom. On his arrival there he brings with him his full array of defects and disruptive behaviors. True, being able at least to sit with his white age-mates may, under certain circumstances (Katz, 1964), bolster his self-esteem, provide him with more competent models to emulate, and significantly improve his academic performance (Coleman, 1966). But integration cannot repair a damaged brain, supply a father, equip a home with books, or alter a family's values, speech habits, and patterns of child rearing. Thus in many cases the Negro child in the integrated classroom continues to be intellectually retarded, unable to concentrate, and unmotivated to learn; initially apathetic, as he gets older he will become resentful, rebellious, and delinquency-prone.

Moreover, in the integrated classroom all of these characteristics of the Negro child have their impact on his white companion. To begin with, unless countermeasures are introduced, they provide an objective basis and an emotional provocation for devaluating and rejecting the Negro, thus reactivating and reenforcing the vicious circle of discrimination and defeat (Coles, 1963; Katz, 1964). But the white child is affected in other ways as well. Although the findings of the Coleman report (1966) indicate that middle-class white children do not suffer academically from attending the same schools as lower-class Negroes, the analysis was not carried out on a classroom basis, nor did it examine other aspects of behavior besides test performance. As has been demonstrated in both field (Polansky, Lippitt, and Redl, 1954) and experimental (Bandura and Walters, 1963) studies, disintegrative and destructive behavior of peers is highly subject to contagion, against which contrasting values and practices of the family provide little immunity. In other words, the white child is likely to take on some of the aggressive and disruptive activities of his Negro classmates. Such developments are of course viewed with alarm by many white parents, who become understandably concerned about the consequences of integration for character development of their children. In short, in the integrated classroom, the problems of the Negro child become, at least in part, those of the white child as well. Thus the costs of inequality to the Negro become the costs of equality to the white.

COUNTERMEASURES AND CONSEQUENCES

These costs do not end with the impact on the classroom of the inappropriate behavior of the Negro child. While the damage already done to the latter by the time he enters school cannot be undone completely, some counteractive measures can be taken within the school environment, or under its auspices, which may entail still further psychological problems for the white community. For example, to a limited but significant extent a male teacher can serve some of the functions of the absent or inadequate father. The high incidence of fatherless families in the Negro lower class argues strongly for the involvement of many more men as teachers at the elementary level. The psychological costs here, to the extent that any exist, lie in the low prestige and the consequent threat to self-esteem that elementary teaching still holds for men in American society. This threat may be alleviated in part by the special need for Negro men as primary teachers. But they themselves may often be resented by the white community, not only on grounds of racial prejudice but also on the basis of their teaching effectiveness. Only a small proportion of Negro teachers have been able to enjoy the same educational opportunities, from early childhood on, as were available to their white colleagues and, for the reasons already outlined, it is the Negro male who is most likely to have been disadvantaged. For this reason if Negro teachers—especially Negro men—are employed in the large numbers in which they are needed, there could be a drop in the general level of instruction, for these teachers will not necessarily have as good command of subject matter as their predecessors, and their speech will deviate from the white middle-class norm. Yet, despite these deficiencies, such persons can do much more for the education of the Negro child than the more middle-class-acculturated white or Negro female who would otherwise be their teacher.

But exposing the Negro child to a male teacher of his own race is not enough. Given the absence of positive male figures in his out-of-school environment, the young Negro requires additional acquaintance with men, especially of his own race, who, by their example, demonstrate the possibility and attraction of masculine competence and constructive conduct in a variety of spheres. This need could be met through programs of after-school activities conducted by persons—both Negro and white—who possess such diverse skills and who have found a place in their community. The objective of such programs would be not so much to take the youngster off the streets (although they would have this effect if successful) as to involve him in patterns of interaction which can develop the basic skills, motives, and qualities necessary for a child to be able to profit from the classroom experience. In other words, these after-school activities are to be viewed as an essential part of the education process falling within the responsibility of those agencies charged with providing public instruction.

It should be stressed that the after-school program here envisioned is not prevocational training. Quite the contrary. The activities would be nontechnical in nature and would begin at levels accessible and attractive to the lower-class child—sports, games, selected movies, outings. In the beginning such activities would have to be conducted by persons trained or experienced in recreational activities, but gradually other adults would participate in them and the child would discover that one was a machinist, another worked in a bank, a third was a reporter on a newspaper, etc. The objective is to expose the child to and induce him to emulate models embodying the values, skills, and aspirations necessary for achievement in school and society.

There is no question that such programs would be difficult to develop and to administer, but there is some evidence that they are practicable. For example, in Soviet schools (Bronfenbrenner, 1962), members of the community are frequently invited to accompany children and participate with them in after-school activities, such as hikes and other expeditions, with the explicit aim of exposing the youngster to intimate contact with adults who combine specialized knowledge or skill with attractive qualities of character (of course from the communist point of view). A related practice long employed in Soviet schools is the involvement of adolescents and preadolescents in activities with young children. Recently, similar utilization of this age group, under appropriate supervision, has been urged in our own country in connection with Project Head Start. An early issue of the *Head Start Newsletter* (1965) pointed to the fact that, in certain respects, high school students can work more effectively than adults with young children because, no matter how friendly and helpful, grownups are still in an important sense a world apart, with abilities, skills, and standards so clearly superior to those of the child as to appear impossible to attain.

It is of course important that persons working in such programs, be they adults or teenagers, not be restricted to one race; but the same consideration applies for the children as well. Unless white youngsters are also involved in after-school programs, the activity once again becomes identified as an operation for second-class, second-rate citizens. Nor is it sufficient if participation is limited to children—Negro and white—from deprived backgrounds. A growing body of research (summarized in Bronfenbrenner, 1962; Millson, 1966) points to the conclusion that peers are at least as effective as adults, if not more so, in their capacity to influence the behavior of the child. From this point of view, it is desirable that children from more favored environments also be included in after-school activities, and, if they are, they are of course exposed to the deleterious as well as to the constructive influences present in that situation.

The after-school program has other difficulties as well. Indeed, some of these difficulties are a direct function of the degree to which the program achieves its objectives. To the extent that the Negro child acquires the skills and values of his new companions, he becomes further removed from his own family. The conflict which such separation can arouse both within the family and within the child himself can undermine whatever progress has been made and lead ultimately to debilitating problems of self-identity. Regrettably, this phenomenon has not yet been investigated systematically by psychologists. The best available data and analyses of the Negro's identity crisis appear in the works of such gifted Negro writers as Richard Wright (1945) and James Baldwin (1962). Because of this danger, it is necessary that, insofar as possible, the child's parents become actively involved in their child's new activities and new world. To modify the pattern of life of parents is of course far more difficult than to influence their children, but some opportunities nevertheless exist. One approach is that being employed in Project Head Start (Report of Planning Committee, 1965), where parents from low-income families participate as "paid volunteers" in a variety of tasks requiring little formal education or experience but at the same time involving close contact with professional workers as they interact with the children. In this manner, some parents—or, more realistically, some mothers—are exposed to new and different attitudes and methods in dealing with young children. The device employed in Project Head Start illustrates a general principle, the validity of which has been demonstrated in a substantial body of research in behavioral science generally and in the study of intergroup relations in particular: that attitudes and behaviors are changed most readily when people work together in pursuit of a common goal to which they are committed (Sherif, 1958; Williams, 1947, 1964). And the goal of bettering life for children is one which most parents are willing to pursue.

If we apply the foregoing principle more generally to the role of parents in programs for disadvantaged children in school and out, we come to a conclusion that should properly give us pause; the principle implies that parental involvement is necessary on the part of not only the underprivileged families, but the privileged as well. It is only through nonantagonistic exposure that the lower-class parent can come to tolerate, understand, and perhaps adopt the different way of dealing with his child employed by those responsible for his education. Accordingly, it becomes highly desirable for parents from more privileged circumstances—Negro as well as white—to become actively involved in programs concerned with the education of their children both in school and out.

We are asking a great deal. As we said at the outset, the psychological costs of quality and equality in education for all children are high. They require a new conception of the scope of public education as extending beyond school walls and school hours. They call for a far greater involvement in education of parents and other members of the adult community. They may even require some sacrifice in academic advancement for children from advantaged families to make possible academic survival for children from disadvantaged families. In short, they demand heavy payment from the haves in favor of the have-nots, not just in money, but in the far harder coin of psychological security and status.

And if we who have are willing to pay, what is achieved? Whatever we pay cannot be enough. Those who receive payment will still feel cheated, and rightly so. One cannot repay to the children of slaves the present costs of ancient bondage.

It is the tragedy and irony of injustice that those who seek to right it gain as much if not more than those who have been wronged. Paradoxically, it is not the disadvantaged Negro alone who would benefit from equality in education, were we truly to achieve it. For the only way in which we can give the Negro child equality is to teach the white child how to treat him equally. This will not happen from mere physical association in the classroom. It will require the actual teaching and practice, in school and out, of the principles of human dignity to which our society is dedicated. It is a sobering fact that in communist schools a deliberate effort is made to teach the child, through concrete experience, the values and behaviors most consistent with communist ideals (Bronfenbrenner, 1962, 1966). In American schools, training for action consistent with social responsibility and human dignity is at best an extracurricular activity. The belated recognition of our educational obligations to the child of poverty, white or black, offers us a chance to redress this weakness and to make democratic education not only a principle but a practice.

REFERENCES

Anastasi, A. Intelligence and Family Size. *Psychological Bulletin* 1956, 53: 187-209.

Ausubel, D. P. Ego Development among Segregated Negro Children. *Mental Hygiene* 1958, 42: 362-69.

Bach, G. R. Father-Fantasies and Father-Typing in Father-Separated Children. *Child Development* 1946, 17: 63-79.

Bacon, M. K., Child, I. L., and Barry, H., III. A Cross-Cultural Study of Correlates of Crime. *Journal of Abnormal and Social Psychology* 1963, 66: 291-300.

Baldwin, J. *Another Country.* New York: Dial Press, 1962.

Bandura, A., and Walters, R. H. *Adolescent Aggression.* New York: Ronald Press, 1959.

————. *Social Learning and Personality Development.* New York: Holt, Rinehart and Winston, 1963.

Barclay, A., and Cosumano, D. R. Father Absence, Cross-Sex Identity, and Field-Dependent Behavior in Male Adolescents. *Child Development* 1967, 38: 234-50.

Bloom, B. S., Davis, A., and Hess, R. *Compensatory Education for Cultural Deprivation.* New York: Holt, Rinehart & Winston, 1965.

Bronfenbrenner, U. Socialization and Social Class through Time and Space, in E. Maccoby, T. M. Newcomb, and E. L. Hartley, eds. *Readings in Social Psychology.* New York: Henry Holt & Co., 1958, pp. 400-425.

————. Soviet Methods of Character Education. *American Psychologist* 1962, 17: 550-64.

————. Response to Pressure from Peers Versus Adults among Soviet and American School Children, in *Social Factors in the Development of Personality.* 28th International Congress of Psychology Symposium, Moscow 1966, 35: 7-18.

Burton, R. V., and Whiting, J. W. M. The Absent Father and Cross-Sex Identity. *Merrill-Palmer Quarterly* 1961, 7: 85-95.

Chein, I. The Roots of Conspiracy. *Society for the Psychological Study of Social Issues Newsletter,* December 1961.

Coleman, J. S., et al. *Equality of Educational Opportunity.* Washington, D.C.: U. S. Office of Education, 1966.

Coles, R. *The Desegregation of Southern Schools: A Psychiatric Study.* New York: Anti-Defamation League, 1963.

Davis, A. *Deep South.* Chicago: University of Chicago Press, 1941.

Davis, A., and Dollard, J. *Children of Bondage.* Washington, D.C.: American Council on Education, 1940.

Davis, A., and Havighurst, R. J. Social Class and Color Differences in Child-Rearing. *American Sociological Review* 1946, 11: 698-710.

Deutsch, M. Minority Group and Class Status as Related to Social and Personality Factors in Scholastic Achievement, *Monograph of the Society for Applied Anthropology,* 1960, No. 2, 1-32.

Deutsch, M., and Brown, B. Social Influences in Negro-White Intelligence Differences, *Journal of Social Issues* 1964, 20: 24-25.

Frazier, E. F. *The Negro in the United States.* New York: Macmillan, 1957.

Garrett, H. E. Klineberg's Chapter on Race and Psychology: A Review. *The Mankind Quarterly* 1960, 1: 15-22.

———. The Equalitarian Dogma. *Mankind Quarterly* 1961, 1: 253-57.

———. Rejoinder by Garrett. *Newsletter of the Society for the Psychological Study of Social Issues* 1958, May 1962, 1-2.(a)

———. The SPSSI and Racial Differences. *American Psychologist* 1962, 17: 260-63.(b)

Glueck, S., and Glueck, E. T. *Physique and Delinquency.* New York: Harper, 1956.

———. *Unraveling Juvenile Delinquency.* New York: Commonwealth Fund, 1950.

Gronseth, E. The Impact of Father Absence in Sailor Families upon the Personality Structure and Social Adjustment of Adult Sailor Sons, in N. Anderson, ed. *Studies of the Family,* Part 1, Vol 2. Göttingen: Vandenhoeck and Reprecht, 1957, pp. 97-114.

Head Start Newsletter. Published by the Office of Economic Opportunity. No. 2, July 1965.

Kardiner, A., and Ovesey, L. *The Mark of Oppression.* New York: Norton, 1951.

Katz, I. Review of Evidence Relating to Effects of Desegregation on the Intellectual Performance of Negroes. *American Psychologist* 1964, 19: 381-99.

Kawi, A. A., and Pasamanick, B. *Prenatal and Paranatal Factors in the Development of Childhood Reading Disorders.* Monographs of the Society for Research in Child Development, 1959, 24, No. 4.

Keller, S. The Social World of the Urban Slum Child: Some Early Findings. *American Journal of Orthopsychiatry* 1963, 33: 823-31.

Kennedy, W. A., Van de Riet, V., and White, J. C., Jr. *A Normative Sample of Intelligence and Achievement of Negro Elementary School Children in the Southeastern United States.* Monographs of the Society for Research in Child Development, 1963, 28, No. 6.

Knobloch, H., Rider, R., Harper, P., and Pasamanick, B. Neuropsychiatric Sequelae of Prematurity. *Journal of the American Medical Association* 1956, 161: 581-85.

Kuckenberg, K. G. Effect of Early Father Absence on Scholastic Aptitude. Doctoral dissertation, Harvard University, 1963.

Lynn, D. B., and Sawrey, W. L. The Effects of Father-Absence on Norwegian Boys and Girls. *Journal of Abnormal and Social Psychology* 1959, 59: 258-62.

McClelland, D. C. *The Achieving Society.* Princeton, N.J.: Van Nostrand, 1961.

McGurk, F. Psychological Tests: A Scientist's Report on Race Differences. *United States News and World Report* September 21, 1956, 92-96.

————. Negro Versus White Intelligence—An Answer. *Harvard Educational Review* 1959, 29: 54-62.

Miller, W. B. Lower Class Culture as a Generating Milieu of Gang Delinquency. *Journal of Social Issues,* 14: 5-19.

Millsom, C. A. Conformity to Peers Versus Adults in Early Adolescence. Doctoral dissertation, Cornell University, February 1966.

Mischel, W. Preference for Delayed Reinforcement and Experimental Study of a Cultural Observation. *Journal of Abnormal and Social Psychology* 1958, 56: 57-61.

————. Preference for Delayed Reinforcement and Social Responsibility. *Journal of Abnormal and Social Psychology* 1961, 62: 1-7.(a)

————. Delay of Gratification, Need for Achievement, and Acquiescence in Another Culture. *Journal of Abnormal and Social Psychology* 1961, 62: 543-52.(b)

————. Father-Absence and Delay of Gratification: Cross-Cultural Comparisons. *Journal of Abnormal and Social Psychology* 1961, 63: 116-24.(c)

Pasamanick, B., Knobloch, H., and Lilienfeld, A. M. Socioeconomic Status and Some Precursors of Neuropsychiatric Disorder. *American Journal of Orthopsychiatry* 1956, 26: 594-601.

Pasamanick, B., and Knobloch, H. The Contribution of Some Organic Factors to School Retardation in Negro Children. *Journal of Negro Education* 1958, 27: 4-9.

Pettigrew, T. F. *A Profile of the Negro American.* Princeton, N. J.: Van Nostrand, 1964.

Polansky, N., Lippitt, R., and Redl, F. An Investigation of Behavioral Contagion in Groups, in W. E. Martin and C. B. Stendler, eds. *Readings in Child Development.* New York: Harcourt, Brace, 1954, pp. 493-513.

Project Head Start. *Report of the Planning Committee.* Washington, D.C.: Office of Economic Opportunity, 1965.

Rohrer, J. H., and Edmonson, M. S., eds. *The Eighth Generation*. New York: Harper, 1960.

Rosen, B. C. Race, Ethnicity, and the Achievement Syndrome. *American Sociological Review* 1959, 24: 47-60.

Scarpitti, F. R., Murray, E., Dinitz, S., and Reckless, W. C. The "Good" Boy in a High Delinquency Area: Four Years Later. *American Sociological Review* 1960, 25: 555-58.

Sears, P. S. Doll Play Aggression in Normal Young Children: Influence of Sex, Age, Sibling Status, Father's Absence. *Psychological Monographs* 1951, 65: (Whole no. 323).

Sears, R. R., Pintler, M. H., and Sears, P. S. Effects of Father-Separation in Pre-school Children's Doll Play Aggression. *Child Development* 1946, 17: 219-43.

Sherif, M. Superordinate Goals in the Reduction of Intergroup Tensions. *American Journal of Sociology* 1958, 53: 349-56.

Shuey, A. *The Testing of Negro Intelligence*. Lynchburg, Va.: J. P. Bell Co., 1958.

Stolz, L. M. *Father Relations of Warborn Children*. Palo Alto: Stanford University Press, 1954.

Tiller, P. O. Father Absence and Personality Development of Children in Sailor Families: A Preliminary Research Report, in N. Anderson, ed., *Studies of the Family*. Vol. 2, Part II. Gottingen: Vandenhoeck and Reprecht, 1957, pp. 115-37.

―――. *Father-Separation and Adolescence*. Oslo: Institute for Social Research, 1961. Mimeographed.

Van den Haag, E. Intelligence or Prejudice? Questions and Answers *National Review* December 1964, 16: 1059-63.

Williams, R. M., Jr. *The Reduction of Intergroup Tensions*. New York: Social Science Research Council, 1947. Bulletin 57.

―――. *Strangers Next Door*. Englewood Cliffs, N. J.: Prentice-Hall, 1964.

Wright, R. *Black Boy*. New York: Harper & Row, 1945.

Chapter 12

ECONOMIC ASPECTS OF POVERTY

David Caplovitz*

The empirical data of a number of studies point up many respects in which the economic behavior of low-income groups is markedly different from that of middle-income groups. For example, the poor are not nearly as likely to be home owners as the rest of the population, although on a national basis the figure is somewhat higher than might be expected: 44 percent of the nation's low-income families owned their own home in 1962, compared with a national average of 60 percent.

Low-income families are not nearly as likely as middle-income families to have life insurance or to be covered by pension plans or to have savings—findings that do not augur well for a secure old age for those now living in poverty. On the matter of savings, my own study of public housing families in New York City in 1960 showed that two-thirds had no liquid assets at all. A more recent study in California of 1,200 families below the poverty line showed that only 9 percent had savings. This study was carried out by Robert Stone and Frederic Schlamp (1966) of San Francisco State College, and dealt with complete families with a male head, half of whom were receiving public assistance—a rate much higher than in my own sample. Interestingly enough, the available data suggest that the poor of a generation ago, during the Depression, were more likely to have savings than the poor of today. Thus the work of Bakke (1940a, b) on the unemployed in New Haven during the 1930's showed that 74 percent had savings, and McConnell, (1942) using the same sample, showed that among

*Professor of Sociology, Hunter College of the City University of New York, New York.

the unemployed laborers of New Haven during the Depression, 40 percent had some savings. If there is indeed a trend away from savings, it may reflect the greater security people have about the future as a result of such governmental programs as Social Security and unemployment insurance. But it may also reflect the increasing skill of American salesmen in inducing the poor to commit whatever spare income they may have to consumer purchases.

Many other differences between the economic patterns of the poor and the more well-to-do can be cited. For example, the poor live in a world of money orders rather than of checking accounts. They spend proportionately more of their income on food and housing and they are not nearly as likely to have telephones as higher-income groups. Although the absolute amount of debt rises with income, the debt-income ratio tends to be negatively related to income. Thus in the California study, some 77 percent of the families had debts, and the median amount was $649.

These differences in savings and expenditures are hardly surprising and can almost be deduced from the income differences alone. But there is one respect in which the patterns of expenditures of low-income families are surprisingly not too different from those of families that are financially better off, and that is in their ownership of certain relatively expensive material possessions, such as TV sets, phonographs, washing machines, and automobiles. In spite of their low income, large numbers of families below and somewhat above the poverty line have such expensive durable goods. My own study in New York showed that fully 95 percent owned a TV set, and the comparable figure in the California study of even more impoverished families is 89 percent. In both the New York and the California studies about half the families had washing machines, and in the California study fully 70 percent of the sample of 1,200 families owned an automobile.

Such findings call attention to what I feel is a relatively neglected aspect of the war on poverty—the role of the poor as consumers. The primary objective of the war on poverty has been to overcome the obstacles that have prevented the poor from achieving a meaningful place in the productive sphere of society. The emphasis has been on how to expand the earning power of the poor through education, job training, and the creation of jobs. But the inability of the poor to earn a decent living is only one side of their economic plight. Also important is how they spend what little income they have. If the poor pay more for the goods they buy—and I am convinced that they do—then they are being forced to live in a world of inflation that more well-to-do citizens are able to escape.

That the poor are consumers of major durables is intimately connected with a highly significant trend in the American economy—the extraordinary growth of installment credit.. Through the mass media, Americans in all walks of life are bombarded with messages to buy now and pay later. "Easy payments" and "no money down" are the slogans luring even the poor into the marketplace, and, in spite of the low credit status of the poor, there are an ample number of merchants who are prepared to extend them credit.

Consumer credit has been the fuel for what George Katona calls the mass consumption society, and its growth in America since World War II has been truly phenomenal. In 1945, the amount of outstanding installment debt was 2.5 billion dollars. A decade later it had climbed to 29 billion, and by the end of 1965 it had soared to 66 billion. It now stands at 74 billion and is increasing at the rate of about 8 percent a year.

The development of consumer credit has brought in its wake a sharp rise in deceptive and fraudulent marketing practices. As long as market transactions depended upon cash, sellers had less opportunity and incentive to employ deception and fraud. The consumer who could afford to pay cash for an automobile or an expensive appliance was probably more deliberate and sophisticated in his shopping behavior, and there was no point in trying to convince the person without cash to make an expensive purchase. All this changed with the advent of installment credit. Whether or not the consumer could afford the purchase became largely irrelevant. Once the contract was signed, the seller could count on the law to enforce his right to payment. Appropriate changes in contract law and regulations governing consumer credit have lagged far behind the growth of our credit economy. The signed contract is sacrosanct in courts of law and the fraudulent techniques used to obtain the consumer's signature, so difficult to prove in court, are largely ignored.

Installment credit has thus been the door through which low-income groups have entered the mass consumption society, and they, more than any other group, have been victimized by the fraud and deception that have accompanied this method of selling. This is so partly because the poor tend to be naive shoppers and partly because they are so eager to share the fruits of our affluent society in a pattern that I elsewhere describe as "compensatory consumption." This readiness to be consumers of major durables makes them highly vulnerable to the exploitative merchants and salesmen.

The marketing system in which low-income groups are forced to operate is in many respects a deviant one in which fraud and deception are the norm rather than the exception. High-pressure tactics, "bait" ads and "switch sales," misrepresentation of price and quality, and the sale of used merchandise as new, all flourish in this special system of sales-and-credit. In the California study that I have mentioned, 22 percent of the impoverished families owned encyclopedias. The authors seem to feel that this is a low rate and interpret their finding as meaning that reading material is not highly valued by the poor. But they tell us nothing about how encyclopedias enter the homes of the poor. My own research has indicated that many poor families are tricked into buying encyclopedias by unscrupulous salesmen who present themselves as representatives of the schools. They convince the family that the school requires an encyclopedia in the home and that unless one is purchased, the child is sure to drop out of school.

Partly because the poor cannot afford the heavy burdens of debt foisted upon them by unscrupulous merchants, and partly because many of them discover that they have been victims of fraud, the system of sales-and-credit frequently breaks down. Payments stop either because the low-income consumer is overextended or, as also happens with some frequency, because he refuses to pay for faulty merchandise. In the latter instance, instead of gaining retribution, the consumer more often than not is subjected to legal sanctions.

Two sets of statistics provide some indication of the increasing frequency of breakdowns in the system of consumer credit. Personal (non-business) bankruptcies have been growing at an alarming rate. In 1948 there were about sixteen thousand personal bankruptcies in the nation; in 1958 there were eighty thousand; and in 1966 there were over one hundred seventy thousand. Garnishments against wages have also been increasing at a rapid rate, although it is virtually impossible to get national statistics on this issue. Each political jurisdiction has its own bookkeeping system, and some keep records of garnishments while others do not. In Chicago, where such records are kept, the number of garnishments has increased from fifty-nine thousand in 1962 to seventy-three thousand in 1966. Extrapolating from the Chicago figures, it would seem that the national figure runs to at least several million a year. It may be noted that personal bankruptcy and garnishment are not unrelated. In states that have harsh garnishment laws, meaning that substantial portions of income can be attached by creditors, the number of personal bankruptcies is high. Apparently many workers have no recourse but to file for bankruptcy in states that permit creditors to take substantial amounts of the debtor's income.

Much has been written in recent years about the inequities in our system of law as it pertains to the poor. Such inequities are particularly flagrant in the consumer field. Violations of legal process are very common in actions brought against defaulting debtors. In most jurisdictions, these lawsuits begin with the service of a summons on the debtor informing him that he must appear in court if he is to defend himself. The process servers often do not carry out their responsibility, especially when the defendant lives in a slum. This happens with such frequency that a term has evolved in legal circles to refer to it: "sewer service." Thus the low-income consumer often does not even know that he is being sued, and when he fails to appear in court a default judgment is entered against him. Default judgments are extremely common; in New York City, where process serving is notoriously bad, more than 90 percent of the cases result in default judgments. The common assumption is that these default judgments are to be expected since the defaulting consumer does not have a defense. But I am convinced that many of them result from the failure to serve process.

Garnishment laws are another example of the inequities in the legal system. All but two states permit creditors to garnishee wages, a system that makes the employer a collection agent for the creditor. Many employers will not be bothered by the nuisance of garnishments and do not hesitate to fire workers whose wages are attached. Each year a number of persons enter the ranks of the unemployed because of garnishments. The exact number is not known. The Department of Labor has recently become concerned with this matter, and its conservative estimate is that at least a hundred thousand people each year lose their jobs because of garnishments. My own feeling is that the true figure is much higher. I am currently involved in a study of debtors who have been sued for not maintaining payments on their installment purchases. This research is being done in three cities that permit garnishment: New York, Chicago, and Detroit. On the basis of a hand tally on the first 250 questionnaires that have been returned, I can report that 10 percent of the debtors lost their job because of their debt problem. It should be remembered that the number of cases handled in these cities each year runs into the hundreds of thousands. We are accustomed to thinking that these credit entanglements arise because people are poor. But it is also true that some families become poor because they have these problems. To lose a job because of garnishment is certainly one way of entering the ranks of the impoverished. The Cook County, Illinois, Welfare Department recently estimated that about 8 percent of the applicants for welfare were persons who had had garnishment problems.

Not only do people lose their jobs because of garnishments, but many become permanently unemployable because of them, for employers are reluctant to hire people with garnishment records. Recently the Department of Labor undertook a study of the unemployed in the twenty largest metropolitan areas. This study found that some of the unemployed were unemployable for reasons in their own personal histories. The unemployable turn out to be mainly those with either an arrest record or a garnishment record. It should be noted that these are statutory stigmas, and the unemployment that results from them might perhaps be called "statutory unemployment." To return this group of unemployed to the ranks of the employed hinges more on changes in the law than on job training programs. Why, for example, should an arrest record, as distinct from a conviction record, be made available to employers, and why should employers be permitted to fire workers because of a garnishment? Or, for that matter, why should creditors have the recourse of garnishment in the first place?

Job loss is not the only severe consequence of debt entanglement. Debt problems also turn out to be a cause of marital instability and of illness as well. S. M. Miller has written several articles reminding us of the considerable heterogeneity of familes that are classified as lower class. In one of his better known papers (Miller, 1964) he develops a typology of the poor based on the dimensions of economic security and familial stability. I would like to suggest that one of the mechanisms leading from Miller's type of the stable poor to the unstable poor is installment debt. That there is a connection between debt and marital instability is suggested by the results of some questions that I inserted in a national survey. In this survey of a representative sample of the population that was conducted by the National Opinion Research Center, the respondents were asked if they knew anyone whose marriage had suffered or broken up because of debt problems. Some 23 percent of the respondents answered in the affirmative. In this same survey, the respondents were asked whether they knew anyone whose health had suffered because of a debt problem, and this time 21 percent answered yes. These same themes were pursued in the survey of debtors that I am now conducting. Again, hand tallies based on the first 250 returns show that marital difficulties and health problems resulting from debt are quite prevalent. Some 40 percent of the respondents indicated that their debt problem had led to quarrels with their spouses, and 7 percent said that their marriage had broken up because of the debt problem. On the issue of health, some 44 percent of these debtors said that their debt problem had caused them some physical illness. On the basis of these results I would like to see all installment contracts contain a warning that says: "Signing your name to this document may be hazardous to your health."

Installment credit is no doubt highly functional for our economy, but, as I have indicated, it has its dysfunctions as well—particularly for low-income groups—such as job and marital instability and even illness. It seems odd that the mechanisms that give the poor some share of our affluent society can also contribute to the vicious circle of poverty.

So much for the poor as consumers. I should now like to make some observations on two other aspects of the economics of poverty: employ-ment or the earning power of the poor, and what, for lack of a better term, I call the economy of poverty areas, by which I mean mainly the economy of our urban ghettos and slums.

DISCRIMINATION IN EMPLOYMENT

As I have noted, the main thrust of the poverty program is directed to-ward increasing the earning power of the poor through job training and educational programs. But I cannot help wondering whether these programs are adequate to cope with the issue of discrimination which is so heavily entwined with our poverty problem. Since Negroes make up only 11 percent of the population, they of course do not account for the majority of the poor. But, as we all know, Negroes are heavily overrepresented among the poor. In fact, almost half of the Negro population falls below the poverty line. What I find particularly disturbing are the surveys that show that for our Negro population the panacea of education has such little significance. The 1966 report on United States Negroes by the Department of Labor shows not only that the unemployment rate is much higher for nonwhites, but that the unemployment rate for nonwhite high-school graduates is higher than the unemployment rate for white high-school dropouts. The same patterns hold for earnings. White high-school dropouts earn more than Negro high-school graduates. The report concludes that many Negro youngsters have more education than they need for the jobs they get.

A study of vocational high-school graduates conducted by Bernard Levenson (1966) of the Bureau of Applied Social Research at Columbia University provides further evidence of discrimination in employment. Levenson's sample consists of youths from low-income families who were sufficiently motivated to succeed to persist with their high-school studies and vocational training to the point of earning degrees from the vocational high schools they attended. Making use of Social Security records on earnings, Levenson is able to show that within each of some trades, the white youths earn more money than the Negroes after graduation. Furthermore, the gap in earnings tends to increase with each successive year.

The training program of Dr. Kenneth Clark's organization, the Workers Defense League, provides a dramatic example of the powerful forces of discrimination. The training program in the past year focused on preparing Negroes for the apprenticeship examinations in the building trades. In trade after trade, the Negro trainees placed high on the unions' entrance examinations. When it came to the examination for the Sheet Metal Workers' Union twenty-six of thirty-two Negroes passed the examination, compared with thirty-six of the 118 white candidates. Thus Negroes constituted almost half of the group that passed the examination. When the results became known, the union disavowed them and claimed that there must have been foul play. Even the educator who designed the tests could not believe the results and considered them untrustworthy.

The issue of discrimination is becoming more and more pressing be- cause of a major trend that is taking place in the job market. Studies have shown that jobs, like middle-class whites, are moving at an accelerating pace to the suburbs. This marked shift in the job market poses serious prob- lems for the philosophy of equal opportunity and fair employment practices. What is the significance of fair employment legislation when the available jobs are increasingly turning up in areas where Negroes, because of dis- crimination in housing, are not permitted to live? There is considerable controversy today about whether urban ghettos should be revitalized or torn down. There is no easy answer to this question, but my feeling is that one dilemma confronting the advocates of revitalization is that such a program might well sustain housing segregation which, in turn, is running counter to the flight of jobs to the suburbs. In short, the battle against discrimination and segregation must be won if significant progress is to be made in the war against poverty, and to formulate the issue entirely in terms of job training and education may well be missing the point.

THE ECONOMY OF POVERTY

Any serious consideration of the getting and spending of money by the poor would have to take into account a topic that we, as social scientists, know comparatively little about, and that is the wide range of illegal and quasi- legal entrepreneurial activities that comprise a substantial part of the slum economy. Included here would also be the various informal patterns of mutual aid among relatives and friends that constitute part of the low- income economy.

Technological advancement and the growth of our bureaucratic society have presumably led to a sharp decline in the number and kinds of petty en- trepreneurs, thieves, and beggars who were so numerous in the nineteenth century—the characters so brilliantly described by Henry Mayhew in his four-volume classic, *London Labour and the London Poor*. Although there may have been an aggregate decline in this kind of economy, it is still very much part of our urban slums. What knowledge we have of it comes mainly from ethnographic studies such as Oscar Lewis' (1966) *La Vida*, or the autobiographical work of such men as Claude Brown (1965) and Piri Thomas (1967), or the work of insightful journalists such as Richard Elman

(1966) in his book, *The Poorhouse State.* While we are rich in anecdotal material, we unfortunately have hardly any systematic, quantitative data on the extent to which slum residents are involved in this economy as producers and consumers of these illicit services. Nor do we know much about the patterns of recruitment into these illicit occupations or the amount of money that is involved. The kinds of occupations I have in mind include writing numbers, running policy slips, loan sharking, pimping, prostitution, drug peddling, supervising gambling activities, trafficking in stolen merchandise, and steering (guiding outsiders who seek unusual diversions). I am told by friends who grew up in slums that each neighborhood and often each block has its own set of entrepreneurs in these activities. And presumably much of this activity is controlled by organized crime.

The term that is used in the ghetto to refer to these illicit activities is *hustling.* It is important to note that what is viewed as crime and delinquency by middle-class society is seen as a means of livelihood by those who for various reasons are cut off from legitimate paths to success. I am convinced that a good deal of the stealing that goes on, even stealing by juveniles, is motivated more by need than by "kicks," or the lure of the easy dollar. Stealing and other forms of hustling are perhaps the only way of surviving for those who have been removed from welfare rolls because of some violation, or who cannot find a job because of a police record. Some evidence for this is provided by a study carried out by Leonard Goodman (1966) of the Bureau of Social Science Research in Washington, D.C., of 124 prison inmates who had been repeated offenders. The prisoners were asked to assess the importance of a number of reasons for giving up a life of crime and "going straight." The one reason that was overwhelmingly endorsed by the inmates was the availability of good jobs.

To my knowledge, the only survey that has included a question on hustling was carried out in 1966 by Samuel Meyers and Ann Richardson (1966), also of the Bureau of Social Science Research. They studied 190 low-income Negro men with a history of unemployment—the so-called hardcore unemployed. At one point in the interview, the respondents were queried about how they get by when out of a job. They were specifically asked whether they "did a little hustling on the side." In spite of the illegality of this activity, some 44 percent of these unemployed men admitted that they have done some hustling. From what we know about respondents' reluctance to admit to deviant behavior, we can assume that the true figure is even higher.

But this is not to suggest that the proportion of full-time hustlers in any slum community is large. Undoubtedly the majority of slum residents depend upon marginal employment for their livelihoods, for, as Richard Cloward has pointed out, access to illegitimate avenues of success may be restricted as well. Since these activities tend to be organized, access depends largely upon sponsorship by those who already are involved in hustling. Presumably teenagers who show promise are recruited by those who are already in the trade, and, after serving an apprenticeship, they may or may not move on to more lucrative activities. But there is undoubtedly a good deal of part-time and temporary hustling as well and, if the number who have at any time engaged in hustling is ever counted, it might well come to a substantial proportion.

Whatever the significance of hustling as a means of livelihood in the ghetto, there is still the question of the involvement of the poor as consumers of the hustlers' services. There seems to be a very large market for at least two types of hustlers: the numbers writer and the loan shark. It is generally believed that a very large proportion of ghetto and slum residents play the numbers, and I suspect that a large number of them also make use of the corner loan shark. I am told that women on welfare often find that they must deal with the loan shark to tide them over until their next welfare check arrives, and many of the small businessmen in ghetto areas, rejected by legitimate credit agencies, find that they must borrow from loan sharks if they are to get the capital they need for their business.

When the full story of recruitment to hustling is told, I am sure that one pattern that will be uncovered is the conversion of consumers into hustlers. The loan sharks' customers who fall behind on their payments are encouraged and even trained to engage in hustling themselves in order to keep up their payments. This, then, is yet another aspect of poverty on the installment plan, although now the creditor is himself a hustler who resorts to force rather than to the law to insure his payments. These facts call attention to what I consider a serious gap in our knowledge about the economy of poverty. If we are to understand this economy, we must develop a sociology and economics of hustling.

Apart from hustling, there is also the question of the significance of informal patterns of mutual aid that follow kinship and friendship lines in the economy of poverty. It is generally believed that such informal patterns of mutual help are widespread, but here, too, we have little systematic data. However, a study by Leonard Goodman focused on just this theme. Interviews were conducted with 335 men between the ages of thirty and forty-five in a low-income area of Baltimore. The results suggested that the significance of these informal systems of assistance may have been overestimated. For example, when asked if they ever received financial assistance from relatives for a month or more after they had finished school, 84 percent answered in the negative. When asked whether they had ever gotten help from a relative on some occasion when they needed money in a hurry or a place to stay, almost two-thirds said no, and an even larger proportion—three-quarters—said no to a question about whether they ever received clothing or food from a relative when they were in need. Since Goodman is interested in the role of the kinship group in social mobility, he limited his study to men in the prime of their occupational careers, and there is still a good deal to be learned about the role of such patterns of mutual help for other segments of the poor.

ORGANIZING THE POOR AROUND ECONOMIC ISSUES

Richard Cloward and Frances Piven (1965, 1966) have written about the extreme difficulties of organizing the poor and converting them into pressure groups and power groups. They have concluded that the ingredients that made organization successful in the labor movement are largely lacking in the lower classes today, and they place their one hope in the prospects for organizing families on welfare, on the assumption that these families have a clear economic interest in welfare policy that can sustain organizational efforts.

I would like to suggest that consumer issues also provide a powerful basis for organizing the poor. Several civil rights and antipoverty groups, such as the Southern Christian Leadership Conference, have already demonstrated the effectiveness of consumer boycotts in pressing civil rights issues. But these boycotts were instituted to win other demands, such as increasing job opportunities for Negroes. I am particularly impressed with the prospects for organizing the poor on the issue of consumer exploitation. Such an organization exists in Philadelphia. Calling itself the Consumer Education and Protective Association, it has used the militant tactic of picketing merchants in order to settle the grievances of consumers. Its membership is made up overwhelmingly of working-class and lower-class persons. The merchants of Philadelphia developed a grudging respect for CEPA, and consider it enough of a threat to have tried on a couple of occasions to obtain injunctions prohibiting CEPA from picketing. But each time CEPA has been successful in getting the injunction lifted, and in so doing it is contributing to the institutionalization of the right of consumers to picket.

What I find particularly impressive about CEPA is that it has dared to enter the political arena. Its members succeeded in collecting enough signatures to enter a Consumers' ticket in the most recent mayoralty election in Philadelphia. Its leaders had no expectation of winning, but they received considerable publicity through their campaign, and in the process they have done much to politicize their membership. Perhaps one key to their success is their very lively monthly newspaper called *Consumers Voice*, which is subtitled, *Let the Seller Beware.* The work of CEPA is beginning to attract attention in nearby communities, and there is some chance that CEPA will develop into a national movement. Should this happen, a substantial base would exist for pressing reforms in consumer laws, and the day may yet come when the poor will not have to pay more.

REFERENCES

Bakke, W. *Citizens without Work.* New Haven: Yale University Press, 1940. (a)

————. *The Unemployed Worker.* New Haven: Yale University Press, 1940. (b)

Brown, C. *Manchild in the Promised Land.* New York: The Macmillan Co., 1965.

Cloward, R. A., and Piven, F. F. The Professional Bureaucracies: Benefit Systems as Influence systems, in M. Silberman, ed. *The Role of Government in Promoting Social Change.* Proceedings of a conference, Arden House, Harriman, New York, November, 1965, published by Columbia University School of Social Work.

————. A Strategy to End Poverty. *The Nation,* May 2, 1966, pp. 510-17.

Elman, R. *The Poorhouse State: The American Way of Life on Public Assistance.* New York: Pantheon Books, 1966.

Goodman, L. H., Miller, T., and DeForrest, P. *A Study of the Deterrent Value of Crime Prevention Measures as Seen by Criminal Offenders.* A Report of the Bureau of Social Science Research, Inc., 1966.

Levenson, B., and McDill, M. S. Vocational Graduates in Auto Mechanics: a Follow-up Study of Negro and White Youth. *Phylon,* 1966, 27(4): 347-57.

Lewis, O. *La Vida: A Puerto Rican Family in the Culture of Poverty— San Juan and New York.* New York: Random House, 1966.

McConnell, J. W. *The Evolution of Social Classes.* Washington, D.C.: American Council on Public Affairs, 1942.

Meyers, S., and Richardson, A. *The Unemployed and Underemployed: A Study of Applicants for Laborer Jobs.* A Report of the Bureau of Social Science Research, 1966.

Miller, S. M. The American Lower Classes: A Typological Approach. *Sociology and Social Research* 1964, 31: 1-22.

Stone, R. C., and Schlamp, F. T. *Family Life Styles below the Poverty Line.* A report to the State Social Welfare Board from the Institute for Social Science Research, San Francisco State College, 1966.

Thomas, P. *Down These Mean Streets.* New York: Alfred A. Knopf, 1967.

United States Department of Labor. *The Negroes in the United States: Their Economic and Social Situation.* Bull. No. 1511, U.S. Government Printing Office, June, 1966.

Chapter 13

PERSONALITY CORRELATES
OF POVERTY

Vernon L. Allen*

In this chapter I shall present a critical, selective review of research on personality and poverty, together with some suggestions for needed research. In selecting and evaluating the research to be discussed, reliance was placed on systematic studies employing appropriate controls (nonpoor or middle-class groups). Many anecdotal and observational studies exist which are so severely limited methodologically as to be totally lacking in scientific merit. This is not to deny that such studies may be valuable in suggesting research ideas, but they clearly are inadequate for hypothesis testing. In reviewing the literature I have attempted to use standards of reasonable scientific rigor without at the same time being blind to potentially useful, if methodologically weak, research.

MENTAL ILLNESS

Perhaps there is an advantage in first discussing differences between the poor and the nonpoor in global personality functioning before focusing on more specific personality traits or dispositions in isolation. Do the poor and nonpoor differ in frequency of occurrence of diagnostic types in-

*Professor of Psychology, University of Wisconsin, Madison. An earlier version of this chapter was presented at a Washington, D.C., conference on Interdisciplinary Research in Poverty in November 1967, organized by Leonard Goodman and sponsored by the Center for the Study of Social Problems, N.I.M.H.

dicative of personality disturbance when all aspects of an individual's behavior are taken into account, as a clinician might, in arriving at a personality assessment?

Only a few studies were concerned with the relation between socioeconomic status (SES) and mental illness (or, to be positive, mental health) prior to the 1950s (Clark, 1948, 1949; Davis, 1938; Warner, 1937). Some studies simply noted the frequency of patients receiving psychiatric treatment according to SES background. Failure to distinguish between treated and untreated cases is so serious a limitation as to render all such research practically useless for the general question of the relation between personality and poverty. The Hollingshead and Redlich (1958) New Haven study is perhaps the best known research project of this type. Unfortunately, due to serious methodological problems (Srole et al., 1962), as well as the more general problem of collecting data only from treatment files, results of this study must be viewed with extreme caution. Results showed a disproportionate contribution from the lowest SES group to psychotic disorders, and a greater proportion of neurosis from the higher SES level.

A few studies have investigated mental illness in the population at large. Perhaps the most ambitious and well-controlled study of this type is the Midtown Manhattan study (Langner and Michael, 1968; Srole et al., 1963). In this study 1,660 adults were randomly selected for an extensive two-hour home interview. Data were subsequently classified by two psychiatrists on a six-point scale of mental health ranging from "well" to "incapacitated." Respondents' SES was found to be highly related to mental health ratings. Proportion of "well" ratings decreased from the highest to the lowest SES group, while the impaired categories increased in frequency. Falling in the two most-impaired categories was 31 percent of the lowest SES level, as compared to only 6 percent of the top SES level.

Of particular interest was the relation between mental health and SES when the six SES strata were extended to twelve. The shape of the mental impairment curve across all levels of the expanded twelve-level SES continuum was very intriguing. Four SES zones were found in which the mental health rating within a zone was very uniform, with abrupt changes occurring between zones. A sharp increase in mental impairment was discernible in the edge-of-poverty group. There was an even sharper increase in impairment in the chronic poverty category, in which few were considered well (4.6 percent) and nearly half were considered impaired (47.3 percent). A turning point in the nature of the life situation is suggested by the sharp discontinuity that breaks the SES continuum into four homogeneous mental health zones. A definite breakthrough point in terms of increase in mental impairment seems to exist at the edge of poverty and again in the poverty group.

Further analyses of data from the Midtown study disclosed a very intriguing set of results concerning the relation between mental health and life stress (Langner and Michael, 1963). Ten empirically derived stress factors (childhood and adulthood experiences) correlated with mental health risk across social-class levels. The number of stress factors was related to mental health in a linear fashion: the greater the number of negative life experiences, the greater the mental health risk. Interestingly, adult stress factors showed a stronger correlation with present mental health than did childhood stress factors. Moreover, the particular pattern of stress variables was not crucial; only the sheer frequency of negative life experiences was important. Stressful experiences affect mental health in a quantitative rather than a qualitative way: not what happened, but how many things happened, is critical.

Differences in observed mental health between lower and middle social classes cannot be accounted for by occurrence of a greater number of stress factors in the life of persons from a low SES background, since only a slight difference in frequency existed between social class levels. But when the number of experienced stress factors was held constant across social class levels, the low SES group still showed a greater mental health risk. That is, as the number of stressors increase, the probability of mental impairment increases more sharply for persons from the low SES level than for persons of middle and upper SES. This suggests that the use of different adaptive techniques might account for the relation between SES and mental health. The poor seem to employ "acting-out" devices: as stress increases, the proportion of psychotics increases uniformly for the poor, but not for the higher SES groups. Conversely, the number of neurotics increases with greater stress in the high SES groups. The reaction of the poor to stress leads to behavior (psychosis) that is more socially incapacitating than the behavior of higher SES groups.

A basic criticism must be raised against research on SES and mental illness. Results of all studies in the area are, in the final analysis, based on judgmental ratings. The type of evaluative decision (diagnosis) made by the psychiatrist is a function of the conceptual and value systems he holds, which may be biased against behavior of the poor even though this behavior may be very adaptive in the lower-class environment. In fact, the entire medical model of behavior and mental illness has come under attack recently from behavioral scientists who seriously question the very conceptual basis of psychiatric categorizations. Sarbin (1967), Scheff (1966), and Szasz (1961) have provided alternative theoretical models.

Related to the genre of research on mental illness, many studies seek to discover differences among SES groups in general personality adjustment, typically measured by an omnibus, multidimensional, self-report personality inventory. Haller (1954) used several methodological criteria in reviewing fifty-six studies dealing with this aspect of personality and poverty. On the basis of results from seventeen of the best-designed studies in the field, Haller concluded that there was a positive relation between personality and SES, with better personality adjustment associated with higher status. In his own study (Sewell and Haller 1956), the positive relation between adjustment and SES existed even when other potentially confounding variables (intelligence, family size, father's age, and age of child) were controlled. Nevertheless, several of the adequately designed studies failed to show a significant relationship between personality adjustment and SES. It is perhaps noteworthy that none of the many studies showed a negative association, i.e., in no instance did the lower SES group have better adjustment than the higher SES group.

One difficulty with this type of research is that the interpretation of *adjustment* or *maladjustment* is evaluative, and usually based on the acceptable behavior patterns of the middle class. Thus, it is almost meaningless to consider a person of low SES maladjusted on the basis of responses to an instrument designed to measure adequacy of personality functioning in an environment quite different from that in which he functions. The problem is common in personality research with the poor. When using a personality inventory, the item content and the standardization group must be scrutinized with care. Otherwise, conclusions about personality might be due to misuse of the validation group or to differences in the information and experience of respondents.

TIME PERSPECTIVE

A number of specific personality traits have been widely assumed to characterize the poor. But rather than merely accepting these assumptions, I will here critically discuss relevant literature with the goal of determining how much is really known, how much is based on incomplete or inadequate information, and how much is myth.

Oscar Lewis' (1961) description of some of the personality characteristics of the poor, based on his observations, would probably not elicit a great deal of disagreement from most social scientists: ". . . a strong present time orientation with little ability to defer gratification and plan for the future, a sense of resignation and fatalism, . . . a high tolerance for psychological pathology of all sorts, . . . gregariousness, . . . authoritarianism. . . ." (pp. xxvi-xxvii).

Consider Lewis first-mentioned characteristic—present-time orientation. It has been quite widely accepted by social scientists that short time perspective and anchorage in the present rather than in the future is a well-documented personality attribute of the poor. The empirical work most frequently cited in support of this contention is Le Shan's (1952) study concluding that lower-class children are less future-oriented than middle-class children. In this study, children were asked to tell a story; time elapsed in the story was then determined. Results must be considered equivocal, however, due to erroneous statistical treatment of the data. A later recalculation of the chi-square from Le Shan's data (Green and Roberts, 1961) showed that results did not reach statistical significance and must be viewed with a great deal of skepticism until replications are conducted.

Very few empirical studies have been conducted on this problem and all, including Le Shan's, used children only. One investigator (Freeman, 1964), using a technique similar to Le Shan's, asked children of three age levels to write six brief stories to pictures. Age had a greater effect on time perspective than social class, with the youngest age group having the longest time perspective! Only in the intermediate age group did social class produce a significant difference in time perspective. Another investigation used a more standardized and less projective technique of measuring time perspective (Judson and Tuttle, 1966). Items with several alternatives were presented. Using middle- and lower-class sixth-graders, these investigators found no significant difference in time perspective. An additional study with sixth-grade boys also failed to find a difference between middle- and lower-class boys using the technique of completing story stems (Maitland, 1966). Employing a fantasy storytelling technique, Reichert (1966) likewise found no difference in time orientation between middle- and lower-class children. Cultural factors of ethnic origin certainly appear to be stronger than social class factors in affecting this personality characteristic. Differences among Anglo, Spanish, and Indian high-school students have been found in degree of temporal extension (Graves 1961).

In a recent study (Kendall and Sibley, 1968), Le Shan's results appeared, at first sight, to receive some corroboration. It was noted, however, that stories that contained more words covered longer time spans. When sixth-grade children of lower and middle SES were matched on length of story, time span did not differ by social class. It might be concluded, on the basis of these results, that any apparent difference in time span as a function of social class could be attributed to the artifact of differential story length. In other words, longer stories tend to cover a greater time span; and middle-class children usually tell longer stories than lower-class children.

In sum, the literature review indicates that the assumption that the poor have shorter time perspective is rather untenable in light of empirical findings.

DELAY OF GRATIFICATION

Related to the time-orientation assumption is the widely accepted belief that impulse gratification is a focal characteristic of the personality structure of the poor. Individuals high on impulse gratification are less inclined to delay immediate, less valued goals for the sake of greater future gains. Such related concepts as impulse control and ego strength play a central role in several theories of personality; ability to postpone gratification is supposed to represent a developmentally more advanced personality structure, in which the reality principle has superceded the pleasure principle.

Several clusters of behavior patterns attributed to the poor have been interpreted as reflecting a personality trait of preference for immediate rather than delayed gratification. Greater premarital sexual experience among the poor (Kinsey et al., 1948), lower educational attainment (Strauss, 1962), lack of financial savings, and pattern of consumption (Schneider and Lysgaard, 1953) have all been accepted as evidence of inability to postpone impulse gratification. Interestingly, the expected behavior of the lower class is generally hedonistic. Adolescent boys were asked in one study to indicate both expectations (what they ought to do) and actual behavior in a number of realistic behavioral situations (Ort, 1952). The investigator evaluated the expectations according to whether or not they offered pleasure and found fewer nonpleasure expectations in the lower-class boys. (But note that the rating was made by the middle-class investigator.) Also, conflict between expectations and behavior was less frequent for the lower-class boys than for the middle-class boys.

Surprisingly little empirical behavioral research—in contrast to inferences drawn from other data—has been conducted directly to test the idea that the poor are more self-indulgent. For the past several years, Mischel has conducted several experimental studies, using a procedure in which a child is presented with a series of choices between receiving a less valuable reward immediately or a more valuable reward in the future. For example, the alternatives might consist of accepting a small candy bar now or a large one tomorrow or next week. In one early study Mischel (1958) showed that for eight- to nine-year-olds a significant positive relation existed between absence of the father from home and preference for immediate reward, but the relation did not hold for older children (eleven to fourteen years). In this study, conducted in the cultural setting of the

southern Caribbean, Negro children showed greater preference for immediate rewards than did Indian children. Mischel explains this difference
in terms of the greater incidence of father absence in the Negro group. All
the children in these two studies were from the lower SES, but we might
be able to extrapolate this finding to the poverty population if in fact a
large proportion of fatherless homes do exist in this population.
Strengthening the importance of the role of parental influence is the
finding that a model—either real or symbolic—significantly alters a child's
preference for either immediate or delayed reward (Bandura and Mischel,
1965). Relevant here is the study investigating white middle-class and
lower-class sixth-graders from organized and "disorganized" homes (Maitland, 1966). Middle-class children made the greatest number of delay
choices, and lower-class disorganized children the fewest. No relation
was found between time perspective and preference for delay of gratification.

Of clear importance in postponability are subcultural variables. Differences found between two Negro groups on the islands of Trinidad and
Grenada are congruent with known cultural attributes of the groups.
Though poorer, the Grenadians were more willing to postpone gratification and had greater trust in promise-keeping (Mischel, 1961). Of three
other cultural groups differing in degree of integration in the American
core culture—Anglo, Spanish, and Indian—the Anglo group was higher in
delay, as based on observation and self-ratings (Graves, 1961).

In spite of its apparent reasonableness, the prediction of a difference
between lower and middle classes on willingness to delay gratification
does not receive unanimous empirical support. At least three studies
failed to find a difference between social classes. Two well-conducted
studies used a behavioral measure of the type developed by Mischel and
sought explicitly to investigate social-class differences in delay of gratification (Seagull, 1964; Shybut, 1963). In both studies, no differences across
social classes were found on several criteria.

Since the ability to postpone gratification is presumably a middle-
class phenomenon, persons who move out of poverty should exhibit this
characteristic more than their less mobile counterparts. A fairly direct
test of the hypothesis was conducted by Beilin (1956) with lower-class
senior boys, all having an IQ of 110 or higher, half of whom intended to
go to college and half of whom did not. Responses to an open-ended
questionnaire were content-analyzed. College-bound boys from lower-
class backgrounds did not see themselves as delaying gratification. In fact,
quite the opposite: they perceived college as a means of achieving the
satisfactions of a desired goal. Certainly no evidence was available of a

conscious postponement of gratification, i.e., no intent to delay immediate satisfactions for future goals. If the presumed pattern of postponability of gratification were a middle-class phenomenon, persons upwardly mobile from poverty backgrounds should reflect this characteristic, which was not the case at all.

ACHIEVEMENT MOTIVATION

Achievement motivation (n Ach) is one of the many personality needs posited in the theoretical system of Henry Murray, and this construct has received a great deal of theoretical elaboration and empirical testing in the last two decades. Responsible for much of the theoretical elaboration and empirical research on n Ach are McClelland (1961) and Atkinson (1958), who devised the fantasy measure, TAT (Thematic Apperception Test), for measuring this personality construct. An individual high on n Ach has a strong impetus to excel, sets high standards for himself, is innovative, and takes moderate risks. A considerable amount of validity has been demonstrated for this motive in terms of school grades, upward mobility, and success in business.

Most studies in this area show that lower-class individuals are significantly lower on n Ach. An early study (Rosen, 1956) on the relation between achievement motivation (measured by the storytelling technique) and social class showed that class V (Hollingshead's lowest classification) scored lowest of all groups. The scores for class II were four times greater than the scores for class V. Dividing data at the median for the entire sample of 120 boys disclosed that 83 percent of the boys in the lowest class (V) had low scores. In another of Rosen's studies (1959), 427 boys from ages eight to fourteen, from four northeastern states, were tested on the TAT for achievement motivation. Achievement motivation was lower, combining across all ethnic groups, in the lower SES group (Hollingshead's V) than in the other SES categories. But here ethnic differences were also significant. Both SES and ethnic membership contributed to the variance, but SES to a larger degree. In a nationwide survey testing achievement motivation (Veroff et al., 1960), persons of lower educational and occupational levels tended to exhibit lower achievement-motivation scores. Most of the studies just described were not conducted with adults, but with children or teenagers. It should be noted that one study with adults found that n Ach was related to the individual's present social class, but not to that of his father (Littig and Yeracaris, 1965).

Other studies have generally found higher n Ach scores for lower-class whites than for lower-class Negroes (Merbaum, 1962; Minigine, 1965). Merbaum (1962) extended the comparison between lower-class Negroes and whites from grades three through eleven. The whites' scores were higher than the Negroes' scores, in general, and the difference increased with age. Negro girls generally had higher *n* Ach scores than Negro boys. In one clever study, level of *n* Ach was found related, under certain conditions, to southern dialect among Negro high school boys of matched IQ from a northern city whose fathers had come from the South (Baehr, 1965). The boys having higher *n* Ach showed less of the southern pronunciation in a formal test (word association) situation. But the difference in dialect between persons high and low in *n* Ach did not appear in the informal interview following the test. These data suggest that high *n* Ach boys were able or motivated to imitate middle-class speech in the more formal situation.

What is the nature of Negroes who are, in fact, high in *n* Ach, which is generally low in this group? A study with urban northern Negroes showed a positive correlation between occupational status and *n* Ach (Nutall, 1964). Father-absence was linked to low *n* Ach. Northern men having high *n* Ach scores were less religious, more militant, better educated, and felt more victimized than those low in *n* Ach. By contrast, the southern Negro high in *n* Ach was more religious, denied feeling victimized, repressed hostility, and was less educated.

If *n* Ach is related to behavior, as considerable research demonstrates, perhaps ways might be devised to increase achievement motivation among the poor. It has been shown, for instance, that high *n* Ach is related to upward mobility from blue- to white-collar occupations (Littig and Yeracaris, 1965). (The relation was significant for women only, though it approached significance for men.) McClelland (1965) contends that *n* Ach can be increased by a proper training regime and has demonstrated his point with a group in India—admittedly a middle-class group. An attempt in this country to increase achievement motivation experimentally for high-school boys was reported by Kolb (1965). An entire summer was devoted to a variety of techniques designed to increase achievement motivation. At a one-and-one-half-year follow-up, the middle-class experimental group had improved significantly in grades over the control, but the lower-class subjects had not improved grades as compared with their controls. As Rosen (1956) takes pain to stress, high achievement motivation may be insufficient to influence performance unless a corresponding set of values and aspirations are also an integral part of the personality organization.

Two methodological cautions on the *n* Ach literature should be mentioned. First, one study found that the significant positive correlation between *n* Ach and SES was reduced to nonsignificance when IQ was controlled (Bruckman, 1966). Second, a recent methodological study suggests that great care should be taken in interpreting *n* Ach scores from different subcultural or SES groups. Stimuli (pictures) used to measure *n* Ach gave less valid measures if they portrayed work settings unfamiliar to the individual. Unfamiliar pictures apparently allow freer play of achievement motives than is possible when responses are restricted or stereotyped due to the person's familiarity with the stimuli. Pictures presenting situations less familiar to the person's occupational background were better predictors of occupational mobility (Veroff, Feld, and Crockett, 1966).

EXPECTANCY FOR INTERNAL VERSUS EXTERNAL CONTROL

A cluster of related personality constructs seems to be subsumable under this single rubric: among the constructs are active versus passive orientation, alienation, anomie, powerlessness, and perceived locus of control of reinforcement. By *internal versus external control* is meant the degree to which an individual perceives that reinforcements are contingent on or follow from his own efforts and actions (internal) versus the degree to which he believes rewards are controlled by forces outside himself—luck, chance, fate, or powerful others (external). The psychological variable of internal-external control seems to be related to the concepts of alienation (Seeman, 1959) and anomie (Merton, 1949).

Using Rotter's (1966) twenty-nine-item internal-external control scale with a national stratified sample, Franklin (1963) found a significant negative relation between SES and feelings of external control. Rotter's internal-external control scale has received substantial construct validation. For example, Negro students willing to join a group of freedom riders have higher internal scores (Gore and Rotter, 1963); persons more internal are more active in union organizations, controlling for age and education (Seeman, 1963); internal persons are more alert to aspects of the environment that might be useful in the future (Seeman, 1967; Seeman and Evans, 1962); and those high on internal control place greater value on skill and ability (Rotter and Mulry, 1965). There is some indication that *feelings of powerlessness* is a useful predictor in community-action work with the poor. One study showed that feelings of internal-external control can be changed through experience in leadership activities (Gottesfeld and Dozier, 1966).

Turning now to studies involving SES as a variable, a projective picture test of external-internal control was used with sixth- and eighth-grade Negro and white children in a study by Battle and Rotter (1963). Middle-class white children were most internal and lower-class Negroes most external. Lower-class Negroes were significantly more external than middle-class Negroes or middle-class whites. A similar trend between the middle-class and lower-class white groups did not reach statistical significance. (It should be mentioned in passing that in one study, using fifth- and sixth-grade children, no difference was found in internal-external control for middle and low SES groups of Negroes and whites [Titus, 1966]). An interesting and suggestive finding in the Battle and Rotter study was that the lower-class Negroes with high intelligence scores were more external than middle-class whites with low IQ. And the external score for high IQ, lower-class Negroes was higher (but not significantly so) than that for the less intelligent lower-class Negro children. Although the finding must be interpreted cautiously in view of the small number of subjects in the groups and the marginal statistical significance, two plausible explanations for the result are evident. First, the intelligent lower-class Negroes may acquire external attitudes as a defensive reaction against perceived deprivation of choice. Second, these individuals may recognize that their lives are, in fact, under control of external factors and respond accordingly.

External-internal control seems to be particularly susceptible to ethnic influences, as shown by results on a related notion, the concept of *mastery* used by Strodtbeck (1958). Strodtbeck showed that class, ethnic, and religious factors affected mastery, with lower-class Italians being distinguished from the upper- and middle-class Jews on this variable. Similarly, in an isolated tri-ethnic community, the most internal were whites, followed by Spanish-Americans, and then Indians (Graves, 1961).

As with the internal-external scale, greater anomie responses—indicating agreement with statements expressing feelings of futility and alienation—repeatedly have been found to be associated with lower-class status (Bell, 1963; Langner and Michaels, 1965; Lefcourt and Ladwig, 1966). Those who score high on the anomie scale are those who are unsuccessful and unprosperous—persons who are, in McClosky and Schaar's (1965) terms, "isolated, deprived and ignorant." McClosky and Schaar (1965) assert that such feelings are due primarily to cognitive, emotional, and attitudinal factors that have impaired learning and socialization. They therefore argue strongly for the basis of anomie in personality factors such as hostility, anxiety, etc., existing independently of social-class level. Whether social-structural variables or personality factors are the conceptual basis for anomic feelings can only be determined by future research. It is likely that variables at both levels interact in affecting the individual's personality structure.

INCENTIVES

It has often been assumed that the poor require external incentives to work and to learn. By contrast, it is assumed that the middle-class person is adequately motivated by performance on the task, and, hence, does not need external, tangible rewards.

Differential responsiveness to a specific category of reinforcement is an aspect of personality of great potential applicability to behavior change. In fact, some theories would maintain that determination of the differential effectiveness of categories of reinforcement is of primary importance for the construction of theories of individual differences. First, the data on the effectiveness of material versus nonmaterial (verbal) reinforcement will be examined. Another way of conceptualizing this type of reinforcer is in terms of degree of abstractness, or in terms of primary (direct) versus secondary rewards.

Most studies testing incentive effects have used simple choice-learning procedures with children. Of twelve studies reviewed in which a tangible, material incentive (candy or money) was compared with an intangible incentive ("right" or signal), results were practically 50-50 as to whether lower- or middle-class subjects performed better with one or the other type of reward. (Two of the most recent and best-designed studies found no difference.) Other studies in this general area compared the incentive value of impersonal feedback ("right") versus more personal feedback (praise or approval) on performance. The few studies on this aspect of incentive are contradictory, too.

Rather minor variations in procedure, instructions, and other aspects of method are known to influence significantly performance on the type of tasks used for studying incentives. Noncomparability among the studies in this respect might contribute to the contradictory findings. Type of incentive has also been shown to interact with age, so differences among studies in age of subjects could also contribute to the overall lack of clarity.

Zigler and Kanzer (1962) suggested that the lower-class child is developmentally lower than the middle-class, in that reinforcers meaning "correct" have not replaced more personal (praise) reinforcers in the response hierarchy. Presumably, emphasis on the importance of being right is a middle-class phenomenon. Data relevant to this hypothesis come from a study in which speed of discrimination learning in middle- and lower-class children of ages five to eleven was compared, when the reinforcement for a correct response was either a light signal or a candy reward, with or without a light (Terrall, Durkin, and Wiesley, 1959). Results showed that middle-class learning was somewhat better with the neutral incentive, but the lower-class children's performance was significantly better with the material reward. In fact, lower-class children receiving material rewards learned faster than either incentive group of middle-class children. Likewise, Zigler and de Labry (1962) found that, on a concept-switching task, lower-class children performed more effectively for a tangible reward (a prize) than for an intangible ("right") reinforcement. Similar results were found by Terrell (1958), Terrell and Kennedy (1957), and Cameron and Storm (1965), using discrimination-learning tasks.

Investigating the same problem, Spence and Segner (1967) employed either verbal reinforcement ("right" for correct and "wrong" for incorrect) or nonverbal reinforcement (candy for correct and sound of a buzzer for incorrect). These investigators failed to find any significant difference between middle- and lower-class elementary school children as a function of type of reinforcer. Bresnahan (1967) also failed to find effects for similar incentives as a function of social class.

Effectiveness of two types of reinforcers, candy and nonmaterial reinforcement, was compared on a simple operant task (Donoviel, 1966). Results showed that lower-class boys and girls were significantly more responsive to candy than to nonmaterial reinforcement (praise and approval). However, in another study three types of incentives   verbal praise, verbal reproof, and candy reward   showed neither a difference between incentive conditions nor an interaction of incentive with social class on IQ test performance (Tiber and Kennedy, 1964). Material reward made no difference in the achievement scores of middle-class subjects in Douvan's (1956) study. A more recent study found no difference, according to social class, in a learning task using candy or a light as reinforcers (Safer and Kornreden, 1968).

In a New Zealand study, subjects performed a speed test with instructions to do as well as possible, or with the instructions plus frequent candy rewards (Storm, Anthony, and Pursalt, 1965). The subjects in both social-class groups scored higher for nonmaterial rewards than for the candy, the difference being greater for the middle than for the lower class. Note that this result disagrees with the Terrell et al. (1959) data in which lower-class boys performed better for material than for nonmaterial reward. Moreover, the results for social-class differences held only for five- to six-year-old boys, but not for those ten to eleven years old.

Looking now at different types of verbal reinforcers, positive feedback may be given by responses directed at the performance ("correct" or "right") or by personal feedback connoting approval ("fine," "good"). Zigler and Kanzer (1962) showed that, for lower-class second-grade children, praise and approval were more effective than responses of "correct" or "right" in a learning task. For middle-class children the reverse was true: "correct" type responses were more effective than praise. Unfortunately, a replication of this study found no difference between middle- and lower-class children in response to abstract versus concrete or personal reinforcers (Rosenhan and Greenwald, 1965). Likewise, social-class differences were not replicated in a second study by McGrade (1966) nor, in this study, was there an interaction between age and type of reinforcer. The lack of an age effect does not support the developmental hypothesis suggesting that children change from initial dependence on tangible, external reinforcements to later dependence on self-reinforcement.

A social interaction view may elucidate these various findings. That is, the source of the reinforcement—who and where—may account for some of the discrepant results. A middle-class child is likely to be familiar and comfortable with middle-class persons and situations that are to a great extent extensions of his home. The lower-class child, however, may be anxious in middle-class institutions such as schools. To test these ideas, Rosenhan (1966) examined the reaction of middle-class and lower-class children to two types of verbal reinforcement, praise and disapproval. Performance of white and Negro first-graders was examined on a binary-choice apparatus. The subject received either praise for the correct response or disapproval for the incorrect response. Results showed that under conditions of approval lower-class white and Negro children's performance substantially improved relative to the effect of approval on white middle-class children, and lower-class whites and Negroes performed more poorly under conditions of disapproval. Approval and disapproval had little differential effect on middle-class whites. (Middle-class Negroes were not tested.) The data are best understood in terms of social class interaction; the lower-class child has little generalized positive expectancy when confronting middle-class persons and institutions. A further example of the importance of the interaction between social class and source of reinforcement is illustrated by the finding that Negro subjects showed a decrement in performance when "blame" feedback ("not so good as expected") came from a white experimenter, but demonstrated an increment in performance with a Negro experimenter (Kennedy and Vega, 1965).

A final comment should be made about research on SES differences in responsiveness to various types of incentives. The reinforcement properties of the social stimuli used in such studies (e.g., the experimenter saying "good") are extremely complex, as Stevenson (1965) has emphasized. Reinforcers may vary widely for different SES groups in terms of their meaning, importance, familiarity, and interest value. To make inferences about personality characteristics of the poor in view of the variety of potentially confounding variables intrinsic in this research is a very risky business indeed.

This caveat (together with the contradictory results found in the review) suggests that no clear conclusion about personality of the poor can be drawn from data now available. Much future research will be required to unravel the complexities in this area.

SELF-CONCEPT

One's view of self would seem to be one of the expected concomitants of poverty. Feelings of low self-concept (self-esteem or self-worth), low self-acceptance, and discrepancy between actual and ideal self are reasonable and common-sense predictions as correlates of poverty. Self-concept is, of course, a product of social learning. The poor are probably frequently exposed to situations in which the relative inferiority of their station in life may be translated into feelings of inferiority and worthlessness. Impressions held by the middle class often attribute maladjustment and unhappiness to the poor (Luft, 1957). This general negative stereotype may be clearly communicated to the lower-class individual in various ways—through direct social interaction or by processes of social comparison.

Most studies in the area of self-concept of the poor are inadequate methodologically, and results are surprisingly negative. Six studies reviewed (excluding merely speculative reports) found no difference in self-concept across social class, and three are confounded and uninterpretable. As an example of the latter, one study (Keller, 1963) found that 65 percent of fifth-grade children from slum areas gave unfavorable self-references; but no control group of nonslum children was provided. That a relevant comparison group is imperative is indicated by data from the same study showing that only 30 percent of the slum white children had negative self-evaluations as compared to 80 percent of the Negroes.

Bieri and Loback (1961) asked male Army reservists to describe themselves. Results showed that the lower-class individuals were significantly lower on a dominance scale (i.e., greater emphasis on submissive and passive self-conception). Contradicting the supportive findings of this single study are several others showing negative results, such as the one by Hill (1957). This well-designed study found no consistent association between social class and self-acceptance. Another negative finding was reported by Silverman (1964). Measuring self-concept by combining the Coopersmith inventory and appropriate semantic differential scales disclosed no difference between middle- and lower-class male children. In another study (Klausner, 1953), sixty self-concept statements were first Q-sorted and then factor-analyzed. Of the three resulting factors, the class and self-concept relationship showed only a suggestive trend. These results should be held suspect, since only twenty-seven boys were used, and the "lower social class" group was actually drawn from the lower middle class.

Some studies reveal results that are no doubt confounded. Several self-concept measures were used by Mason (1954a, b) to study self-worth among persons differing in social class, age, and living conditions (institutionalized or not). The confounding of these variables makes interpretation of social-class data impossible. In the Havighurst and Taba (1949) study a low correlation was found between social class and ideal self as rated on moral values (selfish to altruistic). The moral value ratings were, however, even more highly correlated with IQ than with social-class membership.

Perhaps the most adequate study, in scope and design, was that of McDonald and Gynther (1965), who used over four hundred subjects. Negro and white southern high-school seniors described self and ideal self on a checklist that measured dominance versus cooperative qualities. Results for social class were completely negative, as were results of a previous study by the same authors using a different instrument (McDonald and Gynther, 1963).

In a recent and well-designed study (Soares and Soares, 1968), self-perceptions of 514 children in grades four to eight were compared on five measures: self-concept, ideal concept, reflected-self-classmates, reflected-self-teacher, reflected-self-parent. Half the children were from a school located in a disadvantaged area and half from a school in a non-disadvantaged area. The overall results showed more positive self-perceptions of the disadvantaged children than of the nondisadvantaged children. When analyzed by sex, the overall pattern of the data persisted for boys, but not for girls (i.e., the nondisadvantaged girls had more positive scores than disadvantaged girls).

The self-concept of Negroes does seem to be generally low, though amenable to environmental influence. The self-esteem for matched groups of Negroes living in a residentially desegregated area was significantly higher than for those living in segregated neighborhoods (Haggstrom, 1963). (The validity of the self-esteem measure here is questionable. Self-esteem was measured by a happiness-self-rating scale; but happiness may be caused by reasons other than high self-esteem.) Clark and Clark's (1947) classic research on Negro children's preference for dolls of different colors as a measure of self-concept has been replicated several times (Goodman, 1952; Greenwald and Oppenheim, 1968; Morland, 1962; Radke and Trager, 1950; Stevenson and Steward, 1958). As will be recalled, a large proportion of Negro children tend to prefer the white doll. We recently replicated this study (Asher and Allen, 1969) and failed to find any significant differences between Negro children of low and middle social class. In fact, the middle-class Negro children preferred the white doll slightly more than the lower-class children. Whether this type of projective test is a valid measure of self-concept and acceptance of self is certainly debatable.

The self-concept of lower-class (and possibly middle-class) Negroes does seem to be lower than that of whites of comparable SES, assuming the validity of projective tests with children. But the lack of differences found between lower- and middle-class Negro children indicates that race is probably more important than social class.

The review of available literature strongly points to the conclusion that poverty is not necessarily associated with a more negative self-concept. Such a conclusion runs counter to common-sense expectations and much anecdotal evidence. What can we conclude, in view of present research? Perhaps the poor do possess a low self-concept and perceive themselves as being low in self-worth and self-acceptance; if so, the dimensions of self examined thus far have been inappropriate and the instruments employed too gross and insensitive to detect these SES differences. Then again, there may be aspects of self that are not amenable to measure by direct self-report methods, due to the individual's strong need to maintain a positive view of self. Or lower-class persons may be reluctant to make undesirable statements about self publicly and in the presence of middle-class persons. As another alternative, we can accept presently available data which seem to suggest that the self-concept of the poor does not differ significantly from that of the middle class. Whether the self-concept of the poor (if we assume it is really not low) represents a defensive reaction against anxiety and admission of inadequacy, or is based on other mechanisms (e.g., the use of peers as a reference group for self-concept) remains to be seen. Clearly, here is an important and central area about which we know little, and in which a great deal of research is needed.

CRITIQUE AND SUGGESTIONS

Most of the critical discussion in Chapter 19 is also relevant to research on personality and poverty (particularly the comments about poverty indices, and the role of situational factors), and need not be repeated here.

The quality of much of the research in the personality-poverty area is seriously deficient even when examined with charity. Failure to provide controls for obvious confounding effects (such as influence of social class of the examiner, and intelligence), small and nonrepresentative samples, and measuring instruments of dubious validity within the middle-class group— not to mention validity across classes—are all too common. In many studies sweeping generalizations have been made about poverty and personality on the basis of unsystematic observation and unwarranted inferences. To wound a metaphor, my intention here is not to throw out the few clean babies with the flood of dirty bath water, but to call attention to the paucity of our knowledge about an important subject.

One important fact must not be overlooked: most of the demonstrated relationships between personality and poverty are quite weak. When data are reported in percent of respondents agreeing or disagreeing with an item, the difference between poverty and middle-class groups is frequently about 10 percent. Likewise, correlations between personality scales and SES are typically low. Sewell and Haller's (1959) correlation of 0.25 between SES and the California Personality Test is typical for well-controlled studies. We should not lose sight, also, of the fact that even when statistical significance is obtained, overlap between groups is usually fairly large. Kluckhohn, Murray, and Schneider (1956) have said that every man in certain respects is like all other men, like some other men, and like no other man. Upon finding a slight difference in personality between poverty and nonpoverty groups, it is curious that we often emphasize the difference instead of stressing the even larger degree of similarity.

Apparently a process of leveling and sharpening occurs with respect to research data. Many findings are still widely accepted as valid in the face of data that are ambiguous at best and overwhelmingly contradictory at worst. There seems to be a psychological tendency—perhaps not unique to social scientists nor to data in this area—to sharpen the findings supporting one's preconceptions and to ignore or forget findings that are discrepant. The tendency to simplify and bring order from chaotic conditions is understandable. But, particularly when considering possible policy decisions, it is encumbent upon us to take a long and objective look at available data, with as much freedom from the influence of preconceptions as possible. I cannot escape the impression that much of our "knowledge" about personality and poverty rests on very unstable empirical foundations.

A very significant fact appearing in many personality studies is that large differences exist among ethnic and subcultural groups within the poverty population. It would seem to be very risky indeed, on the basis of present meager results, to generalize research findings across the entire heterogeneous poverty group. More research needs to be directed toward studying variation in personality structure and dynamics within the poverty population. It would seem more important to discover differences within the heterogeneous poor than to continue contrasting the total poverty group with the middle class. Intragroup poverty research might also provide leverage for the investigation of specific life experiences that correlate with personality.

A disproportionate amount of research has been directed toward studying children. This emphasis is understandable. Most psychologists agree that early experience and early personality development are crucial for later behavior; both learning theory and psychoanalytic theory place great emphasis upon the importance of early experience. Possibly a second reason for the disproportionate amount of research with children is more pragmatic: children are easily available as subjects. We should not overlook, however, the contribution of post-childhood experiences to personality and behavior. In Langner's (1963) Midtown Manhattan study, stress factors in adulthood were more strongly related to current mental health risk than childhood stress factors. And Norma Haan (1964) at Berkeley reported that while early (childhood) social status had only a minor effect on adult ego functioning, adult social status and achieved mobility were significantly related to ego function. These data suggest that social learning in childhood may not be as permanent as frequently assumed.

One unfortunate consequence of the unquestioned acceptance of the primacy of early childhood influences on personality is the belief that personality is resistant to change. However, McClelland (1965) has demonstrated that achievement motivation of adults can be enhanced. There is no reason to believe that other aspects of adult personality cannot be similarly changed if appropriate training and subsequent environmental support are provided.

Finally, it must be remembered that not all observed behavior is accounted for by personality (however the term is defined); concurrent environmental stimuli also make a contribution. When we are well aware of environmental differences between two groups, it does not seem reasonable to attribute observed difference in behavior entirely to inferred personality factors alone. Yet this is precisely what frequently occurs in poverty research. In Chapter 19 this issue will be discussed more fully.

REFERENCES

Asher, S., and Allen, V. L. Racial Preference and Social Comparison Processes. *Journal of Social Issues* 1969, 25: 157-66.

Atkinson, J. W., ed. *Motives in Fantasy, Action, and Society.* Princeton, N. J.: Van Nostrand, 1958.

Baehr, R. F. Need Achievement and Dialect in Lower-Class Adolescent Negroes. Presented at convention of the American Psychological Assoc., 1965.

Bandura, A., and Mischel, W. Modification of Self-Imposed Delay through Exposure to Live and Symbolic Models. *Journal of Personality and Social Psychology* 1965, 2: 698-705.

Battle, E. S., and Rotter, J. B. Children's Feeling of Personal Control as Related to Social Class and Ethnic Group. *Journal of Personality* 1963, 31: 482-90.

Beilin, H. The Pattern of Postponability and Its Relation to Social Class Mobility. *Journal of Social Psychology* 1956, 44: 33-49.

Bieri, J., and Loback, R. Self-Concept Differences in Relation to Identification, Religion, and Social Class. *Journal of Abnormal and Social Psychology* 1961, 62: 94-98.

Bell, C. D. Processes in the Formation of Adolescents' Aspirations. *Social Forces* 1963, 42: 179-86.

Bresnahan, J. K. The Effect of Task and Incentive on Concept Acquisition with Children from Two Socio-Economic Levels. *Dissertation Abstracts* 1967, 2886.

Bruckman, I. R. The Relationship between Achievement Motivation and Sex, Age, Social Class, School Stream and Intelligence. *British Journal of Social and Clinical Psychology* 1966, 5: 211-20.

Cameron, A., and Storm, T. Achievement Motivation in Canadian Indians: Middle and Working-Class Children. *Psychological Reports* 1965, 16: 459-63.

Clark, K. B., and Clark, M. L. Racial Identification and Racial Preferences in Negro Children, in T. M. Newcomb and E. L. Hartley, eds. *Readings in Social Psychology.* New York: Holt, 1947, pp. 169-78.

Clark, R. E. The Relationship of Schizophrenia to Occupational Income and Occupational Prestige. *American Sociological Review* 1948, 3: 325-30.

———. Psychosis, Incomes and Occupational Prestige. *American Journal of Sociology* 1949, 44: 433-40.

Davis, K. Mental Hygiene and the Class Structure. *Psychiatry* 1938, 1: 55-56.

Donoviel, S. J. Responsiveness to Maternal Reinforcement in Middle and Low Socioeconomic Children. *Dissertation Abstracts* 1966, 27: 2132.

Douvan, E. Social Status and Success Striving. *Journal of Abnormal and Social Psychology* 1956, 52: 219-23.

Franklin, R. D. Youth's Expectancies about Internal Versus External Control of Reinforcement Related to N Variables. Doctoral dissertation, Purdue University, 1963.

Freeman, S. A. Time Perspective as a Function of Socio-Economic Group and Age. Doctoral dissertation, University of Southern California, 1964.

Goodman, M. E. *Race Awareness in Young Children.* Cambridge, Mass: Addison-Wesley, 1952.

Gore, P. M., and Rotter, J. B. A Personality Correlate of Social Action. *Journal of Personality* 1963, 31: 58-64.

Gottesfeld, H., and Dozier, G. Changes in Feelings of Powerlessness in a Community Action Program, *Psychological Reports* 1966, 19: 987.

Graves, T. D. Time Perspective and the Deferred Gratification Pattern in a Tri-Ethnic Community. Doctoral dissertation, University of Pennsylvania, 1961.

Greene, J. E., and Roberts, A. H. Time Orientation and Social Class: A Correlation. *Journal of Abnormal and Social Psychology* 1961, 62: 141.

Greenwald, H. J., and Oppenheim, D. B. Reported Magnitude of Self-Misidentification among Negro Children—Artifact? *Journal of Personality and Social Psychology* 1968, 8: 49-52.

Haan, N. The Relationship of Ego Functioning and Intelligence to Social Status and Social Mobility. *Journal of Abnormal and Social Psychology* 1964, 69: 591-93.

Haggstrom, W. C. Self-Esteem and Other Characteristics of Residentially Desegregated Negroes. *Dissertation Abstracts* 1963, 23: 3007-08.

Haller, A. Q., Jr. A Correlation Analysis of the Relationship between Status and Personality. Doctoral dissertation, University of Wisconsin, 1954.

Havighurst, R. J., and Taba, H. *Adolescent Character and Personality.* New York: Wiley, 1949.

Hill, T. J. Attitudes toward Self: An Experimental Study. *Journal of Educational Sociology* 1957, 30: 395-97.

Hollingshead, A. B., and Redlich, F. C *Social Class and Mental Illness.* New York: Wiley, 1958.

Judson, A. J., and Tuttle, C. E. Time Perspective and Social Class. *Perception and Motor Skills* 1966, 23: 1074.

Keller, S. The Social World of the Urban Slum Child: Some Early Findings. *American Journal of Orthopsychiatry* 1963, 33: 221-31.

Kendall, M. B., and Sibley, R. F. Social Class Differences in Time Perspective: Fact or Artifact. Paper presented at Eastern Psychological Association Convention, Boston, 1968.

Kennedy, W. A., and Vega, M. Negro Children's Performance on a Discrimination Task as a Function of Examiner Race and Verbal Incentive. *Journal of Personality and Social Psychology* 1965, 2: 839-43.

Kinsey, A. C., Pomeroy, W. B., and Martin, C. E. *Sexual Behaviour in the Human Male.* Philadelphia: Saunders, 1948.

Klausner, S. Z. Social Class and Self-Concept. *Journal of Social Psychology* 1953, 38: 201-05.

Kluckhohn, C., Murray, H. A., and Schneider, D. M. *Personality in Nature, Society and Culture.* New York: Knopf, 1956.

Kolb, D. A. Achievement Motivation Training for Underachieving High-School Boys. *Journal of Personality and Social Psychology* 1965, 2: 783-92.

Langner, T. M., and Michael, S. T. *Life Stress and Mental Health.* Glencoe, Ill.: Free Press, 1963.

Lefcourt, H. M., and Ladwig, G. W. The American Negro: A Problem in Expectancies. *Journal of Personality and Social Psychology* 1965, 1: 377-80.

LeShan, L. L. Time Orientation and Social Class. *Journal of Abnormal and Social Psychology* 1952, 47: 589-92.

Lewis, O. *The Children of Sanchez.* New York: Random House, 1961.

Littig, L. W., and Yeracaris, C. A. Achievement Motivation and Inter-Generational Occupational Mobility. *Journal of Personality and Social Psychology* 1965, 1: 386-89.

Luft, J. Monetary Value and the Perception of Persons. *Journal of Social Psychology* 1957, 46: 245-51.

Maitlund, S. D. P. Time Perspective, Frustration-Failure and Delay of Gratification in Middle Class and Lower Class Children from Organized and Disorganized Families. Doctoral dissertation, University of Minnesota, 1966.

Mason, E. P. Some Factors in Self-Judgements. *Journal of Clinical Psychology* 1954, 10: 336-40. (a)

————. Some Correlates of Self-Judgement of the Aged. *Journal of Gerontology* 1954, 9: 324-37. (b)

McClelland, D. C. *The Achieving Society.* Princeton, N. J.: Van Nostrand, 1961.

————. Toward a Theory of Motive Acquisition. *American Psychologist* 1965, 20: 321-33.

McClosky, H., and Schaar, J. H. Psychological Dimensions of Anomie. *American Sociological Review* 1965, 30: 14-40.

McDonald, R. L., and Gynther, M. D. MMPI Differences Associated with

Sex, Race, and Social Class in Two Adolescent Samples. *Journal of Consulting Psychology* 1963, 27: 112-16.

————. Relationship of Self and Ideal-Self Descriptions with Sex, Race and Class in Southern Adolescents. *Journal of Personality and Social Psychology* 1965, 1: 85-88.

McGrade, B. J. Effectiveness of Verbal Reinforcers in Relation to Age and Social Class. *Journal of Personality and Social Psychology* 1966, 4: 555-60.

Merbaum, A. D. Need for Achievement in Negro and White Children. *Dissertation Abstracts* 1962, 693-94.

Merton, R. Social Structure and Anomie, in *Social Theory and Social Structure*. Glencoe, Ill.: Free Press, 1949, pp. 125-49.

Minigione, A. D. Need for Achievement in Negro and White Children. *Journal of Consulting Psychology* 1965, 29: 108-11.

Mischel, W. Preference for Delayed Reinforcement: An Experimental Study of a Cultural Observation. *Journal of Abnormal and Social Psychology* 1958, 56: 57-61.

————. Father-Absence and Delay of Gratification: Cross-Cultural Comparisons. *Journal of Abnormal and Social Psychology* 1961, 63: 116-24.

Morland, J. K. Racial Acceptance and Preference of Nursery School Children in a Southern City. *Merrill-Palmer Quarterly* 1962, 8: 271-80.

Nutall, R. L. Some Correlates of High Need for Achievement among Northern Negroes. *Journal of Abnormal and Social Psychology* 1964, 68: 593-600.

Ort, R. S. A Study of Role-Conflicts as Related to Class Level. *Journal of Abnormal and Social Psychology* 1952, 47: 425-532.

Radke, M. J., and Trager, H. G. Children's Perceptions of the Social Roles of Negroes and Whites. *Journal of Psychology* 1950, 29: 3-33.

Reichert, L. D. An Investigation of the Relation of Maternal Restrictiveness and Social Class Position as Related to Fantasy, Delay Tolerance, and Time Orientation in Children. Doctoral dissertation, New York University, 1966.

Rosen, B. C. The Achievement Syndrome. *American Sociological Review* 1956, 21: 203-11.

————. Race, Ethnicity and the Achievement Syndrome. *American Sociological Review* 1959, 24: 47-60.

Rosenhan, D. L. Effects of Social Class and Race on Responsiveness to Approval and Disapproval. *Journal of Personality and Social Psychology* 1966, 4: 253-59.

Rosenhan, D., and Greenwald, J. C. The Effects of Age, Sex and Socio-Economic Class on Responsiveness to Two Classes of Verbal Reinforcement. *Journal of Personality* 1965, 33: 108-21.

Rotter, J. B. Generalized Expectancies for Internal Versus External Control of Reinforcement. *Psychological Monographs* 1966, 80: no. 1 (Whole no. 609).

Rotter, J. B., and Mulry, R. C. Internal Versus External Control of Reinforcement and Decision Time. *Journal of Personality and Social Psychology* 1965, 2: 598-604.

Safer, M. A., and Kornreich, L. B. The Interaction of Social Class and Type of Reinforcement in Discrimination Learning. *Psychonomic Science* 1968, 2: 206.

Sarbin, T. R. On the Futility of the Proposition That Some People Be Labelled Mentally Ill. *Journal of Consulting Pychology* 1967, 31: 447-53.

Scheff, T. *Being Mentally Ill: A Sociological Theory.* Chicago: Aldine, 1966.

Schneider, L. S., and Lysgaard, S. The Deferred Gratification Pattern: A Preliminary Study. *American Sociological Review* 1953, 18: 142-49.

Seagull, A. A. The Ability to Delay Gratification. Doctoral dissertation, Syracuse University, 1964.

Seeman, M. On the Meaning of Alienation. *American Sociological Review* 1959, 24: 782-91.

―――. Social Learning Theory and the Theory of Mass Society. Paper read at the annual meeting of the American Sociological Society, Los Angeles, 1963.

―――. Powerlessness and Knowledge: A Comparative Study of Orientation and Learning. *Sociometry* 1967, 30: 105-23.

Seeman, M., and Evans, J. W. Alienation and Learning in a Hospital Setting. *American Sociological Review* 1962, 27: 772-83.

Sewell, W. H., and Haller, A. O. Social Status and the Personality Adjustment of the Child. *Sociometry* 1956, 19: 114-25.

Shybut, J. Delayed Gratification: A Study of Its Measurement and Its Relationship to Certain Behavioral, Psychological and Demographical Variables. Master's thesis, University of Colorado, 1963.

Silverman, M. I. The Relationship between Self-Esteem and Aggression in Two Classes. *Dissertation Abstracts* 1964, 25: 2616.

Soares, A. T., and Soares, L. M. Self-Perceptions of Culturally Disadvantaged and Non-Disadvantaged Children. Paper presented at the Eastern Psychological Convention, Boston, Mass., 1968.

Spence, J. T., and Segner, L. L. Verbal Versus Non-Verbal Reinforcement Combinations in the Discrimination Learning of Middle and Lower Class Children. *Child Development* 1967, 38: 29-38.

Srole, L., Langner, T. S., Michael, S. T., Opler, S. T., and Rennie, T. A. C. *Mental Health in the Metropolis.* New York: McGraw-Hill, 1962.

Stevenson, H. W. Social Reinforcement of Children's Behavior, in L. P.

Lipsitt and C. C. Spiker, eds. *Advances in Child Development and Behavior.* Vol. 2. New York: Academic Press, 1965.

Stevenson, H. W., and Stewart, E. C. A Developmental Study of Race Awareness in Young Children. *Child Development* 1958, 29: 399-410.

Storm, T., Anthony, W. S., and Porsalt, R. D. Ethnic and Social Class Differences in Performance for Material and Non-Material Rewards: New Zealand Children. *Journal of Personality and Social Psychology* 1965, 2: 759-62.

Straus, M. A. Deferred Gratification, Social Class, and the Achievement Syndrome. *American Sociological Review* 1962, 27: 326-35.

Strodtbeck, F. L. Family Interaction, Values, and Achievement, in D. McClelland, ed. *Talent and Society.* New York: Van Nostrand, 1958, pp. 138-95.

Szasz, T. S. *The Myth of Mental Illness.* New York: Harper, 1961.

Terrell, G. The Role of Incentive in Discrimination Learning in Children. *Child Development* 1958, 29: 231-36.

Terrell, G., Jr., Durkin, D., and Wiesley, M. Social Class and the Nature of the Incentive in Discrimination Learning. *Journal of Abnormal and Social Psychology* 1959, 59: 270-72.

Terrell, G., and Kennedy, W. A. Discrimination Learning and Transposition in Children as a Function of the Nature of the Reward. *Journal of Experimental Psychology* 1957, 57: 252-60.

Tiber, N., and Kennedy, W. A. The Effects of Incentives on Intelligence Test Performance of Different Social Groups. *Journal of Consulting Psychology* 1964, 28: 187.

Titus, W. F. Relationship of Need for Achievement, Dependency, and Locus of Control in Boys of Middle and Low Socio-Economic Status. Doctoral dissertation, Indiana University, 1966.

Veroff, J., Atkinson, J. W., Feld, S., and Gurin, G. The Use of Thematic Apperception to Assess Motivation in a Nation-Wide Interview Study. *Psychological Monographs* 1960, 74: no. 12 (Whole no. 449).

Veroff, J., Feld, S., and Crockett, H. Exploration into the Effect of Picture Cues on Thematic Apperceptive Expression of Achievement Motivation. *Journal of Personality and Social Psychology* 1966, 3: 171-81.

Warner, W. L. The Society, the Individual, and his Mental Disorders. *American Journal of Psychiatry* 1937, 94: 275-85.

Zigler, E., and deLabry, J. Concept-Switching in Middle-Class, Lower-Class, and Retarded Children. *Journal of Abnormal and Social Psychology* 1962, 65: 267-73.

Zigler, E., and Kanzer, P. The Effectiveness of Two Classes of Verbal Reinforcers on the Performance of Middle- and Lower-Class Children. *Journal of Personality* 1962, 30: 157-63.

PART FIVE

INTERVENTION STRATEGIES

INTRODUCTION

Some of the approaches available at the psychological level for combating poverty are considered in this section. Each of the five chapters provides examples of the role that psychology can play in intervention programs designed to reduce poverty. Gurin's chapter discusses the application of expectancy concepts to job training; Pareek shows the relevance of the achievement motivation concept to social change; Gordon's chapter analyzes the role of education; Clinard describes the social and personal changes that can be produced by self-help of the poor themselves, and proposes a theoretical model centered around changes in self-concept; and, finally, Pearl argues that the progession of psychology should play a more important role in helping to eradicate poverty. While these psychological strategies hopefully will aid in efforts to eliminate poverty, other approaches—economic, sociological, legal, and political—are not incompatible with programs aimed at the psychological level.

Taking a very broad view, one economist (Lampman, 1965) recommends three approaches to the reduction of poverty. One approach is to prevent the occurrence of events over which the individual has no control. Among specific countermeasures are the reduction of unemployment, retraining and relocation of workers, and remedial measures such as a guaranteed annual income. A second approach to reducing poverty is to remove the barriers that trap particular categories of people in poverty. Specific remedies here include legislation directed toward insuring equal employment practices and equal educational opportunities regardless of class, or race, or other characteristics of group membership. The third broad approach recommended by Lampman is to initiate programs designed to enhance the motivation and ability of persons in poverty in order to improve their chances of escaping poverty through their own efforts. It is, of course, in relation to this third approach that psychologists can make a notable contribution.

In a more detailed survey of strategies for reducing poverty, Pearl and Riessman (1965) describe eight alternatives. All the specific strategies to be mentioned have been seriously proposed at one time or another, and there is no doubt something to recommend each strategy, at least for some subgroups of the poor. The first solution Pearl and Riessman call the optimistic solution: the belief that anything that increases general economic growth will help the poor. This might be called the trickle-down *theory. By way of criticism, it can be said that though a healthy economy may be necessary to eradicate poverty, it may not be a sufficient condition in itself. For instance, quite possibly numerous new jobs could come into existence but not be allocated in such a way as to help the poor. There is another, more pessimistic, solution for poverty. The growth of modern technology might conceivably eliminate the need for unskilled jobs, thus leaving a portion of the population to be wholly supported by the government. A guaranteed annual income scheme or other methods of support would be provided for the nonproductive, now redundant, sector of society. Counseling offers another solution to poverty, the rationale being that persons could succeed if only they were more diligent and took advantage of opportunities available. Other solutions mentioned are specific job training for vacancies that already exist, and a reduced work week to create more jobs. Public works is also an alternative, but unsatisfactory because it would provide only temporary jobs and would probably require only a limited number of unskilled jobs. Still another approach lies in legislation, such as the Economic Opportunity Act, and laws to protect the rights of the impecunious. Pearl and Riessman see their last alternative —education—as a complicated and ambiguous solution that promises much but delivers little.*

To reduce poverty in any significant degree will clearly require a massive and multidirectional attack. Psychological change in itself may be enough to propel some persons out of poverty solely by their own initiative. From studies of social mobility, we know a little about the characteristics of such atypical people. For the vast majority of people, however, escape from poverty is possible only if intervention occurs simultaneously on several fronts with programs complementing one another. Certainly needed are more jobs, an increase in annual income, more effective education, and better housing and physical surroundings. Added to all this must be changes at the psychological level—changes in motivation, values, self-concept, and the like—that will reinforce changes originating at other levels.

The first chapter in Part 5 is an exposition of the implications of expectancy theory for training programs designed for unemployed, usually functionally illiterate, youth. Gurin's description of the organization and goals of early job-training camps is very instructive in pointing out the relevance of psychological factors to any program of intervention in poverty. It is quite clear that underlying assumptions about psychological characteristics of trainees and about the place of psychological variables in obtaining and holding a job determined the direction many training programs took. In some instances, it is clear that psychological assumptions upon which job-training camps were based were quite explicitly acknowledged, and that components of the training were organized intentionally with implications of these psychological assumptions in mind.

Gurin criticizes the early efforts of job-training programs for not giving sufficient attention to increasing job skills that are usable and for not taking into account reality factors governing the job market in the outside world. A major portion of these training programs was designed to resocialize the individual (e.g., to encourage the acquisition of appropriate motivation, attitudes, and behavior concerning work) and to teach some basic educational skills. Unfortunately, the connection between the training programs and the real world of work was rather tenuous.

Gurin uses the framework of expectancy theory to analyze the sometimes unintended consequences of job-training programs for the individual. Extrapolating from results of research in the area of expectancy theory (i.e., internal versus external control of reinforcement, generalization of expectancies, and stability of learned expectancies), Gurin makes some extremely interesting suggestions for organizing job training programs. He points out that the expectancy concept by its very nature is comprised of the individual's dispositions and the objective availability of the goal. Hence, the expectancy concept incorporates motivational and reality factors; it integrates the level of the individual and the level of society. This is an important characteristic of expectancy theory that many other psychological theories lack.

Pareek's chapter in this section focuses on motivational consequences of poverty and suggests methods of intervention designed to change motivational patterns found among the poor. Over the past several years an impressive body of empirical research on achievement motivation has been accumulated, and a highly articulated set of theoretical concepts has been evolved by McClelland (1961), Atkinson (1958), and their associates. McClelland's (1961) application of achievement motivation theory to the interpretation of the economic development of nations contains many relevant and stimulating proposals for reducing poverty.

Many observers have noted that poverty adversely affects motivation—the drive and incentive necessary to reach a desired goal. Achievement motivation—setting high standards and wanting to excel for its own sake—tends to be low among the more disadvantaged groups (Rosen, 1959). Also related to the low level of achievement motivation are feelings of powerlessness, helplessness, and dependence that occur frequently among the poor.

One important source of low achievement motivation comes from parental influence, viz., from the mother's inadequate independence training of the child (Winterbottom, 1958). In addition, Pareek emphasizes the important role of social institutions in maintaining and reinforcing patterns of motivation and expectancy found among the poor. The critical part played by social institutions is illustrated by results of the Indian government's legislation directed towards eradicating caste-based discrimination in that country.

The area of motivation is directly relevant to consideration of techniques of social and individual change described in the last section of this volume. Some extremely intriguing and promising attempts to increase the level of achievement-motivation in adults are described by Pareek. Intensive training programs have been organized in an attempt to teach an individual to think and behave as do persons with high achievement motivation. Whether such explicit training will prove useful or feasible on a wide scale is still uncertain. Research on attitude change sugggests that an increase in achievement motivation as a result of such training may be transitory if group support is not available to help maintain the change.

Gordon provides a critical examination of compensatory education in Chapter 16. Both the poor and the nonpoor have long viewed education as a means of uplifting the disadvantaged and of helping them escape from poverty. Without doubt education has functioned as an antidote to poverty for many poor persons of unusual intelligence and motivation. However, the problem with education as a general antidote to poverty is that the poor do not really have equal educational opportunities because of the inferior quality of schools in disadvantaged areas and because of handicaps inherent in coming from a culturally deprived home environment.

Compensatory educational programs have evolved as a means of providing special help to the child from a lower-class background. Compensatory programs are usually directed toward the preschool child and the high-school dropout. Gordon asserts that compensatory education programs have not really provided anything new educationally. In a critical look at these programs, he concludes that their results have been unsatisfactory, and recommends that more emphasis should be placed on the learning of basic cognitive skills.

Viewing education in a broad perspective, Gordon makes a very trenchant analysis of the role of education in society. It seems that education often merely provides an "entry credential." That is, although school diplomas are usually required for a job, they may be unnecessary; in many instances an individual could perform at the required level of competence without the educational certificate. After critically assessing education as a means of reducing poverty, Gordon comes to the conclusion that education per se is not necessarily needed in order for the poor to succeed in society. (Yet he does acknowledge that basic cognitive skills probably are necessary.) This challenge to our traditional belief about the role of education in poverty should be taken seriously. A long hard look at the "entry credential" function of education is in order, with a view toward possible alternative means of providing such credentials for the poor.

Another very interesting technique for changing conditions of life as-

sociated with poverty is described in Chapter 17. Using data from his research in the urban slums of India, Clinard holds that the poor are able to help themselves very effectively. He maintains that although outside support (from local and federal government, etc.) certainly is needed in order to eradicate poverty effectively, there are still many things that the poor can do to improve their own situation. Merely making services available through outside agencies is not necessarily useful, since the poor often do not take advantage of the social services that are available to them. Without doubt there are many things that the poor can do for themselves better than outsiders, and some things that only the poor can do for themselves.

Clinard feels that among the most critical problems of the slum resident are feelings of apathy and powerlessness and a negative self-image. A conceptual model of social change is presented that stresses the importance of self-concept (or self-identity) as a factor in motivating social change. Also central to the model is the role of new experience (which provides new roles) in initiating change in self-identity. Self-help projects initiated by community members themselves are much more likely to lead to a positive change in self-image than projects initiated by outsiders. Feeling of self-worth can also be enhanced by collective identity-change occurring as a consequence of general community improvements—community members will now think of themselves as different kinds of people. An important element in maintaining and reinforcing any change in self-image is the treatment given the individual by other people; social validation is necessary to confirm a new self-identity. The similarity between Clinard's model and the theory discussed by Sarbin in Chapter 2 should be noted.

Several interesting examples are given from Clinard's research in Indian slums to substantiate his claim concerning the value of self-help programs as a means of producing individual and social change. The Black Muslim organization is mentioned as a good example of the dramatic personal and social change that can result from change in self-identity. It is clear that the theory and techniques discussed in this chapter have direct relevance to poverty in America.

In the last chapter in Part 5, Pearl urges that psychology be more socially relevant, and take a greater share of responsibility for initiating social change to aid the poor. Psychology and other social sciences are criticized for their role in dealing with poverty, and several courses of action that should be undertaken by the social sciences are suggested.

Pearl—himself a psychologist—takes the profession of psychology to task on a number of counts for sins of commission and omission concerning the poor. It is perhaps wishful thinking, however, to believe that *psychology has had sufficient power and influence in affecting the condition of the poor to qualify for the role of villain that Pearl would assign to it. As he acknowledges later in the chapter, poverty is a complex problem that may in the long run be solved only with extensive economic and political readjustments within society as a whole. Still, the social sciences can play an important, though limited, part in broad programs of social change by increasing our understanding of relevant psychological processes involved.*

Federal programs designed to combat poverty also come under severe attack from Pearl. He claims that most federally funded programs have tended to reinforce social inequality rather than eradicate it. In any event, it seems to be generally agreed that the federally funded War on Poverty fell far short of its goal. Certainly, allocation of insufficient funds to the poverty programs was one important source of this lack of success. Pearl makes even more fundamental criticisms aimed at assumptions underlying some of the programs.

Among other areas of action suggested to promote social change, Pearl urges psychologists to challenge myths about the poor, to keep the profession open to all, and to act politically. One way of recruiting more of the poor among the "credentialed industries" (which includes the social sciences) is by using the New Careers technique, discussed extensively by Pearl and Riessman (1965). Using psychology as an example, Pearl demonstrates how a sequence of jobs can be arranged to allow untrained persons to begin at the bottom of a career ladder and proceed upward to more demanding positions as new skills are acquired. Evidence reported in the Pearl and Riessman book suggests that an extensive program of this type would be feasible, and would be of great benefit not only to the poor but to society generally.

REFERENCES

Atkinson, J. W., ed. *Motives in Fantasy, Action and Society.* Princeton, N.J.: Van Nostrand, 1958.

Lampman, R. J. Approaches to the Reduction of Poverty. *American Economic Review* 1965, 55: No. 2, 521-29.

McClelland, D. C. *The Achieving Society.* Princeton, N.J.: Van Nostrand, 1961.

Pearl, A., and Riessman, F. *New Careers for the Poor.* Glencoe, Ill.: Free Press, 1965.

Rosen, B. C. Race, Ethnicity and the Achievement Syndrome, *American Sociological Review* 1959, 24: 47-60.

Winterbottom, M. R. The Relation of Need for Achievement in Learning Experiences in Independence and Mastery, in J. W. Atkinson, ed. *Motives in Fantasy, Action and Society.* Princeton, N.J.: Van Nostrand, 1958, pp. 453-78.

Chapter 14

AN EXPECTANCY APPROACH TO JOB TRAINING PROGRAMS

Gerald Gurin*

A major thrust of the War on Poverty has been a multiplicity of programs devoted to the needs of poverty populations of late adolescence and early adulthood. The target populations for these programs have tended to be in the age range from sixteen to twenty-one, "functionally illiterate" school dropouts, unskilled and unemployed, in most cases Negro or from some other minority group. The programs devoted to these populations have been rather staggering in their variety—the JOBS Corps, the Neighborhood Youth Corps, the special experimental and demonstration programs of the Manpower Development and Training Act, the community programs like Mobilization for Youth. They have been initiated under many different governmental departments and bureaus, with their own approaches and individual orientations fostered by a principle of local autonomy which minimized national integration and often left even the basic design of a given program to the particular local organizations running it.

*Program Director, Survey Research Center, Institute for Social Research, University of Michigan, Ann Arbor. The ideas in this chapter were developed in a series of studies on manpower training programs conducted in association with Dr. John R. P. French, Jr., and Dr. David Bradford. These studies were supported by the Department of Labor contracts OS-64-47 and 82-21-14 and contract OE 5-10-243 of the Office of Education, U.S. Department of Health, Education and Welfare. Thanks are also due to Dr. Patricia Gurin, who formulated a number of the expectancy issues that are discussed in this paper in her study of Negro college students (Gurin and Katz, 1966).

Yet, within this great variety, certain common threads and patterns have appeared. All of these programs have a primary focus on the vocational area, and have as a major objective, the preparation of these youth to take a meaningful place in the job world. Furthermore, in most cases, these programs see the problem of preparation for participation in the job world in general as well as in specific vocational training terms. This general preparation in turn has two aspects. First, it includes education in basic literacy skills, on the assumption that coping in the modern technological world requires a greater level of skill in these areas than most of these youths have acquired in the course of their school careers.

The second aspect of this general preparation has been much more tenuous and ill-defined, but includes a conglomeration of elements that are based on the assumption that in addition to vocational training and basic education, these youths require some major attitudinal and behavioral socialization if they are to be able to handle the world of work. The specific items under this socialization rubric have run the gamut, sometimes within the same program, from lessons in personal grooming, to practice in filling out application forms, to role-playing on how to conduct oneself on a job, to attempts to instill positive attitudes toward work and appropriate habits of work discipline, to ill-defined attempts at broad, general-value socialization —all based on the assumption that the world of work demands certain knowledge, attitudes, and habits that are not available to the trainees in the milieu from which they come, but that they have to learn if they are to make an adequate occupational adjustment.

These three elements, vocational training, basic education, and socialization for the world of work, have not been present in all programs directed toward youth from poverty backgrounds, but this multifaceted attack on the problem has to some extent been the model for such programs.

The reason these programs are particularly relevant to our concerns in this volume is the fact that, for better or worse, the socialization aspect has often been a very central and significant part of the programs, not something tacked on as a rider to what is basically a program for work experience or vocational training. Indeed, many of these programs, particularly in earlier days, expended more effort and money in attempts at socialization than in actual vocational training, which often involved minimal training for rudimentary low-skilled jobs. In a sense, then, the experiences of these training programs provide a laboratory for exploring many of our assumptions about the psychological factors in poverty.

The fact that these programs have been concerned with psychological and motivational problems does not mean they have been clear or in agreement in defining the nature of the problems. Much has been written on this issue, and even a brief review of the literature presents a formidable and bewildering list of concepts that have been used to describe the psychological characteristics of the population that these youth represent.[1] The multiplicity of these views is reflected in the great diversity of activities that has characterized the socialization efforts of these poverty programs, the different activities reflecting different assumptions about the nature of the psychological problems. These varying assumptions and practices have often occurred within the confines of a single program.

A multiplicity of concepts and approaches is not necessarily bad, since these problems do not reflect a single psychological issue and there is no one correct remedial approach. As Rainwater notes in Chapter 1, all the varying perspectives on the problems of poverty populations probably represent partial truths, and there is a certain amount of danger in oversimplifying the issues by casting them in *either-or* terms. However, in the case of the poverty programs, the confusion and uncertainty has to some extent reflected the nature of the underlying problems these programs were attempting to deal with. Poverty programs have perhaps been unjustly criticized for this uncertainty and lack of consistent direction, since the confusion exists in the body of literature that people running these programs have been able to draw upon.

It is not our purpose here to catalog or integrate the many conceptual approaches to problems of poverty. Rather, there will be discussed one framework within which the motivational problems presented by the youth that come to these programs can be viewed, together with some implications of this framework for an analysis of the ways in which these programs are trying to deal with the motivational and attitudinal issues. This framework has as its focus the concept of expectancy that has been central in the motivational theories of people like Atkinson (1964) and Rotter (1954), who have followed the earlier work of Lewin and Tolman. These theorists have stressed that the motivation of any given behavior depends not only on a generalized disposition to approach or avoid a given class of objects and the incentive value of the particular goal or object at issue, but also on the ex-

---

[1]We are referring to the multiplicity of concepts that has been used even among those who have agreed that these populations present certain attitudinal and motivational problems. The diversity of approaches is further extended when we consider that many who have written about these problems have questioned whether people in poverty have any special motivational characteristics and have viewed their problems completely in terms of the opportunity structure and other situational factors. In addition, there is another orientation to these problems, one which does postulate differences among the values and motivations of different socioeconomic class groupings, but sees the characteristics of the poverty group in positive rather than negative terms, as strengths rather than problems, as health rather than pathology. An interesting characterization of these different perspectives appears in this volume in Chapter 1 by Rainwater.

pectancy, or person's estimate of the probability that the behavior will lead to the goal. Without necessarily denying that some of the motivational problems in these disadvantaged groups may come from a low achievement motive or the rejection of some of the achievement goals and incentives in our society, I will focus on their problems of expectancy—the motivational problems that come not from a lack of desire for the goals our society values, but from a feeling that there is little chance of attaining these goals. This approach should be particularly applicable for the youth involved in these training programs who have, after all, volunteered to participate in a program that is appealing to their desire for a share of society's goals, and to values of work and self-help to achieve these goals. Their voluntary participation in these programs suggests that their motivational problems cannot be completely explained away as a rejection of middle-class goals and values.

Granted the severe restrictions and limitations in the choices and opportunities available in the environments of these youth, it would seem obvious to highlight the expectancy aspects of their motivational problems. It is interesting, however, that this has not always been done. The vast literature on differences between middle-class and working-class populations is particularly illustrative of this. In the past the studies in this area tended to emphasize social-class differences in basic values and personality dispositions and traced these differences to early socialization patterns set down in the family and parent-child relationships. It might be noted that this description of social-class differences was not always painted in terms that were disparaging of the less socioeconomically advantaged. Indeed, the reverse was often true, with the anxiety-driven middle-class life compared unfavorably to the more "natural" working-class life. Regardless of the particular value connotation, however, the emphasis was on differences in aspirations, values, and basic approaches to the world.

This focus on class differences in motives and values rather than expectancies is less characteristic of the more recent literature. In current writings and studies the motivational issues in disadvantaged groups have increasingly been viewed as not so much a problem of their basic dispositions and values as a problem of the inability to implement these values. For example, a major focus in the poverty literature these days is on the concept of powerlessness, which points not to lack of appropriate values and aspirations of the poor, but to their inability to achieve them and the frustration that comes from the disparity between aspirations and the ability to implement them. We see this emphasis in the very general day-to-day discussions of these issues which refer, for example, to the outbreaks in the ghettoes as problems of "rising expectations" and unfulfilled hopes, rather than as problems of people with different hopes and aspirations than those in the mainstream in our society. We also see it increasingly in the more theoretical writings and research in this area. For example, in the Coleman report on *Equality of Educational Opportunity*, the critical psychological variable that was most related to Negro elementary and high-school students' educational achievement was a measure of the sense of effectiveness and control over one's destiny (Coleman, 1966). The sense of control is also beginning to figure prominently in the work on early cognitive development of lower-class children, as Hess indicates in Chapter 4 of this volume.[2]

This changing emphasis from a focus on basic personality dispositions and values to one that stresses a sense of effectiveness or powerlessness can be seen not only in the increased attention given to particular concepts, but also in reinterpretations of some old concepts. The "delayed gratification" construct presents a rather striking example of this. A great deal of literature over the past twenty years has pointed to differences in future-oriented behaviors of people from different socioeconomic groupings, with those in lower groupings supposedly more oriented toward immediate gratification and less ready to postpone this gratification for later rewards. Traditional discussions of these supposed class differences viewed them as differences in a basic personality disposition; people wrote of the *inability* to delay gratification as a disposition set down in the early socialization of lower-class children. As Miller et al. (1965) point out in their paper on this issue, the discussions tended to ignore such an obvious issue as class differences in the attainability of the goals for which gratification was being deferred. Traditional approaches to the delayed gratification construct overlooked the very obvious point that people might be less willing to delay the gratification when the payoffs for delay were very tenuous.

Some (although not all) of the current discussion and writings on this construct are more sensitive to the obvious relationship between delay of gratification and the possibility of attaining rewards for the delay. The studies of Mischel (1961) are particularly interesting in the sense that they trace, in the work of the same individual, this historical trend away from the more traditional dispositional approach. In his first studies on delayed gratification behavior about a decade ago, Mischel was interested in the effects of early familial socializing influences, focusing particularly on the effects of growing up without a father in the home. In his latest work Mischel focuses much more on the issue of the expectancies and payoffs for the delay for which gratification is being deferred. More recently his ex-

---

[2]The writings on competence, powerlessness, and sense of control have not usually approached these concepts within an expectancy framework as directly and specifically as we are doing here. However, they are relevant to our discussion because competence and a feeling of control over one's fate are major determinants of a person's expectancies of success.

periments have been concerned with such issues as the child's trust that the experimenter will, in fact, give the rewards for which gratification is being deferred, and with the past success and failure experiences of the individual that affect his confidence that he can attain the gratification for which reward is being delayed (Mischel and Grusec, 1967; Mischel and Staub, 1965).

Perhaps the clearest statement of the more current point of view has come from the studies of Hylan Lewis on the Negro lower class in Washington, D.C. These studies have explicitly taken issue with the view that these people are different in personality or values, and have seen their problems strictly in terms of effectiveness and powerlessness. In Hylan Lewis' words, the problems are "due less to lack of recognition of and affirmation of so-called middle-class values than they are to lack of the wherewithal to support these values" (Lewis, 1967). A particularly eloquent statement of this approach appears in Elliot Liebow's *Tally's Corner* (1966), the report of the intensive anthropological study that was part of Lewis' research.

> . . . The street corner man does not appear as a carrier of an independent cultural tradition. His behavior appears not so much as a way of realizing the distinctive goals and values of his own subculture, or of conforming to its models, but rather as his way of trying to achieve many of the goals and values of the larger society, of failing to do this, and of concealing his failure from others and from himself as best he can.

> If, in the course of concealing his failure, or of concealing his fear of even trying, he pretends—through the device of public fictions—that he did not want these things in the first place and claims that he has all along been responding to a different set of rules and prizes, we do not do him or ourselves any good by accepting this claim at face value. Such a frame of reference, I believe, can bring into clearer focus the practical points of leverage for social change in this area. We do not have to see the problem in terms of breaking into a puncture-proof circle, of trying to change values, of disrupting the lines of communication between parent and child so that parents cannot make children in their own image, thereby transmitting their culture inexorably, ad infinitum. No doubt, each generation does provide role models for each succeeding one. Of much greater importance for the possibilities of change, however, is the fact that many similarities between the lower-class Negro father and son (or mother and daughter) do not result from "cultural transmission" but from the fact that the son goes out and independently experiences the same failures, in the same areas, and for much the same reasons as his father. What appears as a dynamic, self-sustaining cultural process is, in part at least, a relatively simple piece of social machinery which turns out, in rather mechanical fashion, independently produced

look-alikes. The problem is how to change the conditions which, by guaranteeing failure, cause the son to be made in the image of the father.

It is interesting to note, and perhaps no coincidence, that this increasing theoretical concern with issues of powerlessness and effectiveness has occurred during the time that poverty has become an increasing social concern and the energies of the nation have turned toward doing something about it. If we are trying to devise programs to deal with hard-core problems, it is discouraging to view these problems as ones of dispositions and values derived from early socialization. Theoretically, problems of discouragement and sense of powerlessness can be more affected by the environmental and educational influences that these programs can bring to bear than can the dispositions and values formed in early childhood years.[3]

We may grant, then, the relevance of an expectancy framework within which to view the motivational problems that are presented by the poverty program populations and the ways in which these programs are attempting to deal with the problems. In the remaining discussion there will be noted some of the issues that are highlighted when these programs are examined within this framework. Questions that are raised will be stressed more than suggested solutions because both the programs and evaluation research are still in early experimental stages. It is the problems rather than the solutions that are clearest at this time.

THE SITUATION-MOTIVATION DICHOTOMY

Perhaps the most serious and basic question posed by an expectancy framework relates to the underlying assumption of many of the programs for hard-core unemployed youth: that the problems they face can be dealt with effectively in a special program devoted to their problems as individuals —their attitudes, training, and education—isolated from any systematic attempt to affect the opportunity and social structure that the trainees face in the world outside the program. When the literature on poverty is examined, particularly with respect to Negro populations, we find a very striking dichotomy of approaches. One approach stresses the social and institutional aspects of the problem; the other approach, while not denying the original social causes, is mainly concerned with the resultant individual damage and pathology—the lack of education and skills, the motivational deficits. One approach calls for change in the social structure and basic

---

[3]It should be noted that recent work on achievement motive training, particularly that of McClelland and coworkers, raises questions about this.

institutional arrangements; the other calls for the kinds of programs we are discussing here: those which attempt to help the individual, through educational, vocational, and motivational training, to find a more rewarding place within the existing structure. Both approaches, it should be noted, are concerned with the issue of expectancies, but one focuses on the social and the other on the individual determinants of these expectancies.

If we take the expectancy construct seriously, we cannot really separate the motivational and reality aspects of the problems that these youth face, for their motivation is directly tied to the reality-payoffs available to them. This may seem a rather obvious point, but it has been obscured by the tendency to oppose psychological and situational approaches. Even when a concern with psychological motivational problems has not meant ignoring reality opportunities and constraints, the view has usually been that the motivational and reality issues involve different levels of analysis. The point stressed here is that, certainly with respect to the expectancy aspect of motivation, the reality opportunities are an integral part of the motivational as well as the reality analysis. When we focus on expectancies, we integrate the individual and institutional approaches that often have been seen as pointing in divergent directions.

This tendency to separate motivational issues from the question of reality-payoffs was particularly evident in the training programs of several years ago, when the pathological conception of motivational problems tended to predominate. With this as the dominant perspective, many programs focused so much on the trainees' educational and motivational problems that they often neglected the obvious issues of skill competence and provision of jobs. In a number of the early programs skill training was minimal, trainees often were not placed in jobs relevant to their training, and in general, there was very little follow-up provided by the program as the trainees left the project and went out into the job world. This tendency to focus on motivational issues isolated from reality problems was scathingly indicted several years ago by Cloward and Ontell (1965), who were conducting the research on the effects of the Mobilization for Youth program:

> One runs the grave risk of seeming to be ridiculous by calling attention to the possibility that there may be a relationship between the way in which a young person performs in a training program and his expectation that a job does or does not await him on graduation. If it is ridiculous, so be it, for the plain fact is that we act as if the relationship does not exist.

This was probably an overstatement of the case even when it was made several years ago, but it did reflect a tendency for the assumption to be made that meaningful jobs were readily available if the trainees could be made ready for them. The early projects operated essentially as crash programs, lasting from a few months to a year, providing some minimal help and training on the implicit assumption that this might be the crucial influence necessary to pull the trainees out of their rut and despair and get them started toward a meaningful place in the job world. The problems tended to be viewed as in the trainees—in their inadequate educational and vocational skills and in attitudes and behavior patterns that were dysfunctional for the occupational world.

In the past few years, programs devoted to the problems of the hard-core unemployed have reflected a gradually increasing recognition of the relationship between problems of trainee motivation and the actual payoffs available to the trainees in the real world. In contrast with those of several years ago, programs today tend to be much more actively concerned with attempts to articulate the program with the job market. There is increasing concern not only with obtaining jobs for the trainees but with the type of job that might be obtained; jobs are sought that have some skill requirements and mobility possibilities and do not represent the dead-end of unskilled labor. To the extent that the programs maintain a large investment in counseling, there is more emphasis on counseling the trainees out in the job world where the motivational issues can be dealt with around the actual reality problems, as opposed to an approach in which the counselors attempt to operate as socializers within the isolated therapeutic setting of the project.

This greater sensitivity to the tie between motivation and reality-payoffs is also evident in the fact that increasingly programs are not just passively attempting to fit trainees into existing niches, but are aimed at more active job development in helping create the kinds of opportunities that will provide meaningful places for their trainees. There is increasing recognition that it is not enough just to help trainees find available jobs. Perhaps the most striking example of this concern with job development appears in Pearl and Riessman, *New Careers for the Poor* (1965), in which they suggest that the poor could be trained for a vast number of subprofessional jobs in the health, education, and welfare programs that communities are undertaking in carrying out the mandate of the Economic Opportunity Act. But other programs as well have become concerned with job development on a somewhat less ambitious scale.

Perhaps, then, the major contribution of an expectancy approach is to underscore the importance of continuing in a number of the directions already begun in the past few years. However, it should be stressed that these developments are by no means universally accepted in the approaches to the problems of the hard-core unemployed. Thus, in urging a priority for meaningful jobs and skill training, and questioning the value of motivational approaches that focus on socialization in an isolated project setting, this discussion is not just a listing of developments that are by now universally accepted in these projects: the issues are still the subject of active controversy.

MOTIVATIONAL ISSUES WITHIN A REALITY FRAMEWORK

A focus on the expectancy aspect of the motivational problems has led to the consideration of the reality situation that these people face, and to recommendations dealing with these reality issues. In a sense, this may seem a strange conclusion to be reached by a psychologist interested in investigating the motivational issues that these populations present. The major problems in this area are beyond the competence of psychologists to solve.[4] This does not mean, however, that this is all that can be said about the motivational issues. For although their motivational problems are affected by the immediate reality situation, there is more to the motivational problem than that. I have commented that those who have stressed the motivational and psychological issues presented by these trainees have tended to neglect the reality and institutional problems. In a similar vein, those who have approached the problem of poverty with suggestions for changes in social institutions and the opportunity structure have tended to ignore the fact that motivational problems will not automatically disappear with these structural changes. Just as a concern with motivational issues does not necessarily imply a neglect of reality, a concern with reality does not mean that motivational and personality issues are irrelevant. Actually, for psychologists, some of the most interesting and significant theoretical problems just begin when the reality limitations on expectancies begin to disappear.

Thus, the expectancy perspective in which the trainees' motivational problems are viewed in relation to their opportunity situation does not deny the importance of psychological issues. It focuses instead on different types of psychological issues than those that have been emphasized by people who have adopted a more traditional and individually-oriented psychological perspective. The issues that become relevant are those that are major determinants of an individual's expectancies of failure and success—competence, efficacy and powerlessness, feelings about one's ability to affect one's life.

---

[4]This is particularly true if we go beyond the framework of the vocational education program and its assumption that the solution to these problems lies in increasing marketable individual skills. Ultimately a focus on expectancies suggests the limits of an individual competence approach to these problems and raises questions about the need for more drastic system changes to deal with the social and situational determinants of expectancies. At this point the limitations of a psychologist's contribution to recommended solutions become particularly apparent.

And problems remain particularly for a group of people with a history of failure and defeat, even when opportunity and situational factors change, because self-confidence does not automatically increase with an increase in competence, and increased feelings of being able to control one's own fate do not automatically follow the objective reality that this is indeed the case. While I have stressed that expectancies are affected by the immediate objective situational payoffs and are thus subject to change as these situational opportunities change, expectancies also represent the residues of the history of the individual's past experiences with success and failure, and thus influence the way he will react to the realities he faces, and even to changes in these realities. Even in a situation where opportunities are expanding rapidly, some motivational relearning is necessary to change expectancies so that they conform to the present rather than to the old realities.[5]

Thus, the problems of these trainees follow from the fact that expectancy is to some extent a generalized disposition that develops, like other personality dispositions, out of the whole life history of relevant success and failure experiences. This disposition will then affect the way an individual evaluates his expectancies in a particular situation. When expectancy is seen in these general dispositional terms, it may present problems of resocialization and relearning as serious as those of other personality dispositions. People with low expectancies of success, like the hard-core unemployed, will not automatically respond when their situations suddenly change. Once reality-opportunities are expanded, the problem is getting the trainee's expectancies of success (his confidence, sense of efficacy, etc.) to reflect the new opportunities. This means that the issues of motivational theory most critical for these training programs have to do with learning new expectancies and the generalization of this learning from the training situation to the world outside the program. In the following section, we will look at literature that is relevant to relearning and generalizing of expectancies, and the implications of certain findings for job-training programs.

---

[5]Essentially, we are attempting to resolve the usual dichotomy between psychological and situational approaches by focusing on the types of psychological issues that follow from an appreciation of situational and opportunity constraints. It might be noted that some theoreticians who have looked at these problems from a cultural perspective are attempting a parallel resolution between what have usually been viewed as contrasting cultural and situational approaches. Their discussion of the "culture of poverty" focuses on subcultural differences between poverty and other groups, but on differences that represent subcultural adaptations to an environment of constraints and limitations. Thus, they view the environmental constraints as critical, but also recognize that these subcultural adaptations that have served the test of time and history will not automatically change with environmental change, particularly with environmental manipulations imposed from outside. Rainwater is a prominent proponent of this point of view.

THE RELEARNING OF EXPECTANCIES

Although the expectancy construct has an important role in motivational theory, the major motivational theorists have done relatively little work on the learning and transferring of expectancies. For instance, the major focus of McClelland, Atkinson, and their associates has been on the determinants of the motive disposition, not on expectancy. In their studies expectancies have typically been experimentally manipulated as a means of comparing reactions', particularly the risk-taking preferences, of people differing in motive strength. This experimental focus reflects the theoretical orientation which views motives as relatively general and stable personality dispositions and views expectancies as specific and situationally determined. It is only in the later work within the McClelland-Atkinson tradition, particularly the work of Veroff (1965) and Feather (1966, 1968), that expectancy has been viewed as a more general disposition with some of the same problems of resocialization and relearning that are characteristic of other personality dispositions.[6] Thus, the work that is most relevant to our discussion comes from theorists who have worked outside this major motivational tradition.

The one group of motivational theorists that has addressed itself systematically to the issue we are discussing is Rotter (1966) and his associates, who have been particularly concerned with the question of the bases of expectancy—specifically, whether expectancies are seen as deriving from internal or external control of reinforcement—and the relationship of this to problems of learning and generalizing new expectancies. Recently, many people have become interested in the internal-external construct and its relation to issues of efficacy and powerlessness. It has usually been forgotten that Rotter's interest in this variable sprang not from this substantive concern but rather from his theoretical interests in the question of how new expectancies are learned. Looking at this internal-external concept both as a characteristic of a situation and as a personality orientation, Rotter and his associates have shown that where causality is seen as external—

---

[6]It is interesting that in distinguishing between the situationally determined expectancy and the motive disposition set down in early childhood development, the traditional McClelland-Atkinson approach parallels the traditional approaches to poverty and social class differences which, as we have already noted, also separated situational and personality determinants. It is also interesting that the McClelland-Atkinson concentration on the motive disposition and its determinants in early childhood experiences parallels the tendency for the class and poverty literature of the past generation to focus on the personality and value issues supposedly derived from early socialization experiences, rather than on those problems most reflective of ongoing situational limitations. In a similar vein, the motivational theorists' growing interest in the construct of expectancy parallels the increasing interest in the poverty literature in constructs like *efficacy* and *powerlessness*.

that is, as based on chance forces over which the individual has no control, rather than on the person's own internal resources of ability, skill, and effort—one learns less predictably from reinforcement. They have shown that people in experimental situations ruled by chance rather than skill, as well as people who show a disposition to view the world in external terms, are less guided by their experiences of success and failure in learning new expectancies and in generalizing this learning to new situations (Bennion, 1961; James, 1957; James and Rotter, 1958; Phares, 1957; Rotter et al., 1962). This is understandable in simple common-sense terms. If a person feels that his success or failure in a given situation is determined by chance rather than by his own skill and resources, there is no reason for him to utilize this experience as a basis for evaluating future similar situations.

These studies are particularly relevant to our discussion because they focus on a problem that is particularly critical in the groups usually served by these training programs. The research on internal-external control has consistently demonstrated class and racial differences in the degree to which individuals feel they control the reinforcements they receive. Lower socioeconomic groups are more likely to feel that external rather than internal factors operate to control what happens to them in life. Furthermore, the interaction of class and race is such that lower-class Negroes stand out as having a particularly external orientation that is understandable in terms of their life experiences (Battle and Rotter, 1963; Lefcourt and Ladwig, 1965; Coleman et al., 1966). These class and race findings have appeared in studies of all ages—children, adolescents, and adults. Thus, in pointing to the particular problems in learning expectancies that occur among people with an external orientation, Rotter and his associates have underscored a problem that is likely to be particularly relevant in the poverty groups served by these training programs.

What are the implications of these findings? If we are concerned with helping the trainee tie his expectancies to his internal resources and control, the success experiences that the trainees have in the course of their training should be tied to their actual performance. This means programming the tasks in such a way that easy steps come first and trainees learn both skills and expectancies as they proceed through the tasks. It is crucial that their competencies and skills are seen by the trainees as the phenomena that produced their successes so that they develop a well-internalized sense of control that is not easily deflated by subsequent failure experiences.

Therefore, the importance of training in competence and skill is once again underscored, not only to help the trainees with some of their problems in the job world, but as a cornerstone of the approach to their psychological and motivational problems as well. Acquiring competence in a meaningful skill is an essential underpinning for any long-range, stable change in people's feelings about their opportunities in the occupational world.

As has been indicated, this rather obvious point has sometimes been neglected in the concern of some of these programs with socialization issues. Rotter's findings on the implications of an external orientation highlight not only the ineffectiveness of a program that focuses too much on socialization issues, but suggests its possible boomerang effects as well. These programs have often placed great emphasis on teaching the trainees those behaviors that are deemed essential to get along and be acceptable in the world of work. Thus, there is often great stress on grooming, dress, how to behave with a supervisor, and how to take exams that are used in job selection. While such emphases can be helpful, there is a potential danger, particularly if they overshadow the emphasis on skill and competence. To focus on such strategies of manipulation and accommodation to outside forces may encourage the very external orientation that is an important aspect of the problem that these trainees present.

In addition to the issue of internal versus external control, two other issues in the learning of expectancies are of concern: one is the stability of newly learned expectancies and the factors related to this stability; the other is the generalization of newly acquired expectancies.

Interest in stability is obvious. In a training program we are not interested in developing new expectancies that have little stability over time or need constant reinforcement to maintain. Rather, we are hopeful of effecting more permanent change. The studies on expectancy in the literature are rather pessimistic on this point, since they indicate that changes produced by success and failure in specific experimental tasks may be quite transitory. Studies have indicated that in as short a time period as one day after the experimental learning situation, there is a considerable reversal among subjects to the expectancies they held before the experiment (Phares, 1966; Rychlak and Eacker, 1962; Schwarz, 1966). There is also evidence in these same studies the reversals are more likely to occur when the expectancy training was highly discrepant with the person's initial level of expectancy (Schwarz, 1966). For example, among the people who began with very low expectancies, a striking and consistent set of success experiences in the experimental situation could lead to great heightening of expectancy at the end of the experiment, but would have little long-range permanent effect; there would be a greater tendency to revert back to the low expectancy when the subjects were tested again sometime after the experiment.

These findings are particularly relevant since we would expect the trainees to be people with low expectancies. For such people the study findings imply that the training situation should give them enough success experience to provide some basis for a change in their orientation, but not so much success that the training experience becomes divorced from reality and has a minimal impact beyond the period of the training program.

In addition to the question of stability, the expectancy studies raise the issue of when newly acquired expectancies in a specific situation will affect the more generalized disposition regarding chances for success. Just as we are hopeful of promoting more permanent change, we are also crucially interested in training that will transfer beyond the specific training situation. We are interested in providing a set of training experiences that will help the trainees develop a general sense of effectiveness with which to meet the challenges that they face outside the training program.

Although the studies are not clear on this issue, there are some data that are particularly relevant because they refer to people of low expectancies, those we would expect to predominate in poverty groups. The findings of several studies suggest that people with low expectancies are particularly situation-bound. They are very easily affected by success and failure experiences in a given situation, and may more easily generalize to new situations (Crandall, 1963; Crandall et al., 1964). However, this very same situational sensitivity makes them unusually sensitive as well to the success and failure experiences that they then meet in the next situation.

These findings are particularly relevant to the issue of the generalizability from the training program to the postprogram world. Providing a completely supportive environment in the project might help keep the trainee from dropping out, but would not prepare him to handle the realities of the job world. Again, the tying of success (and failure) experiences to actual skill and performance in the training period is helpful on this issue. To the extent that the reinforcement experiences in the training program follow a reality-based pattern of successes and failures, there is a greater possibility for learning expectancies that can handle the realities to be faced after the end of the program.

To deal with the issue of generalizability, then, the environment of the training project should resemble as much as possible that of the job world. The problem of generalizability that we have been discussing is probably best handled by the directions many recent programs have taken, where counseling, education, and vocational training occur not in an isolated program but in an actual job setting. In terms of the psychological issues that have been the concern of this discussion, we wish particularly to support the value of transferring the counseling emphasis from preparatory socialization in an encapsulated project setting to working with psychological problems of confidence and expectancy which will be critically faced in the job world.

There are many other ways in which this realism, and comparability of the two environments, could be encouraged. For example, when many of the issues of confidence and efficacy among Negroes occur in relation to whites, we may question how much a Negro trainee may be expected to transfer the heightened confidence and expectancy built up in a training program when the training program consists of all Negro trainees, as is true of many of these programs.

We might note in this connection that the need for such counseling will likely extend beyond the few months at the beginning of the trainee's first job. The problems surrounding the learning of new expectancies are very difficult ones. The trainees' feelings of confidence are likely to remain fragile and easily deflated for a long period of time, even following a number of success experiences. It is likely that to be maximally effective, the counseling relationships established with the trainees should be maintained over a long period of time.

A cautionary note is important at this point. Making the training realistic is not always synonymous with pointing up the skill-based nature of successes and failures. The nature of the world, particularly for these trainees, is such that rewards do not always follow performance. A training program oriented to the proposition that all situations are skill-based and that success is only a matter of learning new skills would not be adequate training for the realities that these trainees have faced and will face in the future. Expectancy training should also include teaching about the way the social system operates. In some way a trainee should be helped to determine whether a particular situation is skill-based or externally-based or whether a particular failure ought to reduce his internally-based expectancies or not. This raises some questions about complications in the internal-external control area that are usually not considered in the traditional research but which are likely to be highly important in a population that faces a variety of external obstacles. We will discuss some of these complications in the following section.

ISSUES OF INTERNAL-EXTERNAL CONTROL

We have already noted the prominence of the internal-external control dimension in the work of many people studying the problems of poverty groups. In contemporary writings it has become fairly common to view the motivational problems of poverty populations as deriving from feelings of powerlessness in confronting an environment viewed as bewildering and uncontrollable. Despite all the writings and research with this construct, however, and despite the fact that it seems to represent a rather simple common-sense notion, it presents a number of complexities that have usually been ignored, but are important to the issues of concern in this volume.

One of the complexities springs from the fact that the writings in this area have not distinguished between a belief that internal control operates generally in society, and the application of this to a personal situation. It has been assumed in the literature that a belief in internal control represents a feeling of competence, efficacy, and control over one's own fate. For example, questions in the Rotter Internal-External Scale include two types of items that have not been distinguished—those that tap a general belief in internal-external control, and those designed to elicit the respondent's sense of control over his own successes and failures.

In my research, I have found the distinction to be a crucial one. In a study of functionally illiterate inner-city Negro youth in a job training and socialization program, we found that when items were phrased in a very general sense—asking what generally makes for success in life—the great majority of the trainees voice agreement with the ideology that a person can control his own destiny, that hard work rather than luck makes for success in life. In contrast, when the questions were phrased in terms of what control they themselves had over their own lives, the trainees much more often responded in ways that indicated some questioning of this sense of control. More important than these differences in the proportion of trainees responding affirmatively to the two types of questions is the further finding that the two types of questions were differentially related to the success of the trainees in the job world. The questions tapping a general "Protestant Ethic" ideology bore no relation to job success; the questions tapping the trainee's sense of control and powerlessness—those most relevant to the issues of expectancy that we have been discussing—were very clearly related to job success.[7]

There is another implicit assumption in the way the internal-external scale has been interpreted that should be questioned, particularly in its application to poverty groups. It has usually been assumed that internal beliefs represent some kind of positive affirmation. What has been neglected is the fact that an internal orientation may also have negative implications. When associated with success, an internal orientation can lead to feelings of competence and efficacy. When associated with failure, however, it can lead to self-derogation and self-blame. Rotter, in a finding that has tend-

---

[7]The relationship seems to be a circular and mutually reinforcing one. There is some tendency for people who enter the job market with a feeling of some control over their destinies to do better than those who approach it with a sense of fatalism and powerlessness. There is even clearer evidence that this experience of job success feeds back into, and reinforces, these very same attitudes.

ed to be forgotten in our focus on the positive aspects of an internal orientation, noted that the relationship between the internal-external control dimension and personal adjustment may be somewhat curvilinear (Rotter et al., 1962). Because of the potential intrapunitive implications of an internal orientation, people with an extreme internal orientation, as well as those with an external one, tend to be psychologically less adjusted and healthy. This is a particularly important consideration to keep in mind in dealing with the types of people that are likely to be represented in training programs for hard-core poverty groups. For people who have a history of much failure and little success, and whose failures are tied to very real external obstacles they have faced, an internal orientation may be more reflective of intrapunitiveness than of efficacy. An internal response that might be considered normal in terms of the typical middle-class experience may be extreme and intrapunitive in the light of the experiences of the people represented in these programs.

Thus, the implications of an internal or external orientation are complicated by the issue of the reality-bases of the obstacles the individual has faced. This points to a complexity on the external end of the continuum that has not usually been considered in discussions of this dimension. Almost all of the research on internal and external bases of expectancy has examined just two bases—skill versus chance. These may be the most pertinent bases for people whose advantaged position in the social structure limits the operation of other external determinants of success and failure. But low-income groups experience many external obstacles that have nothing to do with chance, such as the operation of the labor market which can lead to layoffs over which individuals have no control. There are class-tied obstacles to all kinds of opportunities, and to resources which open up other opportunities, which may be correctly perceived by low-income persons as external but not a matter of randomness or luck. For low-income Negroes there is also the external factor of racial discrimination that operates over and above class obstacles. It may be perceived as operating quite the opposite of chance—systematically, predictably, reliably.

This distinction on the external side is not just an esoteric issue. I suspect that it matters motivationally for disadvantaged groups whether one talks about chance or about some of these other external factors. Although the literature to date indicates that people who believe in internal control are more guided by reality cues in learning new expectancies, are generally more effectively motivated, and perform better in achievement situations, these same effects may not follow for low-income persons, particularly Negroes, who believe that skill factors are always more important than economic and discriminatory factors in explaining why they succeed or fail. Indeed, a focus on external factors may be motivationally healthy instead of damaging when it concerns assessing one's probabilities for success against systematic and real external obstacles rather than exigencies of fate.

To some extent these considerations may help explain why we found no relationship between our measures of generalized Protestant Ethic beliefs and job success among the trainees in our study. For the trainees to hold such beliefs despite their history of failure in the face of many reality-obstacles may imply an intrapunitiveness and lack of realism that counterbalances any of the possible positive motivational implications that might come from holding such beliefs.

One finding from our study of trainees provides indirect support for the contention that an internal orientation, when it focuses on self-blame, may be associated with negative rather than positive consequences, and a focus on external factors, when it represents real external obstacles these trainees have faced, may reflect a healthy sensitivity to the realities of the world they have to deal with. The group of high-failure trainees—those who completed the program but experienced difficulty getting placed on a job—more often blame their own inadequacies (motivational as well as ability) when asked to rate what things "have kept them from doing as well as they might have done in life." In contrast, the high-success trainees —those who completed the program and were immediately placed on jobs —more often blamed racial discrimination.

This issue was more extensively explored in a study of students in a number of predominantly Negro colleges, which utilized many measures paralleling those used in our study of trainees (Gurin and Katz, 1966). In addition, the college study included a number of items that formed a scale of internal-external control specifically focused on the attribution of blame for failure among Negroes. The internal items stessed the typical—skill, hard work, ability factors; the external items stressed racial discrimination. In general, the findings are consistent with the interpretation that the external rather than internal orientation is associated with positive motivation. For example, there was an interaction effect between a generalized low expectancy and an internal orientation toward the explanation of Negro failure, so that the students with lowest job aspirations and strivings were those who, in addition to their low generalized expectancies, held the internal ideology.

These data, of course, represent only beginning explorations of the issues we have raised in our discussion of some of the complexities in the concept of internal-external control. The issues are critical, however, for they have implications for the way we view the problems faced by these poverty populations and for the solutions we suggest. Most importantly, they serve to remind us that the type of training program we have referred to here, one which focuses on an internal orientation and an individual bootstrap-lifting approach to these problems, is only one limited approach to these issues. It is limited by the possibility that this focus may lead to greater intrapunitiveness rather than competence and efficacy;[8] and even when it does increase individual competence and control, it is limited by the fact that it has not dealt with all of the determinants of the trainees' problems.

In a broad sense, then, the question raised by our discussion of the internal-external dimension relates to the limitations of any program which takes an individual approach to these issues. It is interesting in this connection to contrast the way the youth training programs have approached the problem of poverty with the way in which the other great social issue of our time has been approached. The Civil Rights Movement has been very clearly directed toward assault on the situational and institutional determinants of expectancies calling for action against social and institutional barriers. By its nature, combatting these barriers has demanded group rather than individual action. Thus, in contrast to the individual self-betterment emphasis of programs which focus on the vocational area, the Civil Rights Movement has seen the solution to the motivational and reality problems of powerlessness in terms of group activity directed against the external sources of the problems.

It is interesting, in this connection, that there have been numerous attempts to bring this group orientation to bear on the youth vocational projects in the poverty program. These involve setting up vocational programs not as isolated units but as integral parts of broad communitywide programs attempting an integrated assault on many of the basic problems the communities face. Mobilization for Youth, Har-You, and TWO are examples of broad communitywide action programs which include job training projects as one aspect of the many community problems with which they are concerned. This tendency to place job programs within a broad community-group-action context was intensified under the Economic Opportunity Act, which called for community action programs with a maximum feasible participation of poverty groups affected by the program.

The aim of our discussion of some of these internal-external issues, then, is to underscore the value of programs which attempt to combine the individual betterment and advancement orientation of the job-training program with the group assault on the problem of powerlessness of the social actionists, tying the problem of individual mobility to the success with which

---

[8]This danger would be an issue particularly in programs that focus on socialization issues to the neglect of skill and competence training. To encourage the values and beliefs of an internally oriented Protestant Ethic without training in some of the skills that might help one implement these values is potentially destructive psychologically.

the group attacks some of its external reality problems. To some extent, some of the questions we have raised in this section may serve as cautions and qualifications of the implications we noted in the previous section where we focus on individual-centered approaches to the issues of apathy and powerlessness. It is not that skill training and individual mobility are unimportant; but such an orientation must not be too exclusive.

It should be stressed that participation in group-oriented action against external obstacles is of value not only because it helps to handle some of the real problems these trainees face in their environment, but also because of its effect on the psychological and motivational health of these trainees as individuals. The problems of powerlessness among these ghetto youth are so tied to their identity as Negroes that a focus on external as well as internal determinants and an encouragement of group as well as individual action may be necessary to cope successfully with the problems. The rise of Black Nationalism and Black Power, and even to some extent violence and riots, attest to their desire and need for a group attack on the external sources of their problems. While the tide of recent events does not make an individual competence approach to these problems irrelevant, it should serve to place it in a proper perspective.

CONCLUDING COMMENT

I have attempted to point up the types of issues that are highlighted when we approach the problems of poverty and the suggested solutions within an expectancy framework. More questions have been raised than have been answered because the questions involve issues that theorists in motivation are just beginning to grapple with—issues around the development and re-socializing of motives and expectancies. I may conclude, then, with one final comment. What little psychologists may contribute to programs that are attempting to deal with the problems of poverty is more than matched by what they can learn. The experiences of these programs and a systematic study of them can help clarify many of the issues that motivational theorists are just beginning to explore. Given the resocialization task that many of these poverty programs are attempting, the vast resources supporting the endeavor, and the increasing awareness of the need for controlled and systematic investigation of the process, these programs provide us with a unique opportunity for an integrated pursuit of our social and theoretical interests.

REFERENCES

Atkinson, J. W. *An Introduction to Motivation*. New York: Van Nostrand, 1964.

Battle, E., and Rotter, J. B. Children's Estimates of Their Schoolwork Ability as a Function of Sex, Race, and Socioeconomic Level. *Journal of Personality* 1963, 31: 482-90.

Bennion, R. Task, Trial by Trial Score Variability of Internal vs. External Control of Reinforcements. Doctoral dissertation, Ohio State University, 1961.

Cloward, R. A., and Ontell, R. Our Illusions About Training. *The American Child* 1965, 47: 6-10.

Coleman, J. R. et. al. *Equality of Educational Opportunity*. Washington, D. C.: United States Department of Health, Education and Welfare, U. S. Government Printing Office, 1966.

Crandall, V. C. The Reinforcement Effects of Adult Reactions and Nonreactions on Children's Achievement Expectations. *Child Development* 1963, 34: 335-54.

Crandall, V. C., Good, S., & Crandall, V. J. The Reinforcement Effects of Adult Reactions and Nonreactions on Children's Achievement Expectations: A Replication Study. *Child Development* 1964, 35: 485-97.

Feather, N. Effects of Prior Success and Failure on Expectations of Success and Subsequent Performance. *Journal of Personality and Social Psychology* 1966, 3: 287-98.

————. Changes in Confidence Following Success and Failure and Its Effects on Subsequent Performance. *Journal of Personality and Social Psychology* 1968, 9: 38-46.

Gurin, P., and Katz, D. Motivation and Aspiration in the Negro College. Ann Arbor: University of Michigan, Institute for Social Research, 1966.

James, W. Internal v. External Control of Reinforcement as a Basic Variable in Learning Theory. Doctoral dissertation, Ohio State University, 1957.

James, W., and Rotter, J. B. Partial and 100% Reinforcement under Chance and Skill Conditions. *Journal of Experimental Psychology* 1958, 55: 397-403.

Lefcourt, H. M., and Ladwig, G. W. The American Negro: A Problem in Expectancies. *Journal of Personality and Social Psychology* 1965, 1: 377-80.

Lewis, H. The Family: Resources for Change. Reprinted in Rainwater and Yancy, *The Moynihan Report and Politics of Controversy*. Cambridge, Mass.: M.I.T. Press, 1967.

Liebow, E. *Tally's Corner.* Boston: Little, Brown, 1966.

Miller, S. M., Riessman, F., & Seagull, A. Poverty and Self-Indulgence: A Critique of the Non-Deferred Gratification Pattern, in L. A. Ferman et al., eds. *Poverty in America.* Ann Arbor: University of Michigan Press, 1965, pp. 285-302.

Mischel, W. Father Absence and Delay of Gratification: Cross-Cultural Comparison. *Journal of Personality and Social Psychology* 1961, 63: 116-24.

Mischel, W., and Grusec, J. Waiting for Rewards and Punishments: Effects of Time and Probability of Choice. *Journal of Personality and Social Psychology* 1967, 5: 24-31.

Mischel, W., and Staub, E. Effects of Expectancy on Working and Waiting for Reward. *Journal of Personality and Social Psychology* 1965, 2: 625-33.

Pearl, A., and Riessman, F. *New Careers for the Poor: the Nonprofessional in Human Service.* New York: Free Press, 1965.

Phares, E. J. Delay, Anxiety, and Expectancy Changes. *Psychological Reports* 1966, 18: 679-82.

Phares, J. Expectancy Changes in Skill and Chance Situations. *Journal of Abnormal and Social Psychology* 1957, 54: 339-42.

Rotter, J. B. *Social Learning and Clinical Psychology.* New York: Prentice-Hall, 1954.

———. Generalized Expectancies for Internal vs. External Control of Reinforcement. *Psychological Monographs* 1966, 80: 1-28.

Rotter, J. B., Seeman, M., and Liverant, S. Internal vs. External Control of Reinforcement: A Major Variable in Behavior Theory, in N. F. Washburne, ed. *Decisions, Values, and Groups.* Vol. 2. London: Pergamon Press, 1962.

Rychlak, J. F., and Eacker, J. N. The Effects of Anxiety, Delay and Reinforcement on Generalized Expectancies. *Journal of Personality* 1962, 20: 123-34.

Schwarz, J. C. Influences upon Expectancy during Delay. *Journal of Experimental Research in Personality* 1966, 1, 211-20.

Veroff, J. Theoretical Backgrounds for Studying Origins of Human Motives. *Merrill-Palmer Quarterly of Behavior Development* 1965, 11: 3-18.

Chapter 15

POVERTY AND MOTIVATION: FIGURE AND GROUND

Udai Pareek*

Poverty has been defined in several ways, either in terms of lack of necessary things, e.g., "lack of command over goods and services sufficient to meet minimum needs" (Ornati, 1966, p. 7), or in terms of fear and dread of want (Hunter, 1965, pp. 5-6). One definition suggests a specific criterion: "An income of less than three times the cost of the economy food plan for families of three or more persons" (Ferman et al., 1965). More recently a new concept has been used—a three-level band concept, for "minimum subsistence," "minimum adequacy," and "minimum comfort" (Ornati, 1966). The definition of poverty suggested in the twenties as "an insufficiency of necessaries, or an insufficient supply of those things which are requisite for an individual to maintain himself and those dependent upon him in health and vigour" (Hurry, 1921, p. 1) seems to express well the general concept of lack of adequate conditions of growth behind several definitions. Some typological definitions have also been suggested, distinguishing between primary ("the condition of families whose earnings were insufficient to obtain the minimum necessaries for the maintenance of merely physical efficiency") and secondary ("the condition of families whose total earnings would be sufficient for the maintenance of merely physical efficiency, were not some portion absorbed by other expenditure, either useful or wasteful") (Hurry, 1921, p. 2), or classical (the established culture of poverty), alcoholic (social disintegration), and urban hillbilly

*Professor and Chairman of the Department of Social Sciences, National Institute of Health Administration and Education, New Delhi, India.

(migrants to urban areas unprepared to live in such areas) (Harrington, 1966, pp. 94-96).

Psychologically, poverty can be defined mainly in terms of deprivation and helplessness. The poor are deprived not only of the minimum adequate provisions for physical life, but also of adequate sensory, social, and emotional stimuli necessary for the development of a normal individual. It is now well known that children who are deprived of a variety of stimuli, to which they are maturationally capable of responding, are likely to be handicapped for learning. Language is one such stimulus complex. It has been demonstrated that language plays an important role in the general development of the child, and deprivation of language stimuli in the early years of life handicaps a child in his total development. Poverty, in terms of deprivation of adequate stimuli and experience, produces psychological effects which some authors have mistakenly treated as causes of poverty.

The other important element in poverty is an orientation of helplessness. The poor do not have any control over circumstances, which are controlled by others. Such a condition produces a self-image of helplessness. Solomon and his associates (Solomon and Lyman, 1953) have shown that a dog put in a classical Pavlovian harness loses capacity for avoidance learning for 48 hours following the experiment; in a way, the experience of not being able to control the environment in the Pavlovian harness produces a self-image of hopelessness, and the dog chooses not to attempt to escape the shock later on when he is put in the avoidance learning experiment. Most of the behavior seen in the poor is the result of the environment in which they live, and which conditions their style of responding to the environment.

Thus, poverty (deprivation of stimuli, and control by others) is causally related to behavior, producing a series of behavioral patterns relevant to the conditions of poverty. However, the relationship between the two is not so simple and straightforward. One important variable in this process of conditioning is motivation. Conditions of poverty produce a motivational pattern, which in turn causes behavior of some kind. Although the primary causes in the process are the conditions of poverty, motivation plays an important role and deserves special attention. Before discussing the specific motivational patterns produced by poverty, a general motivational paradigm of human behavior is presented.

A GENERAL PARADIGM OF SOCIAL BEHAVIOR

The paradigm of human behavior proposed here as the basis of understanding the problem of poverty and its influence on people living in poor environment is a simple one. It is suggested that behavior (B) is the result of motivation (*M*) and values (*V*), which are in turn determined and caused by the social system (*SS*) in which the individual lives. The paradigm is represented as (*SS*)→ (*M,V*)→ (*B*) (Pareek, 1967). According to this paradigm a social system produces relevant motivational patterns in the members of the society. These motivational patterns help maintain the social system, and therefore are functional. The motivational pattern produced by a specific social system determines the behavioral patterns of the members of the society. In this way, behavior is a product of the social system in which individuals live, but this is produced through the intervening variable of motivation. The paradigm can be elaborated further, as shown in Figure 1.

Figure 1: General Paradigm of Social Behavior.

The paradigm in Figure 1 shows that a social system produces two different variables at two different levels. At the level of the individual it produces relevant motivational patterns, and at the societal level it produces reinforcing mechanisms. Each social system has its own reinforcing mechanisms, through which it is maintained and reinforced. These mechanisms are responsible for the institutionalization and routinization of those processes which produce reward and punishment systems in the society. Some important mechanisms from this point of view are child-rearing practices, the school system, and other institutions of socialization. Such institutions and mechanisms greatly influence human behavior by producing expectations of behavior being rewarded or punished by the society. For example, in the feudal social system, the reinforcing mechanism of child-rearing practices rewarded behavior of children conforming to dependency on parents, and punished behavior showing independence and initiative. Through such socialization processes, or what I prefer to call reinforcing mechanisms of the social system, rewarding behaviors are selected, and an expectancy framework is built for individuals, i.e., whether a particular behavior will be rewarded or punished.

The expectancy framework influences behavior as much as does motivation. However, motivation and expectancy are not unidirectionally related to the social system and its reinforcing mechanisms. In the course of time, motivation and expectancy frameworks acquire great influence; they not only maintain the social system, but they also begin to determine it to some extent. This is shown in the paradigm (Figure 1) by the dotted arrows from motivation and expectancy toward social system and reinforcing mechanisms. This concept is similar to that of second order conditioning in learning experiments. Motivation and expectancy, acquiring this determining influence, become quite important. The paradigm proposes that the social system is the main causal and determining factor of behavior; behavior is the product of the kind of society in which people live. It also proposes that the social system operates mainly through the motivational patterns it produces and the expectancy frame which is determined by the reinforcing mechanisms. One important proposal which this model makes is that motivation and expectancy are of great importance because they not only determine and cause behavior directly, but they are able to influence the social system and the reinforcing mechanisms in turn. Therefore, motivation and expectancy occupy the central position in the paradigm, although they are intervening variables. One implication of the paradigm is that it is necessary to deal with the problems of change of the social structure and the reinforcing mechanisms; but at the same time the payoff may be greater if motivations and expectancy are also dealt with.

POVERTY AND MOTIVATION: A VICIOUS CIRCLE

In the light of the above paradigm of behavior, poverty can be viewed psychologically both as a structure and as a product (resulting behavior) of a system. In other words, we can start by considering poverty as a structural component of a society, and observe motivations produced by such a structure and the kind of behavior generated by such motivations by certain processes. The patterns of behavior of a large number of persons would produce what has been called the culture of poverty. The conditions of poverty produce a specific pattern of motivation and, through the relevant processes of socialization, the expectancy that can be called the frame of powerlessness. The specific motivational patterns and the expectancy of powerlessness produce behavior seen among the culturally deprived people (the culture of poverty). When we pay attention to poverty (the structure), it becomes the figure and poverty is the ground. The paradigm is given in Figure 2. In either case, the important concept in this paradigm is that poverty is essentially a structural problem producing

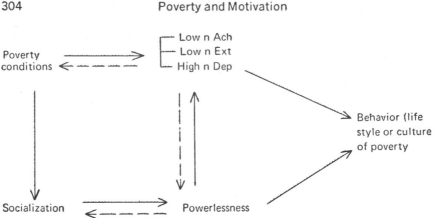

Figure 2: Paradigm of Culture of Poverty.

specific motivational patterns which are also important and deserve attention during consideration of the strategy of dealing with poverty.

According to the paradigm in Figure 2, poverty as a structural component produces a threefold motivational pattern characterised by low need for achievement, low need for extension, and high need for dependence. The motivational pattern produces the behavior described as the culture of poverty. The process of socialization through child-rearing practices and family life plays an important part. Socialization also takes place through informal adolescent groups, gangs, and other important sources of social influence.

Achievement Need

Let us define the three motivational components that are used in this paradigm of poverty: the need for achievement, the need for extension, and the need for dependence. Achievement motivation has been more thoroughly studied than other motives. Not only has it been explored and defined in detail (McClelland et al., 1953), but the relationship between achievement motivation and economic development has been investigated and is now understood more clearly (McClelland, 1961). Moreover, the theory of achievement motivation has been developed and elaborated (Atkinson and Feather, 1966). Achievement motivation is defined in terms of concern for excellence in doing a task, as reflected in competition with the standards set by others or oneself; unique accomplishment; or long-term involvement in a task. McClelland and associates have proposed that the need for achievement can be measured by the analysis of an individual's imagery from such sources as written responses to pictorial cues (e.g., TAT cards). The scoring system for stories and other material used by McClelland and associates includes measures of need or concern for excellence, activities corresponding to such a concern, anticipation of success and failure, perception of difficulties arising both from one's weaknesses or limitations and from environmental factors, active seeking of help to overcome such difficulties, and feelings of elation or depression on success or failure. These measures all indicate the presence of general concern and a striving for excellence. Persons with a high level of achievement motivation have been studied in detail and have been found to have characteristics important for entrepreneurs: seeking help from experts, moderate risk taking, eagerness to have feedback of results of work being done, taking personal responsibility, interest in activities which they can influence rather than those which depend on chance, etc. (McClelland, 1961).

Extension Need

Let us now consider another aspect of motivation—extension motivation. This term is proposed in the absence of another, more appropriate term. Extension motivation is reflected in the need for extending the ego to the society—what McClelland has more recently called "concern for the common welfare of all" (McClelland, 1966), which he has acknowledged, "was also found more often in the children's textbooks . . . used by those countries that subsequently developed more rapidly" (McClelland, 1966).

Extension motivation is reflected in regard for other persons, cooperating with others for achieving a common goal, faith and trust in members of the group, and involvement in goals that concern not only oneself but the society at large. This motivation is particularly low in poor countries and in poor communities in which persons are so conditioned by control from outside that they not only hesitate in taking initiative, but have little faith (justifiably) in other people, including members of their own groups. Lack of faith leads to suspicion, inability to cooperate, and (a justifiable) overconcern with self.

Dependency Need

Dependency motivation has attracted some attention of psychologists. But most of the work on this motivational component has been conducted either in the clinical context or in connection with child development. Dependency motivation comes very close to Murray's proposed *psychogenic need* of *succorance*. According to Murray, the behavioral characteristics of this need are to have one's needs gratified by the sympathetic aid of an allied object; to be nursed, supported, sustained, surrounded, protected, loved, advised, guided, indulged, forgiven, consoled; to remain close to a devoted protector; to always have a supporter (Hall and Lindzey, 1957). He proposed, among several psychogenic needs, one opposite to succorance, *nurturance* (to give sympathy and gratify the needs of a helpless object . . . to support, protect, console). His other pair of related needs is *deference* (to yield eagerly to the influence of an allied other) and *autonomy* (to be independent and free) (Hall and Lindzey, 1957). Sears has defined the dependency motive in terms of *asking movements,* and he measured dependency motivation in children by frequency measures of the following five categories of dependency: negative attention seeking, positive attention seeking, touching or holding, being near, seeking reassurance, comfort, or consolation (Sears, 1963). Some psychologists have proposed the term *independence motive* (Birch and Veroff, 1966; Kasl, Sampson, and French, 1964; Vroom, 1959). Birch and Veroff define independence motive in terms of "accomplishing an activity without help." Kasl, Sampson, and French define independence motivation in Lewinian terms: "For the need for independence, *n* Ind, the valent regions (goals) are the ones in which *P* perceives himself to have a maximal amount of freedom from the control of others" (Kasl, Sampson, and French, 1964, p. 569).

Dependency or independence motivation and power motivation have not been properly distinguished. Birch and Veroff suggest that under the power motivation "a person is resisting someone having control over a decision," while in the independence motive "a person is resisting another person assisting in any given process" (Birch and Veroff, 1966, p. 81).

The concept of dependency motivation proposed here is derived from the general paradigm that a particular social system generates a corresponding motivation, and further that a feudal system generates dependency motivation. Dependency motivation can be characterized in terms of concern for control of decisions in power motivation, and it is expressed through lack of initiative, avoidance syndromes (shifting responsibility to others, exaggerating obstacles), excessive fear of failure, seeking favors of superiors, overconformity, and aggressive rejection of authority (what has been called "counterdependency").

CONSEQUENCES OF POVERTY: EFFECTS ON MOTIVATION

What does the motivational pattern suggested above mean in operational terms? How are the lower needs for achievement and extension reflected in behavior? What is the operational meaning of the higher need for dependence? Answers to these questions could be important in order to know more about the nature of the motivational patterns resulting from the structure of poverty. Let us consider these questions.

Low Need Achievement

If achievement motivation is low in a person, several kinds of behavioral patterns would result. We surmise that the following kinds of behavior could be produced by low need achievement.

Disproportionate Risk Taking. The person with the low need for achievement does not show a moderate risk taking attitude. He may be so afraid of circumstances that he does not take any risk at all and plays very safe. In such cases, the individual may not have enough margin, psychologically, sociologically, and economically, to take risks, and this may result in a tendency not to take any risk at all. On the other hand, an individual with low need for achievement may also take more than moderate risks; in other words, he may gamble. Gambling is indicative of desperation. A person who does not have much at stake has a tendency to gamble. This behavior is, of course, related to other behaviors, some of which are suggested below.

Interest in Chance and Not in Control. An individual with low need for achievement is less interested in an activity in which he can exercise control, probably primarily because he usually does not have an opportunity to exert control. Such an individual may be interested in activities that depend on chance and fate. He may, for example, be interested in games like cards that have a great element of chance, and not in games involving individual control, like chess.

Lack of Interest in Feedback. If the individual has little control over circumstances and does not see himself as influencing them, he may be uninterested in getting feedback from his behavior. Interest in feedback is more likely when the individual can use the feedback in influencing factors in the environment in the manner he desires.

Seeking Company of Friends instead of Experts. It has been found that persons with high need achievement seek the company of experts and not of friends, per se. Persons with low need for achievement seem to show more affiliation motivation through seeking company of friends. They receive comfort through friends who share similar frustrations and similar points of view.

Lack of Activity and Initiative. Persons with high need for achievement take moderate risks, take initiative, and have a high level of activity. On the other hand, low need achievement results in a decrease in activity. The person does not take initiative and consequently does not take much risk. Lack of initiative leads to inaction, creating a vicious circle.

Low Need Extension

Poverty also leads to lowering of the extension motive, which is quite important for improving the operation of a social group. The behavioral consequences of the lowering of need extension may be as follows.

Lack of Regard for Others.   When a person has a low need for extension, he is mostly self-centered and does not pay much attention to others. His self-image is poor, one result of which is lack of respect for others, which in turn leads to many other kinds of behavior.

Lack of Faith or Trust.   One damaging result of lower need extension is that a person becomes so selfish and self-centered that he loses faith and trust in others. For a good social life, trust and faith are important conditions. Experiences of a person living in deprived conditions show him that he cannot rely on circumstances, and that the social conditions would not help him. This results in a general orientation of lack of faith in others.

Lack of Cooperation.   The two behavioral patterns suggested above would result in lack of cooperativeness. This again is a vicious circle. Persons who do not cooperate with members of their group become self-centered and start suspecting others, and this may lead to not cooperating.

High Need Dependency

The structure of poverty leads to the heightening of the need for dependence. This may result in the following kinds of behavior.

Lack of Initiative.   We have already seen that a person with a low need for achievement lacks initiative, and this results in inactivity. Lack of initiative is also a result of a high need for dependence. Instead of himself taking initiative, a person with high need dependency expects someone else to take initiative.

Avoidance Behavior.   A whole syndrome of avoidance behavior results from high need dependency. Avoidance behavior is reflected in such characteristics as shifting responsibility to others (passing the buck). Avoidance behavior is also reflected in the exaggeration of the perception of obstacles.

Fear of Failure.   The person with high need dependency has an exaggerated fear of failure. Different persons deal with fear of failure in different ways. The person with a high need dependency is always afraid that he might fail, which results in lack of initiative and also in avoidance behavior.

Seeking Favor of Superiors.   The person with a high need for dependence is more concerned about gaining the favor of persons of authority (who satisfy his need) than about achieving the goal.

Overconformity.   The person with high need for dependence shows much more conformity to norms. This is probably related to gaining the support or favor of superior persons who are responsible for setting norms.

Counterdependence.   One way of dealing with authority is to aggressively reject it. Counterdependence is the opposite pole of a continuum of dependence. A person with high need dependence may exaggerate the use of the freedom he has by aggressively rejecting authority.

DEALING WITH THE MOTIVATIONAL PATTERN IN POVERTY

As discussed above, changes in behavior can be brought about by change in the social system; this is a necessary condition for any change program. Consequent changes are necessary in the expectancy frame and in the motivational patterns. The problem of changing the motivational patterns will be dealt with in this section. In the paradigm of poverty given above, the motivational pattern caused by poverty consists of low need achievement, low need extension, and high need dependence.

Some work has been done on influencing achievement motivation. McClelland (1965) has suggested a general theory of motivational change. Two significant experiments carried out in India showed that need for achievement can be effectively influenced through specific programs. An experiment with high-school boys has shown that need for achievement can be increased through a ten-day training program for teachers. The purpose of the training was to influence teachers' behavior so that they would encourage boys and give them hope of success rather than reinforce fear of failure. Achievement behavior improved in the experimental schools as compared to the control schools (Mehta, 1968). A similar experiment with adults showed that

need for achievement could be increased through training programs
(McClelland and Winter, forthcoming).

One very interesting experiment at Harvard University attempted to
influence motivational patterns of people in poverty areas. Twenty
persons, all Negro, were invited to participate in a program in motivation development. The program consisted of training components of
achievement motivation. Subjects were given information about
achievement motivation and its relationship to general entrepreneural
behavior, imagery was influenced through continued use of the
achievement categories, and an opportunity was provided for developing some skills of working together. Most of the persons who attended
the program were ex-convicts who showed the typical patterns of poverty behavior. The program resulted in dramatic changes in behavior,
but the main improvement was the change in the self-image. Persons
who attended the program began to see themselves as capable of
achieving, rather than as individuals who consistently failed to achieve
things in life. In other words, the self-image of powerlessness was replaced by an image of being able to control the environment. The
follow-up showed that the program has resulted in several concrete
changes in members of the group. They had steadier jobs after the program, their behavior was more goal-oriented and less purposeless, they
took increasing responsibility, and, more importantly, they took initiative in several ways. Several of the members got together and formed
an enterprising organization called the Massachusetts Achievement
Trainers Corporation. This organization was established in order to
provide the kind of training the group members had received to other
members of their society, and especially to boys. Experts were hired
to help provide programs of motivation development and to plan training programs for improving poverty conditions. This is an example of
how a program of dealing with the motivation patterns that a particular
social condition produces can bring about some change. It certainly
cannot be an alternative to social-structure change, but such programs
can influence the pattern of social change by providing new expectancies, and therefore a greater drive to work for and demand the social
changes necessary to produce change on a larger scale.

The need for extension can also be influenced to a great extent,
though no work has been done on this particular need. However, the
experiments by Sherif (Sherif et al., 1954) have shown that superordinate goals, which help people go beyond their individual needs and individual self, help in reducing conflicts in a group. Superordinate
goals may be important not only for reducing conflicts, but also for
developing a concern for other people and for the community. One important program for this purpose is that of cooperatives. The need for

extension or the concern for other people can be increased through training programs of motivational development that help socially handicapped people set up cooperatives where they physically come together and work for a common goal.

The need for dependence is a great hindrance in the development of initiative, the formation of a positive self-image, and ability to influence the environment. The need is reflected in lack of initiative and expectation of initiative from others, as well as emotionally charged, aggressive behavior towards authority. One method found to be effective in several kinds of situations for dealing with the need for dependence is called the laboratory training method, also known by such terms as sensitivity training, human relations training, etc. (For details, see Bradford et al., 1964; Schein and Bennis, 1965.) Laboratory training helps people to rethink the adequacy of their own behavior. People involved in laboratory training are able to experiment with new patterns of behavior, and such training helps people develop interdependence in place of dependence (Lynton and Pareek, 1967). The problem of dependence is crucial not only among the poor, but in all kinds of organizations. Technologically we are changing very quickly, but changes in patterns of human relationships are not keeping pace with technological changes.

The specific motivational pattern of the conditions of poverty can be tackled through appropriate programs of training. However, providing relevant material conditions is necessary, so that the changes in motivation can be sustained. Motivational programs can work only when people are helped to take initiative and start activities. Motivational programs may be institutionalized, for example, in the form of cooperatives that may help the members take initiative and work for interdependence. Some structural changes are prerequisites for motivational programs. As stated in the Ferman book, "the underprivileged are discriminated against socially and economically. Since poverty is a structural problem, policies must be structure-oriented. If poverty is to be eliminated or drastically reduced, additional measures pinpointing the structural characteristics that have permitted poverty in a relatively efficient economy are demanded" (Ferman et al., 1965, p. 78). One example of structural change is given in the next section discussing a case of changing expectancy.

CHANGE OF EXPECTANCY: A CASE FROM INDIA

An important variable in the paradigm used in this paper is expectancy. Change in behavior can be brought about by changing expectancy frames. One example of an attempt to bring about a major social change by changing expectancy frames is from India. As in any traditional society, a section of people in the Indian nation are underprivileged and discriminated against by people who have had power through several centuries. The classes that have been socially disabled include the low castes and low-caste tribes, and other backward classes, including women. In the highly structured society of India the expectancy framework was clear and well-defined. People who belonged to the underprivileged classes were expected to limit their aspirations to the activities and vocations appropriate to their particular class. For example, a son of a cobbler was limited in his aspirations to becoming a carpenter. Such a well-defined and rigid expectancy produced behavior that made social change among these people most difficult. After independence (in 1947), such distinctions theoretically were abolished and people were free to achieve according to their ability rather than according to the caste or class they came from. Those who framed the constitution and provided the necessary guidelines for the administration of the government felt that the laudable principle of equal opportunity according to ability, if left to itself, would operate only in theory. It was argued that the underprivileged had been conditioned by expectancy for several generations and would not be able to escape the vicious circle of expectancy leading to lower motivation, leading to lower achievement, leading to lower ability, which again leads to lower expectancy. Some positive steps were necessary to remove the social disabilities suffered by persons of such classes. The unique experiment that a large country (current population of over 500 million) undertook on a gigantic scale is quite significant in terms of what expectancy can do for social change.

The change in expectancy was brought about by certain constitutional provisions in the early days of the country's independence. The constitutional provisions were provided for a period of twenty years, and were to be reviewed at the end of this period to assess how much desired change had been produced. The rationale for providing the constitutional provisions was that without positive, specific steps to break old expectations and to develop new expectancy frames, people from these classes would not be able to benefit from the secular and democratic ideals stated in the constitution. It was argued that special efforts had to be made to help people in these classes reach a standard from which they might be able to compete with others without handicap.

I shall limit discussion to the provisions made for persons belonging to special lower castes, known as the scheduled castes, and scheduled tribes. The constitution provided for the abolishment of untouchability in all forms by providing access to all public institutions for people of all races, religions, and castes; by allowing anyone to practice any profession and carry on any occupation, trade, or business; by forbidding any denial of admission to educational institutions, etc.; and by setting up special advisory bodies and administrative mechanisms to look after the interests of the underprivileged classes. As far as the change of expectancy frame is concerned, five articles in the constitution are significant. Articles 16 and 335 relate to the obligation of the state to consider the claims of persons belonging to the underprivileged classes in the making of appointments to public services and making reservations for them in case of inadequate representation. Articles 330, 332, and 334 relate to special representation for the underprivileged in the legislative bodies, both in the central government and in the states, for a period of twenty years. The overall percentages of people belonging to the scheduled castes and scheduled tribes in the country were then 15 percent and 5 percent, respectively.

The three articles in the constitution relating to the representation of these people in the legislative bodies gave them political power and thereby changed their expectancy. They had positive and definite evidence that they could go to the Parliament of the country or to the state legislative assemblies and thereby influence the decision-making process. Their participation in decision making at the legislative level has been a significant and bold step in the direction of building new expectancies. Reservation of seats in the Parliament and the state assemblies for persons belonging to scheduled castes and tribes were proportionate, as far as possible, to their population. Similarly, seats in the legislative assemblies in the various states are reserved according to the ratio of their population. This has been a bold step towards providing opportunities for these people to participate in the political decision-making process. Persons from scheduled castes and tribes have not only been elected, but have been holding important cabinet positions in the central government and in the various state governments. It is obvious that they have obtained a powerful political weapon and that their self-image has changed accordingly. This group no longer feels hopeless, but now realizes it has the capability of influencing major decisions in the country.

As far as expectancy is concerned, the more significant steps were those providing better economic opportunities to persons belonging to the underprivileged classes. The most important provision was the reservation of places for service in the government (government employment in India was, and is still, considered one of the most coveted occupations). It was provided that 12 ½ percent of the vacancies for which recruitment was made in open competition on an all-India basis and 16 ⅔ percent of the vacancies in the government employment to which recruitment was otherwise made, would be reserved for persons belonging to the scheduled castes. Likewise 5 percent of the positions in all types of government employment was reserved for persons belonging to the scheduled tribes. This meant that persons belonging to the scheduled castes and tribes penetrated the various levels of bureaucracy and were able to participate on a mass scale in the total national life of the country. In order to offset the handicap to which these people had been subjected for centuries, and as a result of which they had been conditioned to a life that produced a vicious circle of lower ability and a lack of capacity to compete in the open and free society, special steps had to be taken to help them get into higher positions in various sectors of public life. India has a system of large scale selection for higher bureaucratic positions through promotions from the lower positions and through recruitment to top-level employment in various sectors in open public competition. For direct recruitment through competition several conditions have to be met—age and minimum standards of suitability in terms of physical condition and educational levels. It was argued that these conditions, necessary to assure minimum standards of excellence in the society in general, could not be applied to people belonging to the underprivileged classes because they would not be able to meet these minimum standards. Therefore, another bold step was taken to provide for relaxation of age limit and standards of suitability for people belonging to the underprivileged classes seeking higher jobs either through promotion or through public competition.

Probably the most far-reaching and significant step in terms of the change in expectancy frame was the assurance that persons belonging to the underprivileged classes could participate in the educational development program. This step was the reservation of seats and provision for many other facilities for education at various levels. Special seats for persons belonging to the underprivileged classes were reserved in professional colleges (medical colleges, engineering colleges, technological institutes, etc.). It was also provided that 17 ½ percent of the merit scholarships given to talented students for education in special schools should be reserved for children of the underprivileged classes. Students from the underprivileged classes admitted to medical, engineering, and other professional colleges received free tuition and special stipends to pursue their studies. In several cases, they were also given free books and free midday meals. The students from underprivi leged classes who won foreign scholarships were provided free sea passage to enable them to pursue their studies outside the country.

These various provisions have been in operation for about two decades to help these people change their self-image by changing the expectancy frame which was governing their behavior and producing a special kind of motivation. These provisions have naturally resulted in large-scale participation by people belonging to the underprivileged classes in the wider national life, and have helped in reducing prejudice to a large extent. However, the population of underprivileged classes is quite large in India, and even the constitutional provisions and facilities provided by the government have not completely eradicated prejudice (nor has a complete transformation of these classes resulted). But they have certainly helped to change expectancy and build new expectancies, and have created a new ascending spiral of economic and sociopolitical development in the underprivileged classes, thereby contributing significantly to the national integration and development of a secular democracy.

REFERENCES

Atkinson, J. W., and Feather, N. T., eds. *A Theory of Achievement Motivation.* New York: Wiley, 1966.

Birch, D., and Veroff, J. *Motivation: A Study of Action.* Belmont, Calif.: Brooks-Cole Publishing Co., 1966.

Bradford, L. P., Gibb, J. R., and Benn, K. M., eds. *T-Group Theory and Laboratory Method.* New York: Wiley, 1964.

Ferman, L. A., Kornbluh, J. L., and Haber, A., eds. *Poverty in America.* Ann Arbor: University of Michigan Press, 1965.

Hall, C. S., and Lindzey, G. *Theories of Personality.* New York: Wiley, 1957.

Harrington, M. *The Other America.* New York: Macmillan, 1966.

Hunter, R. *Poverty: Social Conscience in the Progressive Era.* New York: Harper & Row, 1965.

Hurry, J. B. *Poverty and Its Vicious Circles.* London: J. & A. Churchill, 1921.

Kasl, S. V., Sampson, E. E., and French, J. R. P. The Development of a Projective Measure of the Need for Independence: A Theoretical Statement and Some Preliminary Evidence. *Journal of Personality* 1964, 32: 566-86.

Lynton, R. P., and Pareek, U. Training in Human Relations: A Multi-Purpose Design. *Indian Educational Review* 1967, 2: 80-90.

McClelland, D. C. *The Achieving Society.* Princeton, N.J.: Van Nostrand, 1961.

————. Toward a Theory of Motive Acquisition. *American Psychologist* 1965, 29: 321-33.

————. The Impulse to Modernization, in M. Weiner, ed. *Modernization.* New York: Basic Books, 1966, pp. 28-39.

McClelland, D. C., Atkinson, J. W., Clark, R. A., and Lowell, E. L., eds. *The Achievement Motive.* New York: Appleton-Century-Crofts, 1953.

McClelland, D. C., and Winter, D. G. *Developing an Achieving Society* (forthcoming).

Mehta, P. Achievement Motivation Training for Educational Development. *Indian Educational Review* 1968, 3: 46-74.

Ornati, O. *Poverty Amid Affluence: A Report of a Research Project Carried Out at the New School of Social Research.* New York: The Twentieth Century Fund, 1966.

Pareek, U. A Motivational Paradigm of Development. *Indian Educational Review* 1967, 105-11. (Also in *Journal of Social Issues* 1968, 24: 115-22.)

Schein, E. H., and Bennis, W. G. *Personal and Organizational Change Through Group Methods.* New York: Wiley, 1965.

Sears, R. R. Dependency Motivation, in M. R. Jones, ed. *Nebraska Symposium on Motivation.* Lincoln, Neb.: University of Nebraska Press, 1963, pp. 25-64.

Sherif, M., Harvey, O. J., White, B. J., Hood, W. R., and Sherif, C. W. Experimental Study of Positive and Negative Intergroup Attitudes between Experimentally Produced Groups, Robbers Case Study. Norman, Okl.: University of Oklahoma, 1954. Multilithed.

Solomon, R. L., and Lyman, C. Traumatic Avoidance Learning—The Outcomes of Several Extinction Procedures with Dogs. *Journal of Abnormal and Social Psychology* 1953, 48: 291-302.

Vroom, V. H. Some Personality Determinants of the Effect of Participation. *Journal of Abnormal and Social Psychology* 1959, 59: 322-27.

CHAPTER 16

SOME THEORETICAL AND PRACTICAL PROBLEMS IN COMPENSATORY EDUCATION AS AN ANTIDOTE TO POVERTY

Edmund W. Gordon*

Society has always considered educable those categories of persons thought to be needed for participation in its affairs. At one time in the history of man, it was only the religious and political nobility who were considered capable of academic learning. Under the dual pressures of the Reformation and the Industrial Revolution this category of persons was greatly expanded. In the early nineteenth century in this country, during the period of slavery, the "educable" had been expanded to include most Caucasians, but excluded most Negroes. With the end of slavery and the incorporation of the enslaved populations into the available labor force, they too were declared educable. In other words, educability was a function of societal definition, rather than a characteristic of the persons referred to. Of course the schools did not succeed in educating all of these new candidates, but the once narrowly defined concept of educability was now more broadly defined.

For a time even in the twentieth century the uneducated, endowed only with strong backs or skillful hands, were eagerly sought by the economy. In contrast, the economy of the late twentieth century is

---

*Eric Information Retrieval Center on the Disadvantaged, Columbia University, New York.

requiring the ability to manage vast categories of knowledge, to identify and solve highly complicated interdisciplinary problems, and to arrive at infinitely complex conceptualizations and judgments. Students with this quality of intellect and conceptual competence are not
routinely produced in today's schools. In fact, we school people are constantly embarrassed by the large numbers of young people whom we
have failed to prepare for much less complex intellectual and social
functioning than what is required today. We are also under attack in
many quarters for our failure to prepare adequately even many of
those who seem to succeed in our system. Witness the large number
of "successful" people who read inefficiently and without pleasure.
Think of those among us whose skills in arithmetic are limited to simple
computation. Consider the large number of high-school and college
graduates who have difficulty in recognizing a concept and are practically incapable of producing a clear one.

A social revolution has for some time been emerging which is not
unrelated to the growing crisis in the use of intellectual resources and
the management of knowledge. This time the battle is being waged by
Negroes and their allies; soon, no doubt, the poverty-stricken will join
them. What they are demanding is nothing less than total and meaningful integration into the mainstream of our society. Equality of educational achievement (together with equal opportunity to share in the nation's
wealth) is looked upon as a major means of attaining such integrated status.

The production of compensatory education has grown out of a recognition that learners who do not begin at the same point may not have
comparable opportunities for achieving the same goal, even when they
are provided equal educational experiences. To make the opportunity
equal for youngsters who have been handicapped, it may be necessary
to make their education something more than equal: we may have
to compensate for their handicaps before, or at least while, we are providing them with an education of equal quality.

Programs of compensatory education have existed for more than a
decade. Although by now they vary widely in size and scope throughout
the country, they have in common the dual goals of remediating and of
preventing academic, social and cultural handicaps. Unfortunately—
and I should say this at the outset—the most common feature of these
programs has been their tendency to fail. A brief review of some of their
usual strands may help to set in relief a few reasons for their failure.

The principal focus in compensatory programs has been reading
and language development. New reading methods and materials, the
training of teachers to use them, and the extensive employment of remedial reading teachers or reading specialists are all evidence of the

primacy of reading in the school learning hierarchy. The assumed relationship between the quality of oral language and skill in reading has
sometimes led to emphasis on practice in speaking and listening. Where
youngsters do not speak English, there are special methods and materials for developing bilingualism. Finally, some projects have worked to
develop primers featuring racially integrated characters and naturalistic
speech patterns which reflect inner-city life.

Other curricular innovations have been inaugurated with the dual
aim of individualizing instruction and increasing the relevance of classroom materials to the realities of life. Two major types of structural
modification, team teaching and ungraded and transitional classes,
have been widely used to ease children into school or to facilitate
their shift from one school situation to another. Various programs have
provided individual instruction and generally greater flexibility in the
teacher's time. The use of extra classroom teachers, specialists in such
areas as music, science, art or mathematics, and volunteer aides have
all relieved the teacher of some of her burden.

A number of projects have become involved in what might best be
called extracurricular innovation. After-school or Saturday study centers
are widely used, as are clubs organized around sports, science, music,
or reading for pleasure. Cultural events, hobby groups, picnics, and
camping trips have been used to enlarge the experience of disadvantaged
children during the afternoon, evening, and weekend hours. Where
schools have continued their programs into the summer, remediation
and enrichment have been emphasized.

Almost every sizable program of compensatory education now
includes some effort to increase parental involvement in its goals. As
more and more schools serving disadvantaged neighborhoods have
moved toward breaking down the barrier that has separated school and
home, project schools have used home visits by teachers, community
aides, or social workers. These visitors interpret the school program to
families, provide information about school events, suggest ways in
which parents may assist the school program, counsel them about behavioral or school problems, or put them in contact with appropriate
community agencies for such counseling. When meetings are held at
school, they tend to be small and informal, and are often conducted
by the staff persons responsible for home visits or for augmenting
school-family contacts. Adult education courses, clubs, and hobby
groups have also been attempted to bring adults into the school.

The question of community involvement has concerned a number of
schools as they have reached out beyond the parents into the total surrounding community both to offer and to seek help. School doors have

been opened for various community groups as well as for adult education courses. In return, schools have benefited from community volunteers, financial assistance for enrichment programs, and vocational opportunities for their students.

Teacher recruitment and training has given rise to a wide variety of practices designed to attract teachers to disadvantaged schools and to modify their attitudes toward low-income families and communities. Intern programs at problem schools for teacher trainees or for locally based college education majors, orientation programs to acquaint new teachers with the neighborhood, extra consultative personnel or specially qualified teachers to help the incoming teacher, inservice training courses and workshops—all of these practices are designed to give teachers a greater chance of being at ease, and therefore performing better, with their students.

Guidance is the one approach almost universally included in projects for the disadvantaged. Although guidance personnel are unfortunately still hampered by their traditional preoccupation with the misfit, increasing emphasis is being placed on providing quality counseling to all students. A typical well-run compensatory guidance program will combine individual counseling, vocationally oriented group guidance, and, not infrequently, extensive enrichment activities to widen the student's view of the world.

Finally, three new groups of special personnel (many of whose roles are described above) have been added to the project schools. Instructional staff have been employed to provide their particular knowledge in such subject areas as language arts, science, or mathematics, or to offer their special training in work with the disadvantaged. Service personnel are being used increasingly in the areas of guidance and health; counselors, psychologists, psychiatrists, social workers, physicians, nurses, and dental technicians are the most frequent additions in this area. Nonprofessionals have become important, filling such roles as community liaison, teacher assistant, tutor, and study hall supervisor.

These then are eight areas in which innovation has taken place in current compensatory education programs. Probably the most interesting thing about them is the absence of really new or radical innovation in pedagogy. Remedial education programs have been developed, teacher-pupil ratio has been reduced, new materials have been generated, classroom grouping has been modified. All are sensible and appropriate changes, which should be part of any good education program, but they represent no basic alteration in the teacher-learning process. Significantly, much of the current work in the education of the disadvantaged has been directed at preschool children and at high-school dropouts, two groups who stand outside the mainstream of the education process. At times, in fact, one is inclined to think that emphasis on these two groups has been widely accepted simply because they require the least change in the school itself.

I suspect that compensatory education has not worked for a variety of reasons, but one of the main ones is theoretical: the conceptualization has been inappropriate or incorrect. Learning involves at least three categories of function: the first might be identified as basic cognitive processes, the second as affective processes, and the third as achievement systems including the mastery of content or skills. Using traditional methods, much of our work in compensatory education has focused on a modification of basic cognitive processes. But according to work by Zigler and others, it appears that basic cognitive processes are the least plastic or malleable of the three functions. Compensatory education, in putting its emphasis here, may therefore have chosen the very hardest and most impractical of the systems to modify. Zigler, for one, would argue that the motivational or affective system would be more easily modified. In his paper, Dr. Gurin points out that what actually happens in the formal learning situation may be less important than what happens in the individual's total life experience in terms of shifts, changes, and modifications of attitude, of motivation, of expectation in terms of past involvement. He would thus argue that more attention should be paid to modifying affective processes. I am not certain, however, that I would agree that the affective area is the one in which it is easiest for the schools to operate. I would, in fact, place the emphasis on the mastery of skills and content.

However, if we look at developments in educational and industrial technology, and the increasing applicability of the computer, it is conceivable that our traditional concepts concerning the mastery of content and skills may have to shift. Compensatory education, or a good education of any kind, may not involve trying to pour into unready and sometimes unwilling minds a great deal of information, but rather on developing skills for processing, managing, handling, and manipulating that information. I do not think it is a surprise to anyone that the newspaper and television industry, the directions on appliances—most of the media that uses and seeks information in the society—require a quality of technical skills which might well be the test of a good education. If we are trying to prepare people efficiently to move and function in the mainstream, we must first get across the basic communication skills that are presently required for functioning in this society. For many reasons I would also like to see the school not turn its back on the development of an appreciation for art and literature and history. But, if the principal focus of compensatory education now is as an antidote to poverty, I suspect those appreciations are of a secondary order of priority. The first order of priority is to decrease this lack of basic skills.

In a recent publication, Doxey Wilkerson and I suggested that there are certain requirements for survival in the emerging society which the school might use to identify goals, or at least to establish a floor that every child in the school should reach. Included among these mastery goals are basic communication skills, problem solving, the ordering and management of knowledge, management of self and of interpersonal relations, and a category which has to do with respect for continued learning and self-expression which is discussed within the context of the growing need for competence in the use of leisure time. In developing that position, we were suggesting that since the number of persons in our society who are truly mentally defective is probably not more than 3 to 5 percent, there are certain levels of academic achievement that we ought to expect for every youngster except that 3 to 5 percent. At that time I felt that since the lack of prerequisite skills and competencies and entry credentials are serious impediments to upward mobility, we would have gone a long way towards solving the problems of poverty if we could somehow reach this goal.

In rethinking the problem, however, it seems to me that while this position is appropriate as a long-term goal for meaningful living, I am not sure it is appropriate as an antidote to poverty. A brief look at the variety of programs across the country (including Head Start) shows that the educational establishment is not entirely prepared to produce quickly and efficiently enough to achieve the goals that some of us have assumed would be a way out of poverty. It is probably a mistake, therefore, to say to the disadvantaged, "The school is your hope because it is there that you will learn the skills and competencies that will get you out."

Another issue concerns what it takes to get ahead in society. As one who has been concerned with the development of competencies and skills, it is become more and more clear to me that although greater skills and competencies are being demanded, they may not be as important in this society as are the entry credentials. If we look at some of the people who occupy high positions in politics, in commerce and industry, or in social areas, and examine the quality of their day-to-day functioning, I am beginning to be convinced that we have been misleading the poor when we tell them, "You've got to meet this high level of achievement." I still believe in it as a human being and a humanitarian, but I am less convinced that these ideals are the rules of the game that the rest of the world is playing. It may even be that some of our efforts at dealing with certain segments of the population are designed to keep them from really catching on to what the game is about. And the school becomes somewhat immoral when it continues to hold the attainment of these skills as the goal. Those of us who have an opportunity to see how people function in this country realize that it is essential for at least some few to understand what is going on, to be able to solve problems, and to point the direction; unfortunately, most of us are not exercising this quality of intellectual and social leadership.

S. M. Miller has raised the question of whether or not our society is prepared to absorb roughly a third of our population—60 million additional people—into its mainstream. If we succeed in keeping all these youngsters in school, through high school and college, and if we succeed in having them come out as intelligent, well-informed, creative, productive individuals, is the society prepared to absorb them into the mainstream in some meaningful way? I suspect Miller is right in suggesting that we are not. But I suppose the economists and political scientists and other experts will argue this point. In any case, I do not think that we, as educators, should deceive a group of people into participating in the education process because it is an antidote to poverty. It is not. I think it is a way to a better life. By the year 2000, we will probably be less concerned with problems of economic insufficiency than with those of social insufficiency. Hopefully, we will have been forced to arrive at some manner of distributing the wealth so that people at least do not starve in this country. The disadvantaged of that period will probably be the persons who are incapable of relating meaningfully to others, who are inept at using their time in ways that are personally satisfying, and who are unable to relate creatively to nature, to the world of art, or to the world of ideas. I would defend compensatory education or equality of educational opportunity, or a good education, on that basis. As an antidote to poverty, I simply do not see it as a solution.

There is a final note on which I would like to comment, and it has to do with the possibility that if we open the doors to everybody, giving all persons an opportunity to function in the society, many will fail, just as some have failed who have already had this kind of freedom and have gotten into the mainstream. But I also think that there is something about producing and being an active part of a process that develops people. Rather than letting people spend months or years in developing the skills and competencies, it might be more appropriate to take a direct approach and simply let them in. In other words, it might be more appropriate as an immediate antidote to poverty to give the credentials and let the people act as if they were mainstream members. If we look at two and three generations of development in this country, we see that this is a common course. A family that was poor has acquired a bit of wealth by hard work, or stealing, or good luck, and they have moved to the suburbs. While one sees traces of the earlier deficits in their functioning, they have rapidly picked up the characteristics, even some of the skills and competencies, of the people who are already there. The weakness I see in this system is that it tends to settle for and encourage a high degree of mediocrity. It is for this reason that I would prefer to hold to somewhat higher goals for education— understanding once again that they are probably not antidotes to poverty. But again, if one is talking about a way out of poverty, I suspect that we ought to begin to admit that in terms of performance, of skill, and of competency, there is an awful lot of mediocrity in our society; that there are an awful lot of people who can function on this level; and that we should not kid them or ourselves about it.

Chapter 17

THE ROLE OF MOTIVATION AND SELF-IMAGE IN SOCIAL CHANGE IN SLUM AREAS

Marshall B. Clinard*

Slums can be viewed in a number of ways. To some, slums are groups with different values and ways of life; to others, they are groups lacking power; some regard them as groups of disadvantaged people in need of economic and welfare help; to still others, slums represent a physical condition in need of rehabilitation. These various views have affected the perspective or approach of various disciplines. The sociologist is largely concerned with the social structure and patterns of behavior in the slum; the political scientist is interested in their lack of power and influence; the economist is concerned with the relation of the slum to productivity, markets, and real estate; and the planner is primarily occupied with the physical environment. This discussion will largely look at the slum as a social psychological problem of motivation and of the self-images of slum persons and slum communities.

Many have hoped that programs providing more economic and educational opportunities and services to the poor, whether in rural or urban areas, will almost automatically solve their problems. Where conditions have not materially improved, the tendency has been to provide even more funds and technical manpower for opportunities and services, on the continued assumption of a direct relation between the two. Many continue to assume that the problems of the urban poor and the slum arise from the

*Professor of Sociology, University of Wisconsin, Madison.

failure to provide adequate or sufficiently broad services, or what has been termed the *illusion of services* (Hunter, 1964, p. 594).

In the past, in the United States, countless billions of dollars have been spent by private philanthropic and welfare agencies to alleviate or eliminate poverty and slum conditions; in recent years these expenditures have materially increased as government has assumed more of what was originally the result of private initiative. Welfare services in the form of neighborhood centers, adult education, and urban extension programs have been made available to the poor. Schools have been built in the most depressed slum areas, and pressures to improve school programs have often been great. Vocational and job-training programs have been provided in most urban areas.

Despite these large-scale philanthropic and welfare programs over the past half-century, slum areas in American cities have generally continued to resist efforts to change them. A similar situation has occurred in developing countries, where change has not necessarily occurred because services have been offered. A United Nations report (1966) has concluded that in developing countries, "very substantial improvements in living conditions could be achieved if local populations could be brought to adopt certain changes or innovations derived from modern science and technology— changes that do not necessarily require particular skills or expensive equipment." In India, for example, the provision of extensive government services to villages has not necessarily been followed by their adoption. After evaluating the government extension services provided to farmers in India, a leading student of the program, Kusam Nair (1961, p. 192), has concluded:

> Planning in India is framed on the assumption—which in view of the extreme poverty of the people would seem logical—that the desire for higher levels is inherent and more or less universal among the masses being planned for. . . . Generally the lower the level, the more static the aspirations tend to be. . . . Unless a man feels a desire to have more material wealth sufficiently to strive for it, he cannot be expected to have much interest in new techniques; there will be little effort on his part to innovate. He may and often does disdain to engage in activities yielding the highest net advantage even within the available opportunities and restrictions imposed upon him by the society to which he belongs.

The model of human behavior presented by this provision of economic opportunities and services is that human beings, given such means from outside resources, will automatically respond by availing themselves of these opportunities in an effort to improve their situations. They will take advantage of job-training programs, adopt new agricultural techniques, regularly attend and work diligently in schools, use the libraries, and adopt new health and sanitation practices. It is a model of an economic, logical, and rational man—an "as-if" construction of the middle-class planner and professional person about the nature of human motivation. It is a simplication of what is, in actuality, a far more complex problem.

This does not mean to imply that these programs are not important in any permanent solution of slum problems; it is that they have been over-emphasized because of a naiveté about human behavior. Such proposals reflect a lack of acquaintance with the real data of human experience. The assumption that most people of the slum will immediately grasp opportunities for improvement when they are offered is questionable. Many slum dwellers have limited aspirations and feel little desire for education, material achievements, or a better way of life, at least not sufficiently enough to make the effort to achieve them. One writer (Goodenough, 1963, p. 223) on social change has put it bluntly: "Unless people can perceive a good reason to learn something new, they are not going to make the effort and will regard exhortations by others as an impertinent nuisance." As Gans (1967) has pointed out in connection with United States anti-poverty programs, the evidence indicates that "many lower-class people do not share the status aspirations of the middle class. Yet there has been too little sociological criticism of federal antipoverty programs, many of which have proceeded on the assumption that lower-class people have precisely such aspirations." Moreover, the view that poor sanitation, delinquency, drug addiction, and other forms of deviant behavior are necessarily products of poverty, discrimination, or lack of opportunity is not supported by the evidence. The slum way of life, with its norms and values fostering certain behavior patterns, tends to be confused with the prevalent low economic condition.

THE SLUM AS A WAY OF LIFE

Without a doubt slums constitute the most persistent problem of modern urban life: they are the chief sources of crime and delinquency, of illness and death from disease. They are of many types, differing in physical setting, population density, in the permanence or social mobility of their inhabitants, the socioeconomic handicaps or barriers to such movements, the degree of social organization among the residents, and the types of urban problems presented (Clinard, 1966). Each slum neighborhood must be examined in terms of its own uniqueness. Slums may vary in the dominant influence on the life patterns of the inhabitants and the extent to which the slum lives of the residents are shaped through the pressures of environmental and family backgrounds, cultural traditions, and major life concerns.

Although they vary from one type to another, certain general patterns of slum life are universal. Sociologically, it is a way of life with its own subculture. The subcultural norms and values of the slum are reflected in poor sanitation and health practices, deviant behavior, and often a real lack of interest in formal education. With some exceptions, there is little general desire to engage in personal or community efforts for self-improvement. Slum persons generally are apathetic toward the employment of self-help on a community basis, they are socially isolated, and most sense their powerlessness. This does not mean that they are satisfied with their way of life or do not want a better way to live; it is simply that slum apathy tends to inhibit individuals from putting forth sufficient efforts to change the local community. They may protest and they may blame the slum entirely on the outside world, but at the same time they remain apathetic about what they could themselves do to change their world.

Along with a sense of apathy they feel generally powerless to alter their community situations themselves; they feel incapable of influencing either others or themselves. Such powerlessness is accompanied by long-standing patterns of behavior and beliefs that reflect acceptance of their weaknesses. Feelings of powerlessness are derived from the fact that decisions have been made for them by outsiders for so long that they generally have failed to develop the experiences and skills necessary for motivating themselves for social change (Haggstrom, 1965). In the achievement of most goals, slum persons tend to see chance rather than effort, luck rather than planning, as all-important. Producing change in the slum is determined to a large extent by the slum dweller's attitude about getting out of the slum, and by his feeling about the system which controls his existence. It is this that "makes slums a human problem rather than a problem of finance and real estate" (Hunter, 1964, p. 18).

Slum dwellers are constantly reminded of their powerlessness by public and private welfare agencies, by the police as agents of control, by absentee landlords, and even by urban-renewal programs that may drastically alter or even destroy their present physical existence. Clark (1965) has pointed out Harlem's relative lack of power, politically, economically, and in the press. For example, the major social agencies which operate in Harlem depend upon sources outside the community for support; to secure funds it is often necessary to arrange for an agency board to be dominated by white persons. The Chicago Freedom Movement, led by Martin Luther King, Jr., encountered great apathy in 1967 when it first tried to stimulate initiative in the Negro slums of Chicago. King's lieutenant, Hosea Williams, stated that, "We're used to working with people who want to be freed. The Chicago Negro isn't concerned with what the power structure is doing to him. . . . I have never seen such hopelessness. The Negroes of Chicago have a greater feeling of powerlessness than I ever saw. They don't participate in the governmental process because they're beaten down psychologically."[1]

While they are generally apathetic to self and community improvement, feel futile about using services that are offered to them, and have become hostile and suspicious toward the "outside world" and its agents of change such as social workers or representatives of government agencies, slum people have also become disillusioned by the unfilled promises of welfare groups, government agencies, and politicians. They can see little real possibility of bettering themselves. Failure to bring about improvement has affected their hopes for the future, and they have become overdependent on government and private agencies which will, they believe, look out for them regardless of any efforts on their own. This vicious cycle is perpetuated by the lack of effective communication among slum dwellers about local problems. Individually, they may be disturbed about police protection and garbage collection, for example, but there may be little collective expression of this feeling. Consequently, the extent and nature of collective expressions in slum areas by one's reference groups may carry added significance in connection with social change.

MOTIVATED BEHAVIOR AND REFERENCE GROUPS

Motivation for change precedes most successful programs for altering behavioral patterns. People are more willing to participate in action directed at adjusting or changing conditions, such as the adequate utilization of services and programs, if they perceive the desirability of change and are adequately aroused. On the other hand, they may resist change if it appears to threaten their way of life, if they cannot understand the reasons for the change, or if a program is promoted through outside pressures.

Motivated behavior includes what an "individual notices, does, feels, and thinks in more or less integrated fashion while he is pursuing a given goal" (Newcomb et al., 1965, p. 21). The wants and needs of a person or group are not necessarily the same, nor are they necessarily the results of rational decisions. They are responses to feeling states within persons. What a person's needs are depends on the conditions a person wants and the way in which existing conditions differ in terms of achieving them.

---

[1]Comments by Hosea L. Williams, as reported in *The New York Times*, January 16, 1967.

Programs-of-change agents, such as those which provide services to slum dwellers, respond generally to what the agents assume to be observed needs. People's needs are not necessarily their wants. Conceptually, there are not only the "observed needs" of an outsider, but the "felt needs" of a particular people. What people see as being needed to gratify a want depends on their state of knowledge, the situation as they have discerned it, and their organization of reality.

The motives that operate to select attitudes, values, and goals are acquired through social experiences. They are socially molded, usually in accord with the norms prevailing in particular groups to which the individual belongs. People who have grown up in a local community are likely to have had more common experiences and be more alike in their motivations than those who live in other communities. Consequently, members of the same community, such as a slum, no matter how they may differ among themselves, are likely to have more wants in common with each other than they have with outsiders. Reference groups to which an individual belongs, or to which he wants to gain acceptance, have a particularly important bearing on the attitudes of a person and on the possibility of new behavior patterns' or programs' being accepted. If a group is important to him he will often do what is demanded to secure or maintain acceptance. The desire to learn, for example, is acquired through interaction with school subject matter and with those adults and peers who transmit attitudes toward school. Attitudes toward the police are acquired in much the same manner.

Consequently, persons appear to vary in their emphases on given motives, depending on the cultural and subcultural norms which tend to define the behavioral response in a given situation. Slum residents do not respond, for example, to the many services proffered for them simply because they are there. Their response is likely to be in terms of group reactions, for the problems that have developed in these slum areas, and for that matter among the poor generally, have originated in group practices condoned and continued by groups. Thus economic, educational, and cultural improvement programs can be presented to people without their being fully utilized.

Unless behavior can be sufficiently motivated, therefore, social change cannot take place. Such change can, in general, be activated only when groups of persons perceive the need for it and want to cooperate with outside agencies in bringing about this change. Slum neighborhoods often have behavioral norms quite at variance with outside agencies of control—whether they are school teachers, vocational instructors, or social workers—and their norms and goals may be supported, ignored, or ridiculed. School programs to motivate learning in slum areas, for example, cannot be successful without the support of neighborhood people. Conant (1961) pointed out that one had only to visit a slum school to become convinced that "the nature of the community determines what goes on in the school." Moreover, in the social context of ambition, neighborhood influences play a significant role. Turner found, for example, that the differences in the level of ambition between schools in high and low neighborhoods is much greater than can be attributed to differences in individual family-background levels. "The average level of the neighborhood probably has about as much effect as the level of the individual family background in determining how high the child's ambition will be," according to Turner (1964, p. 65).

PERSONAL IDENTITY AND THE SLUM

An important aspect of any person is his self-concept. It is this image of the self (ourselves) in a person that we try to enhance or defend. This self-concept is not static; it is subject to change and modification throughout life. It changes as those with whom one identifies change, or as the expectations of these others are altered. In general, "once established it apparently provides a sense of personal continuity over space and time, and is defended against alteration, diminution and insult" (Brehm and Cohen, 1962; Coopersmith, 1967). This self-image, or identity, either of a person or a local community, embodies those characteristics which are identified as being like or unlike other persons or communities. A man's self-conception, what he means to himself, determines to a great extent how he will act in terms of a given situation or in making a decision. It will determine in large measure the role behavior he will exhibit. He may, for example, reject efforts to improve educational conditions, as he sees them in terms of who he is and what others think. For the most part, a person seeks to achieve personal and social identities which are favorably recognized by others in his immediate area of interaction. The manner in which someone evaluates his identity, as a person who must achieve or not achieve certain societal goals, may be considered as his level of self-esteem in terms of praise or shame.

Many slums constitute subcultures with their own specifications of appropriate social roles, definitions of life goals, and system of meanings for interpreting experiences. Where such a system is internalized or made a part of the self, says Ryan (1963, p. 135), "it forms the elements of the individual's ego identity; his sense of who and what he is, his sense of continuity with the past and with the future and its goals." A challenge to the cultural elements and normative standards of a slum is often a challenge to the ego and conception of self of those who live there. A study of personal identity in a West End slum of Boston (Ryan, 1963) concluded that the values thus reaffirmed in the process of social interaction in the culture were significant in each person's efforts to find coherence and meaning in the world, especially in those aspects of experience which produced anxiety.

Many years ago the distinguished sociologist, W. I. Thomas, wrote that people come to act according to the expectations held of them. This statement has significant implications for planned change of identity. An important way to increase people's motivation for change to take advantage of services provided or to engage in self-help activities is to bring about a change in identity or self-image. Such an identity change can be looked at in two ways—as a change in the self-image of individuals, or as a collective change, for example, in a local community. In the discussion that follows, reference is largely to changes in the identity of slum dwellers, but most of what is said also refers to collective changes in a local slum community. As the individual's self-image is derived largely from social relationships and interactional patterns, so is a local community's self-image influenced by interaction with others from outside the community (Foot and Cottrell, 1955; Strauss, 1955).

The apathy, powerlessness, and lack of confidence in achieving change, all characteristic of slum people, can give way and become modified under newly created self-images which make former ways of life and behavior patterns incompatible with a new self-image. In most instances such change represents a new sense of personal worth and organization of reality. Confidence in their own capabilities must be developed if slum people are to feel their own importance and to recognize the possibilities for changing conditions themselves rather than to rely on outside pressures. After surveying a number of efforts to induce change in various parts of the world, Goodenough (1963, p. 184) concluded:

> People may be unhappy with their lot as members of some ascribed social category and wish that theirs were a different fate. Yet they may not try to avail themselves of proffered opportunities to change their lot because they accept the view that it is their nature to be as they are, that their present identity is something that is beyond human power to change. If trying to be something different can, at best, be only a skillfully executed masquerade, then it offers little promise of accomplishing a change in one's self-image. . . . The fact remains that when people see a proposal as one in which they are pretending to be something they know they are not, they may appreciate its intentions and yet be unable to commit themselves to it.

Social changes in slum areas inevitably rest, then, on identity change and community development as essentially a "process of collective identity change, in which a community's members come to look upon themselves as a different kind of people and on their community as a different kind of place" (Goodenough, 1963, p. 241). One reason for the failure of most planned efforts to alter slums and eradicate poverty has been that there has not been, despite large expenditures of time and money, a real conceptual basis for social change and, above all, that there has often been a failure to recognize the importance of identity change and how it is to be accomplished.

THE PROCESS OF IDENTITY CHANGE: DEVELOPING A NEW SELF-IMAGE

Personal identity or self-image is subject to change and modification throughout life. It changes as those with whom one identifies change, or as the expectations of these others are altered. Both a person's self-image and his public image can undergo alteration. These changes, however, are not readily brought about among slum dwellers. Long-term group and cultural norms in slum areas have tended to make slum dwellers suspicious of, or caused them to reject, the outside and stereotyped change-agencies such as government, welfare, or the school. Continuity with the past and difficulties of estimating future effects make change even more difficult. Expectations and actions that differ from tradition may be rejected. Slum people may not try to avail themselves of opportunities and services to change their way of life because they themselves have accepted the view that their present identities are impossible to change; and when they have built up rationalizations to protect a world that seems comparatively secure and comfortable to them it is even more difficult to change.

In changing slum dwellers, or the poor generally, one must be interested in altering their feelings about themselves as well as in changing their economic and material situation. In this way their potentiality for self-generated improvement can be enhanced, and a new hope for the future and a new confidence in their ability to achieve it can be developed (Batten, 1957, 1965; Taylor et al., 1965). In this identity change, a useful model might well be the following steps: (1) revision of one's view of self through new experiences; (2) commitment to change in self-identity; and (3) recognition of new identities and roles by others.[2]

---

[2]See Clinard (1966, pp. 301-308) for more extensive treatment of identity change. The four steps discussed there have been compressed here into three by combining achieving a desire for change with revision of one's view of self. The theoretical scheme of identity change presented here has been partially derived from Goodenough (1963, Chapter 9).

Revision of One's View of Self through New Experiences

The achievement of desire for change in self-image requires a degree of dissatisfaction among community members with their present identities so that they will reappraise their self-images and reevaluate their self-esteem. Here new and conflicting experiences may often be needed to stimulate some dissatisfaction with the self if one wishes a person to change his present self-image. Consequently, arousing some discontent within slum areas can be not only useful but essential.

Providing new experiences is probably the most effective way to make a person see that his image of himself might be altered.[3] Experiences with new patterns of living may effectively furnish new criteria for self-appraisal and may lead to alteration of the self-image. Through these new experiences and opportunities, the slum dweller may view himself in a different light and often he may develop new wants. The Delhi Project in Indian slum communities, with which the author was associated, indicates the possibilities of the use of new experiences in overcoming apathy among those who live in the slum. The *vikas mandals* were artificially formed slum-citizen development councils of from 1,250 to 5,000 persons, the organization of which was the responsibility of the Department of Urban Community Development of the Delhi Municipal government (Clinard, 1966).[4] In this project, efforts were made to expose people to activities of the "new" India by encouraging visits to the national radio station and various cultural centers and discussions of the five-year plans for the development of the country. Exposure to new methods of child care were also provided.

In the Delhi Project attempts were also made to alter the self-images of slum women who have long played an extremely subordinate role. Independent organizations for women, *mahila samitis,* were formed to carry out self-help activities, and it was hoped that this would help them to assume greater responsibility for changing slum conditions and demonstrate that Indian slum women could display initiative.

Demonstrations of new ways of doing things have long been used in

---

[3]For example, in one New York slum area grade school, Negro airline pilots, stewardesses, doctors, engineers, detectives, and educators were invited to talk to the students and thus to present a new image of the students' capabilities. A survey had shown that the majority had stated that they hoped to earn about $100 a week by the age of thirty-five.

[4]The Delhi project was begun in 1958 under a grant from the Ford Foundation with the author serving as consultant. By 1968, in Delhi there were over 60 citizen development councils involving over 100,000 persons. The project became the prototype for the national program of urban community development which began in 1965 and by 1968 involved nearly a million persons in the slums of 16 cities of India. The project has been described and analyzed in Clinard (1966).

rural extension services to change people's methods of such aspects of life as homemaking or child care. Seeing and learning about major scientific achievements, and opportunities to participate more fully in the outside world, may disturb current ways of living and bring about needed changes. Seeing similar slum areas where people have become more highly motivated for learning, or in controling delinquency, often offers another type of demonstration. To some degree, the Civil Rights movement in the United States has given Negro slum dwellers new views of what they need and are entitled to have; many have become interested in having their identity as Negroes reevaluated by non-Negroes.

The mere fact that community workers and others may ask the opinions of slum residents, and believe them capable of changing many aspects of their lives, may accomplish some of the same results. The vision of possibly doing something for themselves as a group may represent a radically new idea in these slum areas where there has long been dependence on charity, welfare, and government. In the Delhi project, for example, during the worker's initial contact with the Indian slum family, this question was asked: "What problems do you think the people in this area can solve for themselves?" Even though there often were few suggestions, the question itself stimulated discussion among the people about this strange idea of their having any capacity for changing anything themselves. Here were the beginnings of an awareness of the possibility of self-help and of a new view of themselves.

The decentralization of responsibility for certain essential urban governmental services to slum area residents offers still other possibilities for the revision of the slum resident's self-image and consequent social change. Moreover, the successful administration of large cities requires more direct contact between people and those who administer the services. Political units like wards are often too large and the problems too complicated for one councilman or alderman to handle. A controlled decentralization of authority in an urban setting might result in greater support for government, overcome some of the apathy and hostility to government, and clear up misunderstanding of its services on the part of many of the poor living in slum areas.

Such decentralization makes possible wider participation in decision-making processes and furnishes opportunities for the development of more broadly based leadership by average urban citizens. With decentralization, for example, boards of slum residents could largely manage the operation of their local schools. In 1967, in fact, the mayor of New York City recommended to the legislature the establishment in New York of thirty to sixty largely autonomous, locally governed, community school districts, each district to be run by a community school board consisting of six members elected by parents and five appointed by the mayor.[5] The boards would have power to hire school personnel, set educational policy, and allocate funds.

In addition to local school boards, there is a wide range of other possibilities such as local police boards, local decentralized libraries and library boards, local sanitation and health boards, and local planning boards. The supervision, use, and protection of small city neighborhood parks, as has been authorized in New York, could be taken over by local citizen groups.[6] Moreover, decentralized lay panels in slum areas, largely in place of juvenile courts, might deal with juvenile offenders, as is generally the case throughout England and Wales and Sweden. In the latter country, local citizen boards also deal with the problems of alcoholism. The Soviet Union uses an extensive system of worker or citizen courts, located in either factories or neighborhoods, to deal with minor thefts, assaults, or family disputes (Berman and Spindler, 1963). There is also the possibility of wider participation in the supervision of probationers and parolees by local citizen committees as has been developed by the Chicago Area Projects (Kobrin, 1959; Sorrentino, 1959).

It is likely that such a new experience and the assumption of such responsibilities, together with the status attached to such local boards, might do much to change the self-image of slum dwellers and urban persons, consequently changing their attitudes toward school, the library, the police, and the sanitation services. Local school board participation could mean the development of greater interest and an understanding of education and school programs, as well as protection of local schools from vandalism and misuse. Local library boards might encourage more interest in reading and the general use of library facilities in slum communities. Citizen boards attached to police districts could develop changes in community attitudes toward the police and a greater awareness of personal and property protection problems in the area. Out of such work could come greater interest in dealing with youth crime and drug addiction which not only injure the participants, but also the community's image of itself (Alinsky, 1946). Sanitation and health boards could result in greater awareness of sanitation and health problems in the area. Local planning boards could look into the physical and social problems of the area and present plans for their improvement.

Through working with local leadership it is possible to give credit for social change to slum persons. This is important, for unless local people, rather than a welfare or government agency, receive credit for what they

---

[5] *The New York Times*, December 1, 1967.
[6] *The New York Times*, April 29, 1967.

accomplish in changing an area, they are apt to lose their continuing en-
thusiasm for community projects. Conversely, if their efforts do not accomplish what they had hoped it may cause them to re-examine the
community situation to discover the possible reasons.

Commitment to Change in Self-Identity

Exposure to new experiences and new expectations of their capabilities and responsibilities may lead to considerable alteration in the slum
dwellers' view of themselves and it may facilitate the development of a new
identity. New experiences may give rise to new wants. Individuals, however, are often torn between old and new practices—between an old and a
new idea of what is or what is not acceptable as a self-image. Yet the
commitment of a person or local community to new ways of acting, to
rejecting former ways, and to acquiring new skills constitutes the achievement of a new identity.

A commitment to change in self-identity, however, is difficult to make,
for it requires some eradication of the former self. The contents of new
social roles involving the display of initiative and decision making and the
throwing off of attitudes of dependence on others must be learned. Those
who have been accustomed to charity and to being regarded as "poor, unfortunate inhabitants" of the slums may consequently develop a feeling of
independence, self-reliance, and a feeling of personal worth. Commitment
to a new identity may mean that former practices such as poor sanitation,
deviant behavior, and a lack of interest in education may no longer fit a
new image of respectability. The playing of new roles must be developed to
fit a new image of the self.

Successful self-help projects, planned and carried out by those who are
poor, do much, therefore, to enhance the person's conception of his own
worth, to help overcome his feelings of powerlessness, and to commit both
him and his community to a new identity. Such identity is not necessarily
changed if what he does merely enhances the prestige of a private or government welfare agency. People who are able to accomplish self-help projects for and by themselves can be a potent force in identity change. Fortunately, despite government and private programs of doing things for
them, there are many things that people in the slums of urban America
can do for themselves. Changes in slums can be accelerated through the
use of the large potential source of manpower and resources provided by
the slum dwellers' own efforts. There are large-scale possibilities for physical improvements, health and sanitation, education, and recreational and
cultural activities. It is a curious contradiction that middle-class people,
whose problems are not as serious and who often have the funds to ar-

range for help, engage in far more self-help activities, either individually or cooperatively, than do the poor who have greater problems and less ability to pay. People in urban slum areas in the United States could, for example, make minor repairs and improve the maintenance of their housing, whether owned by private or public landlords—perhaps with community-owned tools; improve the sanitation in their neighborhoods and get rid of rats;[7] help to protect public property like schools and parks from vandalism; assist in the control of drug addiction, delinquency, and illegitimacy; establish credit unions and cooperative stores and promote the cooperative ownership of recreational equipment and library materials; and cooperate with teachers and serve as assistants to help with school problems and increase motivation for learning.[8] The protection of local women from sexual assault has been assumed in New York City slum areas by citizen groups, which furnish evening escorts home and maintain citizen patrols. Self-help efforts in job training have also been conducted by some local communities. Some of these things are being done now; but much more needs to be done as a matter of a policy of self-help.

Too often, however, the results of self-help projects by slum people are regarded solely as material accomplishments rather than in terms of the effect in instilling pride and feelings of community respectability, and changing the collective identity of local areas. Professional and well-meaning middle-class persons helping in slum areas are often correct in their view that they can plan and carry out projects more efficiently than the poor. What they fail to realize is that even a poorly planned and carried out project may do much to commit slum persons to a change in self-identity.[9] The dynamics of such successful self-help projects in identity

---

[7]In one large United States city the head of the municipal rodent-eradication bureau recently said that, if the tenement slum dwellers really wanted to get rid of rats, they could do it in a few months. The garbage left about by the slum dweller and his failure to plug entry ways for the rats and to help eradicate them are what make rat control impossible for city administrations.

[8]For example, a group of families or a local community could jointly own an encyclopedia for the children, which is generally too expensive for a single slum family. This approach might increase the children's desire for education and improve their performances in school. In developing countries there is an even wider scope of self-help activities with a consequent effect on self-image. For a lengthy list of self-help activities in the Delhi Project, see Clinard (1966).

[9]A consequence of the self-help in the large-scale Lyari self-help project in the slums of Karachi has been their increased association with the "more respectable" groups of the city because of the achievement of the Lyari group, such as their Girl Guide troop's winning first place in cleanliness and their Boy Scout troop's second in drama in All-Pakistan competitions. These achievements, by increasing community pride, have facilitated other self-help projects.

change have been implied in Haggstrom's (1965) discussion of the development of feelings of power among the poor, in which he says that to be effective, social action programs should have the following characteristics:

1. The poor see themselves as the source of the action.
2. The action affects in major ways the preconceptions, values or interests of institutions and persons defining the poor.
3. The action demands much in effort and skill, or in other ways becomes salient to major areas of the personalities of the poor.
4. The action ends in success.
5. The successful self-originated important action increases the force and number of symbolic or nonsymbolic communications of the potential worth or individual power of individuals who are poor.

Vital to such a concept is a change in identity or self-image of the residents of the slums. In most instances, such a change represents a new sense of personal worth. Self-confidence must be developed so that the slum resident can sense his own importance and recognize the possibilities for changing conditions with some outside help. This can be accomplished, in part, by successful self-help programs and by the assumption of more responsibility for the direction of their own efforts, which gives people a sense of worth and dignity. Change in their ideas of themselves, to be effective, would mean that such practices as poor sanitation, gang delinquency, drug addiction, illegitimacy, and lack of real interest in education, so common in slum areas, may no longer fit the image of people who live in slum areas.

Recognition by Others of New Identities and Roles

Persons, or local communities, may change behavioral patterns, but in order to feel that a change has occurred they must be treated by others in a different manner. Recognition by others of the new identities and roles assumed by residents of slum communities is crucial in maintaining and solidifying identity change, for "it is impossible to play the roles appropriate to one's new identity in a social vacuum" (Goodenough, 1963, p. 240). This means that others no longer demean the individual or local community, for example by referring to them as "poor Negro slum dwellers." They become no longer objects of pity, charity, and failure.

Legitimation of new identities involves approval and praise by individuals and groups who possess sufficient social power in the form of authority and influence. Praise of outsiders plays an important role in such change by helping to develop a new collective identity. On the other hand, attempts to play new roles may be negated if others do not accord a person or community, through role-taking, the new self-image he is trying to cultivate.

Efforts to alter the collective self-image of slum dwellers must successfully deal with the problems of outside recognition of the local community's efforts to alter past roles. Recognition and acceptance by important people in the community, such as government officials, helps to maintain the new image. In the Delhi project, persistent efforts were made to give such prestige to slum dwellers. On occasion officers of citizen development councils reported their accomplishments to area councilmen or to members of the municipal standing committees. Officers of slum organizations were invited to participate in a citywide civic meeting attended by a cabinet officer, the mayor, or other high dignitary. Such meetings recognized that self-help efforts of slum communities and the mingling with people of high prestige served to break down the barriers separating the slum population from others in activities within the city as a whole. In an experimental effort to enhance the feelings of new importance of slum dwellers their officers were invited to the city council chambers of Delhi to report on the activities of their local communities to the city commissioner and the deputy mayor of Delhi.

Through the process which has been discussed in this model, slum people may come to change their motivations and to feel a sense of new identity, an identity that is a product of the new accomplishments of the group. In efforts to live up to this new self-image, further change in ways of life incompatible with effective urban living is possible.

IDENTITY CHANGE AND THE NEGRO: AN EXAMPLE

Recognition of the relation of motivation and self-image is crucial in any effective solution to the Negro ghettos of our large cities. The pre-existing social values of the slums of America's large cities, to which Negroes have moved, have been combined with the ever-present imprint of slavery and discrimination. According to Bollens and Schmandt (1965, p. 251):

> Urban opportunities, triggered by advancing technology and industrialization, have attracted many Negroes from their back-country sharecroppers' cabins to the gaudy neon lights and shabby tenements of the metropolis. Uneducated, unversed in middle-class mores, and flagrantly discriminated against, they have often become social casualties in their new and seemingly hostile environment.

The background of the American Negro is unique not only for the United States but for the western world generally. One would have to go back many centuries to find anything quite like it in Europe. The mark of slavery has influenced the Negro's adjustment to urban living in slum areas; the unstable family pattern of slavery has been carried into the slums, and to this have been added general patterns of violence and serious problems of identity. Living for a long time under slavery and repression has resulted in the development of a subculture or contraculture with its own patterns of attitudes and behavior. The Negro has been effectively prevented from rising out of the slum because of these attitudes, particularly toward self-identity and especially among the lower-class Negroes, and because opportunities to leave have at the same time been restricted by discriminatory practices.

All of these factors, together with a lack of effective group organization in the past, have greatly influenced the urban Negro. Urban Negro life has more and more become characterized by high rates of illegitimacy, juvenile delinquency, theft, assault, criminal homicide, rape, and, more recently, looting in connection with ghetto riots. Most of the victims of these offenses, including rape and assault, are other Negroes. In addition, there are serious problems associated with heavy drinking, drug addiction, health problems, and poor sanitation. Motivation for education and cultural development appear to be lower than for comparable economic groups.

On the whole, Negroes in urban slums have tended to be apathetic to these problems, to approve some, and even to justify deviant behavior as being simply products of discrimination by the whites. The explanation is not this simple, for it also involves a lack of real effort on the part of Negroes to communicate with one another and to deal internally with their problems themselves. To do this requires a change in identity. Among the various occupants of slums in the United States, the Negro alone has had little sense of identity, of ethnic or racial pride. This lack has made it difficult for him to rise above the slum world in the way various ethnic groups have. The American Negro has lost his cultural identity; slavery erased even his knowledge of his exact African homeland (Africa is a large and diverse area from which to come), his past cultural heritage, and often even specific knowledge of his additional biological white ancestry, where this has been added.

The status of the minority-group person is often a reflection of how the person perceives the way that society perceives him. In fact, in the case of the Negro, prejudice and discrimination have affected the attitudes and behavior of the minority-group members toward the standards set by the dominant society, as well as their responses to themselves and their group (Simpson and Yinger, 1965). Studies of Negro children, for example, show that their life experiences have generally given them a negative, inferior conception of themselves. Research has revealed that the drawings, stories, and dramas of young Negro children often reveal a desire to be white; self-esteem has been damaged by the conception that a black skin is inferior. The realization that one's skin is an inferior color soon changes to the feeling that one belongs to an inferior group and that he must act accordingly. Moreover, the damage to a child's esteem appears to be greater for Negro boys than for girls. Northern Negro youths show less self-depreciation than southern youths, which reflects, according to Johnson (1941), a less discriminatory environment and a greater acquaintance with a racial ideology. Teaching materials place little emphasis on the importance of the Negro and his place in the world. Consequently, one writer has concluded that the Negro child, from his earliest school days through his graduation from high school, must have continued opportunities to see himself and his racial group in a realistically positive light. "He needs to understand what color and race mean, he needs to learn about those of his race (and other disadvantaged groups) who have succeeded, and he needs to clarify his understanding of his own group history and current group situation" (Grambs, 1965, p. 21).

Negro adults tend to regard themselves with a sense of inferiority, and this is often shown by their lack of strong motivation to rise in their jobs or their fear of competition with whites; in a sense of impotence in civic affairs as it is demonstrated by lethargy toward voting, community participation, or responsibility for others; and in "family instability and the irresponsibility rooted in hopelessness." Clark (1965) maintains that this self-depreciation is so ingrained that urban Negroes, while identifying with successful Negroes, are suspicious of how they got ahead since they constitute exceptions.

Increasing racial consciousness among lower-class Negroes has brought some feeling of racial pride in recent years. Derogatory remarks about the behavior and inferiority of "whitey" are common, and the concepts of being proudly black, and of Black Power have attracted many adherents. These movements have tended, however, to result from the reactions to the discrimination of the outside world rather than from efforts to deal internally with Negro urban problems through self-help efforts.

Glazer and Moynihan (1963) have also stressed the need for self-help in pointing out that there are tasks that largely only Negroes can do effectively, and these important and necessary tasks have been largely ignored and shirked by Negroes. Any effective change of the situation under which urban Negroes live requires the development of a belief that patterns of life, such as delinquency, drug addiction, and illegitimacy, are incompatible with the Negroes' conception of who and what he is and what he should be

This change in conception of the "New Negro" requires greater effort than merely blaming the whites (who certainly deserve much of it). A concerted effort to present a new image of Negro behavior is needed. Identity change among Negroes, dependent as it is on their own initiative and resources, requires that they: (1) develop a new appreciation of their own worth, (2) effect an individual and corporate identity change, and (3) alter styles of living which are inappropriate to effective urban living.

One Negro group in the United States, the Black Muslims, has attempted to accomplish these objectives, and a number of studies has indicated that their efforts are characterized by considerable success (Essien-Udom, 1962; Lincoln, 1961; Simon, 1963).[10] Working largely in some of the most difficult lower-class Negro slums, this movement basically attempts to change the urban Negroes' image of themselves and, through a subsequent behavior change, to alter the white world's image of the Negro. The Black Muslims believe that the Negro problem stems primarily from "cultural backwardness, moral disposition, and collective image of their place in American society and the world" (Essien-Udom, 1962, p. 283), as well as the appendages left over from slavery.[11] Their spiritual leader, Elijah Muhammad, teaches that for too long Negroes have blamed their situation on the outside and have sought help primarily from the outside white world. He insists that Negroes have the "capacity to redeem themselves and to recover their sense of human worth; that they must take the initiative in their struggle for human dignity. The alternative . . . is continued complacency, moral deterioration, cultural degradation, crime, juvenile delinquency and social and cultural degradation" (Essien-Udom, 1962, p. 363).

The Black Muslims conclude that the only place for the Negro lower class to turn is to themselves, rather than to seek help from the Negro middle class or the white man, whether it be private welfare or government assistance. The Muslim movement attempts to effect a mass identity change in a group of urban slum people who previously had had little sense of identity and pride. The movement emphasizes that blackness is not a badge of inferiority but something positive, something worthy of esteem with a noble tradition and a future. They emphasize the role of the

---

[10] In pointing out the efforts of the Black Muslims to change self-images, there is no endorsement of the anti-white philosophy and tactics of this group.

[11] Commenting on the self-conception of the bush Negroes in Surinam, Derryk Ferrier, a sociologist, has stated (*The New York Times*, December 25, 1967, p. 17) that "they look upon other Negroes as former slaves, while they consider themselves escaped prisoners of war. The bush Negroes are proud of this distinction and view the whites and others as equals."

Negro in history, a role which has largely been left out of school text-books. The slum Negro is given a new status, identity, and pride.

Among Muslims this new identity means that he must live up to his new image and take on new duties and new responsibilities, including work in their small neighborhood mosques and in enterprises supported by the group. Emphasis is put on self-improvement and hard work, collective investment in cooperative enterprises, and responsibility for the welfare of other members by giving assistance to unemployed members and locating positions for others. Some Muslim groups own and operate businesses such as grocery stores, bakeries and restaurants, and various service establishments. Some may even become involved in the operation of their own schools for children, where Negro heritage is stressed.

This application of the process of identity change, although part of a program of a religious sect based on conflict and social separation, is highly suggestive for programs of planned change in slum areas anywhere. This emphasis on racial pride helps to overcome the stigma of a slave background and the void in ancestral pride that had existed among American Negroes, and makes possible the view that slum ways of life, such as delinquency, drug addiction, and a lack of a desire for education and cultural development, are incompatible with Negro pride.

REFERENCES

Alinsky, S. *Reveille for Radicals.* Chicago: University of Chicago Press, 1946.

Batten, T. R. *Communities and Their Development.* London: Oxford University Press, 1957.

———. *The Human Factor in Community Work.* London: Oxford University Press, 1965.

Berman, H. J., and Spindler, J. W. *Soviet Comrade's Courts.* Cambridge: Harvard University Press, 1963.

Bollens, J. C., and Schmandt, H. J. *The Metropolis: Its People, Politics, and Economic Life.* New York: Harper & Row, 1965.

Brehm, J. W., and Cohen, A. R. *Explorations in Cognitive Dissonance.* New York: Wiley, 1962.

Clark, K. B. *Dark Ghetto: Dilemmas of Social Power.* New York: Harper & Row, 1965.

Clinard, M. B. *Slums and Community Development: Experiments in Self-Help.* New York: Free Press, 1966.

Conant, J. B. *Slums and Suburbs.* New York: New American Library of World Literature, 1961.

Coopersmith, S. *Antecedents of Self-Esteem.* San Francisco: W. H. Freeman, 1967.

Essien-Udom, E. U. *Black Nationalism: A Search for an Identity in America.* Chicago: University of Chicago Press, 1962.

Foote, N., and Cottrell, L. S., Jr. *Identity and Interpersonal Competence: A New Direction for Family Research.* Chicago: University of Chicago Press, 1955.

Gans, H. J. Where Sociologists Have Failed. *Trans-Action,* 1967, 4: 2.

Glazer, N., and Moynihan, D. P. *Beyond the Melting Pot: The Negroes, Puerto Ricans, Jews, Italians, and Irish of New York City.* Cambridge, Mass.: M.I.T. Press, 1963.

Goodenough, W. H. *Cooperation in Change: An Anthropological Approach to Community Development.* New York: Russell Sage Foundation, 1963.

Grambs, J. D. The Self-Concept: Basis for Re-Education of Negro Youth, in *Negro Self-Concept: Implications for School and Citizenship.* Report of a conference sponsored by the Lincoln Filene Center for Citizenship and Public Affairs. New York: McGraw-Hill, 1965.

Haggstrom, W. C. The Power of the Poor, in L. A. Ferman, J. L. Kornbluh, & A. Habers, eds. *Poverty in America: A Book of Readings.* Ann Arbor: The University of Michigan Press, 1965, pp. 315-34.

Hunter, D. R. *The Slums: Challenge and Response.* New York: Free Press, 1964.

Hunter, D. R. Slums and Social Work or Wishes and the Double Negative, in B. Rosenberg, I. Gerver, and F. W. Howton, eds. *Mass Society in Crisis: Social Problems and Social Pathology.* New York: Macmillan, 1964, pp. 594-603.

Johnson, C. S. *Growing Up in the Black Belt.* New York: American Council on Education, 1941.

Kobrin, S. The Chicago Area Project; A 25-Year Assessment. *The Annals,* March 1959, 322: 19-29.

Lincoln, C. E. *The Black Muslims in America.* Boston: Beacon Press, 1961.

Nair, K. *Blossoms in the Dust: The Human Element in Indian Development.* London: Gerald Duckworth & Co., Ltd., 1961.

Newcomb, T. M., Turner, R. H., and Converse, P. E. *Social Psychology: The Study of Human Interaction.* New York: Holt Rinehart & Winston, 1965.

Ryan, E. J. Personality Identity in an Urban Slum, in L. J. Duhl, ed. *The Urban Condition: People and Policy in the Metropolis.* New York: Basic Books, 1963, pp. 135-50.

Simon, W. B. Schwarzer Nationalismus in den U.S.A. *Kölner Zeiterschrift für Soziologie und Sozialpsychologie,* Summer 1963.

Simpson, G. E., and Yinger, J. M. *Racial and Cultural Minorities: An Analysis of Prejudice and Discrimination,* 3d ed. New York: Harper & Row, 1965.

Sorrentino, A. The Chicago Area Project After 25 Years. *Federal Probation,* June 1959, 23: 40-45.

Strauss, A. L. *Mirrors and Masks: The Search for Identity.* New York: Free Press, 1955.

Taylor, C. C., Ensminger, D., Johnson, H. W., and Joyce, J. *India's Roots of Democracy: A Sociological Analysis of Rural India's Experience in Planned Development Since Independence.* Bombay: Orient Longmans, 1965.

Turner, R. H. *The Social Context of Ambition.* San Francisco: Chandler, 1964.

United Nations Office of Public Information. *Motivation for Social Change at the Local Level,* Lithograph 49320, November 1966.

Chapter 18

THE POVERTY OF PSYCHOLOGY— AN INDICTMENT

Arthur Pearl*

Psychologists as a group, along with other social scientists, have been guilty of refusing to accept the challenges that poverty presents to a society of unparalleled affluence. In matters of race and class, psychologists are sometimes brash when they should be modest, and often modest when circumstances demand assertiveness. Only when some of the misconceptions about poverty are examined in depth will it be possible to initiate the social changes that are so desperately needed.

MYTHS ABOUT THE INADEQUACY OF THE POOR

Psychologists and other social scientists contribute to at least four mythologies from which emerge programs and policies that prevent the poor from escaping from poverty. These myths assert that the poor are: (a) constitutionally inferior, (b) victimized by accumulated environmental deficits, (c) inadequately socialized, (d) encapsulated within autonomous cultures. Appreciation of the extent to which these mythologies are detrimental to the poor requires further explication.

---

*Professor of Education, University of Oregon.

The Poor Are Constitutionally Inferior

There is a philosophy of perverted Darwinism that—wittingly and unwittingly—psychologists advance. The implication is clear—the poor are poor because of evolutionary factors. Black people are identified as constitutionally inferior to whites because of genetic influences (Shuey, 1966). The primary support for these allegations is test results obtained from instruments developed by psychologists.

Arthur Jensen insists that 80 percent of all intelligence is inherited (Jensen, 1969). Let's follow this argument: if intelligence is measured by tests and if, on these tests, the poor, the black, and the brown score low, then it follows that these are inferior specimens. It also follows that they should be precluded from school programs that lead to college. They should be trained for only menial, low-paying jobs. Such persons can be expected to occupy only second-class positions politically, socially, economically, and culturally. On the basis of this evidence and logic the poor are denied admission to the university and thus are unable to obtain the credential which is the visa out of poverty.

About the evidence of Negro inferiority two psychologists, in a special monograph published by the *Psychological Bulletin* (an official American Psychological Association publication), blithefully conclude: "Suffice it to say that evidence which Shuey marshalls cannot be ignored, and so far as we are aware, has not been given as careful treatment by environmentalists as its own meticulous treatment of the data warrants" (Dreger and Miller, 1968, p. 8).

Their language is impeccable academese: they are open-minded on the issue. They wish the "environmentalists" were not so "violent, interpretive, and extreme" (Dreger and Miller, 1968, p. 8). But they conveniently ignore what everyone who wishes to compare racial groups chooses to ignore: that intelligence cannot be measured. As I have stated elsewhere (Pearl, forthcoming):

> Here we must pause and look at this business of assessing intelligence. At the present time we have no valid way of making such a determination for any group. Nor is it likely that we will ever have a valid means of testing intelligence. We certainly have no valid means to compare ability of different races, social classes or ethnic groups. On the face of it intelligence is much too complex a matter to be reduced to some simple two or three digit code obtained from responses to a relatively restricted universe of inquiry, and yet that is precisely what we do. With scarcely any examination of the underlying assumption governing the determination of intelligence, various testing devices are treated as gospel and from such flimsy stuff a child's life may be ruined. I

am hardly suggesting that all people have identical capabilities, although this possibility should not be dismissed. Boyer and Walsh (1968, p. 78) make a strong point in arguing that until we have evidence to the contrary: "We should base our policy in the most generous and promising assumptions about human nature rather than the most niggardly and pessimistic."

Detached objectivity can be a ploy by which brutal treatment of human beings is justified. The Nazis were also able to conjure up evidence of Jewish inferiority. Psychologists must reappraise the justification of a white, middle-income-dominated class that investigates the poor and the minorities. They should suspect the findings when persons not like them are found to be inferior to those who resemble them. Before such research is continued, investigation into the "intelligence" and values of the investigator is warranted. The psychologist must query whether investigation of Negro research really contributes to theory and practice. And this is the question that "cannot be ignored."

The Poor Are Victimized by Accumulated Environmental Deficit

There is a liberal argument which, from an entirely different set of assumptions, ends up with the same conclusion—that the poor are to blame for their poverty. This group of psychologists does not attribute poverty to genetic influence; they see instead the ravages of sensory deprivation. To them the poor have been deprived in critical early years of important learning experiences. These psychologists draw heavily upon sensory deprivation experiments performed on infrahuman subjects for their conclusions. It is always dangerous to use analogy for scientific conclusion. In this instance the argument is particularly suspect. The experiments involve extreme measures, e.g., when monkeys are isolated in closets and denied light for two years many of them develop irreversible visual defects. Nothing like this happens to poor youth. They are not denied sensory stimulation. They receive as many visual, auditory, and tactile impulses as are experienced by more privileged youth.

The psychologists who claim accumulated environmental deficit limit their argument pretty much to language development. They argue that the poor suffer because their early language experiences leave them crippled for life. The poor, according to Basil Bernstein (1961), have a restricted code, whereas the middle-income class has an elaborated language. It is claimed that poor youth are not taught to label objects, nor are they exposed to complex expressions or to a rich vocabulary.

It is amazing how popular the idea of accumulated environmental deficit is. But it is hardly a parsimonious explanation of anything. The poor of today have at least the stimulation of the affluent of previous generations. They are no more isolated than the pioneers, nor do they have less social contact than the villagers of old, and no one even claims that our current crop of middle-income youth speak or write better than our immediate predecessors.

There are too many talented writers who have emerged from abject poverty to asseverate that they are exceptions to a general rule. There is also the matter of mass media. The very poor come into as much contact with the standard code as the very rich; and the poor child in the ghetto appears to understand Captain Kangaroo equally as well as does the suburban rich kid. The poor have a language; it is an adequate language. It differs in style, tempo, syntax, and vocabulary from the language used by the affluent. It is the height of arrogance to make pejorative statements about that language.

Social scientists present lots and lots of "hard data" to "prove" that the poor have language inferiority. In all kinds of carefully controlled experiments the poor came out second best in language contests with the rich. In every instance the poor are Brand X and that, as one of the more flamboyant exponents of this position likes to say, "is the truth, gang."[1]

It is simply not the truth. The research is flawed. Researchers are making inferences from nonrepresentative behavior. The rich and the poor are not equally comfortable in the experiment. The research is always on the home ground of the affluent—and, as every basketball fan knows, there is an enormous advantage to the home court. Frightened people are not apt to be at their articulate best. People tend to be monosyllabic and restricted in their expression when anxious and in alien territory. Their desire is to run. When the sympathetic nervous system takes over it is ridiculous to make inferences about central nervous system attributes.

The inadequacy of the researcher affects the interpretation of his results. He makes invidious assessments about the structure of a language he doesn't understand. Mark Twain in *Innocents Abroad* stated it as well as anybody (perhaps because by current standards he was culturally deprived): if he spoke in his native tongue an Englishman could not understand him. It is equally true that when the poor speak in their native tongue the psychological researcher is unable to comprehend.

The popularity of the environmental deficit position is not hard to explain. It is a safe doctrine. The onus is placed on the poor child, not on the inadequate institutions. The alternative to acceptance of an inferior

---

[1]Siegfried Engelman, statement at Confontation: 1, at the University of Oregon, March 14, 1969.

learner is the recognition of institutionalized race, class, and ethnic biases in the school. The demand that racism be extricated from American institutions gets a little too close to the bone. There is security in the belief that the poor have been deprived long before they have been exposed to schools. Once we convince ourselves that it is the poor's fault, we can support such trivia as Operation Head Start—whose primary purpose appears to be to get nice middle-class ladies off the street during the summer. Head Start is worse than that. Elsewhere I have commented on the underlying savagery in Head Start (Pearl, forthcoming):

> There is a game that low-income blacks play. It is called *the dozens*. The dozens is a form of verbal assault in which the competitor attempts to score by insulting the opponent's mother. Head Start is a sophisticated form of the dozens. It institutionalizes the attack. In a variety of subtle or not-so-subtle ways the poor child is informed upon entrance into the program that he has a "lousy mother." He is hardly in the position to respond to such an assault. In point of fact, Head Start reflects all the inequity that the poor have had to face in their negotiations with the establishments of society.

The Poor Are Inadequately Socialized

The mythology of inadequate socialization runs parallel to the accumulated environmental deficit. The latter argument attacks the poor on their cognitive deficiencies, whereas the former is more an assault on the affective life of poor people. In this thesis the hypothesized chaos of the poor's social existence leads to disorder of character. The broken home life offers little social support. The child in that condition is unable to develop an adequate ego, thus he is not capable of self-sufficiency. The child, because of the absence of a father, cannot inculcate his social value system, thus he is prone to criminal activity and other social irresponsibilities.

From this well-entrenched mythology many negative attributes of the poor are derived. Here are some most frequently circulated: the poor cannot delay gratification; the poor are security-bound; the poor rely on fate; the poor are action-oriented; the poor are violence-prone; the poor lack impulse control.

The inadequate socialization argument does a great disservice to both social science and society because it is primarily a deflection from what should be the concern. If the poor can be diagnosed as sick then they own the problem. Their condition is a consequence of their infirmity rather than a reflection of inequitable and inadequate social structure. The psychologist then can "cure" the afflicted of their problem. If the patient fails to respond to treatment (i.e., remains poor) this is proof of the severity of his problem. The inadequate socialization thesis not only diverts attention away from the economics of poverty; it is also used to divert much-needed funds away from the poor to the professional who is paid to cure poverty.

The thesis lacks any substantive verification. In the first place there is evidence of much stability in poor families. Surrogates adequately perform the roles that parents perform in middle-income homes (there is also considerable evidence that the middle-class family isn't all that it is cracked up to be). But even more basic than an assessment of inadequate socialization is determination of cause and effect. Is it inadequate control of impulses which causes poverty or vice versa? It is my view that poverty is a problem that poor people cannot solve. The behaviors which are labeled inadequate socialization are, in reality, reflections of a problem which defies solution. There is nothing wrong with the Negro family or the Negro male which a wide range of choice of good-paying careers with upward mobility would not cure. Some years ago I commented:

> The problem for poor youth is not that they lack future orientation, but, indeed, that they lack a future. They are made aware of this early because there is so little meaning in their present. A limited gratification exists in striving for the impossible, and as a consequence poor youth create styles, coping mechanisms and groups in relation to systems which they can and cannot negotiate. Group values and identifications emerge in relation to the forces opposing them. Poor youth develop a basic pessimism because they have a fair fix on reality. They rely on fate because no rational transition system is open to them. They react against schools because schools are characteristically hostile to them (Pearl, 1968, p. 93).

The Poor Are Encapsulated within Autonomous Cultures

This mythology offers to psychology maximum opportunity to opt out of social responsibility. Here the poor are viewed as members of a self-sustaining culture. Now it is argued that the culture generates unique values and norms. The psychologists demonstrate magnificent tolerance by allowing these cultures of the poor to exist uncontaminated by outside influence. It would appear superficially as if this mythology runs counter to the three advanced before. But that is not so. This mythology has the same underlying theme as all the others, and that is that it sustains poverty.

The idea that there are truly autonomous cultures in a mass society is nonsense on the face of it. Mass media penetrate into every segment of society, exercising some influence over language, tempo of life, clothing style, and social values. The economics of a complex society precludes autonomous cultures; the poor, while excluded from participation in the economic life of the community, are not permitted to develop independent existence which is economically self-sustaining, let alone personally gratifying. The saturation of the earth with more and more bodies (nearly three-and-a-half billion by latest count) militates against autonomous cultures—if the world is to generate and distribute sufficient foodstuffs for this population and if it is going to regulate behavior at least to the extent that its people do not kill themselves off with their exhaust, then there must be meaningful communication and negotiation among all levels and divisions of persons. Sophisticated weaponry militates against autonomous cultures. It is clear that isolation of groups from each other is a breeding ground for xenophobia, that suspicions lead rather quickly to open conflict, that the conflict extends to neighboring communities, and that none of this can be tolerated because the destructiveness of weapons means that violent confrontation can no longer be used to resolve differences between groups of people.

There is a warped existentialism that seeps into psychology that goes something like "the poor know what's best for them," which is merely another variant of the old *Reader's Digest* theme that "it's fun to be poor." Cited as evidence of the glory of poverty are the magnificent heroes who emerge to fight it and the renewed efforts of the black and the brown to establish a sense of pride in their history and culture. The point generally missed is that this striving for social identity is necessary because of the persisting racism in the society. The black and brown have to struggle for self-respect in a society which continues to practice social, economic, cultural, and political discrimination. The black and brown people may decide that they do not want to be a part of middle-income white America, but that should be their choice, and their struggles for dignity can never be an excuse to lock them out. They may also decide to participate in the political, social, and economic life of the broader community, but on their own terms, which would require respect for the language, for the norms, for the traditions, and for the values of their culture.

Our society is pluralistic, but our institutions are embedded in the past. We would like to think that affluent America has a culture, and yet any analysis of our media, our art, or our interpersonal interactions must at least consider that we have degenerated into the antithesis of culture. The breaking down of barriers which would allow the locked out populations to "do their thing" may not only offer hope to the poor, but may add vitality to the dominant society.

THE EFFECT OF MYTHS ON SOCIAL POLICY

The myths that psychologists and other social scientists elevate to scientific propositions become translated into social policy. The scientist generates the theoretical support for programs supposedly designed to help the poor, but which in actuality only reinforce institutionalized racism and social inequality. The Economic Opportunity Act and the Elementary and Secondary Education Act provide two cases in point.

The Economic Opportunity Act was grossly misadvertised and we, as psychologists, contributed to this mendacity. The program never was designed to overcome poverty. At the very best it made poverty slightly less painful. At the very worst it made poverty more painful by increasing hope without altering the circumstances of poverty. Nowhere in the Act were significant amounts of money (essential to the relief of poverty) mandated to poor people. On the contrary, the money went to the affluent (psychologists as a group benefited from the poverty program as consultants and as paid functionaries). Job Corps—drawing heavily upon a thesis of inadequate socialization—was created to prepare the structurally unemployed for work in declining industries (primarily mechanical service) without considering competing programs, e.g., Manpower Development Training Act, or Vocational Education, or organized labor's arrangements with employers. Youths were transported thousands of miles from their home base without even minimal protection against hostile communities. As a consequence many returned from the Job Corps with prison records which made them even less employable than when they entered the program. (The criminal record was obtained often for acts which would not even have stirred attention in the inner city from which they came.) Job Corps did, however, offer many thousands of jobs to middle-income credentialed teachers, counselors, social workers, and administrators.

Head Start, the most handsomely funded of the Community Action sections of the Act, drew its inspiration from the accumulated deficit argument and spent a half billion dollars a year on early childhood education. In this program, with very few exceptions, the decent-paying jobs went to middle-income persons with credentials.

The Citizenship Participation section of the Community Action Title ended up as the cruelest delusion of all. The poor were encouraged to get into the act, and then when they responded to the call they were ruthlessly crushed. Social psychologists quite correctly identify as one of the consequences of poverty exclusion from participation in policy-making bodies in the economy. Thus, the aim of maximum citizen participation was laudable, but the naiveté was inexcusable. The program as constructed could, as it did, only lead to disaster. The amount of money made available to the community to eliminate poverty was patently insufficient (and many psychologists are even ignorant of that) but, more importantly, the call for action placed the poor in direct conflict with the established power of the community. To relieve poverty, agencies would have to do a complete about face. They would have to hire differently, allocate resources differently, and change the nature and delivery of service. The politically entrenched have very strong commitments to status quo. The development of a group antagonistic to established practice is viewed by those in control as manifestation of rebellion. They just aren't going to have it. And one thing should be obvious to everyone: government does not fund people to overthrow the government. As a consequence, poor people who got involved in Community Action paid dearly for their involvement, and groups emerged much more violent in their stance as a reflection of bitterness and frustration.

The Elementary and Secondary Education Act also was severely compromised because of the efforts and thinking of psychologists. Under Title I, the section of the law with the lion's share of the funds, money was awarded to local districts according to the numbers of "educationally disadvantaged youth" that could be identified. Ostensibly, the programs generally were to help these unfortunate youngsters, and yet there is no evidence that much value was derived from the two to three billion dollars that was expended. Students were not helped because the money was mainly used to shunt these youngsters out of mainstream education. On the basis of tests constructed and administered by psychologists, students were assigned to special classes, and there left to flounder. On the basis of these diagnoses, students were labeled as minimally educable. Other youngsters were categorized as emotionally and socially disturbed, according to classification systems developed by psychologists, and quarantined from the normal youth. The upshot of it all was that school programs which discriminate and school teachers who discriminate against poor people were allowed to continue to do their business as usual.

The typical ESEA-funded program in a high school is a special class for misfits. In the class the youth are offered no intellectual challenge. They are not in a program with any future perspective. If they are allowed to graduate they are not prepared to "make it" in an institution of higher education. Thus, they are denied access to a credential, and are firmly locked into poverty. The teacher (again the money goes to the nonpoor) has no legitimate function. He is surrounded by students all stamped as *losers*. Because of the limitations imposed by the circumstances, the teacher is driven to desperate measures. He either attempts to oppress by coercive authority, or he defaults completely his leadership role. Both alternatives lead to disaster.

The maintenance of poverty is abetted greatly by psychological theorizing and by psychologists in positions of authority. The support of the unsupportable must stop. We must recognize where our detached objectivity has brought us. Robert Engles, another who is angry with the lack of social consciousness of social scientists, concludes that this stance ". . . is divorced from any deep sense of social urgency and thus from sensitivity to the desperate needs of people on the fringes of an acquisitive society and the equally real torments of those who presumably have made it" (Engles, 1967, p. 197).

A PLEA FOR COMMITMENT

The chronicle of psychologists' failure to be socially relevant could go on endlessly. I hope I have at least made one point: some reflection on current practice and thinking is long overdue. There can be no "sacred cows" in psychology. Those psychologically based theses which inveigh against the poor must be scrutinized carefully and reappraised. Research conducted by middle-income, Establishment-based psychologists against the poor must give way to research investigating those processes and institutions which lock the poor into poverty. Only if representatives of the poor are involved in this research, and also, more importantly, involved in the inferences drawn from the data, can there be some assurance that myths will be challenged. Several areas for action are mentioned below.

The Credentialed Society

In the last analysis poverty is not so difficult to fathom: basically, poverty results when people have little money. In our society people have little money because they either are without jobs or they are in low-paying jobs (or because the allowances they receive in welfare are too small for a life of decency or dignity). One major reason poverty is maintained is that we have evolved into a "credential society." The fastest-growing, highest-paying, and most statusful industries require many, many years of formal training before one is allowed entrance into the lowest rung of the career ladder. Very few poor people can attain that educational status.

Psychology is one of the credentialed industries. The underrepresented must be enlisted into the ranks of the psychologists. This can be done in at least two ways. First, psychology can be reorganized and a hierarchy of functions and duties established. There are things that psychologists do that persons with limited formal training can do just as well. There are some activities that require specific training, and there are responsibilities that should be limited to highly trained professionals. Second, poor people can be recruited into universities and given sufficient encouragement (academic, social, and economic) to remain until they can be certified as full-fledged professional psychologists. Both approaches should be initiated immediately. Both need some more specific explications.

A person must have at least five years of formal training in an accredited institution to be able legally to practice as a psychologist. To be a full-fledged member of the club, at least seven years of formal education beyond high-school graduation is demanded. Nevertheless, much of the training cannot be defended by either logic or evidence; the requirements for credentials frequently relate little to the demands of practice. For some client or subject populations, particularly the racial and ethnic minorities and the poor, psychologists have to be totally retrained in order to function at all. For such populations it may be more efficient to recruit and train the indigenous poor in the skills of psychology rather than to try to sensitize the psychologist to the tempo, style, language, and concerns of the underclasses.

An example may be useful here. I have, in very short periods of time (eight weeks), trained high-school dropouts to be very competent researchers (Pearl and Riessman, 1965).[2] They could do what very few of my graduate students have ever been able to do. They had the skill to obtain data. They could utilize electronic equipment. They could generate tables. They could make permissible inferences from the data. They could design experiments. Their skills ranged from dexterous use of desk calculators to ability to discuss problems of research design, as evidenced by the following incident.

About a year after a group of these dropouts had been engaged in social research, they were asked to pretest a questionnaire that the director of research for Job Corps (a Ph.D. sociologist) had developed. His major concern was whether the language used in the schedule was understandable. The students participated in the pretest, and afterwards they asked the sociologist to explain his research design. Drawing himself up to his full academic elegance, he said, "It is very simple. We will inquire about the employment record, arrest record, and school record of these young men before they enter Job Corps, and contrast their behavior on the same criteria after they come out."

The dropouts responded, "You can't do that. Everybody knows that it is easier to get a job when you are nineteen than when you are seventeen. Everyone who knows anything about delinquency knows that delinquency

---

[2]See also Howard University Center for Youth and Community Studies (1965).

rates fall off after the age of eighteen, and it is impossible to go backwards in school. You won't know from such a design whether you have a treatment effect or a maturation effect. What are you using for a control group?" The sociologist became flustered. "Well, we'll get another group just like the Job Corps kids and compare them on the same criteria." The dropouts responded, "You can't do that. The Job Corps kids volunteered. Your control group didn't. You aren't controlling for motivation. You won't know whether you have a treatment effect or a solution effect." The sociologist phoned me and accused me of sending some Ph.D. candidates to him who pretended to be high-school dropouts, and the dropouts came back and said that "he was in big trouble back there."

Psychologists were not always so exclusive. It was possible for persons with little formal training to be shortcutted into the industry. Erik Erikson, to my knowledge, has no advanced formal training, and yet he is completely accepted as a psychologist of eminence. He was accepted because he was engaged in significant activity in the major concerns of psychology of that time—psychotherapy and personality development. There are many, many talented, uneducated persons learning much in their day-to-day encounters with the focal concerns of today. While most of us ruminate over tired old problems, the black and brown Eriksons of today deal with the factors which currently influence human behavior. They are concerned with effects of denial, social image, bureaucratic intransigence, the frustrations of overcrowding, the impact of segregation, and the ravages of enforced uselessness. They have unique skills, insights, and knowledge.

The psychologist trained in the streets would undoubtedly be restricted in many areas in which psychologists should have competence. But what's new about that? No psychologist of my acquaintance is a renaissance man. If a black worker or migrant organizer were recruited into a psychology department with full rank and privileges commensurate with his talents, he would be encouraged to "do his thing," and should be supported by colleagues with complementary competencies.

When it comes to establishing standards, psychologists have been brash when they should have been modest; as a consequence, practices which at least should be analyzed for class, race, and ethnic bias go unexamined. When it comes to recruiting new talent, psychologists are modest when they should be assertive; as a consequence, persons with sorely needed skills, insights, and knowledge are precluded from admission to the field. There are many good reasons, ethical and scientific, why the poor should be drawn into psychology, and yet no avenues for recruitment have been developed. There are many populations psychologists have not as yet been able to treat or study, and yet no strategy has been developed to attract these populations into the field.

The New Careers Approach

The range of activities that psychologists perform, the training they receive, and the diverse sites where they perform constitute considerable challenge to those who desire change in manpower utilization and deployment. But reorganization, although a difficult and complex matter, is not impossible. There are beacons that point the way. The thinking represented in the New Career approach is one guide. The New Career idea begins with specifying the entry tasks which everyone could be expected to do —there are some clerical and record-keeping functions, and some client and subject interviewing that persons with limited skill, training, and experience can perform adequately. The entry position should be considered the bottom rung of a career ladder. The position should be permanent. The person who occupies the position has all the rights and privileges of any other staff member. He has job security, and if he never aspires to a higher station he has at least horizontal mobility; he can receive salary increments for years of service.

If the person occupying the entry rung has talent, he should be allowed to climb as far as his talents and ambitions carry him. This is the unique feature of the New Career approach—the entry worker is not dead-ended into clerical roles, nor is the position a temporary slot for a student moving on to better things. For the ascension to be a reality, way stations must be created along the route. Each promotion must be readily negotiable. The career sequence may take the form presented in Table 1.

Table 1. Career Sequence for Preparation of Psychologists

Job Title	Duties	Prerequisites
Psychology aide	Clerical functions, interviewing, operation of desk calculators, maintenance of records	None
Psychology assistant	Statistical treatment of data, counseling under supervision, data collection	Two years of appropriate college or work experience
Psychology associate	Supervision of lower echelon staff, research design, report writing, involvement in therapeutic process	Four years of appropriate college or work experience
Psychologist	Team manager, chief tactition in research and clerical activity	M.A. or equivalent
Doctor of psychology	Strategist and planner, staff trainer and supervisor	Ph.D. or equivalent

Depicting the New Career approach in chart form as a career ladder is a deceptively sterile way to present the program. A good New Career program would have more flexibility to it than that presented in Table 1. However, the presentation does bring out all of the problems that will be encountered. There must be a definition of tasks that are going to be performed at each of the rungs in the career ladder. And, finally, the training and the education that New Careerists will need to function at every level must be specified.

The New Career approach can be a means by which the preparation of psychologists can be revitalized. Sequestering persons in universities for upwards of half a decade is hardly the optimum way to prepare people for scientific understanding of human behavior. Such isolation does increase the susceptibility to prejudicial myths. Keeping people in training for many years without allowing them opportunity to use that training is an inefficient procedure to inculcate skills or stimulate conceptual activity. The training offered in New Careers is consistent with most theoretical approaches to learning. Practice would accompany theory: students would be allowed to put into practice what they have been taught, and the training would be a natural outgrowth of problems encountered on the job. Replacing the fragmented and often irrelevant jumble of courses that describes the university program would be coordinated, sequential development of skill and knowledge with payoffs at regularly scheduled intervals. The New Career program is a political reality. Funds have been made available through a variety of legislative efforts. Other fields are venturing forth; psychologists have been most timid. It is past time for psychologists to get involved in New Career programs, and for the American Psychological Association to endorse the concept unequivocally. For a more extensive review of the New Career philosophy, see Pearl and Riessman (1965).

Many factors conspire to lock the poor out of psychology. They have been denied effective precollege education. They are without funds required for an ever-more-expensive higher education. If they do make it to the university or college, they do not have social and academic support that is required for success. They are often asked to pay too high a price—they are asked to give up their values and even their identity for entrance into the field. This last impediment is often disguised as *academic standards* or as a measure of emotional immaturity. Psychology professors too often dismiss legitimately inspired anger on the part of black students as a manifestation of a character disorder.

Each of these obstacles can be overcome. Admission standards can be waived. Many thousands of poor youth are recruited to the community campus, but very little is done for them after they get there. A program can be developed where these youths are sponsored by graduate students and faculty members. Some portion of the funds required for this purpose can be secured from federal financial assistance programs, but some should be obtained from funds provided by psychologists themselves. A meager increase of $10 per year in APA dues, earmarked for scholarships for poor persons desiring to become psychologists, could be a modest but important step. The $250,000 a year raised by this means could be used for seventy undergraduate scholarships and twenty-five graduate scholarships. If these scholarships were awarded in direct proportion to need, within a decade American Indians, Mexican-Americans, and Afro-Americans would be represented in the ranks of psychologists, to a far greater extent than is currently the case. The gains to psychology would be great indeed for such a modest investment.

Psychologists and Social Action

Psychologists must use their influence to keep avenues out of poverty open to all. Rather than using their talents to lock students into second-class educational tracks, they must use their influence to train teachers to educate all. Rather than generating self-fulfilling prophecies of failure through ability or achievement tests, the psychologist must emphasize that no human has functioned close to his capacity and that educational systems fail students, not vice versa.

In a similar vein, psychologists must convince employment agencies and employers that current personnel practices that rely on testing devices are discriminatory because of class, race, and ethnic bias, and must be replaced by measures that offer equal opportunity to all. Our influence in this area is enormous. Failure to act, then, is a monstrous irresponsibility.

Finally, we must act politically to eliminate poverty. The issue of poverty ultimately reduces to politics. To eliminate poverty, income support must be given to those who are truly unemployable, and meaningful career opportunities (where choice can be exercised) must be offered to all those capable of work. Only the government is prepared to do this. Government expenditures have risen from 10 percent of the Gross National Product in the first decade of this century to 30 percent during the 1960s. There is every reason to believe that government will continue to increase in importance in the utilization of manpower, particularly as machines engage in more and more production of goods and man is liberated to human-service activities. Poverty could be effectively eliminated if 40 billion tax dollars were mandated for employment in areas of demonstrated need, and 10 billion dollars more for income support. The 40 billion dollars that would be involved for manpower could be used in education, health services, conservation, welfare, and leisure-time pursuits. If monies were deployed

for these purposes the quality of life would be improved for all, the opportunities to escape poverty would be greatly increased, and the destructiveness that accompanies poverty (crime, violent outbursts, wasted human
life) would be mitigated. There are both social and economic benefits to be
derived from such activity, and yet it is not forthcoming. It is not forthcoming because no political advocacy has emerged to bring it about.

Psychologists, though small in number, can play a leadership role in
reawakening a political conscience. The richer we are as a nation the less
we have become concerned with the plight of the impoverished. We can do
something about that. We have skills of communication. We have access to
mass media. We are called upon to advise Congress. We have a Washington office that lobbies parochially. All of these forces can be used to energize a nation to eliminate an inexcusable condition: poverty, and its bed-
fellow, racism.

REFERENCES

Bernstein, B. Social Class and Linguistic Development: A Theory of Social Learning, in A. H. Halsey, A. Anderson, & J. Floud, eds. *Education, Economy and Society.* New York: Free Press, 1961.

Boyer, W. H., and Walsh, P. Are Children Born Unequal? *Saturday Review of Literature* October 19, 1968, 61-63.

Dreger, R. M., and Miller, K. S. Comparative Psychological Studies of Negroes and Whites in the United States. *Psychological Bulletin,* Monograph Supplement 1968, 70: part 2.

Engles, R. Social Science and Social Consciousness, in T. Roszak, ed. *The Dissenting Academy.* New York: Pantheon, 1967.

Howard University Center for Youth and Community Studies. *Community Apprentice Report.* Washington, D. C.: Howard University, 1965.

Jensen A. R. Learning Ability, Intelligence, and Educability, in V. L. Allen, ed. *Psychological Factors in Poverty.* Chicago: Markham, 1969, Chapter 6.

Pearl, A. Youth in Lower Class Settings, in M. Sherif and C. W. Sherif, eds., *Problems of Youth.* Chicago; Aldine, 1968.

———. *The Atrocity of Education.* Englewood Cliffs, N. J.: Prentice-Hall (forthcoming).

Pearl, A., and Riessman, F., *New Careers for the Poor.* New York: Free Press, 1965.

Schuey, A. M. *The Testing of Negro Intelligence,* 2d ed. New York: Social Science Press, 1966.

PART SIX

PROBLEMS AND PROSPECTS

Chapter 19

THE PSYCHOLOGY OF POVERTY: PROBLEMS AND PROSPECTS

Vernon L. Allen

The objective in this concluding chapter is to add perspective to the specific problems discussed in depth in previous chapters. When appropriate, selected psychological research will be reviewed in the context of discussion of a series of salient issues that cast in bold relief many of the problems and possibilities confronting the scientist engaged in psychological research in poverty. More specifically, I shall comment critically on some conceptual problems that seem to reflect basic issues of present and probably continuing concern, and delineate discernible current trends in psychological research in poverty. At the risk of setting up an occasional straw man, dichotomies will be posed for the sake of discussion. Many of the topics discussed will be somewhat overlapping and interdependent, but for purpose of conceptual clarity each topic will be presented separately.

UNITARY CATEGORY OF POVERTY VERSUS DIFFERENTIATED TAXONOMY

Lest we tend to forget, it is worth emphasizing that poverty is not a psychological concept but an economic one. Using cost-of-living indices and other esoteric measures, economists are able to devise a precise cutoff point that separates the poor from the nonpoor, the sheep from the goats, as it

---

*Professor of Psychology, University of Wisconsin, Madison.

were. However sensible this sharp and quantitative measure may be for economic analysis and for political policy making, the economist's concept of poverty signifies trouble for the psychologist.

The first point that should be made is that the gross category of "poverty" is probably much too broad, even as an economic index. It is a commonly held view that behavior of the most abjectly poor—the most extremely underprivileged—differs from that of others who, though poor, nevertheless seem to share values and behavioral attributes with the middle class above them, rather than with the abjectly poor below them. The erstwhile distinction between the poor and the pauper indicates an awareness of this difference, the pauper often being thought of as apathetic and fatalistic. Likewise, *lumpenproletariat* referred to that portion of the under class seen as devoid of the redeeming revolutionary qualities of the lower class or the working class, being instead viewed as shiftless, undisciplined, and with little desire for change. In sum, many recognize within the poverty group a smaller group, "the disreputable poor" (Matza, 1966), who are subject to severe denigration by the nonpoor as well as by others who economically may differ little from them. It is apparent that discussions of poverty quite often refer to this smaller subgroup, rather than to the entire one-fifth of the population that falls below the poverty line.

If one believes that a relation exists between behavior and economic condition, then psychological differences should also be expected if the poverty group were more finely differentiated according to income. Interesting data from the Srole et al. (1962) study of social class and mental illness support the view that significant psychological differences may exist among groups experiencing different degrees of poverty. When finer than usual differentiations of socioeconomic class were made by Srole, a relationship was found between mental illness and socioeconomic level even within the lower-class group. Implications are clear that for psychological purposes the dichotomy of poor-nonpoor is probably too gross to reflect many important psychological differences that exist within the poverty category.

A second, and even more basic and complex, difficulty can be raised concerning the use of a unitary poverty category. A category of people homogeneous on the economic index of poverty consists on other indices of an extremely heterogeneous lot indeed. Having one characteristic in common—lack of financial resources—does not necessarily imply the common possession of other characteristics (such as psychological traits). The poor include, among others, the child and the aged, the unemployed and the unemployable, the vagrant and the migrant, and the physically sick and the mentally sick. Given the history of discrimination against the Negro in the

United States, race is certainly an important factor deserving separate consideration. It is likely, for example, that the psychological meaning of being poor is different for blacks, who might have lacked objective opportunity, than for whites. For whites, poverty may be more frequently related to personal problems of disturbed personality, intellectual inferiority, or motivational deficits.

Socioeconomic status, though a slightly better index for psychological purposes than the solely economic index of poverty, shares much of its defect by allotting a large weight to income. The reputation (Warner, Meeker, and Eels 1949) method of assessing social class has some advantages for psychological purposes over the more objective socioeconomic index, but the value of both is limited for purposes of psychological research.

Most of the early psychological studies relevant to poverty were usually conducted with samples designated as *lower class* by the use of various socioeconomic-status indices. Because such a global specification of the lower-class sample was used, it is often impossible to determine whether much of this early research has any relevance at all to groups designated as *poor* by the economic criterion used today. Sometimes in past research the lower-lower class was used, and sometimes apparently the upper-lower. Since we are not dealing with a simple or homogeneous population psychologically, care must always be taken to specify which of several poverty subgroups one is referring to. Comparability among studies may well be seriously compromised when such differences exist among samples. Lack of agreement among investigations of the poor sometimes may be more apparent than real because different groups were used for the poverty sample.

Availability of some sort of taxonomy that would classify into reasonable subgroups the varied groups of people now lumped together under a common economic index of *poverty* would be extremely useful. Taxonomic schemes, to be most helpful to the psychologist, should utilize dimensions that possess behavioral significance and implications. One classification, suggested by Miller (1964), consists of two dimensions— stability of family and level of income. Combining the two levels of family stability (stable-unstable) and the two levels of income (adequate-inadequate) produces four groups called the *stable poor,* the *strained poor,* the *copers-skidders,* and the *unstable poor.*

Miller's taxonomy retains the use of the economic index and adds to it a second, noneconomic factor—family stability—that is given equal importance. By holding constant low economic position, classifications can be formed entirely on noneconomic dimensions. Examples of such taxonomies are provided by the work of Deutsch (1967) and Bernstein and Henderson (1969). Deutsch constructed a deprivation index comprised of scores on several variables (e.g., parents' aspirations for children, crowdedness of the house, mother's presence at breakfast, absence of father). Utility of these measures is shown in research demonstrating the independence of the deprivation index from socioeconomic class. A significant correlation was found between scores on the deprivation index and scores on reading level for elementary school children from the slums. Bernstein and Henderson's (1969) classification, again differentiating children within the lower-socioeconomic-class group, is based on the nature of communication patterns in the home, the degree of emphasis on language in the transmission of nonpersonal skills to the child (high or low), and whether emphasis on language is high or low in teaching personal relationships.

It seems clear from present research trends that future efforts will continue toward creating more differentiated and more psychologically meaningful taxonomies for studying poverty. In the past, research typically has simply compared the poor with the middle class; future research will probably make comparisons among several categories of the poor much more frequently.

DEMONSTRATION OF GENERAL RELATIONSHIPS VERSUS SPECIFICATION OF INTERVENING PROCESSES

In very general terms, the psychology of poverty is concerned with the relationship between environment and behavior. To put it another way, the psychology of poverty deals with the interface between the economic system and the individual. Unfortunately, our theoretical and conceptual tools for analyzing such interlevel problems still are unsophisticated and unsystematic.

To find a relationship between environment (e.g., level of income or socioeconomic status) and behavior is not difficult, and has been demonstrated with a diversity of behaviors ranging from sexual activity to religious beliefs. The discovery of a relationship between background (i.e., poverty) and behavior is no longer very satisfactory as an end in itself. Much more worthwhile is an understanding of the means by which environmental conditions produce psychological dispositions, which in turn are responsible for a particular behavior. From merely demonstrating the existence of a relationship, investigators have progressed toward attempting to specify in detail the intervening processes that mediate the relationship between poverty and behavior. Considerable progress is being made in this direction, and it is safe to predict that more and more psychological research on poverty will deal with specific psychological processes and variables that intervene between poverty and behavior. Only two examples need to be mentioned here.

One significant attempt to pursue the specific psychological processes mediating between poverty and behavior was made by Langner and Michael (1963) in their analysis of social class and mental illness. Much research has shown that the poor contribute disproportionately to the incidence of serious mental illness such as psychoses. To analyze the relationship between social class and mental illness, Langner developed a model that employed stress (experienced by the individual as strain) as an intervening variable between environment and behavior. Environmental stress factors, determined empirically, were shown to be positively related to mental illness independent of social-class level. Moreover, and most interestingly, these uncorrelated stress factors operated in a simple additive way in relation to mental illness.

In a series of studies, Deutsch (1967) and associates have attempted to determine the specific psychological processes mediating the relationship between social class and behavior in a quite different area, school achievement in children. Statistics abound that consistently show that children from backgrounds of poverty do more poorly on standard tests and other indices of school achievement than do middle-class children. In addition, the difference between the lower- and middle-class child increases with years spent in school. Thus, difference between a child from the slums and a child from the middle class is greater at the fifth grade than at the first grade, a phenomenon Deutsch calls the *cumulative deficit*.

Deutsch's research aimed at specifying in a detailed manner the psychological processes affected by poverty (motivational, linguistic, perceptual, etc.) while at the same time attempting to determine the skills and abilities required to succeed in particular tasks in school. It was found that children from poverty backgrounds were very retarded in language development, upon which a great deal of school work depends. Less obviously, it was discovered that slum children were deficient in elementary sensorimotor skills, which are basic for the development of more complex cognitive processes. Thus, lower-class children were poorer in auditory discrimination, a skill essential for reading. Moreover, the school experience is often incogruent with the home experience for lower-class children; types of behavior expected in school differ from behavior expected by parents at home. This is not as frequently true for middle-class children. Failure experiences are likely to result when such incongruity exists, with a corresponding decrease in motivation and interest in school work.

The advantage of analysis at the specific and detailed level is clear. When the nature of the psychological processes that mediate between poverty and inadequate school performance are known, then compensatory programs can be designed to accomplish specifiable goals. Thus, preschool enrichment programs for lower-class children need to stress language development, should provide opportunity for improving elementary sensorimotor skills, and must afford success experiences so that school is not a source of frustration.

CULTURE OF POVERTY VERSUS PERSONALITY CORRELATES OF THE POOR

This section deals with two issues: first, the concept of *culture of poverty* will be critically evaluated, and second, empirical evidence will be assessed concerning the relation between poverty and personality characteristics. The concept of culture of poverty has gained prominence within recent years, being particularly emphasized in the writings of social anthropologists conducting research among the poor (Gladwin, 1961; Lewis, 1966). The culture of poverty, or more precisely, the subculture of poverty, refers to a way of life or a design for living that is handed down across generations. Oscar Lewis (1966) states that slum children have acquired the basic values and attitudes of their subculture by the age of six or seven. The culture-of-poverty concept accounts for the behavior of the poor by positing a system of values different from the middle class in many (but not all) respects—a normative system that is self-perpetuating. The culture of poverty supposedly transcends social, racial, regional, and even national differences: the poor are expected to be much the same the world over. Lewis identifies seventy traits comprising the culture of poverty; the most important ones for our purposes are the values and character structure of the individual.

The most frequently mentioned psychological themes referred to in the culture-of-poverty concept are: strong feeling of fatalism and belief in chance; strong present-time orientation and short time perspective; impulsiveness, or inability to delay present gratification or to plan for the future; concrete rather than abstract thinking processes and concrete verbal behavior; feelings of inferiority; acceptance of aggression and illegitimacy; and authoritarianism.

Several criticisms can be raised against the concept of culture of poverty. For one thing, behavior cannot be equated with values. In other words, simply because a person behaves in a certain way does not mean he desires to do so or does so because of his beliefs or values. Another problem is that the concept is tautological: values inferred from behavior are used to explain the same behavior. To be useful for explaining behavior, values should be measured independently of the behavior to be explained, or no advantage can be claimed for the gratuitous labeling of behavior. Another difficulty is that the concept of culture of poverty implies a certain degree of homogeneity and consensus, certainly a matter for empirical investigation.

At this point, let us examine available data to determine whether consistent differences do in fact exist between the poor and nonpoor in areas of personality and values covered by the concept of culture of poverty. In Chapter 13 I reviewed available empirical data on several personality concomitants of poverty and concluded that a considerable number of the data are ambiguous at best and overwhelmingly nonsupportive at worst. Many presumed relationships between personality characteristics and poverty simply are not supported by reliable data. This statement should not be taken so strongly as to suggest a firm and final conclusion. Many available studies suffer from methodological shortcomings, and often do not investigate the group of extremely poor who might be most likely to manifest differences from the middle class. On the other side of the coin, evidence alleging the existence of differences between the poor and nonpoor has often been based on data obtained from a single family by self-report or through participant observation. For reasons too obvious to enumerate, broad conclusions about the culture of poverty based on such evidence should be viewed with extreme caution bordering on skepticism.

On the more specific question of whether the poor share common values with the rest of society, there also has been empirical dispute. Some investigators point to evidence of the acceptance of a common value system in some areas by the middle class and by the poor: Goode (1960) on illegitimacy, and Taft (1950) on juvenile delinquency. Other investigators have concluded that value differences are not shared between classes: Hyman (1953) on attitudes and aspirations, Henriques (1953) on illegitimacy, and Miller (1958) on delinquency. Rodman (1963) proposed a way of resolving these contradictory conclusions by the concept of the lower-class "value-stretch." He suggests that while the poor do not abandon the general values of society, at the same time an additional or alternate set of values is developed. In other words, the general values of society are stretched to afford an adjustment to the situation of the poor, resulting in the existence of a wider range of values than that found in the middle class. The value-stretch concept is useful in preventing an oversimplified either-or conceptualization, and again points to a limitation of the concept of culture of poverty.

The culture-of-poverty concept seems to be viewed sometimes as a causative factor in poverty, sometimes as a result. In general, psychological factors in poverty may be viewed as either dependent or independent variables. Viewed as dependent variables, they may be interpreted as consequences of a set of adverse environmental conditions to which the individual has been subjected over a long period of time. As independent variables, the same psychological factors may be viewed as having contributed to the individual's present condition.

When viewing psychological factors as independent variables, we are on somewhat insecure conceptual and empirical ground. It may be appealing to assume that psychological factors have contributed to an individual's plight; it is then an easy—but unwarranted—step to conclude that intervention programs should be directed to alter the psychological characteristics presumed detrimental to the individual. Regardless of the degree of truth in such an analysis (and there may be some), there is a more general problem at issue here. It is often assumed implicitly that internal psychological characteristics are causally related to important patterns of behavior. How closely related in a causal manner are internal psychological states and behavior? Does a change in the internal psychological state produce a concomitant change in behavior for either the poor or the non-poor? Answers to these questions are equivocal. For example, on the basis of the known association between achievement and school grades, a program to increase achievement motivation should improve school grades. An attempt to accomplish this end showed that achievement training increased grades for middle-class high-school students, but not for lower-class students (Kolb, 1965). For most dispositions, little or no attempt has been made to observe their relation to some specifiable behavior, and even less is known about the relation between individual psychological change and social change. Without such knowledge we are unable to affirm that changing a particular psychological disposition would have social utility for the poor, regardless of how appealing such an analysis may be for those persons inclined to a psychological interpretation of poverty.

INTRAPERSONAL (PSYCHIC) VERSUS SITUATIONAL DETERMINANTS OF BEHAVIOR

An issue that continues to recur in one form or another concerns the relative contribution of psychological (intrapersonal) as opposed to situational factors in determining behavior. The problem is often posed as whether behavior patterns observed among the poor are due to internal characteristics (personality) of the poor or to reality factors, i.e., the inevitable pressures of objective life conditions. The issue is frequently phrased in an all-or-none fashion, which is not only an obvious oversimplification—it is simply wrong. Most psychologists would affirm that behavior is always a joint function of the external situation and of personal dispositions, the determination of the relative weight being admittedly difficult in specific instances. (See, for instance, Gurin's chapter in this book.)

The trend within psychology certainly seems to be toward greater recognition of the important role played by situational factors. Thus, for example, difference in behavior of a single person across situations is often greater than difference in a given behavior across people in the same situation. Generality and consistency of behavior across situations is often not high, and much of the observed difference in a person's behavior can be accounted for by changes in the situation or stimulus context (Hunt, 1965). In a cross-cultural study of child rearing, situational constraints seemed to be more important determinants of the mother's behavior toward her children than psychodynamic factors or beliefs (Minturn and Lambert, 1964). For instance, the mother exhibited less affection and warmth toward the child when the number of persons per living unit was high. Situational variables such as living arrangements, family size, household composition, and sex of child were critical factors associated with variation in maternal behavior.

The problem of internal dispositions versus situational stimuli manifests itself in several forms in the psychology of poverty. One form is in the all-or-none sort of interpretation or reinterpretation of a given set of findings. A set of behaviors that has been observed to occur among the poor is interpreted, on the one hand, as being due entirely to internal psychological dispositions possessed by the poor. In contrast, other persons may deny totally that any role at all is played by internal psychological characteristics, claiming instead that environmental conditions constitute the single causal factor.

The presumed inability to delay gratification (impulse-following) by the poor is a good case in point. Several clusters of behavior patterns attributed to the poor have been interpreted as reflecting the personality trait of preference for immediate gratification: greater premarital sexual experience among the poor (Kinsey, 1948); lower educational attainment (Strauss, 1962); and lack of financial savings and an inefficient pattern of consumption (Schneider and Lysgaard, 1953). Let us assume that agreement can be reached on the assertion that the poor and the middle-class do differ on the set of behaviors listed above. Even so, the meaning of the behavior, that is, the alleged causal basis of the behavior, often takes one of two extremes. In one instance, a personality trait may be posited as the causal force—the poor are seen as impulsive because of a character trait. In the second instance, behavior may be attributed to the inevitable pressures of environmental forces, pressures that would presumably produce the same effect on most people under such conditions.

Miller, Riessman, and Seagull (1965) take the latter tack, pointing out many alternative explanations for the alleged impulsiveness of the poor. Most of their explanations are in terms of situational pressures. For example, although statistics show that lower-class adolescents leave school earlier, this may not indicate inability to defer gratification. The school, with its middle-class structure, probably is less enjoyable for the lower-class student. Moreover, economic problems make it more likely for the lower-class youngster to be forced to leave school. Furthermore, experimental studies of ability to delay gratification have not found social-class differences, though both groups respond similarly to situational variables such as trustworthiness of the experimenter. Miller et al. conclude that the poor are not "psychodynamically constrained" to prefer immediate gratification; instead, other realistic factors can parsimoniously account for the same behavior.

As the example demonstrates, even if objective differences in behavior can be shown to exist between the poor and the nonpoor, positing an internal psychological state to explain the behavior may be unnecessary. Among alternate explanations for the behavior are situational factors that impinge in a similar manner upon all people living under conditions of poverty. A person's behavior may represent, then, the most rational (and perhaps the only) response that could be made under conditions of pressures from the real world.

Another form taken by the situational versus intra-individual problem is methodological. In this version of the issue, alleged psychological differences between the poor and the nonpoor are minimized or discounted as being invalid because situational variables contribute differentially to the observed performance of the two groups. Intelligence testing is an ideal case in point. Results of intelligence tests tend to show quite consistently that children from poverty backgrounds score lower than children from the middle class. These data, in themselves, have not been in dispute; but whether the data really do indicate true differences in innate intelligence (leaving aside for the moment what intelligence means)—that is, whether the tests are valid for the poor—certainly has been in dispute. Many years ago, Allison Davis (1948) pointed out that intelligence tests, like the institution of the school itself, have a heavily middle-class bias. Thus, intelligence tests tend to be composed of items whose language and content are more common and familiar in the experience of middle-class children, who also tend to have more often taken tests similar in content and in emphasis on speed. In other words, middle-class children are apt to have had more practice at test taking and to have greater knowledge of the optimal strategy to follow for obtaining high scores. Also, the test-giver is usually a middle-class person with whom the lower-class child taking the test is likely to have less rapport and whom he would be less motivated to please, which is to say that test taking is a social situation (Kroger, 1967). All these factors, and others, have been shown to affect performance on intelligence tests, and other types of tests as well.

These comments are meant to imply that situational influences may differ in the cases of the poor and nonpoor, and that these situational influences in addition to the real level of the individual's hypothetical capacity or intelligence may be contributing to the test results.

In a very impressive series of experiments, Haggard (1954) demonstrated the influence of simple situational variables in a quite rigorous way. In three one-hour training periods, several hundred eleven-year-old lower-class boys received practice in taking tests. In addition, positive motivation was enhanced by creating rapport with the examiner and by giving rewards for doing well. Providing the children with only this very limited amount of instruction and practice produced significant and quite dramatic increases in scores on intelligence tests.

The example given with intelligence testing can be generalized to any instance in which, due to differences in rapport with the examiner, understanding of instructions, level of motivation, familiarity with the measuring devices and procedure, and other similar factors, the resultant data on performance may not indicate true differences in underlying psychological structure between the poor and the nonpoor, but reflect instead artifactual differences due to the unequal weight of known and unknown situational factors. This dilemma is interestingly similar to that confronting the cross-cultural researcher who wants to be sure that his results are not due to unintended artifactual differences in response to procedure, language, etc. And, in a sense, research comparing the poor and the nonpoor perhaps should be thought of as cross-cultural—or cross-subcultural—to draw attention more prominently to this problem. Attempts have been made to construct culture-free instruments. Whether a test and a testing procedure can ever be totally culture-free is very doubtful indeed, which makes measuring the "true" internal psychological dispositions of persons from different cultural backgrounds an extremely difficult endeavor.

The psychic versus situational alternatives are often discussed in terms of *psychological* versus *reality* factors, which confuses the issue by assuming that there is an objective reality uninfluenced by cognitive and perceptual processes. The truth no doubt lies somewhere between the polar extremes of intra-individual and situational; the problem of research in poverty is to determine the relative importance of individual and situational factors in accounting for a particular behavior. Internal psychological predispositions may be paramount in determining some behaviors; situational and stimulus factors are doubtless of predominant influence in other behaviors.

Extrapolating from recent trends, we would expect that theory and research in the future will emphasize situational variables to a much greater extent than in the past. Such research holds the advantage of being particularly appropriate for understanding poverty; environmental conditions of deprivation are certainly of great centrality in the life of the poor. The situational approach also has the advantage of suggesting that changes ought to be made in the environment or social structure in order to change behavior. Changing long-enduring psychodynamic structures of individuals is likely to appear more difficult to accomplish than changing environmental conditions, and thus less likely to lead to programs of action by society.

PSYCHOLOGY OF PEOPLE
VERSUS PSYCHOLOGY OF POOR PEOPLE

By this rather odd heading I intend to raise questions concerning alternative strategies for psychological research on poverty. It seems unnecessary to affirm that we can learn about the poor by studying the poor themselves. Yet it may also be true that our understanding of poverty can be enhanced by application of basic psychological theory and data. The poor, after all, are not a species apart. Many examples could be given to support the contention that advances in general psychology might in the long run make more important contributions to the understanding of a social problem than direct research on the problem itself. (It should also be said that research in poverty can enrich basic psychological theories.)

Since the necessity of direct research on the poor presumably needs no defense, I shall therefore attempt to emphasize the importance of general psychological theory and research for furthering our understanding of poverty. One very significant trend that has occurred within psychology during the past decade is the greater emphasis now given to cognitive processes. There has been a great increase in interest in intelligence and learning in the poor, and also much more interest in the role of language. That language, thought, and learning are very closely interrelated is becoming quite clear (Bernstein, 1960; Deutsch, 1967).

Previously, cognitive processes received little attention relative to motivational processes, both in general psychological research and in social-class research. Thus, past studies have attempted to find differences between lower- and middle-class children on aggression, dependency, conscience development, and the like. Much of the earlier emphasis stemmed from the influence of psychoanalysis, a motivational theory. Although the change in emphasis within psychology may have been part of the zeitgeist, much of the credit for establishing the conceptual foundations for research in cognition belongs to Piaget (see Flavell, 1963) and Hunt (1961). The pendulum clearly is swinging away from preoccupation with motivational processes toward an increased interest in cognition; manifestations of this trend are evident in research on poverty.

Psychologists have now come to realize that the human organism is highly malleable and easily affected by transactions with the environment, especially in the early years of childhood. There seem to be stages in the development of sensorimotor, perceptual, and linguistic skills; lack of optimal stimulation at one of the early preverbal stages may retard development at a later stage. Hence, early experience is of extraordinary importance in determining the course of a child's cognitive development. Awareness of the importance of early sensorimotor stimulation in cognitive and intellectual growth has led to a great deal of research on learning in the poor, and has inspired the creation of programs designed to provide compensating experiences for the inadequate perceptual and cognitive stimulation found in the homes of the poor. A variety of preschool enrichment programs of the Head Start variety has been a practical outgrowth of research interest in cognition and cognitive development.

Several cognitive theories in psychology and sociology emphasize the importance of relativistic considerations for behavior. Poverty is a relative or subjective, as well as an objective, condition of life; certainly the effects of privation and deprivation depend to a considerable extent on the condition of others around us. In affluent countries such as the United States the condition of those labeled *poor* would be envied by a large portion of the people of most countries of the world. One has only to compare the descriptions of poverty in the nineteenth century (e.g., Hunter, 1904) and in the twentieth century (e.g., Harrington, 1962) to realize that in the past the lot of the poor was, in absolute terms, much more execrable than now. The lot of the rest of the population has, however, been rapidly improving, too, and the poor person assesses his position in life relative to the position of others about him.

Since poverty is a relative condition, cognitive theories that deal with the consequences of evaluating one's place in life relative to the situation of others should be applicable to research in poverty. Social comparison theory, relative deprivation theory, and reference-group theory all assume that the meaning attached to a given behavior or situation depends upon the individual's evaluation of his behavior or situation relative to another individual or group. In a very useful article, Pettigrew (1968) shows the interrelation among all these concepts, and subsumes them under the rubric of *social evaluation*. Pettigrew has indicated the potential value of these concepts by using them to explain various aspects of racial integration, and by suggesting some useful research. Social evaluation theories should have direct applicability to the psychological study of poverty, and are likely to become more important conceptual tools for poverty research in the future.

We have asserted that poverty is a relative condition. However, this can perhaps be overemphasized. For many physical and psychological needs, the failure to reach some absolute minimal level may have serious consequences, regardless of one's situation relative to others. For example, a minimal level of nutrition is required for adequate physical and mental functioning. More attention should be paid to the effects of different absolute levels of environmental deprivation. The relative view of poverty can be pushed so far as to become absurd in some cases (e.g., where almost everyone in a society has practically nothing at all).

The social evaluation theories mentioned above employ other persons or groups against which one can compare himself. As a great deal of research indicates, expectations of other persons are extremely important in determining one's behavior and view of self. It is quite surprising that in our research on the poor so little attention has been devoted to the attitudes and expectations of the nonpoor about the poor. The behavior and self-concept of the poor are doubtlessly influenced strongly by expectations held by other people, both poor or nonpoor. A recent study shows the dramatic impact that expectations of others can exert on behavior. Rosenthal and Jacobson (1968) led teachers to believe that, according to test results, certain lower-class children would show unusual intellectual gains during the year. Actually these children were randomly chosen and retested four months and one year later to determine whether teachers' expectations led to improved school work and gains on intelligence test scores. Children for whom teachers held positive expectations did in fact show gains in their test scores. Interestingly, the children were also perceived more favorably by teachers in terms of personality characteristics.

The examples discussed above show that new basic findings in psychology may have important implications for understanding the behavior of the poor. In terms of the knowledge required to guide programs of social change more effectively, available psychological theory and data at this point must be declared incomplete. While research with the poor should continue vigorously, we should stay ever alert to opportunities for applying basic findings from all areas of psychology to the problems of poverty. Both basic and applied research can be useful in ameliorating the situation of the poor.

Within this country and around the world poverty continues to be a cause of untold suffering and needless waste of human potential. The existence of oppressive inequality demeans the life of an entire people, the affluent as well as the poor. Social science cannot remain aloof from important social problems, of which poverty is only one. Knowledge need not be cloistered from the rude world; it can be utilized for the betterment of human life. We can with Roger Bacon lament that ". . . the greatest error of all the rest is the mistaking or misplacing of the last or farthest end of knowledge. . . ." The seriousness of social problems now confronting us demands that theory be conjoined with practice, that knowledge proceed to understanding, and that understanding engender change.

REFERENCES

Bernstein, Basil. Language and Social Class. *British Journal of Sociology* 1960, 11: 271-76.

Bernstein, Basil, and Henderson, D. Social Class Differences in the Relevance of Language to Socialization. *Sociology* 1969, 3: 1-20.

Davis, Allison, *Social-Class Influences upon Learning.* Cambridge, Mass.: Harvard University Press, 1948.

Deutsch, Martin. *The Disadvantaged Child.* New York: Basic Books, 1967.

Flavell, John H. *The Developmental Psychology of Jean Piaget.* Princeton, N. J.: Van Nostrand, 1963.

Gladwin, Thomas. The Anthropologist's View of Poverty, in *The Social Work Forum.* New York: Columbia University Press, 1961, pp. 73-86.

Goode, William J. Illegitimacy in the Caribbean Social Structure. *American Sociological Review* 1960, 25: 21-30.

Haggard, E. A. Social Status and Intelligence: An Experimental Study oi Certain Cultural Determinants of Measured Intelligence. *Genetic Psychology Monographs* 1954, 49: 141-86.

Harrington, Michael. *The Other America.* New York: Macmillan, 1962.

Henriques, Fernando. *Family and Colour in Jamaica.* London: Eyre & Spottiswoode, 1953.

Hunt, J. McV., *Intelligence and Experience.* New York: Ronald Press, 1961.
———. Traditional Personality-Theory in the Light of Recent Evidence. *American Scientist* 1965, 53: 80-96.

Hunter, Robert, *Poverty.* New York: Macmillan, 1904.

Hyman, H. H. The Value Systems of Different Classes: A Social Psychological Contribution to the Analysis of Stratification, in Reinhard Bendix and Seymour M. Lipset, eds., *Class, Status and Power.* Glencoe, Ill.: Free Press, 1953, pp. 426-42.

Kinsey, Alfred C., Pomeroy, Wardell B., and Martin, Clyde E. *Sexual Behavior in the Human Male.* Philadelphia: W. B. Saunders, 1948.

Kolb, D. A. Achievement Motivation Training for Underachieving High-School Boys, *Journal of Personality and Social Psychology* 1965, 2: 783-92.

Kroger, R. O. The Effects of Role Demands and Test-Cue Properties upon Personality Test Performance. *Journal of Consulting Psychology* 1967, 31: 304-12.

Langner, Thomas S., and Michael, Stanley T. *Life Stress and Mental Health.* New York: Free Press of Glencoe, 1963.

Lewis, Oscar. The Culture of Poverty. *Scientific American* 1966, 215: 19-25.

Matza, David. Poverty and Disrepute, in R. K. Merton and R. A. Nisbet, eds., *Contemporary Social Problems*. New York: Harcourt, Brace & World, 1966, pp. 119-69.

Miller, S. M. The American Lower Classes: A Typological Approach, in Arthur B. Shostak and William Gomberg, eds., *Blue-Collar World: Studies of the American Worker*. Englewood Cliffs, N. J.: Prentice-Hall, 1964, pp. 9 23.

Miller, S. M., Riessman, Frank, and Seagull, A. A., "Poverty and Self Indulgence: A Critique of the Non-Deferred Gratification Pattern, in Louis A. Ferman, Joyce L. Kornbluh, and Alan Haber, eds., *Poverty in America*. Ann Arbor: University of Michigan Press, 1965, pp. 285-302.

Miller, Walter B. Lower Class Culture as a Generating Milieu of Gang Delinquency. *Journal of Social Issues* 1958, 14: 5-19.

Minturn, L., and Lambert, W. M. *Mothers of Six Cultures*. New York: Wiley, 1964.

Pettigrew, Thomas F. Social Evaluation Theory: Convergences and Applications, in D. Levine, ed., *Nebraska Symposium on Motivation*. Lincoln: University of Nebraska Press, 1968, pp. 241-311.

Rodman, Hyman. The Lower Class Value Stretch. *Social Forces,* December 1963, 42: 205-15.

Rosenthal, Robert, and Jacobson, Lenore F. Teacher Expectations for the Disadvantaged. *Scientific American* 1968, 218: 19-23.

Schneider, Louis, and Lysgaard, Sverre: The Deferred Gratification Pattern: A Preliminary Study. *American Sociological Review* 1953, 18: 142-49.

Srole, Leo, Langner, T. S., Michael, S. T., Opler, S. T., and Rennie, Thomas A. C. *Mental Health in the Metropolis: The Midtown Manhattan Study*. New York: McGraw-Hill, 1962.

Straus, Murray A. Deferred Gratification, Social Class, and the Achievement Syndrome. *American Sociological Review,* June 1962, 27: 326-35.

Taft, Donald R. *Criminology,* rev. ed. New York: Macmillan, 1950.

Warner, W. Lloyd, Meeker, Marchia, and Eells, Kenneth. *Social Class in America*. Chicago: Science Research Associates, 1949.

Index of Authors Cited

Topical Index